FRENCH NATIONALISM IN 1789 ACCORDING TO THE GENERAL CAHIERS

FRENCH NATIONALISM IN 1789
ACCORDING TO
THE GENERAL CAHIERS

BY

BEATRICE FRY HYSLOP

(New Printing, with Additions and Corrections)

1968
OCTAGON BOOKS, INC.
New York

Reprinted 1967

by special arrangement with Columbia University Press

OCTAGON BOOKS, INC.
175 Fifth Avenue
New York, N. Y. 10010

Library of Congress Catalog Card Number: 67-18768

Printed in U.S.A. by
NOBLE OFFSET PRINTERS, INC.
NEW YORK 3, N. Y.

TO

MY "INTERNATIONALIST" FRIENDS
IN FRANCE

PREFACE TO THE OCTAGON EDITION

Between the original edition of this volume and its present edition, more than thirty years have elapsed. Hitler and the Nazis developed nationalism along lines rejecting the liberal nationalism of 1789, as shown in the *cahiers de doléances*. The Second World War and the movements for independence of subject and colonial peoples have led to a renewed interest in the study of nationalism. Much has been written on the meaning and implementation of nationalism, but the author of this book believes that the analysis and findings published in the 1930's continue to be valid today.[1]

The general cahiers manifested the elements of a modern nationalism, present more or less in all classes and regions, but only a minority showed a fusion of these elements into a well-formed national sentiment, overriding class or regional loyalty. Most of the national elements corresponded with liberal reform objectives. Progressive leaders in the assemblies of all three classes, but notably from the third estate, advocated reforms that implied liberty and equality and a fraternity of national unity to achieve these goals. The French Revolutionary and Napoleonic wars fused these national elements into the French nationalisms of the nineteenth and twentieth centuries, and stimulated nationalisms in conquered territories or wherever French or Napoleonic influence was felt. Nationalist reaction to Napoleonic rule in the Germanies, Italy, the Low countries, and Spain helps to explain nineteenth-century history of these countries. Thus, the French Revolution was a key event in

[1] When this volume was first published, Carlton J. H. Hayes was the acknowledged historian of nationalism, and this study was prepared under his guidance. He accepted the importance of the French Revolution era to the development of nationalism. Professor Hans Kohn, who had not yet published his *The Idea of Nationalism,* (Macmillan, 1944), is now publishing a volume entitled: *Prelude to Nation-States: The French and German Experience, 1789-1815,* in a sense a sequel to his earlier classic. The volume will be published by Van Nostrand simultaneously with this second edition, but the present author was able to see proof of the volume. Although Professor Kohn delineates nationalism in France in 1789, he devotes far more attention to the wars of the French Revolution. Points made on nationalism in the general cahiers formed a background of his thinking on the spirit of 1789 and the development of French nationalism. His use of the cahiers of 1789 harmonizes with mine published in 1934.

the development of nationalism, both French nationalism and that of other European countries.

The general cahiers are a unique and invaluable source of analysis of national sentiment in France on the eve of the Great Revolution. Since the method of convocation of the States-General in 1789 resulted in leaders of the clergy, the nobility, or the third estate exercising great influence in the electoral assemblies, the general cahiers are an expression of dominant opinion in the spring of 1789, and provide a platform of the reforms that were to be undertaken in the National Assembly after the transformation of the States-General. The general cahiers of the third estate present the program of the middle class rather than of the peasantry, whose views were better expressed in parish cahiers and not always faithfully repeated in the general cahiers. Evidence of a national outlook was always present in the general cahiers of the third estate, whereas the preliminary cahiers and especially parish ones were frequently concerned with local reform. Since the deputies of the general assemblies were to introduce the reforms advocated in their *cahiers de doléances,* these documents are the best gauge of public opinion of French leadership in 1789. In the renewed interest in the *cahiers de doléances,* there is now, perhaps, a little more recognition of the value of the general cahiers than there was in the 1930's.

The first edition of *French Nationalism in 1789* utilized some general cahiers not hitherto published, but whose texts were given in *A Guide to the General Cahiers.*[2] After World War II, the author prepared the *Supplément au Répertoire* (the *Répertoire* having appeared in 1933), which was published in France in 1952,[3] and a further article that appeared in the *Annales historiques de la Révolution française,* 1955, pp. 115-23. The texts of general cahiers that have been found since the first edition of this volume are from different classes, different regions in France, and essentially do not

[2] The *Guide* was published by Columbia University Press in 1936 and is being reprinted with corrections simultaneously with the present volume.

[3] The *Répertoire* was printed by the French Government, Paris: Ernest Leroux; 1933, and has long been out of print. The *Supplément,* which must be used with the *Répertoire,* also appeared in the official series of *"Collection de documents inédits sur l'histoire économique de la Révolution française,"* printed by Firmin-Didot, and can be obtained from Presses universitaires. The author has microfilm of the *Répertoire* should any interested reader wish a copy.

alter the generalizations made in 1934. The one really significant cahier among those not known in 1934 is that of the third estate of Rouen. However, since the town of Rouen was allowed to send its cahier, which was classified as Radical, the general cahier of the bailliage, which resembled it closely, would reenforce radicalism in Normandy (see p. 211). It is possible that the third estate of Hennebont might be placed in the Radical column, adding to those of Rennes and Vannes in the generality of Rennes. However, the author is loath to attempt to recapture after thirty years the frame of reference that led to the classification at that time.

The author will not attempt to insert implications of the ten cahiers that have been found into the text, nor will she write a supplementary chapter summarizing the implications of these particular general cahiers. IBM analyses of the general cahiers are currently being undertaken by Sasha Weitman of Johns Hopkins University and John Markoff of Boston College, under the direction of Gilbert Shapiro, professor of sociology at Boston College. Such a study may well shed new light on public opinion in France on the eve of the Revolution. The present author will, however, provide corrections of statistics and references to the general cahiers to be added to the 522 used for the first edition. Additions and corrections precede the index of this edition.

August, 1967. BEATRICE F. HYSLOP

Hunter College of the City University of New York

PREFACE

One is sometimes astonished at the slight utility of preceding States-Generals. Read the early cahiers of the *bailliages:* one may there discover the reasons for the meager results of these national assemblies. True principles were not known; the cahiers present, from one epoch to another, only contradictions of the constitutional order; and besides, each *bailliage,* isolated within its particular interests, failed to include the whole of France in the same glance.[1]

Nationalism, in its widest sense, has been a great distinguishing feature of modern political evolution. The dynamic force and self-conscious manifestations of nationalism in the twentieth century, and especially in recent years, have led historians to define it, to search its origins and to trace its development. Other loyalties characterized earlier periods, but the building of national states, with a corresponding growth of national spirit, has been a special characteristic of the modern era. Although nationalism has shown certain common tendencies, wherever manifested, its development has displayed differences peculiar to each national state, and quite naturally nationalism does not today exhibit the same elements or strength in all countries. Each country has its particular national history.

The key position of France in contemporary world politics and the cogency of its nationalism give a particular interest to French nationalism. Carlton J. H. Hayes, professor of history, Columbia University, has described the general evolution of nationalist philosophy and has devoted some attention to French contributors to its development.[2] Additional light upon French nationalism can best be provided by a series of specialized studies, some of which have already appeared.[3] Especially illuminating may be such a

[1] Quotation from the *cahier de doléances* of the nobles of the *sénéchaussée* of Ponthieu, in northern France, drawn up in 1789; for the text, see *Archives Parlementaires* (Paris, 1867), Vol. V, p. 431, col. 1.

[2] Hayes, C. J. H., *The Historical Evolution of Modern Nationalism* (New York, 1931).

[3] The discussion of nationalism in the seminar conducted by Professor Hayes at Columbia University has already led to several theses and volumes touching different

study of the eve of the great French Revolution of 1789. That eve was marked by an economic depression, a social and political awakening among the masses, and a new orientation of French history. It was at once a national crisis and a landmark in the evolution of French nationalism. Although various elements in the highly conscious nationalism of the present day existed prior to the eighteenth century, an essentially national spirit was produced in France on the eve of the Revolution. The nobles of Ponthieu, whose statement is quoted at the beginning of this preface, bear witness to a contemporary recognition of this fact. According to this group, administrative confusion and regionalism had dominated France in the sixteenth, and in the early seventeenth century, and only in its own day, that is to say, on the threshold of the Revolution, were the philosophy and psychology of nationalism appreciated. In the interval between the States-General of 1614 and the one which ushered in the Revolution in 1789, two major forces had modified the spirit of the French nation—the Grand Monarchy and eighteenth-century enlightenment. From the fusion of these were preexisting national currents, modern French nationalism was born.

The present study aims to determine the trend of national sentiment in France on the eve of the Revolution. One French custom affords us an admirable means to this end—the custom of making *cahiers de doléances*. Every electoral assembly throughout France was authorized to draw up lists of complaints or recommendations of reform as guides for the deputies to the States-General. Whereas Professor Hayes has emphasized the development of nationalism among statesmen and philosophers, and other students of the subject have pursued a similar policy, the cahiers should afford us a gauge of popular opinion. As sources, however, the cahiers present difficulties which have led to much controversy among historians concerning their utility. As a preliminary to the present analysis, therefore, it has been necessary to study the cahiers as historical sources and to discover how they may properly be employed for the purpose in view. For, after a careful examination of these docu-

individuals and periods. See, for example, under Cole, Barzun, and Van Deusen in the bibliography, pp. 308, 309.

ments,[4] the present author is convinced that there is a proper, and really significant use of them for the study of nationalism.

During the one hundred and fifty years since the making of the last *cahiers de doléances* in France, none of the innumerable summaries or analyses has dealt separately with the two large classes of cahiers—the general cahiers and the preliminary cahiers. The resulting confusion explains a tendency to discredit the cahiers altogether. In preceding analyses, also, attention has been centered upon some one phase of opinion—the religious, the financial, the industrial, etc.—without any attempt to evaluate national opinion as a whole for all France. Consequently, little heed was paid to whether a complete number of cahiers had been consulted, to the geographic and class distribution of ideas, and to the collective impression of individual cahiers. For a study of nationalism, the general cahiers alone afford certain advantages which would be lost were an attempt made to use the entire number of cahiers prepared in 1789. Our first aim has been to evaluate the general cahiers.

Use of the cahiers of 1789 has been handicapped by disorder, incompleteness, and inadequacy in the secondary works dealing with them, and by confusion among the original documents themselves. Rather than augment the manuscript of the present volume whose major concern is with French nationalism, it has seemed desirable to reserve detailed documentary information for a *Guide to the General Cahiers of 1789*,[5] which will be published shortly. One chapter of the present study has been devoted, however, to an ex-

[4] In the course of the author's documentary study of the cahiers, much information was accumulated relative to the convocation of 1789 and to the composition of the cahiers. Moreover, the French Commission for the publication of the *Documents inédits sur l'histoire économique de la Révolution française* appointed the author to prepare an inventory of texts of the cahiers of 1789. During the preparation of that volume, which has already appeared (*cf. infra*, note 5), access was had to supplementary materials and information that facilitated the determination of the value of the cahiers.

[5] Three works already published are indispensable for a study of the cahiers: the little volume by Champion, E., *La France d'après les cahiers de 1789* (Paris, 1897), a general survey; Brette, A., *Recueil de documents rélatifs à la convocation des Etats-généraux de 1789* (Paris, 1894-1915, 4 vols.), which reprints or summarizes the convocation and electoral material, and the official inventory, Hyslop, B., *Repertoire critique des cahiers de doléances de 1789* (Paris, 1933), which indicates where all known texts of cahiers may be found.

position of what the cahiers were, the distinctions between general and preliminary cahiers, and an appreciation of the limitations and special values of the general cahiers for the present study.

The analysis of the general cahiers of 1789 for French nationalism involves four aspects: (1) the range and intensity of ideas and practices indicative of nationalism; (2) the general trend of nationalism expressed by the cahiers; (3) the geographic and class distribution of the various shades of national opinion; and (4) the influence of the cahiers upon the growth of nationalism. By limiting the analysis to the general cahiers—a specific number of documents—it has been possible to utilize a qualified statistical method and to verify general impressions by specific information. Every effort to insure accuracy and to overcome the difficulties inherent in the utilization of the cahiers has been made.

In respect to the documentary phases of the thesis, special thanks are due to Camille Bloch, professor at the Sorbonne, former supervisor of French archives, and member of the commission for publication of French sources relative to the French Revolution. The archivists and librarians of the *Archives Nationales* and *Bibliothèque Nationale,* as well as of numerous departmental archives and libraries, offered helpful assistance and coöperation. Charles D. Hazen, professor of history, Columbia University, also gave helpful criticism.

For general supervision of the thesis and for generous and constructive criticism, special appreciation is due to Carlton J. H. Hayes—the recognized authority on nationalism. Virginia Thompson (Ph.D., Columbia University) and Mary Bradshaw (Ph.D., University of Wisconsin) offered helpful suggestions, and Stephanie Locke (M.A., Columbia University) furnished invaluable assistance for the statistical and technical phases of the manuscript. The final draughtsmanship of the maps is the work of Theodore R. Miller of Columbia University. The printing of the thesis has been facilitated by the grant of the Mary E. Woolley Fellowship of Mount Holyoke College.

May the courteous collaboration of so many minds have produced a work that will merit the attention of serious historians, and contribute some constructive considerations to the study of French nationalism and of the French Revolution.

BEATRICE FRY HYSLOP

COLUMBIA UNIVERSITY
March 15, 1934

CONTENTS

ABBREVIATIONS

Arch. Nat. *Archives Nationales* at Paris.

Arch. Dept. *Archives Départmentales.* Sometimes, *Arch.* has been followed simply by the name of the department whose archives have been consulted.

AP. *Archives Parlementaires,* edited by Mavidal and Laurent (Paris, 1867-75), 7 vols. *Cf.* bibliography, p. 292.

Bib. Mun. *Bibliothèque Municipale.*

Bib. Nat. *Bibliothèque Nationale* at Paris.

C clergy.

CN clergy and nobles (combined).

CT clergy and third estate (combined).

D.I. A volume in the official series of *Documents inédits sur l'histoire économique de la Révolution française.*

Gen. *généralité.*

MS manuscript.

N nobles.

NT nobles and third estate (combined).

PR printed.

p.v. *procès-verbal,* or *procès-verbaux.*

T third estate.

U the three orders (combined).

V *ville,* or town.

3 O. the three orders.

References to specific electoral districts and quotations from cahiers have been given according to the class and the name of the district, without designation as to whether its official status in 1789 was a *bailliage, sénéchaussée, comté, gouvernance, intendance, siège royal,* etc. The official status may be checked with Brette, A., (*Recueil des documents relatifs à la convocation des Etats-généraux de 1789,* Paris, 1894-1915, Vol. I), or Hyslop, B., (*Repertoire critique des cahiers de doléances de 1789,* Paris, 1933). The omission has been made in order to save space and to eliminate unnecessary detail.

When reference has been made to the electoral districts, the word which applied to the majority of districts, the *bailliage,* has been used.

Attention may be called to the fact that French accents are not generally used with capital letters. Consequently, such names as Etampes, Etain, etc., appear without an accent over the "e."

CHAPTER I

THE USE OF THE GENERAL CAHIERS OF 1789 IN A STUDY OF FRENCH NATIONALISM

The practice of making *cahiers de doléances* was an essential feature of the French States-General. Although the custom of holding States-Generals in France dated back to the medieval period, their positive influence upon the trend of events was chiefly between 1484 and 1615, during which time six important meetings were held.[1] Before 1484, written memoranda had been given to the persons summoned to the States-General, but in that year, election by *bailliage*[2] was substituted for personal summons. Thereafter, with each new convocation, the royal authorization for the preparation of instructions by each elective assembly became increasingly concrete, and by 1614, it was a well established tradition that the electoral districts should give their deputies written instructions—*cahiers de doléances*. Three types of cahiers may be distinguished: cahiers composed in the preliminary assemblies to be taken to the assemblies of the *bailliages;* cahiers prepared in the *bailliage* assemblies to be taken to the States-General; and the national cahiers composed by each order of the States-General itself[3] for presentation to the king. Thus, by a series of steps, the will of the people was supposedly made known to the king.

THE CAHIERS AS DOCUMENTS

When Louis XVI took the momentous step of summoning the States-General for 1789, it was quite natural that the traditional

[1] The scholarly study of the early States-General by Georges Picot (*Histoire des Etats-généraux,* Paris, 1888, 5 vols.) is especially recommended. The six meetings of prime importance between 1484 and 1615 were: 1484, 1560, 1576, 1588, 1593-96, 1614.

[2] The French word for the judicial unit which formed the electoral district—the *bailliage*—will be preferred to the nearest English equivalent—"bailiwick."

[3] The procedure in 1484 was exceptional. All three orders concurred in one national cahier.

procedure should exert a marked influence. The actual method of convocation adopted was a compromise between the traditional course and the newer principles of uniformity and equality, but the practice of making cahiers was revived, and their composition officially prescribed in the royal regulations.[4] As a great quantity of pamphlet propaganda was issued during the electoral period,[5] some of which bore the misleading title of *cahier de doléances,* a criterion for the distinction between official cahiers and private pamphlets was necessary. In 1905, when a commission for the official publication of source materials of the French Revolution was formed by the Ministry of Public Instruction, the commission issued the following definition of a *cahier de doléances:*

l'ensemble des écrits contenant voeux, plaintes, doléances, rédigés en 1789 dans les assemblées électorales qui avaient un caractère de légalité reconnu, soit parcequ'elles avaient été convoquées en exécution d'ordres royaux, soit parceque les députés élus en conséquence de ces assemblées furent admis à l'assemblée nationale.[6]

The first requisite of a cahier, according to this definition, was that the document emanate from one of the legally constituted electoral assemblies. Unless an assembly was authorized by the royal convocation, or subsequently recognized by the National Assembly,[7] it was not legal. The documents themselves furnish the evidence as to whether or not they were the product of an official electoral assembly.[8]

[4] For reprints of the royal acts of convocation, consult Brette, Armand, *Recueil des documents rélatifs à la convocation des Etats-généraux de 1789* (Paris, 1894-1915), Vol. I, *passim.* The text of the regulation which formed the general type, issued on January 24, 1789, appears pp. 64-87. On the composition of the cahier, *cf.* arts. 21, 24, 28, 33, 34, 38, 40, 43-45, 49.

[5] The first act of the royal convocation, an order in council of July 5, 1788 (*ibid.,* pp. 19, *et seq.*), implied freedom of the press. Although the Parlements suppressed the more radical pamphlets, the large degree of freedom allowed until the opening of the States-General, led to the publication and circulation of extensive electoral propaganda.

[6] Circular sent out by the commission, reprinted in *La Révolution française, revue,* 1908, Vol. LV, p. 74.

[7] Recognition by the National Assembly is a necessary criterion of legality in the cases of the principality of Arches and Charleville, the district of Bassigny-Barrois, and of the several French colonies.

[8] A cahier gave the following information about its composition in the title and the formal ending:—the class and electoral district that made it, the date of adoption, the committee who drew up a draft to be discussed by the assembly, the signatures of the members and officers of the assembly, verification by the royal

A second feature of the definition is the phrase, *ensemble des écrits*. There were three parts to this *ensemble*. In addition to the document bearing the specific name of *cahier de doléances*, were the minutes of the assembly which made the cahier.[9] The *procès-verbaux* of the electoral assemblies are an indispensable supplement to the cahier not only for its verification and for the discussion and modification of the cahier by the assembly, but also for an understanding of the influences on its composition. Included in the cahier, in the *procès-verbal*, or appearing as a separate document, was the third part of the *ensemble*—the mandate.[10] This was the grant of powers to the deputy, which either broadened or restricted the instructions of the cahier. In rare cases, one should also consult special *mémoires* and the preliminary cahiers which the assembly voted to annex to the general cahier.[11] Any careful study of the cahiers of 1789 must, therefore, include the minutes of the electoral assemblies, the mandates, the cahier, and any supplementary material given to the deputy.

THE DISTINCTION BETWEEN GENERAL AND PRELIMINARY CAHIERS

The method of indirect election used in the convocation of the States-General of 1789 leads to the classification of the cahiers into two groups: those issuing from the preliminary assemblies to be taken to the next successive assembly, and secondly, those issuing from the general assembly of the *bailliage*, Provincial-Estates,[12] or other electoral unit,[13] to be carried to the States-General itself.

---

officers of the *bailliage*. To be accepted as authentic, a cahier must have at least some of these marks, which should be compared with the minutes of the electoral assembly.

[9] Minutes were prescribed by the royal regulation. *Cf.* type regulation, Brette, *op. cit.*, Vol. I, p. 86, art. 49.

[10] For examples: a mandate included in the cahier, N. Angers (see table of abbreviations, p. xix), Mavidal and Laurent, *Archives Parlementaires* (Paris, 1867-75), Vol. II, p. 37, col. 2; a mandate in the *procès-verbal*, C. Aix, p. v., MS, *Arch. Nat.* Ba 9; a mandate as a separate document, T. Blamont, MS, *Arch. Nat.* C 21/110.

[11] For instance, the third estate of Senlis sent a memoire on provincial administration with their cahier, while the clergy of Alençon and the third estate of Agen, etc., voted to send preliminary cahiers with the general cahier.

[12] "Provincial-Estates" will be used to translate *états-provinciaux* in order to avoid confusion with *assemblée provinciale*.

[13] *Cf. infra*, p. 8, on the method of convocation, and electoral units.

To the first group belong cahiers of church chapters, regular orders, priests without office, curates, parishes, gilds, towns, assemblies of secondary *bailliages,* and preliminary assemblies of principal *bailliages.* To the second group belong all the cahiers made in the last series of successive assemblies before the States-General, together with those specially authorized to be taken to the States-General.[14]

The failure to distinguish between these two large groups has led to much confusion and inaccuracy in studies of the cahiers of 1789. This division was less clearly drawn in the minds of the makers of the cahiers than in ours, since even the smallest electoral unit hoped that its demands would reach the king. The classification into the two groups arises from the method of composition of the cahiers, their content, and their actual use. One may cite four main differences between the preliminary and the general cahiers.

The first essential difference is one of procedure. The general cahiers of the clergy and of the third estate were compilations of the preliminary cahiers of each *bailliage.* A committee of the assembly was appointed to which the preliminary cahiers were given. At least a day later,[15] the committee submitted a draft of the cahier based upon the consensus of opinion in the preliminary cahiers. The assembly discussed the draft, and often altered it before final adoption.

A difference in the length and scope of the cahier resulted from four factors—the procedure, the pressure of time, the education of the members of the assembly, and influences brought to bear upon the composition of the cahier. The preliminary cahiers were almost invariably shorter, less comprehensive, and more local in their focus than the general cahiers. The latter represented a selective summary of the important issues in the preliminary cahiers. They gave greater relative space to the big national problems, and fuller discussion of the reasons for the reforms demanded.

A third difference between the preliminary and the general

[14] *Cf. infra,* p. 8, note 26. This condition would apply to districts favored by special royal concessions, for example, T. Rochefort-sur-mer, etc.

[15] One can learn from the *procès-verbaux* the approximate time taken by the committees for the preparation of the cahier. In some cases, several days were required.

cahiers reflects the relative degree of education of the members of the assemblies. Whereas illiteracy often existed in the rural districts, the members of the general assemblies were the leaders of their locality and usually the better educated. The parish cahiers often showed a defective knowledge of French, the presence of a popular dialect, bilingual conditions, and in the signatures of the members of the assembly, they revealed the presence of some illiterates.[16] On the other hand, with rare exceptions for the bilingual areas[17] and for some isolated *bailliages,*[18] the general cahiers of 1789 used the official language, French, uniformly and intelligibly.[19] The likelihood of the adoption outright of models or of undue personal influence on the cahier was far greater in the parishes and other preliminary assemblies than in the general assembly of the *bailliage,* where compilation was the method used, and where all members were more enlightened.

A fourth difference between the two classes of cahiers concerned the publicity given to them. The preliminary cahiers were seldom printed, and the texts usually remained in the local archives. On the other hand, many of the general cahiers were printed, and their widespread circulation gave them an influence in 1789[20] which the preliminary cahiers could not have had.

A fifth difference was not inherent in the two classifications but is an accident of time—the preservation of texts. Since 1789, many of the preliminary cahiers have disappeared.[21] Even when the

[16] Until recently, editors of parish cahiers have modernized the spelling and the grammar of the original texts. An examination of the original manuscripts justifies the above generalizations. The author has seen many collections of parish cahiers in the departmental archives visited. *Cf.* Bibliography, p. 292.

[17] The bilingual areas were the northeast (French and German), north (French and Flemish), southwest (French and Basque), Brittany (French and Breton), and Corsica (French and Italian).

[18] There is reason to believe that there were illiterates in the general assemblies of the third estate in six *bailliages*—Agen, Annonay, Cambrésis, Sisteron, Hyères, Toulouse. In no other case, does the cahier or *procès-verbal* indicate their presence.

[19] The editors of the *Archives Parlementaires,* the most complete edition of general cahiers, also modernized the orthography and punctuation. *Cf.* Hyslop, *Guide to the General Cahiers.*

[20] On the printing of the general cahiers, *cf. infra,* pp. 16-17, 229-31.

[21] *Cf.* Hyslop, B., *Repertoire critique des cahiers de doléances de 1789* (*Documents inédits* . . . , Paris, 1933). This official inventory lists under each *bailliage* the texts of all cahiers for which an original or a reprinted text is known. The number of parishes differed for each district, but a cursory glance shows the large number of

general cahier was not printed, several copies were usually made,[22] so that at least one of the original texts of nearly every class and district has come down to us. Any study of France in 1789 requires as complete a picture as possible for all classes, and all parts, of France. Fairly complete collections of the parish cahiers exist for only one third of all the *bailliages,* many gild cahiers are unknown, and the preliminary cahiers of the clergy have been poorly preserved.[23] There were no preliminary cahiers of the nobles. An analysis of the preliminary cahiers for a study of nationalism would have to be by district, and in any case, there would be too many gaps for an adequate synthesis for the whole of France.

In contrast to this, out of the six hundred and fifteen general cahiers of 1789[24], five hundred and twenty-two are now available.[25] The number of general cahiers is based upon the electoral process, an analysis of which shows that two hundred and thirty-four districts (including Corsica, but not the French colonies) made cahiers to be taken directly to the States-General.[26] The map opposite illustrates not only the distribution of the electoral districts and their grouping by *generalities,* but also their relative geographic

---

cahiers that have disappeared. Large collections of parish cahiers exist for about 150 out of over 400 *bailliages.*

[22] The original was given to the chief deputy. Copies were usually made for the other deputies, and one copy kept in the local archives.

[23] *Cf.* Hyslop, *op. cit., passim,* and also *Guide to the General Cahiers of 1789.*

[24] The number of general cahiers made in 1789 is a controversial question. For a full discussion, *cf.* Hyslop, B., *op. cit., passim.* The alphabetical list of general cahiers calculated on the basis of the method of convocation, and a list by *generality* may be consulted in the appendix of this thesis, pp. 312 *et seq.,* and 237 *et seq.*

[25] *Cf.* Tables in Appendix, pp. 237 *et seq.*

[26] The method of convocation in 1789 was so intricate that the computation of the number of districts is a complex affair. Although there was one type regulation —that of January 24, 1789—there were so many exceptions and variations, that the elections proceeded according to one of seven methods: (1) those that followed the type regulation or a similar method, whereby a general assembly by separate orders, or by united orders, of a principal *bailliage* held elections to the States-General and made the general cahiers; (2) those where several *bailliages* met at a common center for the final elections, but gave each of the *bailliage* cahiers to the deputies; (3) those where the Provincial-Estates carried on the elections and made the cahier; (4) privileged towns; (5) several small districts granted special right of direct representation; (6) Brittany and Corsica; and (7) two districts in France and the French colonies, that had been omitted from the royal convocation but held elections subsequently recognized by the National Assembly. For a full discussion of these seven methods, *cf.* Hyslop, B., *Guide to the General Cahiers. . .*

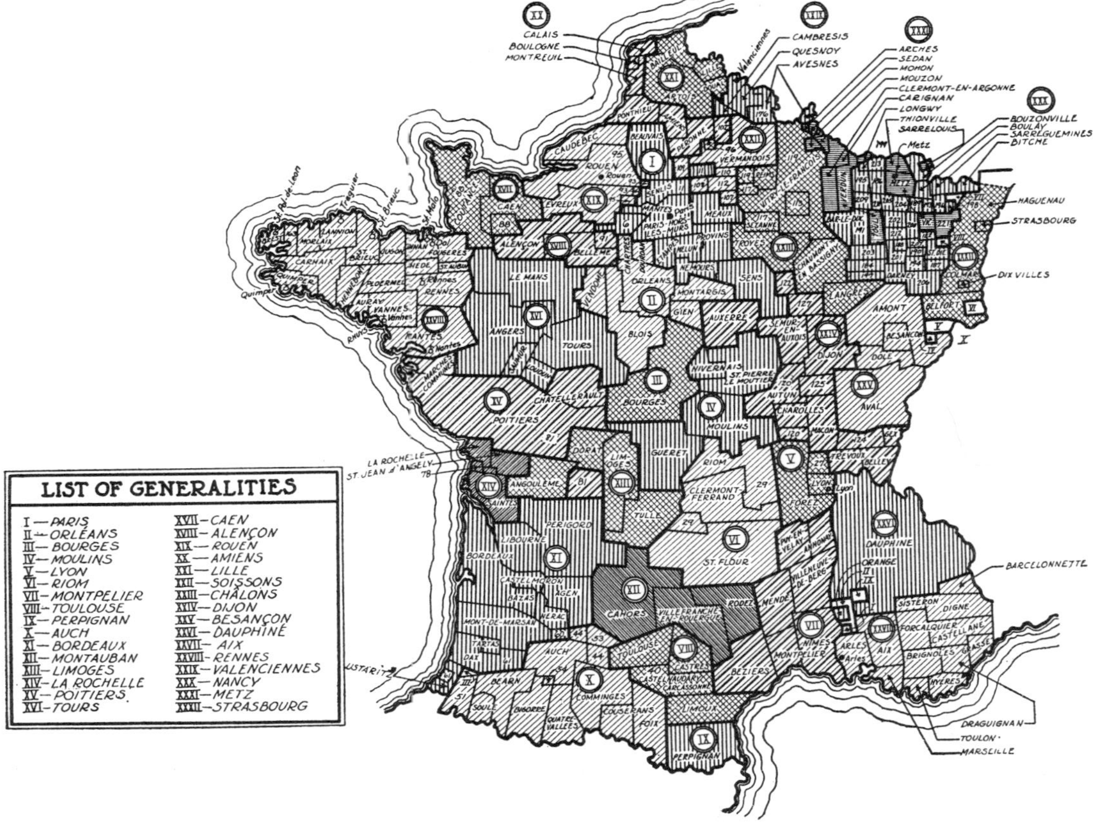

GENERAL ELECTORAL DISTRICTS OF 1789

The white areas with small Roman numerals indicate foreign jurisdictions. For the key to the numbers, and for the general explanation of the map, see Appendix, pp. 247 *et seq.*

size. Due to the method of convocation,[27] more cahiers in proportion to the population were sent to the States-General from the northeast, the southeast, and from the lower clergy and third estate of Brittany than from the rest of France, but it is also in these same districts that more of the cahiers have been lost. Ninety-three cahiers are missing—thirty-six cahiers of the clergy, twenty-eight of the nobles, twenty-three of the third estate, four of the three orders united, and two of the nobles and third estate combined. Of the five hundred and twenty-two available, one hundred and fifty-eight are of the clergy; one hundred and fifty-four, of the nobles; one hundred and ninety, of the third estate; fourteen, of the three orders united; three, of the clergy and nobles united; one, of the clergy and third estate united; and two, of the nobles and third estate united.[28]

The cahiers of the colonies need to be considered separately from the rest of France.[29] Of the nine made for the National Assembly, only four have been preserved.

In view of the differences between the preliminary and the general cahiers, and of the relatively complete number of general cahiers available, the general cahiers offer a more representative study for all of France than do the preliminary cahiers.

THE VALUE OF THE GENERAL CAHIERS FOR A STUDY OF FRENCH NATIONALISM

Granted that the general cahiers are more useful for our analysis than the preliminary cahiers, there yet remains the question of how valuable the former are. In view of the controversy over the utility of the cahiers of 1789, what are the limitations upon their value, and what, if any, is their special contribution to a study of nationalism?

LIMITATIONS.—The limitations of the general cahiers[30] are in

[27] Consult the details of the electoral process of the second and sixth types.

[28] *Cf.* Table, Appendix, p. 244.

[29] A good many documents bearing on the colonial elections have been lost. This fact, together with the difference in time between the regular elections and those of the colonies, makes it advisable to treat the latter separately. See the *Guide* for fuller information, and the appendix of this volume, pp. 243-44, for list of colonial cahiers.

[30] Hereafter, the various generalizations apply to the general cahiers. The preliminary cahiers will not be considered.

part those that apply to any one class of source materials, those that can be remedied by the proper documentary verification of individual cahiers, and those shortcomings that result from the particular nature of the cahiers.

Any historian who attempts to get a well-rounded picture of life and thought in a given country at a specific period, would consult all available sources. He would examine the executive archives, judicial records, the laws, letters, diaries, and the writings of the times. Each source would illuminate the others, while any class of sources by itself would give an imperfect and often one-sided view. The *cahiers de doléances* represent a very circumscribed set of documents, composed for a common purpose during two months of 1789,[31] and designed according to a common legal framework. They could not tell the whole story. For a full appreciation of nationalism in 1789 on the eve of the Revolution, it would be desirable to check and supplement the cahiers with all the other sources of the period.

The purpose for which the cahiers were made imposes a second limitation upon their value. Composed as platforms of reform, the cahiers presented a series of proposals not necessarily accompanied by explanations or justification. Some of the cahiers were simply brief, unembellished articles.[32] Others slipped in philosophical reasons here and there, or amplified the demands. Recognition of the fragmentary character of the philosophical statements is particularly necessary for a study of nationalism. The ideas bearing upon nationalism were scattered throughout the cahier without evidence of conscious connections. The brevity and the form of the cahiers impose an important limitation upon their utility.

A third limitation is the incompleteness of the cahiers. By virtue of the synthetic method of composition, many items in the preliminary cahiers were omitted. The absence of a demand did not

[31] With few exceptions, all the general cahiers were made in the months of March and April of 1789.

[32] Contrast, for example, the bald articles of the cahier of the third estate of Calais (AP, Vol. II, pp. 510 *et seq.*) with the fullness of the third estate of Bar-sur-Seine (AP, Vol. II, pp. 253 *et seq.*). An extreme brevity is illustrated by the cahier of the nobles of St. Pierre le-Moutier (AP, Vol. V, p. 635, two articles only), while an example of exceptional length is that of the cahier of the third estate of Nemours (AP, Vol. IV, pp. 112-215). AP is the abbreviation which will be used for the *Archives Parlementaires.*

mean that the thought was lacking to the assembly, but merely that it seemed to them of secondary importance. Had the central government sent out questionnaires to the electoral assemblies, one would have found all the questions answered in every cahier. This, however, was not the case. Although there had been widespread political campaigning, there was no official model.[33] Consequently, the makers of the cahiers selected salient items from a multitude of topics. Thus, the cahiers of 1789 show what was uppermost in the minds of the French electorate, but do not give a complete picture of every phase of public opinion. The variety of demands and the omission of obvious ones complicates the problem of a national synthesis.

A fourth limitation lies in the unoriginal character of the general cahiers. Eighteenth-century philosophy was popularized on the eve of, and during, the elections by hundreds of pamphlets.[34] In view of this literature, and the many other influences upon their content—the pressure of time,[35] the personnel and method of the committee, prominent leaders in the assembly[36]—the cahiers contained no statement and no philosophical reasoning that could not be found elsewhere in the written works of the eighteenth century. The vital fact for the value of the cahiers was their adoption by the electoral assembly. The minutes of the electoral assemblies indicate that, in the majority of cases, the members of the assembly discussed and amended the text submitted by the committee before giving the final text its official approval. The vote of the assembly gave the cahier an official sanction lacking to other contemporary expressions of opinion. Consequently, the interest of the cahiers does not lie in any startling new theory or demand, but in the degree and frequency with which certain ideas occur. Since the general cahiers came from all parts of France and from all three

[33] Consult the *Guide.*

[34] The flood of pamphlets was particularly copious after the order in council of July 5, 1788, which allowed publication.

[35] Late publication of the regulations for the convocation, the pressure of local duties of church service, spring planting, etc. and the distance and difficulties of travel were among the influences which affected the time at the disposal of the *bailliage* assemblies.

[36] It could be shown that most of the leaders that were later prominent in the National Assembly were influential in their respective electoral assemblies. However, a distinction should be made between the natural leadership of the intelligentsia, and domineering, self-seeking individuals. *Cf.* the *Guide.*

of the classes, they show the distribution of elements in the national consciousness.

Among the five hundred and twenty-two available general cahiers of 1789, there are twenty-seven cahiers that are distinctly less reliable as gauges of the opinion of the assembly which made them.[37] Reservations on these particular cahiers are necessary for one of the five reasons. In the case of three cahiers, there is evidence that the text was tampered with, or another one substituted for the one adopted by the assembly.[38] In three cases, there was undue influence on the part of some person or faction, with insufficient evidence that the assembly adopted the text which comes down to us.[39] Two cahiers, the originals of which have been lost, are mere summaries of articles or topics of reform.[40] The larger number of unreliable cahiers are ones for which there is evidence that the cahier was adopted by a small majority with the obvious conclusion that opinion differed on specific articles.[41] The cahier of the third estate of Nemours, while authentic, is an exceptional one.[42] Although a committee compiled the parish cahiers with great care, and the assembly voted upon the text, the unusual length and fullness of philosophical expression were undoubtedly due to the influence of Dupont de Nemours.[43] Some reservation should also be made for the documents from the Dauphiné. The original cahier has been lost and we possess only a summary of its articles inserted in the *procès-verbal* of the Provincial-Estates, which, in this case, drew up the cahier. In point of time, the elections of the Dauphiné were exceptional, as they took place early in January, 1789,[44] while a few cahiers were composed after the regular elec-

[37] *Cf.* list, Appendix, p. 237.

[38] T. Périgord (interference of *lieutenant-général*); N. St. Pierre-le-Moutier (interference of *bailli*); T. Perpignan (trouble between the town and the rest of the assembly).

[39] T. Chaumont-en-Bassigny (influence of royal officers); T. Mont-de-Marsan (turbulence in the assembly); T. Puy-en-Velay (*idem*).

[40] C. and T. Tours.

[41] For example, T. Poitiers, T. Agen, etc.

[42] *Cf.* text, AP, Vol. IV, pp. 112-215.

[43] *Cf.* the *procès-verbal* of the assembly (*Arch. Nat.* C 21/112[1]), the text of the cahier, and compare with writings of Dupont de Nemours.

[44] *Cf.* Brette, A., *Documents rélatifs à la convocation des Etats-généraux de 1789,* Vol. I, pp. 280 *et seq.,* for reprint of regulations on the convocation of the Dauphiné. *Cf.* also, the *Guide.*

toral period, but these were in remote districts where news of the events at Versailles and Paris had evidently not penetrated.[45] The cahier of the principality of Arches and Charleville presents a contrast in point of time, for it was drawn up in December, 1789, and its makers were evidently cognizant of the trend of affairs in the National Assembly.[46]

Despite reservations of judgment for the twenty-seven cahiers mentioned, and for a few exceptional cases, these cahiers will be included in the present study. In the first place, these texts were used by the deputies fully as much as the completely authentic cahiers, and they therefore contributed to the general trend of opinion. The second reason is that in most cases, the items bearing on nationalism were little affected by the doubts raised by the texts. Where there was conflict between bishop and curates, the disagreement was more significant for ecclesiastical questions than for nationalism. A small majority of the nobles of Dijon preferred vote by order to vote by head, but this fact does not invalidate the rest of the cahier.[47] One should, however, keep the reservations in mind, and allowance will be made for these particular cahiers when the reason for their unreliability affects general conclusions.

Some historians have discounted the cahiers of 1789 because of their alleged pessimism. Any platform or reform proposes changes that should be made, and tends to pass over in silence the practices that are satisfactory. Because the cahiers gave long lists of reforms covering so inclusively the institutions of the old régime, they have been branded as one-sided. It is, however, a minority of the general cahiers[48] that accompanied their demands with graphic descriptions of deplorable conditions prevailing in their particular locality. The important point for a study of nationalism in the cahiers is their subjective, and not their objective, value. Although conditions may not have been as bad as they were represented by some of the cahiers, and although demand for thorough-going re-

[45] C, N, T, Soule, for example.

[46] *Cf.* Brette, *op. cit.*, Vol. I, p. 300, and the *Guide.*

[47] *Cf.* the cahier, AP, Vol. III, pp. 127 *et seq.*, and the *procès-verbal, Bib. Mun. Dijon, Fonds Juigné,* no. 44, Vol. V.

[48] More of the parish cahiers emphasize the bad local conditions than do the general cahiers.

forms was not balanced by praise of existing institutions, the vital factor is that the assembly thought things were as the cahiers expressed them. Nationalism is a state of mind. Precisely for this reason, the pessimism of a few cahiers and the reforming optimism of others are both significant.

The sixth limitation upon the utility and value of the general cahiers may be disposed of by proper documentary verification. Despite the extensive literature on the cahiers, access to the complete number of authentic texts has been extremely difficult. The intricacy of the problem, the inadequate and partial publication of texts of cahiers, and the dispersion of the documentary facts among many analyses have hampered accurate consultation of the cahiers. For these reasons, the author has prepared a complete *Guide*[49] and will give here only an explanation of how the general cahiers were actually used for the present work.

When the number of general cahiers had been ascertained, special effort was exerted to find each and every text.[50] The author has verified the texts reprinted by the *Archives Parlementaires*, which were so defectively edited; and where errors or omissions affect the use of individual cahiers for the study of nationalism, a note to that effect has been given. As the limits of the text are not always clear unless the original has been consulted, the inclusive pages for a cahier will be indicated.[51] Attention has already been called to the fact that three documents constitute a cahier. Since an official inventory of the *procès-verbaux* and cahiers has already been published,[52] it has not seemed necessary to indicate where the original *procès-verbaux* and cahiers may be found. As the mandate was nearly always in one of the two foregoing documents, no mention will be made of it, unless it existed as a third, supplementary

[49] Hyslop, B., *Guide to the General Cahiers of 1789.*

[50] Thirty-four unedited texts will be reprinted in the *Guide.* The table of texts in the Appendix, pp. 312 *et seq.*, indicates all reprints used, and is especially valuable for ambiguous cases, or isolated texts.

[51] The cahier was sometimes in two divisions. In other cases, the editors of the *Archives Parlementaires* have given misleading reprints. *Cf.* table of cahiers used, in Appendix, pp. 312 *et seq.*

[52] *Cf.* Hyslop, B., *Repertoire critique des cahiers de doléances de 1789.* The organization of information on the cahiers differs from that of the table in this Appendix, but contains all the necessary material.

document.[53] By means of the table of texts, anyone can consult all the extant texts.

It is not only important to have the full and the authentic texts of the general cahiers, but the way in which the cahiers are read has a direct bearing upon their utility. The cahiers should be read by *generality*,[54] and the cahiers of all three orders of a single *bailliage* should be reviewed consecutively. By this method, similarities and differences between cahiers of the different orders and of all cahiers of a locality can be detected. A synthesis of national opinion must be based upon regional analyses. The order of *generalities* used for the present thesis[55] begins with Paris, and proceeds clockwise through all the *generalities* that were *pays d'élection*,[56] and then takes those that were *pays d'état*[57] in similar order. Such a method is the logical one for analyzing the general cahiers, and especially for bringing out regional, as well as national, sentiment.

Of the six limitations on the utility of the general cahiers, three—the lack of originality, pessimism, and the difficulty of consulting the general cahiers—have been overcome by analysis and verification. The remaining three are inherent in the nature of the cahiers but are more than offset by certain special values for a study of nationalism.

ADVANTAGES.—The primary value of the general cahiers for a study of French nationalism lies in the fact that these documents form a unique body of historical sources for the period. Journalism, as we now know it, did not exist prior to the Revolution. Neither the writings of eighteenth-century philosophers, the large number of election pamphlets, the official *Gazette de France*, the *Mercure*, nor

[53] For example, N. Aix, Appendix, p. 312.

[54] The regulations for the convocation of 1789 went to the grand *bailli* of the *généralité*, who distributed them among the *bailliages* in his jurisdiction. The *généralité*, translated as *generality*, corresponded with the areas called *intendance*, *pays d'élection*, and *pays d'état*. The name applied to an area depended upon its historic and administrative status. *Generality* will be used as the class name, just as *bailliage* is used to designate all electoral districts.

[55] *Cf.* table in Appendix, pp. 237 *et seq.*

[56] *Pays d'élection* had no rights of local administration. The *generality* of Auch combined both types of provincial administration, but its cahiers were read with those of the *pays d'élection*.

[57] *Pays d'état* dealt with certain local matters through the Provincial-Estates.

other publications of the era reveal the mind of the French masses. Court records, correspondence of French administrative agents, personal letters, and diaries are similarly inadequate for a complete picture of popular opinion. In contrast with all the other sources of the period, we possess a nearly complete series of documents representing the collective opinion of groups all over France. Although the loss of cahiers has left some gaps in the class and geographical picture,[58] there remains an excellent basis for a comparison of opinion from five hundred twenty-two groups. For this reason, the general cahiers afford us the most adequate measurement of mass opinion in France on the eve of the Revolution.

A second advantage lies in the possibility of comparison of the general cahiers of 1789 with the similar class of sources from previous States-Generals. The survival of cahiers written for the States-Generals from 1484 until 1614 affords a means of comparison and contrast between similar documents at different historical intervals. Too few of the *bailliage* cahiers of the early States-Generals have survived to make useful a comparison with those of 1789.[59] We do, however, possess the texts of the national cahiers drawn up by the separate classes in all of the important States-Generals of the period of their effective activity. Had the traditional procedure been pursued in 1789, whereby each of the orders held separate sessions, drew up a national cahier for its class, presented these to Louis XVI and left all deliberation to the king and his council, a comparison would have been possible between completely analogous documents, but then, there would have been no revolution. There could be no national cahiers after the oath of the Tennis Court and the transformation of the States-General into the National Assembly.

With some reservation for difference in kind between the national class cahiers of preceding States-Generals and the *bailliage* cahiers of 1789, their similarities, as well as their differences, afford some illuminating points. A comparison helps in the evaluation of national sentiment among the masses in France, and throws into relief certain trends in the cahiers of 1789.

A third special value of the general cahiers arises from their use

[58] Even in the ninety-three cases where the cahier proper has been lost, we nearly always possess the *procès-verbal* and supplementary election material.

[59] Consult the bibliography, p. 298, for cahiers of the early States-Generals.

at the outset of the Revolution. In the first place, the printing of many of the general cahiers made possible their widespread circulation. Nearly one-half of their number were printed in 1789.[60] The size of the average edition was four or five hundred copies,[61] although some numbered several thousands of copies.[62] There is every evidence that the cahiers were widely read and discussed. To be sure, Gouverneur Morris fell asleep during the reading of the *Declaration* of the higher clergy and the nobles of Brittany (in fact not a long document),[63] but Arthur Young was more indicative of the attitude of the French intelligentsia.[64] The texts of cahiers were avidly sought in Parisian bookshops, while their readers frequented cafés where discussion of politics was the order of the day. In the provinces, where books and pamphlets were less plentiful, the printed cahiers may have received additional attention.[65] The texts of separate cahiers were soon supplemented by newspaper discussions[66] and by published summaries.[67]

The first impression from reading the cahiers, both in 1789 and today, would be of their striking similarity, indicative of a like-mindedness among the French people. Camille Desmoulins expressed the common verdict of every perusal of the general cahiers:

> Listen to Paris and Lyon, Rouen and Bordeaux, Calais and Marseille; from one end of France to the other, the same cry (*cri*), a universal cry, is heard. . . . The Nation has everywhere expressed the same will. All wish to be free.[68]

In the course of the analysis of nationalism in the cahiers, it will

[60] Two hundred and sixty-three out of 615 general cahiers. *Cf.* list, Appendix, p. 244.

[61] The *procés-verbal* usually designated how many copies should be printed.

[62] Many districts issued several editions (e.g., C. Agen, N. Artois, etc.). The largest single edition was voted by the third estate of Bailleul, which authorized 5,000 copies (p.v., *Arch. Nat.* Ba 18).

[63] Morris, G., *Journal pendant les années 1789-1792* (Paris, 1901), p. 21, April 26.

[64] Young, A., *Voyages en France en 1787, 1788 et 1789* (edition by H. Sée, Paris, 1931), Vol. I, p. 314, June 27.

[65] Various *procès-verbaux* show that cahiers of distant districts were known (e.g., N. Charmes knew the cahier of N. Bordeaux, *cf.* p. v., *Arch. Nat.* Ba 53). In addition, scattered references in contemporary diaries, correspondence, etc., and present-day collections in provincial libraries are evidence of the circulation of general cahiers in the provincial towns.

[66] For example, the *Mercure* discussed the cahiers in an article in the issue of May 2, 1789.

[67] See works of Dupont de Nemours, Prudhomme, Grille, etc., in the bibliography, pp. 300-301.

[68] Desmoulins, C., *La France libre* (s.l. 1789), p. 2.

become obvious that the general cahiers differed both in regard to the aggregate import of particular cahiers and in the topics treated. This fact does not, however, detract from the general impression which inevitably results from the similar form of the cahiers and the constant repetition of certain items and phrases. The belief in the unity of the French nation engendered by the reading of the cahiers was a force in the contemporary enthusiasm of the period. The sentiment of national amity and harmony made possible the subordination of class and regional loyalties, and the transformation of the States-General into a National Assembly.

The general cahiers are also important as an index of nationalism because of their rôle in the States-General itself. The change to the National Assembly challenged both the traditional practice of drawing up national cahiers by order and also the binding force of imperative mandates. After the transformation to the National Assembly, there could be no national cahiers. Although the *bailliage* cahiers would not serve thereafter as the bases for summaries to be presented to the king, nevertheless the deputies did make use of the general cahiers. A great many of the cahiers of all three orders had been reënforced by imperative mandates, that is to say, by the prescription of certain action, with the threat of disavowal for disobedience.[69] Many deputies of the clergy and of the nobles refused to join the Third Estate during the struggle for domination in the States-General because of their imperative mandates for vote by order. Throughout the months of May and June, adherence to imperative mandates by the two upper classes signified an appeal to tradition, class interest and regionalism as opposed to national interest.[70]

When the third estate triumphed, and the king ordered the clergy and nobles to join it, he gave permission to the deputies holding imperative mandates of contrary import to ask their constituents

[69] Consult the *Guide* for a full discussion of mandates There were three kinds of mandates, on the basis of their binding force: general mandates; special mandates which emphasized certain articles of the cahiers; and imperative mandates which enjoined obedience to the instructions of the cahier or the mandate.

[70] Although some members of the third estate had imperative mandates for vote by head, their uncompromising attitude and stubborn demand for the union of the orders was based upon national interest rather than upon their imperative mandates.

for new powers.[71] The Oath of the Tennis Court automatically repudiated imperative mandates. To safeguard the deputies against violence or corruption, which had been motives for issuing imperative mandates, the National Assembly declared the persons of the deputies inviolable.[72] Thus, the stand of the revolutionary party was against imperative mandates, while the conservatives adhered to them.

The question still remained after the royal order for new mandates, as to whether the National Assembly should expressly repudiate imperative mandates. After much discussion on July 7-8, the view of Siéyès was carried.[73] He held imperative mandates to be *ipso facto* null and void by virtue of the sovereignty of the National Assembly, and hence, that no resolution on the matter was necessary. Acceptance of Siéyès' opinion was therefore a negative acquiescence in the sovereignty of the National Assembly and a repudiation of imperative mandates. It also signified the recognition of the deputies, once admitted, as representatives of the nation at large, and not as the delegates of a particular class and *bailliage*.

The legal rejection of imperative mandates did not mean, however, that the cahiers ceased to influence the procedure of the National Assembly. After the nullification of mandates, the binding character of the cahiers was psychological rather than specific. The deputies used them as general guides. The continued importance of the cahiers was best shown in their use by the committee on the constitution. On July 27, 1789, Clermont Tonnerre,[74] in behalf of that committee, gave a summary of the cahiers before the National Assembly.[75] This was a tacit acceptance of the cahiers as

[71] *Cf.* minutes of royal séance of June 23, 1789, PR, *Arch. Nat.* AD I 11, art. 5, and text of royal order reprinted, Brette, *op. cit.*, Vol. I, pp. 56 *et seq.*

[72] *Procès-verbal de l'Assemblée nationale constituante* (Paris, s.d.), Vol. I, no. 5, p. 3. June 23, 1789.

[73] *Ibid.*, Vol. I, no. 17. *Cf.* also, Bailly, *Memoires* (Paris, Année XII, 1804), Vol. II, p. 37.

[74] Deputy of the nobles of Paris *intra-muros*.

[75] See *Procès-verbal de l'Assemblée nationale constituante,* Vol. II, for the complete text of the summary. The *Point du Jour* barely mentioned the report (*op. cit.*, Vol. I, pp. 315 *et seq.*) and the *Journal des Etats-généraux* made no mention of it (*op. cit.*, Vol. II, pp. 196-210).

guides for the order of business. This report, though short and undoubtedly based upon an incomplete number of the general cahiers, was astute and fair. Clermont-Tonnerre began with the statement that all the cahiers agreed on the necessity for a regeneration of France, but that they differed on the means to achieve it. He proceeded to cite the articles on which there was virtually unanimous agreement, and then the points wherein the cahiers differed. The emphasis upon the first part must have impressed the National Assembly with the unanimity of opinion on the vital problems then before it—constitutional recognition of the hereditary monarchy, legislative power vested in the National Assembly with the royal sanction, taxation by the National Assembly, the establishment of Provincial-Estates in all provinces, and such rights of citizens as personal liberty, inviolability of property, safeguards for the mails, and personal security from arrest.[76] The cahiers were thus consulted as guides in the preparation of the constitution, and the report showed the deference of the National Assembly to the wishes of the nation at large, of which the cahiers were considered the gauge.

After July 27, occasional reference was made to the cahiers in the deputies' speeches on the constitution,[77] but less frequently as time passed. Thereafter, although interest in the cahiers continued,[78] they ceased to exert a direct influence upon the course of events. Whatever their individual differences, the cahiers contributed to the enthusiasm for unity and to national sentiment during the opening months of the Revolution.

SUMMARY OF THE USE OF THE GENERAL CAHIERS

Along with the development of the States-General in France grew the practice of giving written instructions to the deputies. When the States-General was summoned for 1789, the revival of

[76] The report appeared less important in the session of the National Assembly than the proposals of Mounier, another member of the committee on the constitution, but it is significant that the cahiers were consulted at all.

[77] For example, *cf.* the quotations selected on the question of the veto, in Andrews, G. G., *The Constitution in the Early French Revolution* (New York, 1917), *passim.*

[78] Besides the publication of summaries, references to the cahiers in contemporary memoires, etc., there exists an unfinished manuscript summary of the cahiers begun at the command of the keeper of the seals. *Cf. Arch. Nat.* Ba 89.

this traditional procedure led to the composition of *cahiers de doléances* in all the electoral districts of France. Out of the total number of cahiers composed, six hundred fifteen were designed as the specific instructions for the deputies direct to the States-General. These may be called the general cahiers, and possess greater value for the present study than the remaining group.

The cahiers represent a special class of source materials for a study of the Revolution. Six limitations upon their value should be recognized—the limitations of any circumscribed class of documents, the brevity and topical character of the cahiers, the omission of obvious problems combined with the infinite variety of topics expressed, the unoriginal character of the cahiers, alleged one-sidedness, and difficulties of consultation. These limitations are in part removed by documentary analysis, and are more than overbalanced by special advantages.

Three special advantages of the cahiers as documentary sources render them an indispensable part of any study of the Revolution. The absence of a more adequate source of mass opinion for the period, the possibility of comparison with cahiers of the early States-Generals in respect of general national trends, and the use of the cahiers in the early Revolution give them special significance. Despite their limitations, the general cahiers of 1789 are an invaluable gauge of national sentiment and are also important for their influence in increasing nationalism.

CHAPTER II

CERTAIN BASIC ELEMENTS IN FRENCH NATIONALISM

The word "nationalism" seems to have first appeared in French in 1798, when the Abbé Barruel was quoting from the German illuminist, Weishaupt.[1] *Amour national* or *nationalisme* was considered by the German cosmopolite as synonymous with an egotistical, aggressive nationalism, while the Frenchman defended a humanitarian nationalism that would combat Jacobinism. The philosophy of the national state antedated, however, the use of the word "nationalism." In the middle of the eighteenth century, the Swiss, Zimmermann, had published in German a little handbook called *Vom Nationalstolz*.[2] This went through several editions in German, appeared in French translation in 1769, and was also translated into other languages. *Considérations sur l'orgueil national,* the title of the French edition, was a keen, impartial analysis of national sentiment, including both its good and bad features, and could very well have appeared under the title *Nationalisme*. The actual forces of nationalism had, however, been operating long before the collective name had been invented, and before political writers recognized its collective force.

Nationalism has been, indeed, the chief motivating ideal of political development throughout the modern era. In the ancient world, history unfolded the oriental empire, the Greek city-state, and the Roman Empire. The medieval period was characterized by the ideal of a universal Christian empire combined with feudal or local loyalty, while modern times have been marked by the

[1] Attention was called to this first appearance of the word *nationalism* in French by F. Baldensperger, in the *Révolution française, revue,* 1905, Vol. XL, pp. 263-64. He quotes the passage from the Abbé Barruel's *Mémoires pour servir à l'histoire du jacobinisme* (Hambourg, 1798), Vol. III, p. 184, where Weishaupt was describing the duties of the *Epopte*.

[2] J. G. Zimmerman, *Vom Nationalstolz* (Zurich, 1758). The fourth edition, appearing in 1768, was enlarged, and served as the basis of the French translation (Paris, 1769).

emergence of self-conscious nationalities, all of which have sooner or later sought to establish national states. Nationalism has substituted the national unit for universal empire, and national patriotism has taken precedence over personal allegiance and local fealty. Internationalism, a corollary of nationalism, began when a number of the European states had achieved the unification of their respective nationalities, and were forced, therefore, to recognize the separate existence of other national states. It may be that some generations hence, historians will distinguish an international era. Without regard, however, to the future, which is the concern of the prophet rather than the historian, the whole trend of modern history has been toward the development, and the culmination in the twentieth century, of nationalism as a political theory and a political fact.

The historical development and the present manifestation of nationalism differ in the various national units. It is hardly necessary to cite such commonplace facts as the achievement of political unity by the French nationality before 1500, and its delay in Germany until the nineteenth century. The measure of governmental unity reached in England under the Tudors was scarcely consummated in France before the reign of Louis XIV. In the seventeenth century, while the Englishman was in revolt against absolutism, the Frenchman submitted to the sway of the *Roi Soleil*. Patriotism, to Luther, meant German Protestantism versus papal supremacy, and also an appeal to the German nation against Catholic princes and rebellious German peasants alike, while to Jean Bodin, patriotism meant support of the French monarchy as a means of unifying the French nation, irrespective of religion.

One might continue to recite the truisms of modern history that demonstrate the contrasting developments of the various modern national states. We are concerned, however, with the particular national development of only one of these states—France. Nor can we attempt to trace the full evolution of French nationalism. Our interest is to note the distinguishing characteristics of present-day French nationalism, and then to examine the stage of development reached on the eve of the great French Revolution.

There is a tendency, especially in France, to look upon nationalism merely as the chauvinistic aspect of national patriotism and national policy. Nationalism has had its chauvinistic moments, its chauvinistic defenders, to be sure. The word "chauvinism" came into use in the Napoleonic period to designate a ridiculously exaggerated devotion to a cause. Today, chauvinism means boastful aggressiveness, but that has not been the exclusive monopoly of modern political evolution. There was Athenian chauvinism under Pericles; Hellenistic, under Alexander; Roman, under Caesar; Frankish, under Clovis; French, under Philip Augustus and Louis XIV; Hohenstaufen, under Frederick Barbarossa; Florentine, under the Medici; Papal, under Caesar Borgia; Spanish, under the *conquistadores;* and so forth. To identify chauvinism and nationalism as synonymous is to forget the different derivations and meanings of the two words, and, far more important, to misinterpret or ignore a most vital trend throughout modern history. Nationalism is the really appropriate term to describe the general change in governmental policy and in popular sentiment toward emphasizing the principle of nationality and devotion to the national state. It may, or it may not, involve "chauvinism."

In its historical significance, therefore, nationalism may be viewed as a psychological force, a policy and a method of building up the national state and intensifying national feeling. The continuous thread of modern French history displayed first, the building of the national state, and once this was achieved the intensification of national sentiment. Twentieth-century French nationalism combines four elements, whose proportional combination distinguishes it from the nationalism of other European states. Consciousness of nationality and national patriotism are universal elements of all nationalism. To these two, France added democracy and *étatisme.* It is to a large extent the development of two specifically French factors, and their interaction upon the two universal elements, that have characterized the last hundred and fifty years of French history, and which give a special color to contemporary French nationalism. Let us examine a bit more closely each of the four marks of French nationalism.

It is needless to review all the uses of the word "nationality."

There have been three main uses—the juridical, the racial, and the politico-sociological. The juridical conception of nationality implies merely the jurisdiction of any sovereign state over its citizens, and from the point-of-view of the individual, the possession of rights, privileges, and duties as a citizen of that state. In this sense, every person possesses nationality in some state.[3] Juridical nationality is individualistic and legalistic, whereas the other two conceptions of nationality are social.

Nationality has also been used in a racial sense, to imply subdivisions of the human race into groups with more or less defined physical characteristics. The racial use of the word has given rise to great abuses. Majority traits have been looked upon as universal, and rigid physical lines have been drawn and exclusive characteristics claimed. It is this use of the term that has led to popular delusions that all Englishmen are like the fictitious John Bull; all Frenchmen, short, vivacious, jealous, mercurial; all Italians, dark-complexioned, sensuous, given to extremes. Experience and analysis have failed to eradicate these popular misconceptions.

The third use of the word "nationality" is the politico-sociological, the one most properly applicable to actual phenomena of nationalism. Carlton J. H. Hayes has given an adequate definition of this concept. According to him, a nationality is

> a group of people who speak either the same language or closely related dialects, who cherish common historical traditions, and who constitute or think they constitute a distinct cultural society.[4]

The strong consciousness of French nationality (in this sense) which is well nigh instinctive in the average Frenchman today, has been a slow growth stretching back into medieval history. The factors which have produced this common consciousness are: (1) geography, (2) race, (3) language, (4) religion, (5) traditions, and (6) "community spirit." The essential basis of nationality is psychological. The first five factors may coexist without necessarily making people aware that they belong to one and the same na-

[3] International law is attempting to remedy the conflict of laws which has made possible citizenship in two countries, and also loss of citizenship.

[4] Hayes, C. J. H., *Essays on Nationalism* (New York, 1926), p. 5.

tionality. When the sixth factor begins to operate—when community spirit appears—the concept of nationality becomes a self-conscious power.

Democracy is one of the distinguishing features of present-day French nationalism. It was prominent in the political philosophy of the eighteenth century, and has since then received progressive application. Democracy affected both the character and the intensity of French nationalism by promoting a leveling of the classes and a form of political equality within the state. The result of an increase in the active participation of the individual in the state and of the development of democratic machinery of government has been to increase the popular interest in the national state, and popular loyalty to it. Democracy has been an integral part of French liberal thought since the French Revolution, and of majority opinion and practice since the establishment of the Third Republic. Although France has retained social aristocracy, individualism—the basis of political democracy—is an essential feature of French nationalism today.

Etatisme means the supremacy of the secular state over individuals or groups within its jurisdiction. This involves an exalting of the state and an enlargement of its functions. *Etatisme* is opposed to both the feudal and the clerical concept of the state, to any doctrine of plural sovereignty, and it is also opposed to the liberal concept of the state as a "passive policeman," a "necessary evil." In proportion as the secular state has subdued all other forces within its dominion, the sentiment of nationalism has taken a more coherent form, and has been purposefully propagated by the state. A philosophical conflict exists between *étatisme* and democracy. *Etatisme* subordinates the individual to the state, while democracy (in theory) subordinates the state to the individual. The secular state in France has gradually increased its functions, and has grown, in a general way, more "socialistic," in the sense that it has increasingly regulated the individual both for his own and for the national benefit. This movement has, however, been paralleled by an increasing participation of the common man in government, an active popular criticism of government, a flexible ministerial system, and an actual repudiation of infringements on individual liberty and independence. *Etatisme* and democratic individualism are coexistent in contemporary French life, and the balance maintained between them is a distinctive characteristic of French nationalism.

Patriotism, the fourth element in nationalism, needs no definition. Like consciousness of nationality, it is primarily a psychological force. The *patrie* of patriotic devotion has differed at various historical epochs. There has been loyalty to an oriental monarch, to a loosely wrought empire, to a city-state, to a feudal lord, to a feudal state, to a nationality, and to a national state. The national state is peculiarly a phenomenon of modern history,[5] and consequently, national patriotism has been, above all, a mark of the modern era. At the opening of modern times in France, royal patriotism—loyalty to the king—was nascent. Feudal loyalty and regionalism prevailed long after the Middle Ages, and impeded the development of national unity. During the French Revolution, patriotism ceased to be royal patriotism, although that form survived in the legitimist movement of the nineteenth century, and has continued to a degree among present-day French monarchists. Regionalism long survived in the periodic manifestations of federalism. The sentiment of national patriotism is today so conspicuous and so cogent that its slow evolution may be overlooked.

The fusion of nationality and patriotism in France was gradual. Although the development of democracy and *étatisme* accelerated the movement, one must not ignore the distinction clearly drawn by Frenchmen between the *patrie* and the state. It is this distinction which gives to modern French nationalism its verbal aggressiveness and its physical defensiveness. The Frenchman will give his life for his *patrie,* but not for the state. He maintains his individualism against an aggressive state at home but will sacrifice completely his individualism in defense of France. Democracy holds French *étatisme* and patriotism in check, and prevents an excessive consciousness of French nationality from resulting in a completely chauvinistic patriotism. French nationalism today displays an unusual fusion of these four elements.

[5] This might be challenged with respect to the ancient Hebrew kingdom, the Roman state before its expansion outside of Italy, etc., but historians would recognize a difference at least in degree between all early national states, and the modern form.

Consciousness of nationality and national patriotism developed earlier than democracy and *étatisme* in French nationalism. It was not until the nineteenth century that all four elements coöperated and created the distinctive, and extraordinarily potent, nationalism of contemporary France. Previously, such nationalism had been the conscious philosophy of some individuals and of some groups; and, it must be borne in mind, the separate elements were developing long before their fusion into nationalism was generally appreciated. It is our purpose to discover what stage in its evolution French nationalism had reached on the eve of the French Revolution.

CHAPTER III

NATIONALITY AND THE GENERAL CAHIERS

French nationalism today embraces all the six elements which in the preceding chapter we have associated with the concept of nationality. Frenchmen believe in a physical unity of their country, *la belle France,* and regard themselves as a racial unit possessing a common language, influenced by a common religion and common traditions, and, above all, characterized by a distinctive French spirit. By an analysis of the testimony of the cahiers on these separate elements in the concept of nationality, we may discover how far they were recognized and expressed on the eve of the Revolution.

FRANCE AS A DEFINED TERRITORY

The France of 1789 did not extend to the "natural boundaries" which were achieved under the Convention, and which have been the goal of French ambition ever since. Furthermore, the general boundaries enclosed several areas subject to foreign sovereignties,[1] while the territory actually governed by the French monarch was divided and subdivided by the diverse, irregular, and overlapping administrative units of the old régime. What was the attitude of the cahiers toward territorial disunity?

A great many cahiers referred to France as a positive entity,[2] but without clear association between French nationality and a defined territory. The rare expressions involving geographic area took one of three forms, indication of the consciousness of frontiers, reference to foreign jurisdictions within the boundaries, and an occasional statement against a change of boundaries. The makers of the cahiers were too anxious about domestic reforms to be much concerned with rectification of external frontiers.

[1] Consult Brette, Armand, *Les Limites et les divisions territoriales de la France en 1789* (Paris, 1907), for an excellent discussion of the territorial eccentricities of France in 1789. Diagrammatic maps at the end of the book give the ten foreign districts inside French frontiers, and the complex administrative divisions.

[2] For example, T. Saintes, AP, Vol. V, p. 670, col. 1.

Expressions of consciousness of the frontiers came largely from the border provinces and were economic or strategic. In the northeastern provinces—the Barrois, Lorraine, Trois-Evêchés, and Alsace—only twelve cahiers out of ninety-eight available for the four districts expressed frontier consciousness.[3] Two instances illustrate the attitudes taken: the third estate of Thionville[4] spoke of its location on the highway between the Austrian Netherlands and Germany, and pled for proper fortification and military maintenance,[5] while the nobles of Nomény gave the fullest statement of frontier consciousness by relating problems of taxation, emigration, roads, and debts to their frontier position.[6]

In the south, only one cahier of Provence indicated the proximity of the frontier,[7] while four of the southern districts noted the nearness of Spain.[8] In the north, four cahiers gave evidence that they came from frontier territories.[9] Other than these few citations, the overwhelming mass of general cahiers ignored the matter.

A similar lack of concern over the foreign jurisdictions within France characterized the cahiers. A few cahiers mentioned the case of Avignon, which was papal territory,[10] while three cahiers of the northeast—two from Alsace[11] and one from Lorraine[12]—referred to foreign principalities in the vicinity.

Although a few cahiers expressed content with French boundaries as they then were,[13] the center of interest was not geographic

[3] The twelve are exclusive of the cahiers that recognized the special customs status of these provinces (*Cf. infra*, pp. 56-57). The twelve cahiers are: N. Bouzonville, C, N, Colmar, T. Dieuze, CN. Lixheim, T. Longwy, N. Nomény, N. Nancy, T. Sedan, N. Sarrebourg, T. Thionville, U. Villers-la-Montagne.

[4] All general cahiers issued from *bailliages, senechaussées,* or corresponding administrative units. In the interest of simplicity, a cahier will be cited by the proper name of the district without indication of the official title of the jurisdiction.

[5] AP, Vol. III, p. 777, art. 20.

[6] AP, Vol. IV, p. 93, art. 16. (See Appendix, p. 323, under Nomény).

[7] T. Barcelonnette, AP, Vol. III, p. 366. This district bordered on the Kingdom of Sardinia.

[8] U. Navarre, N. Perpignan, T. Bigorre, Ustaritz.

[9] C, T, Artois, N. Quesnoy, N. Vitry (not directly north).

[10] N, T, Forcalquier, T. Marseille, T. Toulon. The loss of the cahiers of the *sénéchaussée* of Arles deprives us of opinion from the district nearest Avignon.

[11] C, N, Colmar.

[12] T. Longwy.

[13] T. Bailleul, N, T. Corsica, T. Mâcon, N. Trévoux, U. Villers-la-Montagne. For example, the third estate of Mâcon would require the consent of the nation for aggressive warfare (AP, Vol. III, p. 628, art. 17).

unity, but the right of the French nation, rather than of the monarch, to determine territorial limits.

These scattered references to territory were the only indications of a relationship between nationality and a defined geographical area that the general cahiers of 1789 contained. The many references to France, as an entity, ignored its pertinence to the map of Europe. One must therefore look into the other elements of nationality for any widespread consciousness of this factor in 1789.

RACE

The word *nation* appeared constantly in the general cahiers. This was the term used both in a sociological and a political sense to signify the French people, the French nationality. The political meaning of *nation* will be discussed later.[14] In its sociological import, it was synonymous with the present use of *nationalité*.[15] There is no doubt that the makers of the cahiers believed vaguely in a definite subdivision of the human race, for the ethnic group was implied whenever *la nation* and *les français* were mentioned.[16] The physical conception remained, in most cases, undefined, since the words appeared without interpretation. Some of the cahiers did, however, indicate certain attitudes which throw light upon their notion of nationality. These were the attribution of certain qualities of character to the French nation, attitudes on citizenship, and interest in the increase of population.

TRAITS OF CHARACTER.—A small number of the general cahiers of 1789 claimed a great many different virtues for the French nationality. Generosity,[17] dignity,[18] fidelity,[19] devotion to public welfare,[20] enlightenment and humanitarianism,[21] vivacity,[22] deli-

[14] *Cf. infra*, pp. 65-71.

[15] The *Dictionnaire* of the Encyclopedists gave no definition for *nationalité*, whereas it said that *nation* was "the collective word to express a large number of people who inhabit a certain territory, with certain limits and subject to the same government." Furthermore, it said that each nation had particular characteristics, e.g., "frivolous as a Frenchman," "jealous as an Italian," etc. (*op. cit.*, Vol. XI, p. 36).

[16] For examples, *cf.* U. Montfort l'Amaury (AP, Vol. IV, p. 38, col. 1), T. Rustaing, (AP, Vol. II, p. 367, col. 2), T. Caudebec-en-Caux (AP, Vol. II, pp. 580-81), etc.

[17] N. Clermont-en-Beauvoisis, AP, Vol. II, p. 750, col. 2.

[18] T. Beauvais, AP, Vol. II, p. 301, col. 2.

[19] T. Calais, AP, Vol. II, p. 514, col. 1.

[20] N. Clermont-en-Beauvoisis, AP, Vol. II, p. 750, col. 2.

[21] N. La Rochelle, AP, Vol. III, p. 483, art. 69.

[22] N. Rouen, AP, Vol. V, p. 504, col. 1.

cacy,[23] sensibility,[24] were considered to be outstanding characteristics of the French nation. The two qualities which were most often repeated were a love of fame[25] and a high sense of honor,[26] both of which suggest a widespread influence of Montesquieu. There was reference both to national honor, and to the individual sense of honor. Frenchmen possessed so keen an appreciation of personal honor that an appeal to it should be sufficient reward for virtuous service.[27] National honor was being violated by certain irrational and inhumane legal practices,[28] and by the use of foreign methods of discipline in the French army.[29] Reform of such practices, these cahiers said, would restore the real sense of honor of the French people.

A few cahiers went further than isolated characteristics and spoke of the "genius" of the French,[30] the "national character,"[31] or the "national spirit."[32] Such references occurred most often in connection with discussion of reform in military discipline.[33] The close link between the laws of a state and national character, voiced by both Montesquieu and Rousseau, was reflected in several cahiers. The third estate of Paris *intra-muros* stated that law should be framed in conformity with national character.[34] The clergy of Nivernais suggested the origin of the French nationality, "The condition of persons in France is not the result of accident; it has been determined by the genius of the nation, by ancient customs, by possession and by the laws."[35] A great many cahiers were

[23] T. Beauvais, AP, Vol. II, pp. 308-9.

[24] *Loc. cit.*, note 23.

[25] For example, N. Orléans, in Bloch, C., *D.I., Cahiers de doléances . . . d'Orléans . . .* (Orléans, 1906-7), Vol. II, p. 433, art. 7.

[26] The third estate of Alençon gave a humorous twist to the question of honor, when they said, ". . . if honor is the father of the nobility he was born in the bosom of the third estate." (AP, Vol. I, p. 719, ch. x, art. 1.)

[27] For example, C. Montreuil, AP, Vol. IV, p. 59, art. 6.

[28] For example, N. Paris *intra-muros,* AP, Vol. V, p. 274, col. 1.

[29] For example, N. Artois, AP, Vol. II, p. 83, art. 12. *Cf.* also, *infra,* p. 163.

[30] For example, N. Caen, AP, Vol. II, p. 491, art. 25.

[31] For example, N. Castres, AP, Vol. II, p. 567, art. 16.

[32] For example, N. Castelnaudary, AP, Vol. II, p. 558, ch. v.

[33] *Cf. infra,* p. 163. The discipline in use was considered contrary to French honor, national character or genius.

[34] AP, Vol. V, p. 288, col. 1, art. 1.

[35] AP, Vol. IV, p. 248, art. 10. Few of the cahiers were expressed in literary prose. There will be an attempt in the translation of the French to preserve some of the quaintness of their eighteenth-century phraseology.

aroused over the decline in public *moeurs,* and believed that their reform would regenerate the national character.[36] According to the clergy of Alençon, the States-General should "work for the re-establishment of the public *moeurs;* it is upon these that the prosperity of empires depends."[37] The cahier of the third estate of Agen[38] opened with an optimistic prophecy that "reason, philosophy, and humanity" were about to be revived, and that, thereafter, the French would no longer be a "group of men" but would become "a free nation."[39] One cahier went further than all the others, and claimed a "male" character for French ancestry.[40] We miss, however, any hint in the cahiers of the effect of climate and geographic conditions upon national character, the outstanding contribution of Montesquieu.

Despite the many different characteristics assigned to the French nation, their insertion was incidental to requests for reform, and less than one seventh of the total number of general cahiers included such phrases.[41] It is significant, however, that any of the cahiers devoted time and space to expressions of national qualities. One is led to believe that such ideas were much more widely held than the brief cahiers indicate. If one were to judge from the cahiers alone, the concept of nationality was more concrete among the nobles than among the clergy or the third estate.

Citizenship.—Did all the inhabitants of France comprise the French nationality? What was the relationship between French citizenship and the possession of French characteristics?

The traditional basis of citizenship in France prior to the Revolution and the Civil Code of 1804 was *ius soli* with some rare extensions of the principle of *ius sanguinis.*[42] Although the convocation of the States-General of 1789 had been based upon French nationality, whether by birth or by naturalization,[43] the problem of

[36] *Cf. infra,* p. 106.
[37] AP, Vol. I, p. 708, art. 3.
[38] See reservations on certain cahiers, *supra,* pp. 12 *et seq.,* and Appendix, p. 237.
[39] AP, Vol. I, p. 686.
[40] C. Longwy, AP, Vol. III, p. 772, art. 12.
[41] *Cf.* Table I, Appendix, p. 250.
[42] Rouard de Card, *La Nationalité française* (Paris, 1922), *passim.*
[43] *Cf.* the regulation of January 24, 1789, in Brette, A. *Documents inédits relatifs à la convocation des Etats-généraux de 1789* (Paris, 1894-1915), Vol. I, pp. 76-77, art. 25.

the appearance of foreign holders of French fiefs arose, and the central government interpreted the convocation on the basis of property and not of nationality.[44] Outside the foreign property owners, there were large groups of foreign residents in France, who were subject to consular jurisdiction, hampered by economic and social impediments, and who had little chance to acquire French status.[45]

The cahiers of 1789 seldom touched the subject of juridical citizenship. Opposition to foreigners took the form of hostility to the privileges enjoyed by foreign property owners,[46] to the appointment of foreigners to French offices and benefices,[47] and to the facility of naturalization.[48] One cahier from the interior of France denounced "cosmopolites."[49] Only about twenty-five cahiers in all indicated opposition to foreigners, and almost all of these were from the northeastern provinces.[50]

More cahiers were inclined to let down the bars for foreigners than to discriminate against them. A favorable attitude toward foreigners was indicated by the demand for the abolition of the *droit d'aubaine*,[51] for the extension of naturalization,[52] or for the same protection of law for foreigners as for French citizens.[53]

The widespread absence of statements relative to foreigners, and the presence of scattered items favorable to them,[54] indicate the

[44] Trouble arose in the assemblies of the nobles of Avesnes, Quesnoy, and Gex. In each case, the keeper of the seals decided that representation was a prerogative of property-owners, irrespective of nationality.

[45] Mathorez, J., *Les Etrangers en France sous l'ancien régime* (Paris, 1919-21), *passim.*

[46] For example, T. Belfort, AP, Vol. II, p. 318, art. 59.

[47] For example, U. Villers-la-Montagne, AP, Vol. II, p. 245, art. 14.

[48] For example, N. or T. Longwy, MS, *Arch. Moselle, cf.* reprint in the *Guide.*

[49] N. Limoges, AP, Vol. III, p. 567, ch. iv, art. 6.

[50] 22 cahiers, 4 C, 6 N, 11 T, 1 U. N. Bailleul, C, T, Belfort, T. Belley, N, T, Bouzonville, C, N, T, Colmar, T. Dix Villes, C, N, Limoux, C. Longuyon, N, T, Longwy, T. Haguenau, T. Nîmes, N. Paris *hors-les-murs,* T. Sarrebourg, T. Sarreguemines, T. Tours, U. Villers-la-Montagne.

[51] The *aubaine* was a tax paid by foreigners on inheritances, and for the right to engage in commerce. The clergy of Orléans approved of this tax, but seven cahiers asked for its abolition: C. Péronne, N. Orléans, T—Angers, Cahors, Charolles, St. Quentin, Toulon.

[52] For example, C. Bailleul, AP, Vol. II, p. 169, col. 2, note 1.

[53] For example, T. Besançon, AP, Vol. II, p. 338, arts. 16, 17.

[54] The importance of the number of cahiers favorable to foreigners lies less in their number than in their appearance in cahiers from different parts of France. To the list of cahiers, note 51, add—C. Bailleul, N—Metz, Sens, T—Aval, Digne, Besançon.

general prevalence of a form of cosmopolitanism. The hostility to foreigners existed almost exclusively in Lorraine and Alsace. The majority attitude of the cahiers of 1789 contrasted with the attitude of the Convention in 1793. In pursuance of the policy of the cahiers, the *aubaine* had been abolished before 1793,[55] and naturalization had been granted to foreigners who favored the Revolution,[56] but when foreign war came, the cosmopolitanism of the early Revolution gave way slowly to an anti-foreigner policy.[57]

The criterion of a common religion was the basis for the exclusion of Protestants and Jews from the spiritual unity of Frenchmen. These two non-Catholic groups in the French population were not, however, classed together. The nobles and the third estate were generally favorable to the civil rights granted Protestants by the edict of 1787,[58] and thereby tacitly included them in the French nation. On the other hand, the opposition of the clergy to the edict implied their exclusion. Only one cahier, that of the clergy of Meaux, specifically ostracized Protestants.[59]

While the Protestants found some defenders among the two lay orders, there was almost always discrimination against the Jews. Mention of the Jews was limited to cahiers from Alsace, Lorraine, and Trois-Evêchés (plus one exception, the cahier of the nobles of Paris *intra-muros*). Three cahiers showed a liberal attitude,[60] as against forty-five that were hostile to the Jews.[61] Antagonism was not religious, however, but economic. Their money lending, usury, acquisition of property, and intermarriage with

[55] The *aubaine* was abolished by the laws of August 6, 1790, and April 8-12, 1793.

[56] Mathiez, A., *La Révolution et les étrangers* . . . (Paris, 1918), ch. ii, iii.

[57] *Idem,* pp. 129 *et seq.*

[58] *Cf. infra,* p. 45.

[59] Large sections of the original cahier were omitted by the editors of the *Archives Parlementaires.* The section on the edict of 1787 is one of these. *Cf.* MS, *Arch. Nat.* C 20/97, under *Edit des Protestants,* and *Guide.*

[60] U. Rozières, T. Dieuze, T. Verdun. In addition, the cahier of N. Paris *intra-muros* was noncommittal, merely asking that the status of Jews be examined.

[61] *Gen.* of Nancy: C. Bitche, C, T, Boulay, C, T, Bouzonville, T. Châtel-sur-Moselle, T. Château-Salins, N. Darney, C. Dieuze, U. Fenestrange, CN, T, Lixheim, N, T, Mirecourt, C, N, T, Nancy, T. Pont-à-Mousson, C, N, T, Sarreguemines, T. St. Dié, T. Vézelise.

Gen. of Metz: T. Metz, C, N, T, Sarrebourg, N, T, Sedan, N, T, Thionville, N, T, Toul, C, N, Verdun, C, T, Vic.

Gen. of Strasbourg: C, N, T, Belfort, C, T, Colmar, T. Dix Villes, T. Haguenau, T. Strasbourg.

Christians were considered detrimental to French prosperity.[62] The aim of these cahiers was to increase the restrictions against Jews and thereby to complete their exclusion from the French nationality.

In conclusion, one may say that the cahiers showed little hostility toward foreigners in France, but that animosity against them and against Jews did exist in the northeastern provinces.

Were Frenchmen who had emigrated to the French colonies still Frenchmen? Very few of the cahiers dealt with the matter. It was, however, implied in the request of twenty-three cahiers that the colonies be represented in the States-General.[63] For these, at least, French colonials were an integral part of the French nationality. The colonists themselves naturally claimed French citizenship.[64]

It is obvious from the foregoing that juridical citizenship was not prominent in the minds of the electorate of 1789. Had the abuses of the old régime been traceable to foreign residents or officials,[65] a great many cahiers would undoubtedly have discussed foreigners. The paucity of expressions on the subject leads one to the conclusion that racial exclusiveness was not then an important factor in the consciousness of French nationality.

THE INCREASE OF POPULATION.—A great outcry against depopulation came in the nineteenth century, but even in 1789, the French expressed some interest in increasing the number of Frenchmen. In this, their motives were both humanitarian and patriotic.

[62] The following examples of demands affecting the civil status of the Jews may be cited: (1) opposition to the increase in the number of Jewish families (e.g., T. Boulay); (2) proscription of intermarriage between Jews and Christians (e.g., C Colmar); (3) exclusion of Jews from the acquisition of property (e.g., T. Boulay); (4) limitation upon the occupations that might be chosen (e.g., T. Bouzonville); (5) supervision of money lending (*e.g.*, T. Colmar). In practically all cases of opposition to the Jews, the hostility was attributed to their usury, money lending, or what was considered to be their bad moral influence.

[63] 23 cahiers: 2 C, 11 N, 10 T. C—Paris *hors-les-murs*, Paris *intra-muros;* N—Angers, Artois, Auxerre, Melun, Nemours, Orléans, Paris *hors-les-murs*, Paris *intra-muros*, Périgord, Provins, Tours; T—Clermont Ferrand, Chaumont-en-Vexin, Melun, Orléans, Paris *hors-les-murs*, Paris *intra-muros*, Rochefort-sur-mer, St. Brieuc, Senlis, Ustaritz.

[64] The fact that the colonies held elections, even though omitted from the convocation, was an indication that the colonists considered themselves Frenchmen.

[65] The contrary was the case. Many cahiers praised Necker.

In the first place, numerous cahiers suggested ways for increasing the birth rate. A double tax on bachelors was recommended,[66] a more equitable arrangement of dowries,[67] and a general encouragement of marriage.[68] Preference in employment should be given to fathers of families, according to the third estate of Rochefort-sur-mer.[69] Another method of raising the birth rate was to lower taxes or pay bonuses to large families.[70] According to the clergy of Dourdan, laws against suicide and enforcement of the prohibition against duelling would also prevent depopulation.[71] The favorable influence of general prosperity on the increase of population was recognized by the third estate of Draguignan.[72]

Besides this interest in an increase of population, the cahiers also showed a desire for the preservation of the living. Concern for health and sanitation led to demands for maternity hospitals,[73] and was one of the motives for a widespread request for training and regulation of midwifery and surgery. The clergy of Limoux stated in lucid terms the effect of the prevailing conditions on the population:— "The inexperience of mid-wives takes away every day a multitude of saints to heaven, and deprives the state of subjects, and the *patrie* of citizens. . . ."[74] It is a moot question whether piety or the desire to increase the Catholic population of France led the clergy of Aix to ask that midwives be not only skilled but Catholic.[75] A variety of other requests were aimed at improving public health, but none of them brings a smile today like that of the nobles of Castres, or of the nobles of Bailleul. The former stated that "The conservation and the health of a precious part of your subjects require a change in the sale and distribution of to-

[66] For example, T. Villefranche-de-Beaujolais, AP, Vol. II, p. 283, art. 8.
[67] For example, C. Péronne, AP, Vol. V, p. 355, col. 1.
[68] For example, T. Aix, AP, Vol. I, p. 696, col. 2, art. 2.
[69] AP, Vol. III, p. 487, vol. 2, art. 3.
[70] For example, T. Castres, AP, Vol. II, p. 569, col. 2.
[71] AP, Vol. III, p. 245, art. 25. Several other cahiers denounced duelling, but no reference to the effect on population was made.
[72] AP, Vol. III, p. 261, col. 2.
[73] For example, C. Melun, AP, Vol. III, p. 736, cols. 1-2.
[74] *Cf.* text in Dom de Vic, and Vaissete, J., *Histoire de Languedoc* (Privat, 1872-92), Vol. XIV, p. 2617, art. 10.
[75] AP, Vol. I, p. 692, art. 9.

bacco,"[76] while the nobles of Bailleul said that tobacco had become a necessity.[77]

A few cahiers were anxious to prevent emigration, which resulted in loss of population and the transference of citizens to a foreign jurisdiction. According to the nobles of Quesnoy, the heavy taxes in Hainaut and the low taxes in the neighboring Austrian provinces encouraged emigration,[78] while the nobles of Nomény recognized a similar danger with regard to adjacent German kingdoms.[79] A few cahiers denounced exile as a punishment.[80] Sentiment against emigration was infrequent, however, since the desire for individual liberty was stronger than concern for population.[81]

A total of forty cahiers showed, by some one of the foregoing demands, an interest in increasing the population of France.[82] The methods later advocated by nationalists were all to be found in one or another of these cahiers. Interest in the numerical increase of the French nationality came from all parts of France, and more frequently from cahiers of the third estate.

TRADITIONS

Expression of the territorial unity of France, of national characteristics, of exclusive citizenship, and of concern for the preservation and increase of the French nationality were relatively rare and scattered among the cahiers of 1789. A far more important element in the concept of nationality on the eve of the Revolution was an appeal to common traditions. French history was capable of varied interpretation and it served the cahiers of all three orders as support for their demands.

[76] AP, Vol. II, p. 567, art. 21. Tobacco was used for cattle, but both these cahiers considered its use by human beings. The T. Bigorre denounced its use (AP, Vol. II. p. 360, art. 11).

[77] AP, Vol. II, p. 172, art. 29.

[78] AP, Vol. V, p. 507, art. 28.

[79] AP, Vol. IV, p. 93, art. 16.

[80] For example, T—Artois, Bailleul, Etampes, Lille.

[81] *Cf. infra,* pp. 92-94.

[82] 8 C, 7 N, 24 T, 1 U. C—Dourdan, Libourne, Limoux, Melun, Nérac, Péronne, Tours, Villefranche-de-Beaujolais; N—Blois, Lille, Montargis, Montreuil-sur-Mer, Nîmes, Nomény, Quesnoy; T—Aix, Bigorre, Blois, Bourmont, Castres, Châtillon-sur-Seine, Château-Salins, Château-Thierry, Corsica, Dijon, Draguignan, Lixheim, Mantes, Nérac, Paris *hors-les-murs,* Reims, Rennes, Riom, Rochefort, Quimper, Sens, Toulon, Vermandois, Villers-Cotterets; U—Rozières.

THE CONSTITUTION.—In 1789, the general cahiers referred to various French customs, but the basic consideration behind an appeal to tradition involved the popular attitude toward a constitution. Did France possess a constitution or was it necessary to make one? A minority affirmed directly that France had a constitution. The clergy of Châteauneuf-en-Thimerais made the assertion very positively:

> Perfectly content with a constitution to which the French empire, for fourteen centuries, owes its status, its happiness and its prosperity, we ask that the States-General immediately plan with the sovereign the means to render it indestructible.[83]

By far the greater majority of cahiers referred to a customary constitution by its various principles, which they believed should be reaffirmed by the States-General. The cahier of the nobles of Evreux opened with several paragraphs that illustrate this point of view:—

> The assembly of the order of the nobles of the *bailliage* of Evreux,
>
> Considering that the evils that afflict France to-day arise from the repeated violations of the constitutional laws of the kingdom and of the imprescriptible rights of the nation, which are an integral and essential part of the constitution;
>
> That these laws have fallen into disuse only because, not being assembled into one body, they have made it easy for ministers to deceive our sovereigns. . . .
>
> Considering finally that the times, the abuses, the innumerable illegal acts of the sovereign authority have hidden from sight the true principles of the monarchy, and have substituted the use of arbitrary power. . . .
>
> The assembly thinks that the first, the unique means that can be or ought to be employed to remedy efficaciously the present evils of the State and to prevent others with which it is menaced, is to recall the French constitution to its true principles. . . .[84]

Again and again the electorate of 1789 affirmed the existence of constitutional principles and the prime necessity of their reaffirmation before other business should be undertaken by the States-General.[85] The majority had perhaps come under the influence of

[83] AP, Vol. II, p. 639, col. 1. [84] AP, Vol. III, p. 295.

[85] For example, *cf.* C. Meaux, AP, Vol. III, p. 722, col. 1. Many more than half of the general cahiers asked for the confirmation of the constitution before the States-General proceeded to other business, and especially to taxation.

the contract theory and felt the need of a formal, solemnly promulgated constitution, but the same cahiers also appealed to traditional principles of French history.[86]

The principle most often referred to as fundamental was the institution of monarchy. The cahier of the clergy of Dourdan put the appeal in graphic terms:

> The monarchical government being the firm constitution of the nation, the form most appropriate to its internal tranquillity and to its external security, the most suitable to the extent of its provinces, the best adapted to the character of its peoples, who, at all epochs, have distinguished themselves by their love and attachment to their sovereigns: we will never concur in anything that would tend to alter the form of this government. . . .[87]

The nobles of Mantes expressed the same thought when they said that monarchy was the most appropriate for large empires, and for the physical situation and moral character of France.[88] Almost invariably, the cahiers stipulated adherence to the monarchy as the first article of the constitution.[89]

A second precept of French constitutional tradition was an appeal to the rights of the nation. According to the third estate of Draguignan, there were reciprocal rights between the nation and the king.[90] The right of the States-General, as representative of the nation, to regulate the taxes was *almost universally* affirmed.[91] For example, the nobles of Beauvais asked that the constitution be enacted before any taxes were granted, and the first and third articles of their proposed constitution would state:

> Art. 1. That the States-General, representing the nation, has legislative power conjointly with the king.
>
> Art. 3. That to the States-General alone belongs the right to establish and to extend the taxes. . . .[92]

Many cahiers cited the right of the nation as exercised in the

[86] For example, *cf.* N. Carcassonne, AP, Vol. II, p. 527, art. 2.

[87] AP, Vol. III, pp. 243-44.

[88] AP, Vol. III, p. 661.

[89] Even where there was no specific mention of a constitution, nearly every cahier affirmed adherence to monarchy.

[90] AP, Vol. III, p. 256, col. 1.

[91] No cahier omitted express or implied rights of the nation as exercised through the States-General.

[92] AP, Vol. II, p. 294, arts. 1 and 3.

past as justification of articles on the convocation, functions and procedure of the States-General. When the two privileged orders prescribed vote by order, they appealed invariably to traditional practice.[93]

All three orders, but more especially the clergy and nobles, claimed the division of the French people into three orders, as fundamental to the French constitution. The words of the nobles of Coutances were typical;

> It [the assembly of the nobles] accepts, therefore, as fundamental that the French constitution is composed of the King, supreme head of the nation, and of the three orders, essentially distinct and separate, equal, free, individual, except for subdivision, and mutually independent.[94]

According to the clergy of Mâcon, the aim of the States-General should be—

> to maintain as far as possible . . . the peace and harmony which ought to reign between the three orders, in opposing, however, anything that would disturb the position assigned by law to each of them, or anything that would efface the line of demarcation which separates them.[95]

Even the third estate sometimes recognized the division into three classes as an article of the French constitution.[96]

The cahiers of the privileged orders also referred to the historic rights of their classes. The nobles of Montpellier said that the rights of the classes were imprescriptible, just as were the rights of the nation.[97] According to the nobles of Ponthieu, the prerogatives of the nobles came down from the privileges exercised by the original Franks over conquered tribes.[98] Many cahiers of the clergy agreed with their spokesmen of Saintes, who claimed that the clergy had always been the first order in the states.[99]

[93] For example, C. Caudebec-en-Caux, AP, Vol. II, p. 573, col. 1. The third estate of Villers-Cotterets, one of two cahiers of that class that advocated vote by order, appealed to the traditional method (AP, Vol. VI, p. 191, art. 1).

[94] Bridrey, E., *D. I., Cahiers de doléances . . . de Cotentin* (Paris, 1912), Vol. III, p. 510, art. 3.

[95] *Arch. Nat.* B III 77, p. 287, art. 6 of the mandate.

[96] For example, T. Meaux, AP, Vol. III, p. 728, col. 2. The third estate seldom state that the French constitution required three classes, but they frequently implied that the division was customary. For example, T. Agen, AP, Vol. I, pp. 687 *et seq.*

[97] AP, Vol. IV, p. 48, col. 1.

[98] AP, Vol. V, p. 432, art. 14.

[99] AP, Vol. V, p. 659, art. 2.

A great many of the cahiers included statements of individual rights as articles of the constitution. Sometimes these were given as supplementary articles[100] while sometimes emphasis was laid upon the enactment of a formal Declaration of Rights.[101] Although the origin of such a declaration was never cited, undoubtedly the makers of those cahiers had been influenced by Locke and by English law. Wherever a formal Declaration of Rights was asked for, reference was tacit or explicit to principles of natural law and the rights of mankind. Such cases generally appealed to universal history, but there were also cahiers that appealed to French traditions in support of the rights of citizens. In speaking of liberty, the nobles of Carcassonne desired "to see flourish again that ancient constitution."[102] Security of property was looked upon as traditional by the privileged orders,[103] while a few claimed that guarantees against arrest had once existed in France and only needed revival.[104]

In their discussion of a constitution for France, a very large number of cahiers appealed to French tradition at the same time that they were actually creating a new tradition. France tried many constitutions before she achieved that of the third French Republic, but at each new attempt, one party or another looked back for inspiration to the constitutional principles enunciated in the cahiers of 1789.

A Common Religion.—Catholicism was considered by many cahiers as a distinctive French tradition, and in some cases, as an essential of the French constitution. The clergy of Nivernais gave the strongest affirmation of this:

> The Catholic religion has been at all times the religion of the state of France. It was raised to the throne with our first sovereigns; their successors promised at their coronation, before God and their people, to maintain it in the kingdom and to eradicate the errors which it pro-

[100] For example, T. Clermont Ferrand, AP, Vol. II, p. 769.

[101] For example, T. Paris *hors-les-murs,* AP, Vol. V, pp. 238 *et seq.*

[102] AP, Vol. II, p. 527, col. 1.

[103] For example, N. Paris *intra-muros,* AP, Vol. V, p. 272, col. 1. The third estate was almost equally anxious to confirm inviolability of property, but less often as an article of the constitution.

[104] For example, the nobles of Saintes claimed that the right of trial by jury was traditional in France (AP, Vol. V, p. 668, col. 1).

scribes. This holy religion has thus become, for the welfare of the nation, one of our fundamental laws. . . .[105]

Although the majority of cahiers tacitly[106] or specifically recognized Catholicism as the traditional religion of France, several attitudes were reflected regarding its future maintenance. At the time, France was overwhelmingly Catholic, but with the gradual decrease of persecution and the promotion of toleration by eighteenth-century philosophers, non-Catholics had reappeared in France. An edict in 1787 had permitted Protestants to carry on private ownership, and had given them civil rights.[107] In 1789, Protestants in appreciable numbers occupied the northeastern provinces,[108] the region of La Rochelle, and the southeast. Jews were largely concentrated in the northeastern provinces.[109] Since the general cahiers represented the opinion of the majority in the electoral assemblies, they were the oracles of Catholic opinion. One would have to look elsewhere for the expression of non-Catholic views.[110]

The Catholic majority evinced three attitudes toward the problem of future religious uniformity: the positive desire for uniformity, the superior claim of liberty of conscience and toleration, and the simultaneous championship of the principles of uniformity and toleration. The first—the demand for the maintenance of Catholicism as the only religion in France—took several forms. A large number of the general cahiers, especially those of the clergy, agreed with the clergy of Lyon who gave as the first article of the constitution the following article: "That the Catholic religion, which is the national and constitutional religion, shall be the only

[105] AP, Vol. IV, p. 246, col. 1.

[106] Tacitly, by the reforms asked.

[107] For the terms of the edict, see Isambert, *Recueil général des anciennes lois françaises* . . . (Paris, 1822), Vol. XXVIII, p. 472.

[108] According to a pamphlet in circulation in Alsace, one third of the population of that province was Protestant. *Cf. Mémoire pour les magistrats protestants des Villes ci-devant libres et impériales d'Alsace,* MS., *Arch. Nat.* Ba 11.

[109] According to a similar *mémoire,* there were 5,000 Jewish families in the provinces of Lorraine, Trois-Evêchés, and Alsace. *Cf. Mémoire pour la nation juive régnicole établi dans la généralité de Metz, d'Alsace, et de Lorraine,* MS., *Arch. Nat.* Ba 11).

[110] Only the cahier of T. Amont included demands of non-Catholic groups in the electorate (Goddard and Abensour, *Cahiers de doléances . . . d'Amont* (Besançon, 1927), Vol. II, p. 552, art. 84.

public cult."[111] Some of these cahiers used more forceful terms and contemplated the exclusion of all other forms of worship.[112] A number of cahiers, chiefly those of the clergy, desired uniformity of ritual as a means to fortify Gallican Catholicism.[113] The clergy of Condom stated that in order to

maintain among the clergy the most perfect harmony, it is desirable that there be only one catechism, one uniform theology, one ritual, one breviary, one ceremony.[114]

In its similar demand, the aim of the clergy of Poitiers was not only that of ecclesiastical concord, but the welfare of the church as a whole.[115] The celebration of the mass depended upon the education of the clergy; uniformity would remedy such defects, and at the same time increase the prestige of the church. Opinion favorable to Catholic supremacy was further strengthened in many cahiers of the clergy by their opposition to the edict granting civil rights to non-Catholics. Hostility to the edict of 1787 was in part the passion for uniformity and intolerance of exceptions to the dominant religion, and in part, opposition to activities carried on by Protestants under cover of the edict. The clergy complained of the extension of Protestantism through illegitimate influence on the appointments to Catholic benefices,[116] of intermarriage with Catholics,[117] and of their educational activities.[118]

One hundred and twenty-four cahiers, of which nearly 80 percent were those of the clergy, expressly desired the active maintenance of Catholicism by one or more of the methods just described.[119] Many others implied their preference for Catholicism

[111] AP, Vol. III, p. 600, art. 1.

[112] For example, C. Mantes, AP, Vol. III, p. 652, art. 1.

[113] The majority of cahiers asking for a uniform ritual also stated that Catholicism was the state religion, but at least thirteen made this demand without any reference to the state religion: C—Beauvais, Bigorre, Coutances, Libourne, Mont-de-Marsan, Nantes, Nérac, Toulouse, Villefranche-de-Beaujolais, Villers-Cotterets; T—Forez, Nantes, St. Quentin.

[114] AP, Vol. III, p. 33, col. 1, art. 1.

[115] AP, Vol. V, p. 391, art. 19.

[116] For example, C. Limoges, AP, Vol. III, p. 560.

[117] For example, C. Paris *hors-les-murs,* AP, Vol. V, p. 231, art. 4.

[118] For example, C. Chartres, AP, Vol. II, p. 622, art. 1.

[119] *Cf.* Table III, Appendix, p. 252.

by the detailed reforms asked. Let us see how these figures compare with those for toleration.

Approval of toleration took the form either of an outright adherence to liberty of conscience, or of an indorsement of the edict of 1787. The clearest expression of the former came from the third estate of Nîmes, where Rabaut St. Etienne, a pronounced Protestant, was chosen deputy and was very probably influential in making the cahier;

> It shall be represented, in respect to liberty of thought, that nothing is more worthy of the wisdom of His Majesty than to permit the free profession of every religion based on sane ethics, the sole method to enlighten men and to lead them toward virtue. . . .[120]

The article continued by approving the edict of 1787 and favoring its extension. The third estate of La Rochelle also stated concisely the principle: "Universal toleration ought to be admitted in an enlightened nation."[121] It was however, a minority of the cahiers that made such general statements of principle, or that included freedom of religion among the rights of man.[122] A favorable attitude toward toleration was more often shown by approval of the edict of 1787, without reference to the general principle, and without an assertion for Catholic uniformity. Such cases implied approval of civil toleration, without favor either for Catholicism or for Protestantism. Only thirty-five cahiers advocated general or civil toleration, without other implications.[123]

Unqualified statements of religious toleration were, however, comparatively rare. Economic and social considerations complicated the religious issue. Consequently, many more cahiers supported Catholicism and at the same time approved of the edict in favor of non-Catholics. Such cahiers desired religious uniformity

[120] Bligny-Bondurand, *D.I., Cahiers de doléances . . . de Nîmes* (Nîmes, 1909), Vol. II, p. 596, ch. iv, art. 2. In their introduction, the editors claimed that Rabaut St. Etienne wrote the cahier of the third estate of Nîmes (*Loc. cit.*, I, p. xxx-xxxi). He was a member of the committee that drew up the cahier, but the *procès-verbal* indicates that the cahier was thoroughly discussed by the assembly before adoption. (*Cf.* p. v, MS, *Arch. Nat.* Ba 57.)

[121] AP, Vol. III, p. 485, art. 102.

[122] For example, *cf. infra*, p. 93.

[123] *Cf.* Table III, Appendix, p. 253.

but recognized the expediency of civil toleration. How this might be true is well illustrated by the cahier of the third estate of Bar-sur-Seine. After favoring Catholicism as the sole religion, it stated:

> Liberty of conscience derives from natural law: each is responsible only to God for his religion. What men who live under one state demand of one another, is that no one disturb the order of their society, and the interest of states is to assemble in their midst all those who, by their knowledge, their skill, their industry, are capable of fostering abundance and prosperity; it is therefore desirable that France offer to all sectarians of the different religions a lot similar to that which the edict of November, 1787, affords to non-Catholics.[124]

A later passage in the same cahier showed that toleration was a means of winning new converts to Catholicism, and "to regain the children she had lost."[125]

Of the two hundred and three cahiers that faced directly the question of a common religion versus toleration, about 60 percent favored uniformity, about 30 percent approved of toleration, and about 30 percent expressed both opinions simultaneously.[126] It is obvious at once that less than half the available number of general cahiers broached the problem. Almost every cahier included some demands relative to religion, but most of them were irrelevant to the problem of uniformity, and to Catholicism as a French tradition. The silence of the majority of the cahiers on the edict of 1787 must be interpreted as acquiescence in the *status quo,* that is, preference for Catholicism and consent to civil toleration. It was natural that the clergy should affirm the fundamental character of Catholicism more often than the lay orders, and also that the latter should exhibit a more widespread toleration.

The tabulation of convictions regarding religious uniformity brings out some interesting facts about the geographic distribution of opinion.[127] The clergy of the majority of *generalities* were for uniformity, but those of the *generalities* of Nancy, Metz, and Strasbourg gave few expressions of opinion. In view of the presence of large numbers of Protestants in these districts, the silence of the

[124] AP, Vol. II, p. 256, art. 18.
[125] *Idem.*
[126] *Cf.* Table III, Appendix, pp. 252-53.
[127] The following generalizations are deduced from Table III, Appendix, pp. 252-53.

cahiers of the northeast signified a greater degree of toleration. The *generalities* of Lyon, Besançon, and Lille were predominantly for uniformity, even among the lay orders. The strongest toleration appeared in the lay cahiers of the *generality* of La Rochelle, with a close second in those of the *generalities* of Montpellier, Orléans, and Amiens.

The failure of many cahiers to discuss Catholicism as the one religion for France and the division of opinion among those that did consider it, indicate that, whereas the tradition of a common religion played a relatively important part in the concept of nationality among the clergy, it was subordinated to other considerations by the majority of the nobles and of the third estate. The dubious support of Catholicism in the cahiers contrasts with their universal championship of the French monarchy. Catholicism was a French tradition, but, in the future, liberty might compromise its ascendency.

A COMMON LANGUAGE.—The general cahiers of 1789 were singularly silent on the subject of language. In the first place, they are a poor gauge of linguistic conditions. The general assemblies comprised the better educated members of a *bailliage,* and were therefore cognizant of the official idiom. As early as 1539, the edict of Villers-Cotterets had required the use of French in the courts. During the seventeenth and eighteenth centuries, the French Academy had done much to standardize French and to spread its usage at the expense of local *patois,* while the *salons* and literary societies of the eighteenth century also promoted the official language. It is not, therefore, surprising that the majority of general cahiers give the impression of a widespread use of French and of a high degree of literacy and linguistic uniformity.[128]

Aside from peculiarities of spelling, punctuation, and occasional complexity of phraseology, which may have been due to the particular registrar or secretary, the major exceptions to a uniform

[128] Due to the policy of correcting small eccentricities when texts of cahiers have been published, minor differences that appear on the manuscript of the original may not always be detected in the reprints. Cahiers of the third estate of Brittany, some of the southwest and of the northeastern provinces, and those of the clergy of the southeast often showed imperfections in their French.

use of French appeared in the bilingual areas. The general cahiers gave evidence of the common use of two languages in Alsace, Lorraine, Trois-Evêchés, the Pyrenees sections, Brittany and Corsica,[129] but they gave no indication of the use of Flemish along the northern frontier. We know from other sources that the common people of France often used a *patois*,[130] but the general cahiers illustrate, rather, a widespread knowledge of French.

Of the districts that were bilingual, Alsace and Roussillon wanted their privileged status maintained,[131] while the other districts passed over the issue in silence. On the other hand, there were only half a dozen cahiers that desired the extension of French and the encouragement of uniformity in language. Two cahiers asked that the laws be published in French,[132] while the third estate of Paris *hors-les-murs* wanted public prayers to be read in French.[133] The other cahiers approached the question from an educational viewpoint. Two cahiers asked that more attention be given to French and less to Latin in the schools,[134] while the clergy of Autun, in the assembly of which Talleyrand was an outstanding member, were the strongest champions of the use of French. Their cahier asked that all children be given a knowledge of their language in the primary schools.[135]

From these isolated references to language, it is obvious that

[129] Eight districts of Alsace showed by the *procès-verbal* or the cahier a bilingual character: N, T, Belfort, C, N, T, Colmar, N, T, Haguenau, T. Dix Villes. Two districts of Lorraine (T. Sarreguemines, p. v, MS, *Arch. Nat.* Ba 77, and C. Bouzonville, protest of curates against the elections, MS, *ibid.*); one of Trois-Evêchés (T. Sarrebourg, cahier, MS, *Arch. Meurthe-et-Moselle,* art. 37); five districts near the Pyrenees (Béarn, T. Montpellier, T. Perpignan, U. Navarre, T. Ustaritz); four of Brittany (T. Rennes, C. St. Malo, C. Tréguier, T. Vannes), showed their bilingual character, while all three orders of Corsica used Italian for their *procès-verbaux* (*Cf.* MS, *Arch. Nat.* C 18/60[1] and Ba 34).

[130] Arthur Young gave conclusive proof of the imperfect use of French among the common people (*Voyages,* Vol. I, p. 352, July 26, 1789).

[131] The Alsatians wanted Alsatians appointed to office (e.g., C. Colmar, AP, Vol. III, p. 7) or asked that German be allowed in the courts (e.g., T. Colmar, AP, Vol. III, p. 10, art. 26). A request relative to education in the cahier of the third estate of Perpignan (AP, Vol. V, p. 374, col. 2, paragraph 3—on teaching of Latin), signified a desire to continue the bilingual status.

[132] N. Condom, T. Toulon.

[133] AP, Vol. V, p. 241.

[134] T. Bordeaux, T. Rennes.

[135] Charmasse, A., *Cahiers de doléances . . . d'Atun* (Atun, 1895), p. 373.

language played very little part in the concept of nationality on the eve of the Revolution, nor did the cahiers give any strong indication of the aggressive policy for the exclusive use of French later advocated by Barère and the Abbé Grégoire. Eighteenth-century French philosophy had ignored the element of language in national consciousness, and the cahiers offered no marked advance. The fact that French was the language of the educated classes in all countries of Europe,[136] may have accounted for indifference to linguistic uniformity.

A COMMON EDUCATION.—Historians have differed markedly upon the state of education at the end of the old régime, and consequently upon the merits of the work undertaken during the Revolution.[137] The general cahiers are not a fair gauge of the existing status, but they do show that everyone wanted improvement. A great many of the cahiers recognized education as a factor of primary importance in the development of national character and were consequently aware of the shortcomings of the institutions and methods then in use. By the application of principles of unity and uniformity to education, they believed that the homogeneity of the French nation would be increased.

The outstanding demand pertinent to the relationship between education and nationality was a national plan of education. The words of the joint cahier of the nobles and third estate of Péronne were, "that the States-General consider the means to procure an education that would be truly national for all classes."[138] Other cahiers suggested that a national committee be appointed to work on a scheme which would be acted upon by this States-General

[136] The common use of French among the intelligentsia is evidenced not only by the correspondence of the philosophers with rulers of Germany, Russia, etc., and among savants of different states, but also by the prize awarded in 1783 to Antoine de Rivarol by the Academy of Berlin. In his essay *De l'universalité de la langue française,* Rivarol maintained the superiority of the French language, and claimed that France was the center of the world, not by reason of her patriotism or egotism, but by virtue of history and events. France had played a superior rôle.

[137] The various authorities cited for education in the bibliography, p. 306, range themselves into two groups, those who hold that education under the old régime was good and that the early years of the Revolution marked a step backwards, and those who maintain that education before the Revolution was defective, and that the Revolution accomplished wonders.

[138] AP, Vol. V, p. 358, art. 5.

or by its successors. In all these cases, emphasis was laid upon a uniform program for the whole of France.[139]

Another demand which showed the psychology of national unity was the request for textbooks. Uniform texts should be prescribed. According to the clergy of Forcalquier,

> . . . the government will choose capable persons, friends of religion and of the *patrie,* whom it will charge to compose elementary books for a public and uniform instruction.[140]

Conceded a uniform education, how far was it to be universal or general? The cahiers emphasized the extension of education to all classes. Education should no longer be a class privilege, and opportunities for education should be extended to everyone. According to the clergy of Sézanne:

> That there should be provided free education for the rural poor, by appropriating a sum levied on the industries of the parish where they are sufficiently endowed, and by establishing scholarships in the colleges and seminaries of episcopal towns for poor children who display talent.[141]

There was little demand for extension of university training,[142] or for an increase in the number of colleges and seminaries. The chief interest was in primary education and the establishment of adequate schools in the country districts.

Were both boys and girls to receive education under the reformed régime? Thirty-three cahiers recommended the development of education for girls, without specifying its nature.[143] Presumably, this would apply only to elementary education. In view of the absence of any similar interest in the early cahiers, and in view of the multiple problems on the eve of the Revolution, it is astonishing that any attention whatsoever was paid to feminine training in the cahiers of 1789. Feminism is a recent development in France.

[139] For the propagation of patriotism by education, *cf. infra,* pp. 179 *et seq.*

[140] AP, Vol. III, p. 325, under art. 7.

[141] AP, Vol. V, p. 763, col. 1.

[142] The cahiers contained demands on the detailed organization of the universities and their course of study, but demand for the actual extension of opportunities of higher training was always indirect, except where a few cahiers asked for the establishment or reëstablishment of a university in a specific town (e.g., N. Clermont Ferrand, AP, Vol. II, p. 767, art. 17).

[143] 16 C, 9 N, 8 T, cahiers, scattered geographically.

Although many cahiers gave suggestions for reform and for the extension of education, none came out directly for universal education. By facilitating opportunities of education, instruction would be accessible to the majority of Frenchmen, but only a score of cahiers seemed to contemplate universal education, and that only as regards the primary grades.[144] Among the large number that asked for reforms in education, only one-fifth of the general cahiers gave constructive suggestions that would have resulted in a uniform national education.[145] These cahiers alone may be said to have appreciated the value of education in the formation of the national life. It is striking that the clergy were more concerned with a national education than the two lay orders. The most constructive advice came from the *generality* of Paris. Eight *generalities* of different parts of France were relatively unconcerned in national education.[146]

The detailed suggestion of the cahiers, as well as their general principles, were reflected in the work of the education committees of the National Convention, which undertook a thorough reform and the establishment of a national education. The value of a common education was appreciated by at least a portion of the electorate in 1789, and later became one of the important instruments of nationalization.

A majority of the cahiers of 1789 appealed to French traditions, but some cahiers paralleled this by an appeal to universal principles and history, and others by an appeal to provincial and class traditions.[147] The most widely cited common tradition was the French monarchy, while recognition of Catholicism was a close second. The rights of the nation were constantly appealed to, and the traditional division into three classes was frequently accepted. Appreciation of the common language as an element in French tradition was almost non-existent, while only a fifth of the cahiers appreciated the value of a common education. One should not be surprised that the appeal to tradition was stronger

[144] 20 cahiers, 7 C, 6 N, 7 T. C—Aix, Chartres, Longwy, Mans, Orléans, Rouen, Sarreguemines; N—Corsica, Clermont-en-Beauvoisis, Lyon, Mantes, Nîmes, St. Mihiel; T—Annonay, Castelnaudary, Corsica, Nemours, Nivernais, Sens, Toulouse.

[145] *Cf.* Table IV, Appendix, p. 253.

[146] Auch, Alençon, Caen, Lille, Limoges, Poitiers, Montauban, Strasbourg.

[147] On provincial and class traditions, *cf. infra*, pp. 183 *et seq.*, pp. 191 *et seq.*

(relative to the number of opinions available) among the privileged orders than in the third estate.[148] The astonishing fact is that the latter expressed as strong a traditional sentiment as they did. In their appeal to common French traditions, the cahiers demonstrate a degree of homogeneity of the French nation in respect to the fundamental basis of French nationality.[149]

THE DESIRE FOR UNIFORMITY

The cahiers indicated the presence in 1789 of one element in their national psychology which no longer appears in the twentieth century. In fact, the present-day tendency in France runs in the opposite direction. The sentiment to which we refer is the desire for unity and uniformity. This was the natural reaction in 1789 against the complex, heterogeneous organization of France under the old régime. The trend of French history from medieval times onward had been toward unity and centralization. Despite the efforts of Richelieu, and of the grand monarchy of Louis XIV, the old régime represented a compromise between national unity on the one hand, and local diversity on the other. All sorts of irregularities and exceptions were practiced. Privilege and arbitrary power throve and annulled the spasmodic attempts at systematization. The very irregularities of the old régime created abuses and injustices.

The reaction against existing conditions may be summarized in the desire for uniformity, equality, and liberty which characterized the cahiers of 1789. The mutual relationships of these three desires involved contradictions, and no one of them could be completely applied without sacrificing one or both of the others. We are not, however, concerned for the moment with the philosophical conflict, which the cahiers themselves failed to appreciate. The fact remains that the electorate of 1789 set forth uniformity as the goal of many of the reforms asked. This implied a consciousness of the conflict between disunity of administration and spiritual integrity of the nationality. The Revolution

[148] *Cf.* Table II, Appendix, p. 251.

[149] *Cf.* Table II, Appendix, p. 251. This does not include cahiers where the appeal to other than national traditions was dominant.

actually carried out many of the demands of the cahiers, and with the establishment of uniform practices, removed obstacles to a greater national unity, which in turn extended the consciousness of a common nationality. The sentiment for uniformity in 1789 pertained to many institutions, but especially to certain legal, administrative, and economic phases of organization.

LEGAL AND ADMINISTRATIVE UNIFORMITY.—The widespread demand for a constitution or for the reaffirmation of that already existent, showed the desire for a unified legal system. The cahiers went further, however, and wanted the whole body of the administrative law to be systematized and formed into one great national code.[150] The third estate of Lyon indicated this as a goal, and also suggested a means of accomplishing it:

> There shall be formed a national code, adapted to our customs and to our government, which prescribes the forms to be followed in civil and criminal matters, and which will conciliate as far as possible Roman law and the diversity of customary law [*coutûmes*]; and to accomplish this, the States-General will choose commissioners among the most capable lawyers of each province.[151]

The substitution of a unified code for the complex practices in use would not only allow the layman to know the law, but would also simplify its enforcement.[152] A small group of cahiers applied the same principle of legal unification to provincial law, where the customary law was also in hopeless confusion.[153] The cahiers contained an almost universal demand for the abolition of exceptional jurisdictions of all kinds. Over two-thirds of the cahiers, from all parts of France, denounced the extraordinary courts, *committimus, évocation,* and *prévention.*[154] By implication, they would substitute a uniform system of law administration, in which inequalities, privileges, and arbitrary exemptions would be eliminated.

The application of uniformity to the administration of France

[150] Approximately forty general cahiers from all parts of France, but chiefly of the third estate, asked for a national law code.

[151] AP, Vol. III, p. 610, sec. 2.

[152] For example, T. Draguignan, AP, Vol. III, p. 257, col. 2.

[153] For example, T. Reims, AP, Vol. V, p. 532, art. 47.

[154] Seligman, E., *La Justice pendant la Révolution* (Paris, 1913), for good definitions of these terms, Vol. I, pp. 44 *et seq.* 77 C, 116 N, 155 T, 9 U—357 cahiers denounced these practices.

was expressed by both direct and indirect means in the general cahiers. In the first place, the ideal of simplicity and uniformity prompted a demand for the suppression of superfluous offices. The individual officer most often denounced was the intendant.[155] At first sight this might appear to be a contradiction of the prevalent wish for uniformity, since the intendants had been the great agents of the centralized bureaucracy initiated by Richelieu. The cahiers, almost without exception, asked for the establishment of Provincial-Estates throughout France,[156] and these bodies, by taking over the powers of the unpopular intendants, would render that office superfluous. The provincial governor was another official condemned in the cahiers of 1789.[157] Aside from these two major offices, a whole regiment of small financial, supervisory, and minor judicial officials aroused expressions of disapproval.[158] Quite a large number of cahiers were concerned that the notarial records be improved, and therefore, they prescribed higher qualifications for holding the office of notary, and stipulated that uniform formulæ be used.[159] As one reads the general cahiers, one is impressed with the desire to reduce the number of officials, not only for the sake of government economy, but also in the interest of simplicity and unification.

More fundamental in the organization of a uniform system than the suppression of individual offices, were demands asking for the reorganization of the administrative machinery. The chief consideration of the cahiers in the provincial reconstruction contemplated was the establishment of an equitable status among the territorial divisions of France. The third estate of Draguignan left no doubt of their aim:

[155] One hundred and twenty cahiers (20 C, 35 N, 58 T, 5 U, 2 NT), asked for the suppression of the intendants. The demand was more frequent from the *pays d'état,* but appeared quite commonly in all *generalities.*

[156] *Cf. infra,* pp. 77, 183-84.

[157] This office had long been a sinecure. It had been denounced by the third estate in 1614 (Lalourcé and Duval, *Cahiers des Etats généraux, Paris,* 1789, Vol. IV, p. 309). For example in 1789, N. Cahors (AP, Vol. V, p. 489, col. 2).

[158] For an example of many suppressions asked, N. Angoulême, Boissonnade, P., *D.I., Cahiers de doléances . . . d'Angoulême* (Paris, 1907), pp. 506 *et seq.,* beginning with art. 34. *Procureurs, juré-priseurs, huissiers,* minor seignorial officers, etc., were among those under the ban of the cahiers.

[159] About eighty cahiers from all three classes and from all parts of France, but especially the southwest were anxious for an improvement in the office of notary.

Uniformity of administration throughout the kingdom is still a very desirable goal; it will be useful as a means to simplify it, to establish, in all provinces, Provincial-Estates really representative of the three orders. . . . It will be superfluous to emphasize the advantages which this form of administration, simpler and everywhere the same, presents.[160]

Uniformity in the new provincial administration was advocated by one-tenth of the general cahiers.[161] Another way in which uniformity would be applied to the provincial system was by a redivision of France along uniform lines. The third estate of Forcalquier, without using the word "uniformity," was specific:

The diversity of the composition of the provinces of the kingdom, the work of chance, of conquest, of successions, presents a singularity prejudicial to unity, to economy of administration and to good order, which it is proper to introduce in a monarchy such as France. The deputies are to ask for the reduction of the forty provinces to about twenty. . . .[162]

The application of uniform principles to the redivision of France and to the establishment of a new régime would be one way to combat privilege and complexity.

In respect to the legal and administrative system of France, the principle of uniformity was a dominant note in about one-sixth of the general cahiers of 1789.[163]

ECONOMIC UNIFORMITY.—France has always been, and still remains, primarily an agricultural country. Her economic system in 1789 partook of the same diversity as the other phases of her national existence. The advantages that France might have enjoyed by virtue of her soil and climate had been impaired by the cumbersome and intricate legislation of an exaggerated mercantilism. The ill-fated remedies of Turgot, which presaged the actual reforms made during the Revolution, only served to complicate matters. The whole economic system of the old régime was based upon privilege and regulation. The government licensed privileged companies and regulation was carried on both by the government

[160] AP, Vol. III, p. 256, art. 4.

[161] An equal number of cahiers of the nobles and of the third estate emphasized uniformity in the provincial system. The attitude was common to most of the *generalities,* but lacking in those of the northeast, and, except for one cahier, in those of the *generality* of Auch.

[162] AP, Vol. III, p. 330, cols. 1-2.

[163] *Cf.* Table V, Appendix, p. 254.

and by the privileged company. The gilds had once possessed virtual sovereignty in their small sphere, but they had declined noticeably in the eighteenth century. They continued, however, to struggle more or less successfully for a monopoly of the production and sale of manufactures. It was the government itself that had first inaugurated a policy of uniformity. The mercantile system had been designed to control the entire economic machine for the benefit of the whole, even though within its limits the creating of privileges had defeated uniformity.

As in the case of other phases of the national life, the desire for change in the economic organization was expressed in the cahiers much more often than any positive scheme of uniformity. Two demands which received widespread expression had already been voiced in earlier cahiers,[164] uniformity of weights and measures, and the abolition of interior customs barriers. These, therefore, did not represent a new development in the eighteenth century, but the fact that both reforms were undertaken during the Revolution and that they helped to unify France economically, makes it desirable to examine the cahiers of 1789 for these two items.

The request for the establishment of one uniform standard of weights and measures appeared in one hundred and eighty-four cahiers, of which the overwhelming number were from the third estate.[165] The existence of local standards not only complicated the exchange of produce, but was a factor in local privilege barring the way to a national economy. Not a single cahier defended the existing diversity, and the strength of the demand for uniformity was such that in 1793 (obligatory after 1795), the metric system replaced the old practices.

A second demand, voiced in the cahiers of 1614, and one which would help to build national economic unity, was a request for the abolition of interior customs barriers. The appearance of both of these demands in the cahiers of the seventeenth century as well as in those of 1789, is proof that they were not due to the influ-

[164] Weights and measures: *cf.* *Lalourcé* and Duval, *op. cit.*, Vols. I-IV, *passim*, under N, T, 1560, N, T, 1576, T, 1588, C, T, 1614. Internal customs: C, T, 1614, *ibid.*, Vol. IV, pp. 110-11, and pp. 384-85.

[165] 18 C, 32 N, 128 T, 5 U, 1 NT. The demand for uniformity was strongest in the *generalities* of Paris, Orléans, Moulins, Lyons, Montauban, Châlons and Dijon, and weak in Auch, Lille, Metz and Strasbourg.

ence of eighteenth-century economic liberalism, but to a natural protest against the complex hindrances to commerce. Uniformity should replace diversity and privilege. Opinion was not, however, unanimous on the question of customs duties, as it had been on weights and measures. Over one-half of the cahiers were for their abolition.[166] This included all the districts subject to the five great administrations (*grosses fermes*),[167] as well as the southern *generalities* and those of Besançon and Rennes, which were outside of that régime.[168] Opinion in the Barrois, Lorraine, and the Trois-Evêchés was divided between a wish to maintain the privileged status which those provinces enjoyed,[169] and the desire for its abolition.[170] The *generalities* of Lille and Valenciennes, on the northern frontier, outside the Five Great Administrations, were divided in opinion. Their prevailing attitude was that, if abolition were enacted, the provinces[171] should have some compensation.[172] One *generality* which enjoyed a privileged régime was unanimously opposed to dropping the bars within France with the inevitable result of raising the tariff between itself and the German States. Alsace, or the intendance of Strasbourg, repelled any change in the existing system.[173]

[166] There were approximately 291 for abolition, 24 cahiers opposed, and 13 for abolition with qualification.

[167] Half of France was administered under a system called the *Cinq Grosses Fermes,* with customs duties for the passage of goods from within, to the districts of France outside this régime (*provinces réputées étrangères* and *provinces d'étranger effectif*). *Cf.* Shepherd, W., *Historical Atlas* (New York, 1929), p. 146, second map, and Marion, Marcel, *Dictionnaire des institutions de France . . .*, under *traites.*

[168] The *generalities* of Moulins, Riom, Lyon, Grenoble, Aix, Montpellier, Toulouse, Auch, Bordeaux, Montauban, Limoges, La Rochelle, Rennes, Besançon, Dijon were outside the Five Great Administrations (in whole or in part). All these districts, however, favored abolition of customs duties within France. One cahier (C. Gex) of the *generality* of Dijon, and one of Besançon (N. Besançon) opposed abolition.

[169] These provinces, called "foreign," levied duties on goods from the rest of France, but levied none on goods coming from outside France. Opinion was probably influenced by the place from which the bulk of commerce came. These three provinces involved the *generalities* of Nancy and Metz.

[170] In the *generality* of Nancy, seventeen cahiers favored abolition and seven maintenance of customs barriers. In the *generality* of Metz, seven approved, and eight opposed abolition.

[171] The boundaries of provinces and *generalities* did not coincide, but the cahiers spoke of provinces when they referred to privileges.

[172] In the *generality* of Lille, three cahiers favored abolition, and three abolition only with compensation. Four cahiers of the Valenciennes favored abolition, and two abolition with compensation.

[173] Seven cahiers of Alsace opposed abolition.

It is obvious from the foregoing that the majority of France favored a uniform régime with tariffs only on the frontiers, but the privileged sections along the northern and north-eastern frontiers dissented. Uniformity was to the economic advantage of the majority, while the maintenance of privilege was profitable for the sections opposed to uniformity. Interior customs duties were actually abolished in 1790 when the departments were organized.

Besides these requests affecting the commercial activity of France, a number of demands bore upon uniformity in the fiscal system. The dominant idea regarding taxation was an equality of status as between provinces and as between individuals, based upon the capacity to pay.[174] A number of cahiers, however, emphasized the principle of uniformity in the taxes to be levied. In the words of the third estate of Lyon, "not only the equality of the tax should be established, but even more its uniformity as far as possible. . . ."[175] The widespread demand for the abolition of many specific taxes, like the demand for the suppression of useless offices, showed an inclination toward uniformity.[176]

The problems of the currency were little appreciated in 1789, as proven by the subsequent difficulties of the National Assembly, but twenty-two cahiers asked that a national bank be instituted.[177] The nobles of Bailleul drew their model from the Bank of England, but felt that some modifications for France would be necessary.[178] Four cahiers went so far as to ask for a unified currency.[179] Many asked for a national treasury (*caisse*), but the motive of this demand was to give control to the nation instead of to the king.[180] These rare expressions pointed the way to a future development toward uniformity in financial matters.

If the various expressions in behalf of economic uniformity are taken together, about one-half of the general cahiers showed a

[174] *Cf. infra*, pp. 77-78, 84.
[175] AP, Vol. III, p. 601, art. 5.
[176] *Cf. supra*, p. 54.
[177] 2 C, 7 N, 12 T, 1 CN. C—Melun, Moulins; N—Calais, Château-Thierry, Bailleul, Mantes, Montpellier, Limoux, Sarrebourg; T—Brest, Carhaix, La Rochelle, Mâcon, Mantes, Nancy, Dieuze, Etain, La Marche, Neufchâteau, Paris, *intra-muros*, Sarrebourg; CN—Lixheim.
[178] AP, Vol. II, p. 171, art. 14.
[179] T—Langres, Reims, Troyes (all of the *generality* of Châlons), and Dijon.
[180] For example, T. Chaumont-en-Bassigny, AP, Vol. II, p. 727, art. 13.

marked approbation. Although equality was more often the goal, nevertheless one hundred and sixty-two cahiers made uniformity an important note in their economic program.[181] The sentiment for economic uniformity was much more frequently expressed by cahiers of the third estate, as might be expected, in view of their greater interest in taxation and commerce. The frontier provinces were less anxious than the rest of France for uniformity, while the *generalities* of Perpignan and Strasbourg were definitely opposed to it.

SUMMARY OF THE CONSCIOUSNESS OF NATIONALITY

From the foregoing analysis, one may see that some consciousness of France as the territorial basis of nationality existed. The notion of race was demonstrated in the occasional ascription to the French of national characteristics and in a concern for increase of the population, but was limited at the same time by a vague cosmopolitanism that avoided exclusive delineation of the French nation. Behind and beyond any specific characterization of the French was, however, the basic idea of the nation as a unit. This was expressed in a very large number of the general cahiers of 1789. Similarly, there was a widespread appeal to tradition, to the existence of a French constitution or fundamental principles. Monarchy was accepted *almost unanimously* as an essential in the French polity. The clergy and a large group of the lay orders regarded Catholicism as equally fundamental, but a small minority placed toleration above uniformity of religion. The rights of the nation and of the individual were enunciated, but the appeal to traditions in these cases was less clear than in discussion of the monarchy. On the other hand, there was an appreciation of the value of a common education to weld the French nation together, and a very widespread desire for the substitution of legal, administrative, and economic uniformity for the existing diversity. All of these attitudes implied a consciousness of the unity of the French nation.

What light does a comparison of the cahiers of early States-Generals with those of 1789 throw upon the conception of nation-

[181] *Cf.* Table VI, Appendix, p. 255.

ality manifested in 1789? In the first place, the greater territorial unity of France in 1789 contrasted with expressions used by the early cahiers. The three orders united in 1483, referred to the "kingdom, Dauphiné and adjacent countries [*pays*]."[182] Although the nobles in 1560 spoke of the nobility of France and of the kingdom, they merely listed the *bailliages* that coöperated to make the cahiers.[183] From 1560 on, France was spoken of as a kingdom (*royaume*), a unity made by common subjection to the king.[184] By comparison with these statements, the cahiers of 1789 conceived of some geographic unit with which the French nationality was associated.

A contrary conclusion regarding the development of citizenship in relation to nationality would result from a comparison of the early cahiers with those of 1789. Demands for discrimination against foreigners were recurrent in the early cahiers. Their exclusion from high public office,[185] from church offices,[186] from military command,[187] from banking,[188] and discrimination against them in the commercial world[189] were reiterated in the requests of successive cahiers of the fifteenth, sixteenth, and seventeenth centuries. This may probably be explained as a protest against the influence of Italians and Spaniards, as well as of foreign Protestants, who played so prominent a part in the history of the time. By comparison, the few demands against foreigners in 1789 pale, and demonstrate the greater relative force of cosmopolitanism in the eighteenth century.

The early cahiers had shown some consciousness of distinctive characteristics of the French nationality, but rarely, and always vaguely. In 1576, the nobles had referred to the traditional services rendered by the nobility to the king,[190] and in 1614, they

[182] *Cf.* text, Mayer, C., *Des Etats-généraux* . . . (La Haye, 1788-89), Vol. IX, p. 314.

[183] Lalourcé and Duval, *Recueil des cahiers généraux des trois orders aux Etats généraux* (Paris, 1789), Vol. I, pp. 121 *et seq.*

[184] Compare the various cahiers of the early States-Generals, *loc. cit., passim.*

[185] For example, N. 1560, Lalourcé and Duval, *op. cit.,* Vol I, pp. 210, 240.

[186] For example, N. 1576, *ibid.,* Vol. II, pp. 125-26; C. 1588, *ibid.,* Vol. III, pp. 13-14.

[187] For example, C. 1576, *ibid.,* Vol. II, p. 74.

[188] For example, T. 1560, *ibid.,* Vol. I, p. 436.

[189] For example, T. 1576, *ibid.,* Vol. II, p. 333; T. 1614, *ibid.,* Vol. IV, p. 469.

[190] *Ibid.,* Vol. II, p. 180.

showed some pride of birth in their opposition to what they considered to be treatment "unworthy of Frenchmen and noblemen."[191] In 1614, also, the third estate showed a feeling for French *moeurs,* French law, and mentioned the beauty of French flowers.[192] These were only faint beginnings, although one must not forget that the *bailliage* cahiers of the early States-Generals may have included expressions omitted in the composite cahiers drawn up by each class in the States-General. By comparison with the spirit shown in 1614, or earlier, the cahiers of 1789 showed a decided development in the consciousness of traits of nationality.

Monarchy had been recognized in the early cahiers, but less often as a national tradition than in 1789. The cahier of the three orders in 1483 had spoken of the king as the "protector and defender of the rights and liberties of the church, of his realm and of Dauphiné,"[193] but throughout the period of the civil wars, the cahiers said little about Catholicism as a tradition of France. The appeal to Catholicism in 1789 was, therefore, more significant, but simultaneously civil toleration made its first appearance in the cahiers of that year. The belief in a traditional constitution as a concrete part of French national life was much more marked in the cahiers of 1789 than in earlier ones. The appeal to traditions on the eve of the Revolution was both more varied, and more conscious.

Like cosmopolitanism and toleration, the awareness of population and the desire for its increases were new developments after 1614. There was not the slightest hint in the early cahiers of concern for the preservation or numerical increase of the French nationality.

As we have already noted, the early cahiers expressed some sentiment for uniformity,[194] but the principle was applied in 1789 to many more phases of national life. The consciousness of a united nation, struggling against the centrifugal forces of the old régime, was also much more marked in 1789.

A comparison of the early cahiers with those of 1789 not only

[191] *Ibid.,* Vol. IV, pp. 248-49.
[192] *Ibid.,* Vol. IV, p. 271.
[193] Mayer, *op. cit.,* Vol. IX, pp. 317, 322.
[194] *Cf. supra,* pp. 56 *et seq.*

brings into prominence as new elements in the national consciousness—a geographic unity called France, a degree of cosmopolitanism and of toleration, interest in national traits of character and in increase of population, but it places a new emphasis upon consciousness of national traits, the appeal to national traditions, an appreciation of the value of a national education and a desire for greater unity. Of far greater importance than these separate items, however, was the marked conception of the *nation* as a generic whole in the cahiers of 1789. Not only was the word rarely used in the early cahiers but there was no substitute. France had been composed of subjects of the king, of classes, of an agglomeration of peoples, according to the early cahiers, whereas the majority of cahiers of 1789 conceived of a united nationality. Thus, consciousness of nationality had spread among the French masses by 1789. Individual philosophers of the eighteenth century had depicted fuller conceptions of nationality than were anywhere expressed in individual cahiers of 1789, but the French electorate as a whole had made great strides since the last States-General in 1614.

What was the geographic and class distribution of the consciousness of nationality shown in the cahiers of 1789? One must recognize three degrees. It may be said that all cahiers showed some vague notion of nationality. Its elusive character may have been due to the nature of the cahiers themselves. A very large number, however—two-thirds of the number of *general* cahiers available—gave several statements indicative of a consciousness of nationality.[195] In proportion to the number of cahiers available for each *generality,* five *generalities* showed a marked consciousness of nationality, the *generalities* of Paris, Orléans, Riom, Alençon, and Besançon.[196] The *generalities* along the frontier lagged in their concept of French nationality, and mingled appeals to provincial and class status with such statements as they made. All three classes of France showed about the same proportion of consciousness of nationality. In their respective concepts, however,

[195] Three hundred and twenty-six cahiers, 97 C, 104 N, 115 T, 7 U, 1 CN, 1 CT, 1 NT.

[196] Paris: 31 out of 35 cahiers; Orléans: 15 out of 21; Riom: 7 out of 8; Alençon: all 9; Besançon: 10 out of 11.

the element of tradition was stronger in the cahiers of the clergy and nobles, while the psychology of race preservation and of uniformity was more marked in cahiers of the third estate.

One needs to be constantly reminded that the cahiers were composed of a series of practical articles and did not represent a succinct philosophy. The ideas bearing on any one topic may denote a major or a minor importance in relation to the total impression made by a cahier. Thus, out of the many cahiers that voiced ideas about French nationality, only twenty-eight showed a marked self-consciousness.[197] The nobles and the third estate were about equally represented in this group, but the clergy lagged. The *generalities* of Paris, Orléans, and Lyon formed the centers of this strong consciousness of nationality.

About the same amount of time has elapsed since 1789 as elapsed from 1614 to the Revolution. When the concept of nationality and its prevalence in 1789 are compared with present-day French thought, it is obvious that a consciousness of nationality has since clarified and increased in astonishing proportions. One misses in the cahiers of 1789 expressions of the love of French soil, the definite delineation of the French nationality and the astonishing development of a belief in inherent characteristics, and in the consistent evolution of French history along the lines of these guiding traits. The present-day conception of all of these elements of nationality is so marked that their beginnings seem very elusive and amorphous. Perhaps the cahiers, by reason of their nature, fail to indicate the full range and strength of ideas on nationality held in 1789. Taken in the perspective of five hundred years of French history, however, they show not only the existence of national consciousness on the eve of the Revolution, but a more comprehensive and a firmer popular conception of nationality than that for which we have any evidence before that time. They also reveal the embryonic development of all the ideas which have since become vital factors in French nationality.

[197] 3 C, 11 N, 12 T, 3 U: C—Dourdan, Nivernais, Villefranche-de-Beaujolais; N—Artois, Blois, Calais, Castres, Château-Thierry, Clermont Ferrand, Clermont-en-Beauvoisis, La Rochelle, Lyon, Paris *intra-muros,* Orléans; T—Beauvais, Nemours, Orléans, Paris *hors-les-murs,* Paris *intra-muros,* Pont-à-Mousson, Quimper, Reims, Rennes, Rochefort, Sens, Vézelise; U—Bourg-en-Bresse, Rustaing, Villers-la-Montagne.

CHAPTER IV

DEMOCRACY AND THE GENERAL CAHIERS

In a recent book, André Siegfried, a widely accepted interpreter of national developments, has said:

> The France of 1789, which is still a reality, works unceasingly for democracy all over the world, teaching the doctrine of equality and dignity of the individual—a doctrine which in reality is revolutionary. But the spirit of France even today is aristocratic. . .[1]

As contrasted with France under the old régime, a great many democratic principles are applied now in France. The movement which has brought about the present curious compromise between social aristocracy and political democracy began as a three-fold operation: the adoption of popular sovereignty, the equalization of provinces and classes, and, lastly, emphasis upon the rights of the individual against the existing political order. In view of the events of the Revolution, the slow progress of democracy in France during the nineteenth century, and present-day conditions, one would not expect startling expressions of democracy in the cahiers of 1789. Such statements as did appear, were largely a matter of degree, strengthening guarantees against arbitrary government, leveling classes and provincial privileges, and assuring individual liberties. The cahiers of 1789 were pro-democratic on a relative scale and indicated most of the lines along which democracy advanced in the next century, but their general tone was conservative.

DEMOCRACY AND GOVERNMENT

The propositions in the general cahiers bearing upon a more democratic government fall into four categories: the principle of

[1] Siegfried, André, *Impressions of South America,* translated by H. H. and D. Hemming (New York, Harcourt, Brace and Co., 1933). This quotation occurs as part of an appeal to the French to develop their interests in South America. (*Loc. cit.*, p. 190.)

popular sovereignty, the elective principle, equality among the provinces, and miscellaneous suggestions for democratic machinery of government. In each case, we shall see the advance of ideas over that of previous centuries, but radical expressions appeared in only a small minority of cahiers.

POPULAR SOVEREIGNTY.—Ideas and practices which would place the power of the state in the hands of the greatest number point towards democracy. In the cahiers of 1789, the fundamental statement implying popular sovereignty was the assertion that the States-General should be the agent of sovereignty. More or less power *vis-à-vis* the king may have been recommended by each cahier, but *not one* defended royal absolutism.[2] All the cahiers contemplated limitations upon the monarchy,[3] with the States-General as the voice of the sovereign people. The theory was given terse expression with the following words, "All power emanates from the nation, and can only be exercised for its welfare."[4] Another cahier stated the corollary equally briefly, "The States-General is the organ of the will of the nation."[5]

The failure to establish as a constitutional principle the control of the purse strings by the States-General had led to the downfall of that body.[6] This failure was universally recognized in 1789, and led to a unanimous affirmation in words resembling those of the clergy of Paris *hors-les-murs,*

> Art. 7. That no tax and no loan may be made without the free consent of the States-General.
>
> Art. 8. That the taxes freely consented to by the States-General cease *ipso facto* at the period indicated by it.[7]

Not only was the States-General to control the purse strings, but it should also possess chief legislative power.[8] According to the third estate of Etampes,

[2] Occasionally a cahier used words in support of the monarch as if absolutism were approved, but elsewhere in the same cahier, there always appeared the conventional checks. For example, C. Melun, AP, Vol. III, p. 733.

[3] The cahiers desired a constitutional monarchy. *Cf. infra,* pp. 152 *et seq.*

[4] AP, Vol. V, p. 281, by T. Paris *intra-muros.*

[5] C. Provins, AP, Vol. V, p. 446, art. 1.

[6] *Cf.* Picot, G., *Histoire des Etats-généraux* (Paris, 1888), *passim.*

[7] AP, Vol. V, p. 232, col. 2.

[8] Some cahiers stated that the king and the nation jointly possessed the legislative power, but only a handful of cahiers discussed a royal veto. The main emphasis in all cases was upon the power of the States-General.

The first and the most essential object is to establish the legislative power on an invariable basis; that power belongs incontestably to the nation; it has been deprived of this for a long time, and it is to this dispossession that the disorders which have troubled the peace of the state should be attributed; we desire, therefore, that this power be restored to the nation forever, and that the assembly of its representatives be henceforth charged with the making of all laws by which it will be governed. . . .[9]

Aside from these fundamental assumptions of the sovereignty of the nation through the organ of the States-General, there were five measures almost universally advocated that would assure mastery to the States-General. These five were: (1) the establishment of a constitution recognizing the status and powers of the States-General, prior to the voting of any tax measures;[10] (2) periodic or permanent meetings of the States-General for the future;[11] (3) no intermediate commissions between the sessions, or if allowed, the activity of such commissions to be valid only until the next meeting of the States-General; (4) the preparation of a national budget with responsibility of all officials to the States-General; and (5) responsibility of all officials to the States-General. By these several means, the king would be effectively limited, and in the resulting constitutional monarchy, sovereign power would rest with the nation.

Although the States-General was to become the voice of the nation, the question arises, Who was the *nation?* Was the nation numerically all the people? Where would the power in the States-General lie? The cahiers advanced claims of popular sovereignty against theories of monarchical absolutism, but opinion was far from unanimous upon the practical application of democracy to the States-General itself. The attitude of the cahiers upon the composition of the French nation (in its political sense) is an ex-

[9] AP, Vol. III, p. 283, art. 1.

[10] The fact that reform legislation had been issued by the king only after the adjournment of the States-General made it impossible for the latter to insure that the king would carry out his promises once the States-General had voted money for the royal treasury.

[11] The majority of cahiers wanted a periodic States-General, with the maximum interval of from three to five years between sessions. Only a few asked for a permanent States-General, while only one cahier (CN Lixheim, AP, Vol. V, p. 714, art. 5), asked that it meet automatically two months of each year.

cellent illustration of the relative, and not absolute, democracy of 1789. Compared with the old régime, public opinion among the third estate was moving in the direction of individualist political democracy, but aristocracy was still dominant among the clergy and the nobles.

The balance of power in the future States-General, and hence in the nation as a whole, depended upon the method of voting in that body. Should the States-General sit in three separated groups, with two of the orders empowered to overrule the third?[12] Or should the count be taken by head, irrespective of class, with majority opinion prevailing? The cahiers prefigure the events which actually ushered in the transformation of the States-General into the National Assembly. We possess the opinion of five hundred and forty-five electoral assemblies[13] and these foreshadowed the attitudes taken in the first months of the Revolution.

One hundred and fourteen of this number evaded the issue.[14] Ninety-two assemblies omitted any instruction upon the method of voting.[15] A few agreed that either vote by head or by order was permissible,[16] while some others sidestepped the difficulty by leaving to the States-General itself the decision on the method to be used.[17] Most of the latter group were cahiers of the clergy and the nobles, which fact implied a more conciliatory attitude, since it allowed acquiescence in vote by head in case the States-General adopted it. Thus, one-fifth of the districts tacitly or expressly left the problem to the States-General.

Two hundred and twelve opinions favored vote by order. Sixty per cent of these were cahiers of the nobility. Only two cahiers of the third estate asked for vote by order,[18] while one other cahier

[12] The problem was aggravated by the probability that the two privileged orders would agree, and thus overrule the third estate, which was numerically double, and represented the largest portion of the nation.

[13] The number of opinions does not correspond with that of the available general cahiers because the *procès-verbal* sometimes indicates the opinion where the cahier itself is now missing, and other irregularities exist.

[14] *Cf.* chart, *infra,* p. 68.

[15] One might predict the opinion from the tone of the cahier, but that would be unhistorical.

[16] For example, N. Blois, Cauchie and Lesueur, *D.I., op. cit.,* Vol. II, pp. 432-33.

[17] For example, C. Bazas, AP, Vol. II, p. 267, art. 21.

[18] T. Longwy, T. Villers-Cotterets. The latter safeguarded vote by order by requiring consent of all three orders.

of the same order asked for vote by head on taxes, but the traditional method for all other business.[19] In the case of thirty-one assemblies of the clergy and nobles, no expression of opinion was given, but their imperative mandates indicated their conservative attitude, and one may conclude that they preferred vote by order.

On the other hand, two hundred and nineteen cahiers indicated preference for vote by head.[20] Nearly 80 per cent were of the third estate, as might be expected, while 14 per cent were of the clergy and only 6 per cent of the nobles.[21] The whole picture of opinion on voting in the States-General will be more graphic, if the summary of the statistics is given here:

Cahiers missing, no opinion: 33 C, 16 N, 22 T, 2 U, 2 NT.	75	
Cahiers omitting opinion: 52 C, 12 N, 21 T, 4 U, 1 NT, 2 CN.	92	
Cahiers leaving matter to States-General: 4 C, 8 N, 1 T.	14	
Cahiers agreeing to either method: 4 C, 1 N, 3 T.	8	
TOTAL: CAHIERS MISSING OR EVADING THE QUESTION: 61 C, 21 N, 25 T, 4 U, 2 CN, 1 NT.		114
Cahiers for vote by order: 61 C, 114 N, 2 T, 1 NT, 1 CN.	179	
No mention in cahier, imperative mandate: 11 C, 20 N.	31	
Vote on tax by head, otherwise by order: 1 C, 1 T.	2	
TOTAL: CAHIERS FOR VOTE BY ORDER: 73 C, 135 N, 2 T, 1 CN, 1 NT.		212
TOTAL: CAHIERS FOR VOTE BY HEAD: 32 C, 14 N, 165 T, 7 U, 1 CT.		219

A glance at this table shows that the nobles were overwhelmingly for vote by order,[22] the third estate almost unanimously for vote by head, districts where joint cahiers had been made largely for vote by head, and the clergy divided between the two camps. The majority of the cahiers of the *generalities* of Lyons, Amiens,

[19] T. Strasbourg.

[20] A detailed tabulation for the privileged orders and joint cahiers has been made for the districts favoring vote by head. *Cf.* Table VII, Appendix, p. 256.

[21] The cases where the nobles expressed preference for vote by order, but would acquiesce in majority opinion, have been given as approving vote by order. (For example, N. Sens, AP, Vol. V, pp. 752-53.)

[22] The opinion within an assembly was not always unanimous, but the cahier represented the majority. In the case of the nobles of Bruyères, fourteen voted for vote by head, and eight for vote by order, while a majority of three only approved vote by order among the nobles of Dijon.

and Aix preferred vote by head, the more progressive attitude.[23] Otherwise, distribution of the various opinions among the classes of the different *generalities* was proportional to the total number of opinions.

It is hardly necessary to recall that in May and June of 1789, the States-General was similarly divided, that part of the clergy showed a conciliatory spirit and went over to the third estate, and that a small group of the nobles, after much delay, joined the third estate. After that event, it was necessary to nullify the imperative mandates before the conservatives could be won over to the National Assembly.[24] The victory of the third estate was a victory of the greatest number, and signified a step toward democracy and popular sovereignty.

The appeal of the cahiers which preferred vote by order was to tradition. The nobles of Paris *hors-les-murs* put it clearly:

> The deputies will adhere to the ancient form of opinion by classes independent of one another, which the nobles will always regard as the constitutional safeguard of the liberty of the States-General.[25]

The clergy of Etampes argued that vote by order was really to the advantage of the third estate,[26] while the nobles of Tartas looked upon vote by head as anti-monarchical.[27] The advocates of vote by head appealed to reason, if they discussed their motive at all. Many looked upon it as the only way to discover the general will,[28] while a few districts justified it as expedient in the existing crisis.[29]

Ten cahiers stated the revolutionary doctrine that the third estate alone should be sovereign.[30] By ignoring the privileged orders, these cahiers expressly regarded the third estate as the *people,* the *nation.* Some of the ten emphasized the fact that the

[23] Compare table no. VII with the number of cahiers available for each *generality,* pp. 256, 237 *et seq.*

[24] *Cf. supra,* pp. 18-19. This was, of course, what took place.

[25] AP, Vol. V, p. 235, art. 2.

[26] AP, Vol. III, p. 279.

[27] AP, Vol. I, p. 700, art. 12.

[28] For example, T. Clermont Ferrand, AP, Vol. II, p. 769.

[29] For example, T. Etampes, AP, Vol. III, p. 283, art. 3.

[30] T. Auxerre, Angers, Dijon, Dorat, Mâcon, Nîmes, Nivernais, Nemours, Quimper, Rennes.

third estate comprised the bulk of the French electorate.[31] Some instructed their deputies that, in case of refusal of the clergy and nobles to vote by head, the third estate should withdraw and declare itself the States-General with the king.[32] The cahier of the third estate of Rennes, upon whose wording Lanjuinais undoubtedly exerted an influence, contained the strongest statement of the sovereignty of the third estate:

> It is by a disastrous error that what is called the third estate, actually comprising more than ninety-nine hundredths of the nation, has been styled an order and put in balance with the two privileged orders! This error ought to cease, and what has thus far been called the third in the realm, shall henceforth, with or without the privileged orders, comprise the people or nation, the only true name which accords with the dignity of the people.[33]

The third estate of Angers was prophetic of the events of May and June; it asked that the name of *Communes* be substituted for that of *Tiers Etat*.[34] The chamber of the third estate did actually take the name of the *Communes* despite the opposition of the chamber of the nobles.[35] The dispersion in France of the ten radical cahiers that voiced the sovereignty of the third estate suggests that a similar opinion may have been much more widely held, but that anxiety for union of the orders against arbitrary power outweighed the determination to place power in the hands of the common people. The sentiment of national unity was greater than that of democracy on the eve of the Revolution.

To summarize opinion on popular sovereignty, the cahiers of all orders agreed that the reformed government should be a constitutional monarchy, and that the States-General should be the agent of the sovereign power. When it came to a definition of who was the "people," opinion divided sharply. The numerical advantage was on the side of the third estate, which gave the interpretation that the "people" comprised all the classes together, with representation and power proportionate to numbers, and there-

[31] For example, T. Nîmes, Bligny-Bondurand, *D.I., op. cit.*, Vol. II, pp. 591-92.

[32] For example, T. Auxerre, AP, Vol. II, p. 120, art. 1.

[33] Sée and Lessort, *D.I., op. cit.*, Vol. IV, p. 240, art. 2.

[34] AP, Vol. II, p. 38, art. 3.

[35] *Cf.* Aulard, F. A., *Récit des séances des députés des communes* . . . (Paris, 1895), pp. 64 *et seq.*

fore, predominance of the third estate. Only a few cahiers took the more radical stand that the privileged orders could be ignored, and that the third estate alone was the *people* or the *nation*.

THE ELECTIVE PRINCIPLE.—For office-holding, the old régime in France relied upon inheritance, appointment, or purchase. By contrast with the existing system, the cahiers of 1789 contained many pro-democratic suggestions for the employment of election to public office.

The cahiers applied this principle to the kingship in three of their demands. In the first place, the hint of an elective monarchy was contained in the demand for the automatic summons of the States-General in case of a regency.[36] This demand touched not only the problem of succession to the throne, but also the inherent sovereignty of the States-General. The majority of cahiers had accepted the hereditary monarchy according to the Salic law as the traditional form in France.[37] A few cahiers stated that henceforth the king should take his coronation oath before the States-General, and no longer before an assembly whose members were summoned by the king on the basis of birth or public office.[38] Ten cahiers went further and claimed the right of the States-General to designate the line of succession in default of heirs.[39] In view of the failure of the States-General of 1593 to elect a king, this claim could hardly be supported by an appeal to past history. All three of these demands pointed toward the application of election to the monarchy. Irrespective of whether the States-General was itself really representative, the application of election to the monarchy in nearly one hundred cahiers[40] reënforced the principle of the sovereignty of the States-General.

A second institution to which the elective principle should apply, according to the great majority of the cahiers, was the new

[36] 92 cahiers. 9 C, 47 N, 33 T, 2 U, 1 NT.

[37] *Cf. supra,* p. 40. Mention of the Salic law was widespread.

[38] For example, C. Bellême, AP, Vol. V, p. 321, art. 13.

[39] 2 C, 4 N, 4 T. C—Dijon, Reims; N—Châtillon-sur-Seine, Coutances, Dijon, Evreux; T—Bellême, Moulins, Nantes, Senlis.

[40] Only three cahiers (1 N, 2 T) need to be added to the list of those asking for convocation of the States-General for a regency, *i.e.,* a total of ninety-five cahiers. All the other cahiers that spoke of the coronation oath before the States-General or the right of that body to elect the king, also asked for the States-General in case of a regency.

system of Provincial-Estates to be established. The provincial assemblies instituted by the edict of 1787 had fallen short of the popular demand in this respect.[41] There had been an elaborate combination of royal appointment and restricted election. The new plan which was almost universally solicited, involved the election of the members of the Provincial-Estates,[42] and also of the presiding officers.[43] Furthermore a number of requests relative to such elections signified that the new provincial bodies would be more democratic and not the bulwark of the privileged classes. Numerous cahiers asked that the Provincial-Estates be established on the model of that of Dauphiné where the principle of doubling the third estate applied.[44] Other cahiers would extend the suffrage of the lower clergy,[45] and of the lesser nobility.[46] The application of the elective principle to the provincial government was one form which federalism took in the cahiers of 1789.

A third application of election was implied in the almost universal denunciation of the sale of offices.[47] This had constituted one of the great abuses under the old régime and had been denounced by the early States-General,[48] but never so forcefully as in 1789. Appointment on merit was the remedy usually suggested, but election was also contemplated. According to the clergy of Alençon, "the suffrage of public opinion" should replace venality.[49] Election was applied by the cahiers especially to municipal offices, for city government had degenerated into venal oligarchy. The demand for freely elected municipal officers was widespread.[50]

[41] *Cf.* Renouvin, P., *Les Assemblées provinciales de 1787* (Paris, 1921), pp. 97, 111, *et seq.*

[42] For example, C. Bellême, AP, Vol. V, p. 321, art. 2.

[43] For example, T. Bigorre, AP, Vol. II, p. 361, art. 5.

[44] For example, T. Crépy-en-Valois, AP, Vol. III, p. 77, art. 7.

[45] For example, C. Provins, AP, Vol. V, p. 446, art. 10.

[46] For example, N. Rivière-Verdun, AP, Vol. V, p. 585, col. 1.

[47] 223 cahiers denounced venality: 52 C, 50 N, 116 T, 4 U, 1 NT. There was no special geographic distribution of the demand.

[48] U, 1483—Mayer, *op. cit.*, Vol. IX, p. 371; T, 1576—Lalourcé and Duval, *op. cit.*, Vol. II, p. 295; C, N, T, 1614, *ibid.*, Vol. IV, pp. 97, 206, 366.

[49] AP, Vol. I, p. 709, col. 2, art. 10.

[50] Two hundred and seven cahiers asked for this: 28 C, 49 N, 124 T, 6 U. The demand appeared very often in the *generalities* of Auch, Bordeaux, Dijon, Nancy, and Metz, less often in those of Paris and Orléans, not at all in those of Poitiers and Grenoble, and only once in the *generalities* of Bourges, Caen, and Aix.

Seven cahiers would extend election, either directly, or by one of the bodies of the local government, to the judiciary.[51] The third estate of Alençon made the strongest appeal in this respect,

> That no judge may be established except by the suffrage of the citizens, whose election will be confirmed by the king, and to this effect, the abolition of venality of offices of the judiciary is asked, on condition, however, of a preliminary reimbursement.[52]

A few cahiers would go so far as to include the lower ecclesiastical offices in the range of those filled by election.[53]

The one institution of the old régime in which the elective principle had been applied was the States-General. Although there were innumerable protests against the method of convocation applied in 1789, the cahiers were conservative and suggested no fundamental changes in the theory of representation. The theory was warmly advocated in general terms by the nobles of Mantes, as follows:

> A complete and equal representation being the sole basis of every legitimate constitution, we require our deputy to take measures such that, in the following sessions, the deputies will be elected by the majority of citizens of each territory; and, in consequence, he will ask that a representative constitution from the parish assemblies to the national assembly be established.[54]

With the exception of four cahiers,[55] which in a vague way suggested universal suffrage, the cahiers did not contemplate any great change in suffrage qualifications.[56] Ownership of property or the payment of taxes was accepted universally as the requisite for voting. As the nobles of Clermont-en-Beauvoisis put it, "Property gives the first interest in public affairs."[57] Even the cahier of the third estate of Nemours, which lauded the elective principle, showed a Physiocratic conservatism on suffrage, and

[51] C. Montreuil; T—Alençon, Amiens, Carhaix, Paris *hors-les-murs,* Rennes, Vannes.

[52] AP, Vol. I, p. 717, col. 1, art. 1.

[53] *Cf. infra,* p. 104.

[54] AP, Vol. III, p. 662, col. 2, art. 1.

[55] T. Bordeaux, Chatellerault, Montpellier, Rennes.

[56] It may be remembered that the original qualifications for suffrage in the convocation of 1789 had been wide. This basis was approved. *Cf. Guide.*

[57] AP, Vol. II, p. 753, col. 1.

would require a tax and a property qualification for voting.[58] One cahier seemed to include women in a wider suffrage; the third estate of Chatellerault asked "that the assembly be formed on an equitable basis; in consequence, that all the citizens of both sexes and of all ages have the right equally to concur in the deliberations and the nomination of deputies. . . ."[59] It may be remembered that nuns and women property owners had been represented by procurators in the electoral assemblies of the clergy and nobles in 1789,[60] but this had been due to their holding of property and not to their sex. The basis of universal suffrage is the individual. So long as representation was based upon class or property, there would be little advance toward democratic suffrage. The cahiers of 1789 were far from democratic on the fundamental qualifications for suffrage.

The cahiers were equally uncritical of plural voting which the convocation of 1789 had allowed.[61] The only demands which were pro-democratic on the subject of elections had to do with indirect elections and the units of election. The idea of indirect elections was denounced in only seven cahiers,[62] although some others would limit the elections to two degrees.[63] The more frequent concern was that the method of election be made symmetrical so that all districts would receive similar representation. The redivision of France was urged, not only for the sake of theoretical uniformity, but also for practical administrative purposes. The injustice of the principal and secondary *bailliages* would be eliminated and all would be put on an equal basis.[64] The principle was stated by the third estate of Vitry-le-françois:

[58] AP, Vol. IV, pp. 173 *et seq.*

[59] AP, Vol. II, p. 691, col. 1.

[60] *Cf.* art. 20 of January 24th regulation.

[61] Clergy and nobles possessing fiefs had the right to be represented wherever they held property (Regulation of Jan. 24, arts. 17, 21). Such a privilege was particularly significant in such cases as that of the Duke of Orléans, whose active campaigning and influence were increased by representation in several *bailliages.* The Duke was actually elected to the States-General by several assemblies (*Cf.* Brette, *op. cit.,* Vol. II, p. 260).

[62] C. Calais; T—Briey, Caudebec, Coutances, Dijon, Nemours, Vermandois.

[63] For example, T. Paris *intra-muros,* AP, Vol. V, p. 239, art. 9.

[64] The principle of classification into principal and secondary *bailliages* was adopted in 1789 from the method applied in 1614. One indirect step in the elections was added thereby for the third estate of secondary *bailliages.* The classification was

The astonishing medley in the composition of the *bailliages* and just motives for complaint which the greater number of citizens feel against their lack of representation in the States-General, determine them to ask His Majesty to ordain that, in the future, the convocation for the States-General be made by the Provincial-Estates and by districts equal either in population or in taxation.[65]

A number of cahiers described a hierarchy of assemblies which would thereby retain indirect elections but would function on the basis of equality.[66] The third estate of Rennes set forth a complete system of progressive election by parish, canton, or district.[67] In other cases, where the *bailliages* would be retained, their status should be equalized.[68] By a great variety of measures, whose details differed, numerous cahiers signified a desire for the elimination of privilege and the establishment in its place of the principle of equality in the elections to the States-General.

Not only were the cahiers conservative upon the suffrage and indirect election, but the majority of them made no open attack upon election by class. In most cases, the issue was passed over in silence. The power of each class relative to the others was the major concern with even the more radical cahiers. The third estate of Rennes, whose discussion of representation was more thorough than that of most cahiers, was exceptional, and made the following statement:

Art. 13. The States-General will be composed of the deputies of the entire nation completely and uniformly represented throughout the kingdom without distinction of class . . .[69]

On the other hand, some cahiers expressed fear of the extension of democracy. The clergy of Villefranche-de-Beaujolais spoke of

---

based largely upon historical status or practice, and it did not correspond in 1789 with the density of population. The attempt in the convocation of 1789 to base the number of deputies to the States-General upon population was sincere, but vitiated by the many exceptions and privileges, by the limitation of representation of the third estate to double the number granted the privileged orders, by ignorance of the electoral units, etc. *Cf. Guide,* also Brette, *op. cit.*, Vol. I, *passim.*

[65] AP, Vol. VI, p. 212, art. 9.

[66] It is quite possible that this method was inspired by the pamphlet of Siéyès, *Déliberations à prendre . . .*, which formed a part of the electoral propaganda of the Duke of Orléans.

[67] Sée and Lessort, *D.I.*, *op. cit.*, Vol. IV, p. 242, arts. 13-17.

[68] For example, T. Montargis, AP, Vol. IV, p. 26, art. 7.

[69] Sée and Lessort, *D.I.*, *op. cit.*, Vol. IV, p. 242, art. 13.

the elimination of classes in government as leading to democracy or to despotism, both of which they considered equally undesirable.[70] The nobles of Briey said that too much influence in the hands of the third estate would cause the government to degenerate into democracy, "a form of government opposed to our constitution and to our true interest."[71] What would the curates of Bouzonville have said about our modern democracy when they complained that the elections of the third estate of their district were made in the night, and "that strangers to the assembly entered, indecently, with pipe in mouth, and elbowed, made speeches, and influenced the elections."[72] The third estate itself was much more concerned with achieving equal power with the other two classes than with sponsoring democratic measures.

Thus, although the extension of the elective principle was widely demanded, its practice would still be aristocratic. It is not surprising, in view of the attitude of the cahiers, that the principle of universal manhood suffrage first appeared in the Constitution of 1793 and not in that of 1791.[73] In one respect, some cahiers indicated the changing trend toward personal, numerical representation in the States-General. Once the deputies were elected, they would represent, thereafter, the nation at large, and not a class or a *bailliage*. In the words of the nobles of Montargis,

> The representatives to the States-General, of whatever province they come, once united in the national assembly, can no longer regard themselves as other than representatives of the entire nation.[74]

This democratic attitude was expressed by only twenty-eight cahiers.[75] Fear of arbitrary action against the States-General, as

[70] AP, Vol. II, p. 279, col. 1.

[71] AP, Vol. II, p. 203, col. 2.

[72] P. v. MS, *Arch. Nat.* Ba 77. Protest of the curates on March 27.

[73] *Cf.* the comments of Meuriot, *La Population et les lois électorales en France de 1789 à nos jours* (Paris, 1916), pp. 4-5.

[74] AP, Vol. IV, p. 22, art. 4. This cahier had an imperative mandate attached to it which was designed as a safeguard against arbitrary action, and not as a guarantee of class or provincial privileges.

[75] 3 C, 12 N, 11 T, 1 U, 1 NT. C—Beauvais, Bellême, Lyon. N—Auxerre, Castelmoron d'Albret, Dôle, Etain, Forcalquier, Mantes, Montargis, Nemours, Nivernais, Paris *hors-les-murs,* Provins, Riom. T—Caudebec-en-Caux, Clermont Ferrand, Grasse, Limoges, Nemours, Nîmes, Orange, Paris *hors-les-murs,* Paris *intra-muros,* Ponthieu, Rennes. U—Rustaing. NT—Péronne. One would question this curious indi-

well as class and regional spirit, was still too strong for any widespread assertion of national representation.

The elective principle, an essentially democratic tenet, should be extended according to the cahiers of 1789, but its application would be limited by other considerations. Its advocacy was pro-democratic, but true democracy was far in the future.

Equality and the Provinces.—The French state on the eve of the Revolution was composed of many provinces, brought together over a period of centuries and gradually welded together, until, as we have seen, some sentiment of common nationality had been achieved. The relationship of each province to the whole was, however, a complex of inequalities, both administrative and economic. Until this diversity had been eliminated, together with the regional sentiment which sustained it, there would be little chance of a strong national sentiment.

Advocacy of provincial equalization took several forms in the cahiers of 1789. The retention of the existing provincial boundaries was tacitly accepted by the majority of cahiers. Even those that asked for a redivision of France had in mind the *bailliages* or other units of administration rather than the provinces.[76] The desire was for a similar machinery of local administration for all provinces, proportionate equality in taxation, and economic equality rather than for provincial equality in size, population, or economic resource.

We have already noted that numerous cahiers asked for the establishment of a uniform provincial régime.[77] Equality was the underlying principle. Similarly, the demand for the establishment of Provincial-Estates in all provinces came from the same motive. These bodies had been the agency of self-administration in the *pays d'état,* and the envy of the other provinces. By their institution in each of the provinces, all of France would enjoy the same right of local self-administration.[78] In respect to provincial taxa-

---

cation that democratic philosophy had gone further in the ranks of the nobles than in those of the third estate.

[76] *Cf. supra,* p. 55.

[77] *Cf. supra,* pp. 54-55.

[78] *Cf. supra,* p. 54 and *infra,* pp. 183-84.

tion, the general principle of equality was well stated by the clergy of Péronne, who asked:

> That all provinces of the kingdom, participating equally in the public protection, in the national rights, and the grace of the king, contribute for the future to all the charges of the state in the most exact equality, without any exception whatsoever.[79]

The cahier went on to explain that equality was to be proportioned to the capacity to pay, but in no way to be based upon privilege. Whenever the status of the provinces was discussed from the standpoint of taxation, the principle of equality on the basis of ability to pay was voiced.

Demands for the abolition of internal customs barriers were further indication of the sentiment for an equalization of the provinces. According to the nobles of Beziers, the existing régime made "The different parts of the same state appear to be in a condition of permanent war, rather than governed by the same king and the same law."[80] We have already seen that the greater part of France rejected this régime, whereas the districts along the northern and eastern frontiers were inclined to continue the unequal conditions.[81]

Besides the desire for administrative and economic equality, three cahiers were conscious of the political factor. The third estates of Sarrebourg[82] and of Melun (a district of the *generality* of Paris)[83] protested against the influence of Paris, while the nobles of Périgord deplored the growth and expenses connected with the city of Paris.[84] The third estate of Melun definitely asked that an equilibrium be established between the province of the Ile de France and the other provinces.[85] Although Paris had enjoyed considerable prestige before the Revolution, it became the center of attention once the National Assembly established its headquarters there, while the revolutionary influence of the commune of Paris further increased the rôle of that city. A few cahiers

[79] AP, Vol. V, p. 348, art. 3.
[80] AP, Vol. II, p. 348, art. 14.
[81] *Cf. supra*, p. 57.
[82] Cahier, MS, *Arch. Meurthe et Moselle*, art. 28; *generality* of Metz.
[83] See note 85.
[84] AP, Vol. V, p. 340, col. 1.
[85] AP, Vol. III, p. 743, col. 1, art. 18.

seem to have resented the power of Paris even under the old régime.[86]

By a synthesis of the demands for equality of taxation, representation, administration, and influence, we discover that one hundred and twenty-one cahiers were concerned with an equalized régime for the provinces.[87] This movement was fairly widespread, though less marked in the provinces that were already *pays d'état*. During the Revolution, the organization of the departments was an effort not only to establish an equitable administrative basis, but also to break down provincial feelings. Such regionalism as survived, has been largely cultural.

Democratic Machinery of Government.—The advocates of nineteenth-century democracy utilized certain instruments in order to attain and operate democracy. The cahiers of 1789 mentioned nearly all of these without, however, any one of them appearing in more than a handful of cahiers. It is surprising perhaps to find so many suggestions of the kind in view of the fact that other aspects of democracy were elusive in the majority of cahiers.

In the first place, there was some anticipation of the devices of initiative and referendum. Beside occasional assertions of the right of petition,[88] numerous cahiers contained proposals for the submission of plans of reform to the States-General by committees appointed by the States-General, the provinces, or interested parties. The principle of initiative was behind such statements as that of the nobles of Armagnac who asked "that there be named a commission of magistrates, lawyers, military authorities, and other enlightened and instructed citizens, to work upon and report their work [a law code] to the next assembly of the nation, which work of the commissions will be made public a year before the assembly of the States-General."[89] Some cahiers proposed com-

[86] Aulard pointed out that the Girondists and the Mountain both aimed at the glory of France, but the former would achieve this through the action of the provinces in a federated union in which Paris was merely one of the units, whereas the latter would give Paris the major rôle. (Aulard, A., *Histoire politique de la Révolution française,* Paris, 1926, *passim*). Opposition to predominance of Paris was one form of federalism.

[87] *Cf.* Table VIII, Appendix, p. 256.

[88] A clear statement of the right of petition was made by the third estate of Paris *hors-les-murs,* AP, Vol. V, p. 239, art. 27.

[89] AP, Vol. II, p. 71, art. 40.

mittees to draft legal reforms,[90] others for military reforms,[91] while still others for miscellaneous reforms.[92] As it was largely cahiers of the nobles that suggested the submission of plans to the States-General, we would hesitate to call their motives democratic. They were democratic only in that they were recommending an extra-governmental method of initiating plans and of getting the opinion of enlightened groups directly before the States-General. Initiative later became a significant tenet of democracy.

Referendum, outside of its application to the provinces which inclined toward federalism and regionalism rather than democracy,[93] was less often recommended than the initiative. The third estate of Clermont-Ferrand combined both initiative and referendum in their request that a committee should draw up suggestions for a national law code, but that the States-General should not act upon it until the plan had been printed, circulated, and the judgment of the public obtained.[94] According to the nobles of La Rochelle, the Provincial-Estates should act not as an arbiter of the decisions of the States-General, but as a convenient agency for preliminary discussion, and as an index of public opinion on the proposals by the States-General.[95] The third estate of Agen proposed a general protest against infractions of the constitution, guaranteed reciprocally by the provinces, and if no action was taken, "the nation ought to assemble immediately, to legislate in its own interests."[96] This was not a mere variant of the contract idea so often voiced in the cahiers, and which showed the common currency of Rousseau and other contract philosophers. The national assembly which would meet as a result of the circumstances described by this cahier would represent a national censure of the government.

The plebiscite, introduced by Napoleon I and revived and claimed by Napoleon III as a democratic principle of the first empire, was essentially the application of a principle implied by

[90] For example, T. Vitry-le-françois, AP, Vol. VI, p. 216, art. 7.
[91] N. Montpellier, N. Reims.
[92] For example, T. Clermont Ferrand, AP, Vol. II, p. 772.
[93] *Cf. infra,* pp. 183 *et seq.*
[94] AP, Vol. II, p. 772, col. 1, art. 1.
[95] AP, Vol. III, p. 473, art. 7, and p. 475. col. 1.
[96] AP, Vol. I, p. 682, art. 6.

the few cahiers suggesting referenda. In the illustrations cited, may be seen the use of the referendum for specific questions, and also, its use for a general change of policy or government.

A total of twenty-eight cahiers contained hints of the future development of the principles of the initiative and referendum.[97] These opinions came from different parts of France, and almost exclusively from the two lay orders.

When applied to changes of boundary or national loyalty, the plebiscite involves self-determination of peoples. Six cahiers stated that no changes in the boundaries of France should be made without the consent of the peoples concerned, or the consent of the States-General.[98] The clearest statement came from the third estate of Bailleul, a district on the Flemish frontier,

> In the future, there should be no change of boundaries without having first heard the inhabitants of the districts which are to be exchanged, in order that they may make known the inconveniences which might result.[99]

It was not a far cry from this to the Declaration of November, 1792, for the liberation and self-determination of peoples.

Democracy in the judicial branch of the government was envisaged by two demands in the cahiers of 1789.[100] The first of these was a demand for the institution of the jury. Trial by jury had been established in England in the twelfth century, but in France it had never been generally in use, even though two cahiers claimed that it was a traditional institution there.[101] Approximately thirty cahiers, most of which were from the third estate, asked for the establishment of juries.[102] Jury trial for criminal offenses was

[97] 1 C, 14 N, 13 T. C—Sézanne; N—Agen, Bordeaux, Bourmont, Darney, La Rochelle, Limoges, Lyon, Montpellier, Nîmes, Provins, Reims, Rouen, St. Mihiel, Toulouse; T—Angers, Bordeaux, Caen, Clermont-Ferrand, Colmar, Mantes, Nemours, Paris *hors-les-murs,* Rennes, Rodez, Villefranche-en-Rouerque, Villers-Cotterets; V. Rouen.

[98] T. Bailleul, N, T, Corsica, T, Mâcon, N, Trévoux, U. Villers-la-Montagne.

[99] AP, Vol. II, p. 176, art. 29.

[100] There were few positive assertions of the separation of powers (e.g., T. Forez, AP, Vol. III, p. 367), the measure so strongly advocated by Montesquieu.

[101] N. Saintes, N. Dôle.

[102] 28 cahiers, 2 C, 14 N, 10 T, 1 U, 1 NT. C—Autun, Villefranche-de-Beaujolais; N—Angers, Artois, Corsica, Coutances, Dôle, Etain, Foix, Mantes, Melun, Ponthieu, Riom, Saintes, Sarrebourg, Semur; T—Alençon, Autun, Bigorre, Bordeaux, Draguignan, Melun, Nemours, Paris *intra-muros,* Rennes, Toulon; U—Rustaing; NT—Péronne.

actually adopted in the legal reform organized on the plans of Thouret, in September, 1791.

A second demand for judicial reform which reflected democratic thinking was for the establishment of justices of the peace. This was not only an indirect stab at seignorial justice, but pointed in the direction of a more democratic local justice. According to the third estate of Nantes,

> There shall be established, in the rural districts, justices of the peace, who shall be nominated each year in a general assembly of the inhabitants of each district; they shall reside in the district; they shall take an oath before the royal judges; they shall administer justice without charge because they will be appointed by the parishes; they shall have a definite competence, and in cases where the judges entering office cannot exercise jurisdiction, the case shall be taken before the first justice of the peace retiring from office.[103]

Although the third estate of Poitiers mentioned the institution as one of common practice in Prussia,[104] it is probable that more cahiers looked toward England, where, however, the justices of the peace were not then a democratic institution.[105] Justices of the peace in France would, nevertheless, remove from feudal justice many of its petty cases, and on the basis of popular election, would extend the jurisdiction of the local government.[106] Justices of the peace were actually instituted in August, 1790.[107]

A practice which became an important accompaniment of nineteenth-century democracy—the secret ballot—was mentioned only twice in the general cahiers of 1789.[108] The usual procedure at the time was public voting in all assemblies, except for the actual election of deputies, which was done by written ballot. In the earlier States-General, the customary method had been to take the vote orally by governments, starting with the Ile de France or ter-

[103] AP, Vol. IV, p. 95, art. 43. Although the *Archives Parlementaires* have given the text of the town of Nantes, this article is the same in the general cahier.

[104] AP, Vol. V, p. 411, col. 1.

[105] In the eighteenth century, the justices of the peace were members of the country gentry and dependent upon royal appointment from nominations made by the local aristocracy. Miss Bertha Putnam, of Mount Holyoke College, authority on the justices of the peace during the medieval period, conveyed this information to the author.

[106] About 50 cahiers, chiefly of the clergy and third estate asked for justices.

[107] Seligman, *op. cit.*, Vol. I, chap. vi, *passim*.

[108] T. Rodez asked for oral voting (AP, Vol. V, p. 557, art. 7).

ritory around Paris. This gave a certain prestige to Paris and a cumulative force to the voting. By their silence on this matter, the cahiers of 1789 acquiesced in oral voting. It is probable that the fear of corruption and the absence of any other check on the obedience of deputies to their instructions led the electors of 1789 to adhere to the traditional method. When the fear of arbitrary power had been removed and literacy extended, the secret ballot came into widespread demand.

Various suggestions for some democratic machinery of government appeared in approximately seventy-five cahiers of all three classes,[109] mainly surrounding Paris, and hardly at all from districts of the north and north-east, from the upper classes of the south or from Brittany. Although the ideas were fragmentary, incidental, and their democratic import never fully grasped, it is interesting to note how much of the later machinery of democratic government was foreshadowed in the cahiers of 1789.

EQUALITY AND THE CLASSES

In discussing French traditions, we noted that many cahiers deemed the division of the French nation into three classes as fundamental to the French constitution.[110] So long as the existing class system prevailed, complete national unity was impossible. Comparatively few cahiers, however, attacked the class system at its root. The majority accepted class divisions and worked for equalization among them. As the third estate of Longuyon said, apropos of voting by head, the third estate "does not seek absolute equality, all that it asks is that consideration and respect for the law and before the law be equal for all."[111] "Egalitarianism," like ideas of democratic government, was relative in the cahiers of 1789, and almost never absolute.

There were, nevertheless, a few scattered attacks on classes as such. The philosophical principle of equality was occasionally enunciated in connection with some concrete egalitarian demand. For example, the third estate of Trévoux, in discussing ennoble-

[109] 22 C, 20 N, 33 T, 1 NT.

[110] *Cf. supra*, p. 41.

[111] Cahier MS, *Arch. Moselle,* end of 2d paragraph, or reprint in *Guide.*

ment, declared: "Nature has made men equal, and it is only their personal qualities that can raise some above the others."[112] Such declarations were, however, usually made to fit into the class framework. One attack upon classes took the form of demands for a readjustment in their number or their membership. A few cahiers suggested the addition of a fourth order composed of the rural population.[113] Others suggested a reduction to two classes,[114] either by the union of the privileged orders into one class,[115] or by the division of the clergy between the nobles and the third estate.[116] Nevertheless, such suggestions were rare, and although they attacked the existing system, were hardly egalitarian.

Within the framework of the class system, egalitarian demands took several forms. The outstanding desire was for proportionate equality in taxation. Such egalitarianism was clearly expressed by the clergy of Puy-en-Velay who asked for equality between classes as well as between provinces:

> All the French are members of the same family; they participate equally in the advantages of government; they ought therefore to share equally the costs. No privilege ought or should take precedence over public interest; the State has equal and imprescriptible rights over all individuals and all property which it protects. The fundamental principle of society is that all its members who have common interests to sustain and to defend, have also equal charges and duties to perform.[117]

The demand for proportionate equality of taxation was well-nigh *unanimous* in the cahiers of 1789,[118] but it appears to have been more often the result of fraternity and patriotism than of a devotion to abstract equality.

Proportionate equality would mean the elimination of the fiscal privileges of the two upper orders. The clergy of Châlons-sur-Marne declared quite definitely:

> The order of the clergy, in order to prove to the king and to the nation that it has shown such strong attachment to former practices

[112] AP, Vol. VI, p. 69, col. 1.

[113] For example, N. Montargis, AP, Vol. IV, p. 21, col. 2, ch. iv, art. 1.

[114] Cahiers desiring only two orders were: N—Aval, Briey, Metz; T—Aix, Auray, Brest, Montargis, Strasbourg, Verdun.

[115] For example, T. Montargis, AP, Vol. IV, p. 26, art. 7.

[116] For example, N. Metz, AP, Vol. III, p. 763, art. 1.

[117] AP, Vol. V, p. 465, art. 7.

[118] *Cf.* Table IX, Appendix, p. 257.

only because it looked upon them as the last monument of the former national liberty in the matter of taxation, and that it has never considered its distinctive privileges as a means to escape the public charges, not only consents, but solicits the suppression of every distinctive tax, and the substitution of a tax common to all three orders.[119]

Both the nobles and the clergy made occasional reservations to their fiscal altruism. The clergy sometimes offered equal liability to state taxes on condition that the state assume the church debt,[120] or that the clergy retain the right to apportion among themselves the tax allotted to their order.[121] The nobles would reserve feudal privileges,[122] on the assumption that these constituted property rights and historic exemptions based upon service to the monarch. Numerous cahiers agreed with the nobles of Châlons-sur-Marne, who avoided the fundamental issue of equal liability by conceding equality for *new* taxes, but retention of the current privileges.[123] The cahier which defended most strongly the privileges of the nobles has unfortunately come down to us in a mutilated condition, for the rats of Auvergne found the assertions of the nobles of St. Flour nourishing, and have perhaps deprived us thereby of even more substantial statements of class privilege.[124]

Parallel with demands for equal tax liability went a renunciation of privilege. Very frequently, the two were coupled together, but the latter also occurred alone.[125] One finds four types of statement: those in favor of complete renunciation of privileges; those with reservation of property rights; those renouncing financial privileges but retaining honorary privileges; and those that opposed renunciation.[126] The vagueness of the phrase "renunciation

[119] Laurent., G., *D.I., Cahiers de doléances . . . de Châlons-sur-Marne* (Epernay, 1906), p. 831, art. 1.

[120] For example, C. Châtillon-sur-Seine, AP, Vol. II, p. 702, art. 16.

[121] For example, C. Clermont-Ferrand, AP, Vol. II, p. 764, art. 36.

[122] For example, N. Lyon, AP, Vol. III, p. 604, art. 1.

[123] Laurent, *D.I., op. cit.*, p. 841.

[124] The only surviving copy of this cahier exists in the departmental archives of Cantal. The *Archives Parlementaires* has reprinted it with indications of parts missing, due to the work of the rats.

[125] *Cf.* Table IX, Appendix, p. 257.

[126] The cahiers that opposed renunciation of privileges by direct statement were: C—Gien, Bourmont; N—Montargis, Guéret, St. Flour, Armagnac, Comminges, Dorat, Châtel-sur-Moselle. On those making reservations, *cf.* Table X, Appendix, p. 258.

of privileges" was perhaps less illusive in 1789 when privilege affected every daily act, than it is today.[127]

Recommendations for a renunciation of privileges appeared quite frequently in the cahiers of the clergy and nobles, although more often in the latter, and only rarely in the cahiers of the third estate.[128] The third estate wished to retain whatever advantages it enjoyed, while acquiring those of the privileged orders. While the upper class benefits would be scaled down, the third estate would be raised to their level.

The renunciation of privileges or advocacy of equal liability to taxation, or both, occurred in the overwhelming majority of cahiers of the clergy and nobles. In view of the reservations made, it is not surprising that when the first enthusiasm manifested during the electoral period and culminating in the dramatic night of August 4th, had cooled, such reservations should re-emerge to color the altruism of the upper classes. Absolute equality was certainly not the aim of the renunciation, and when the full bearing of the principle was seen, many districts drew back from the egalitarian statements made in the electoral assemblies.

Egalitarianism was also expressed in several other ways. Over one-fifth of the cahiers stated that henceforth there should be no distinction before the law between members of the different classes.[129] There should be the same protection and the same punishment irrespective of class. According to the nobles of Artois,

> Liberty, which only consists in dependence upon law, requires also that all citizens be equally subject to the law. The nobles of Artois demand that no accused be excepted from the ordinary forms of procedure . . . which shall be regulated for all citizens without distinction; that the difference in penalties be determined only by the nature of the offense and not by the quality of the person. . . .[130]

The demand for the abolition of class qualifications for office

[127] Privileges possessed by the clergy included exemption from certain taxes, the right to apportion the financial quota required of them, the privilege of trial in ecclesiastical courts, certain prerogatives of office-holding and of suffrage. The privileges of the nobles were feudal, official, military, fiscal, and social. As compared with the upper classes, the third estate did not possess privileges, but within its own ranks, members of gilds, municipal corps and members of monopolistic companies enjoyed advantages not shared by other members.

[128] *Cf.* Table IX, Appendix, p. 257. Four hundred and eighty-two cahiers favored one or both of these demands.

[129] *Cf.* Table XI, Appendix, p. 259.

[130] AP, Vol. II, p. 80, art. 7.

holding was another form of egalitarianism in the cahiers of 1789. Appointment on merit should replace class eligibility. As the clergy of Reims said,

> Every individual of talent and virtue, of whatever order he be, may attain any employment—civil, ecclesiastical, or military; ordinances or regulations to the contrary should be revoked. There is no surer means nor any more efficacious to reawaken patriotism and to regenerate the entire nation.[131]

The third estate of Nîmes expressed the thought that there might be distinctions and prerogatives for each profession, but "the right to be useful to the *patrie*" should no longer be a caste privilege.[132] The assertion in favor of appointment based on merit irrespective of class was a corollary to the denunciation of the purchase of office,[133] and was expressed by more than fifty cahiers, including some cahiers of the privileged orders.[134]

Other demands for democratization of the classes were less in the nature of general principles applicable to all the orders, than expressive of a desire for the gradual removal of distinctions within a class. For example, the cahiers of all three orders were concerned with the betterment of the status of the lower clergy,[135] whereas the cahiers of the clergy, more often than the lay cahiers, recommended a more equitable distribution of church offices[136] and revenues,[137] and protested against plurality of office.[138] There

[131] AP, Vol. V, p. 523, art. 5.

[132] Bligny-Bondurand, *D.I., op. cit.,* Vol. III, p. 602, art. 5.

[133] *Cf. supra,* p. 72.

[134] 60 cahiers; 15 C, 7 N, 38 T. C—Avesnes, Château-Salins, Dijon, Forez, La Marche, Mans (le), Mantes, Nantes, Reims, Rennes, Rodez, Saint Malo, Soissons, Villefranche-de-Beaujolais, Vitry-en-françois; N—Châteauneuf-en-Thimerais, Château-Thierry, Corsica, Metz, Paris *intra-muros,* Sarreguemines, Villeneuve-de-Berg; T—Aix, Artois, Bailleul, Bar-le-duc, Bazas, Bellême, Belley, Bordeaux, Bourmont, Bouzonville, Briey, Caen, Calais, Castelnaudary, Castelmoron d'Albret, Châteauneuf-en-Thimerais, Dijon, Dorat, Foix, Forcalquier, Forez, Longuyon, Longwy, Lyon, Mantes, Meaux, Nantes, Nemours, Neufchâteau, Paris *hors-les-murs,* Paris *intra-muros,* Ploërmel, Quatre-Vallées, Rennes, St. Pierre-le-Moutier, Semur-en-Auxois, Toulouse, Verdun.

[135] For example, N. Alençon, AP, Vol. I, p. 714, col. 2, art. 11. (The number of this article in the MS text is art. 9, *Arch. Nat.* Ba 11.)

[136] For example, C. Moulins, AP. Vol. II, p. 443, arts. 3 and 5, or N. Bouzonville, AP, Vol. V, p. 702, cols. 1-2.

[137] For example, C. Châlon-sur-Saône, AP, Vol. II, p. 601, art. 8. Denys-Buirette also argued that the demands relative to the *dîme* showed a democratic movement (*loc. cit.,* Part I, ch. 4, *passim*).

[138] For example, C. Moulins, AP, Vol. II, p. 443, art. 2.

were also demands to give the lower clergy an equal voice in the ecclesiastical assemblies and likewise to give due recognition to the rank of curate.[139]

In regard to the nobles, the cahiers of all three orders contained one demand pointing directly toward democracy. This was the demand for the abolition of ennoblement by purchase, and the substitution of ennoblement for service of France. Members of all classes would thereby be eligible on the basis of merit. The clergy of Dourdan put the thought concisely, "That nobility be no longer acquired by a money payment, but that it be the recompense of real and important services to the *patrie*."[140] This demand was not an attack on the old hereditary nobility, but its application would gradually transform aristocracy into an *élite* of public servants, to which distinction all alike could aspire. The fact that nearly 36 percent of the general cahiers expressed this opinion shows how widespread was the democratic principle of reward for merit rather than superiority based upon birth or favor.[141]

Whereas demands in behalf of the curates interested all classes, solicitude for the lot of the lesser nobility appeared almost exclusively in cahiers of the nobles themselves. In the words of the nobles of Bourges, "The deputies will be especially concerned for all that touches the interests and the glory of the nobles of the provinces, the least accessible to the favors of the court."[142] Obviously, the motive here was more selfish than egalitarian. There were, however, various other suggestions aimed at equal justice for all nobles, and at a democratization within their own ranks. Some cahiers suggested that education be facilitated,[143] careers in the army opened,[144] or trade be permitted without loss of caste.[145]

One must not lose sight of anti-egalitarian demands appearing in cahiers of the nobility. Reservation of the honorary distinc-

[139] For example, C. Castelnaudary, AP, Vol. II, p. 552, art. 3. Consult Table XII, Appendix, p. 260, for the list of cahiers demanding a democratization of the clergy.

[140] AP, Vol. III, p. 245, art. 13.

[141] 188 cahiers; 24 C, 101 N, 56 T, 5 U, 2 NT.

[142] AP, Vol. II, p. 322, art. 5.

[143] For example, N. Limoux, AP, Vol. III, p. 579, art. 29.

[144] For example, N. Chaumont-en-Bassigny, AP, Vol. II, p. 725, arts. 35, 36.

[145] For example, N. Provins, AP, Vol. V, p. 450, art. 18. As many as fifty-eight cahiers made this demand (6 C, 34 N, 16 T, 1 U, 1 NT).

tions of the nobles was usually made when renunciation of privileges was affirmed.[146] The verification of titles of nobility was also motivated by selfish interests.[147] Thus, although various democratic measures regarding the nobles appeared in many cahiers, the nobles themselves were more anxious for improvement of the nobility than for egalitarian reforms affecting their relative status among the orders.[148]

Demands for equality within the third estate were somewhat different from those of the clergy and nobles. The third estate was more eager than the upper orders for the general reforms affecting all classes, but their motive was more frequently self-interest than the lofty ideal of equality. Although the third estate was less of a unit than the other two orders,[149] it presented complete harmony in its desire for equality with the two upper orders.

Whereas a few cahiers of the third estate had asked that there be no exclusions from office on the basis of class,[150] over four times this number asked merely for the removal of all disqualifications against the third estate.[151] The demand for representation of the third estate on all governmental bodies[152] equal to that of the two privileged orders combined, may appear conservative in view of the fact that the third estate comprised much more than half of the French nation, but the fundamental idea was equality between the classes. A third demand that would benefit exclusively the third estate was a request for the removal of humiliating differences in the ceremonial of the States-General and of royal audiences.[153] The third estate had been required to kneel, while the other two orders stood. The disappearance of this mark of in-

[146] *Cf. supra,* pp. 85 *et seq.*

[147] For example, N. Beziers, AP, Vol. II, p. 347, art. 13.

[148] A comparison of the number of opinions from cahiers of the nobles bearing upon democracy and the classes supports this conclusion.

[149] The *procès-verbaux,* and sometimes the cahiers, gave evidence of conflicts within the third estate between the richer bourgeoisie and the rest, between gildsmen and unorganized labor, between town and country, etc.

[150] *Cf. supra,* pp. 86-87.

[151] Compare list, p. 87, note 134, with Table XIII, Appendix, p. 260.

[152] The most frequent demand for the doubling of the third was with respect to the States-General, but the demand was also made in respect of the new Provincial-Estates, while eight cahiers would also apply it to courts (C—Lunéville, St. Mihiel; T—Angers, Carhaix, Rennes, St. Dié, Sarreguemines; U—Rozières). 121 cahiers asked for the doubling of the third estate (11 C, 7 N, 98 T, 5 U, 1 CT).

[153] Seventy-five cahiers made this demand: 3 C, 9 N, 61 T, 2 U.

feriority would remove one of the most galling inequalities and would be symbolic of political equality. Another practice which was considered humiliating by the third estate was the levying of *franc-fief,* a tax collected on non-noble owners of fiefs. This received widespread denunciation, and not alone from the cahiers of the third estate.[154] In the third estate's opposition to the feudal régime, more emphasis was placed upon its infringement of the state's sovereignty and on its financial burden than upon the principle of equality.[155]

The cahiers of all three orders were more attentive to demands that would help their own class than to those affecting the other two orders. It is significant that the clergy and nobles were slightly more altruistic than the third estate. Although individual egalitarian demands appeared quite widely in 1789, only a very few cahiers were consistently democratic with respect to the classes.[156] Only one-tenth of the general cahiers were predominantly democratic, and of these, two-thirds were cahiers of the third estate.[157] The upper classes showed some pro-democratic tendencies, but were essentially aristocratic and conservative, while the third estate was more interested in its own advancement than in general equality. All egalitarianism was within the framework of the class system.

INDIVIDUALISM

Although radicalism in any age has gained force by an initial appeal to the individual, and though in France individualism was inherent in the antifeudal movement and in the wars of religion,

[154] 179 cahiers asked for abolition of *franc-fief* (22 C, 23 N, 126 T, 6 U, 1 CN, 1 NT).

[155] *Cf. infra,* pp. 114 *et seq.*

[156] The cahiers may not have appreciated the interrelations of various democratic and aristocratic demands. For example, the clergy of Villefranche-de-Beaujolais voiced a fair number of the democratic items mentioned, but denounced democracy when discussing voting in the States-General.

[157] 52 cahiers. 7 C, 7 N, 36 T, 1 U, 1 NT. C—Alençon, Chatellerault, Châtillon-sur-Seine, Dol, La Marche, Péronne, St. Mihiel; N—Châteauneuf-en-Thimerais, Clermont-en-Beauvoisis, Mantes, Nemours, Paris *hors-les-murs,* Paris *intra-muros,* Sens; T—Amiens, Angers, Auray, Autun, Bordeaux, Brest, Briey, Carhaix, Castelmoron d'Albret, Castelnaudary, Chartres, Chatellerault, Châteauneuf-en-Thimerais, Coutances, Dinan, Dijon, Forez, Gien, La Rochelle, Lyon, Mâcon, Mans(le), Mantes, Montpellier, Nantes, Nemours, Paris *intra-muros,* Ploërmel, Reims, Rennes, Rodez, St. Pierre-le-Moutier, Saintes, Vannes, Villeneuve-de-Berg, Vitry-le-françois; U—Villers-la-Montagne; NT—Péronne.

it was during the French Revolution that individualism, so distinctive a feature of French nationalism today, received its great impetus. How far was this development heralded in the general cahiers of 1789?

The general cahiers were the result of collective efforts, and the need of the moment was coöperation against arbitrary power, with the subordination of the individual to the general welfare. One would, therefore, hardly expect from them outstanding assertions of individualism. It was implied, however, in the emphasis of many cahiers upon individual rights. Frenchmen in 1789 desired the affirmation not only of the rights of the nation, but also those of the individual.[158] The cahiers identified the universal rights of all men with the rights of French citizens. In so far as all Frenchmen were to enjoy the same rights, the individual likewise benefited. The entire movement for affirming and guaranteeing the rights of French citizens drew for its ultimate philosophy upon individualism.

A great many cahiers that asked for the reaffirmation of the French constitution, or for the establishment of a new one, requested also a formal declaration of rights—a charter of individual liberties—similar to those contained in English constitutional law.[159] The words of the nobles of Beziers were typical of the cahiers that asked for such a declaration;

> that the general assembly examine, as a preliminary object, the making of a declaration of the rights of man and of the citizen, a declaration which will serve as a basis for all laws, political or civil, which may emanate at present or in the future from all national assemblies.[160]

Whether these principles should form one compact section of the constitution, or should merely follow along after the articles dealing with the national organization was unimportant.[161] Their sig-

[158] For example, N. Château-Thierry, AP, Vol. II, p. 659, art. 6. *Cf.* also *supra*, p. 42.

[159] The cahiers themselves gave no clue to the origin of their interest in a declaration of rights. Authorities have differed about the explanation. Jellenik ascribed the origin to American state constitutions, while Marcaggi made out a good case for Physiocratic doctrine. (See bibliography, p. 305.)

[160] AP, Vol. II, p. 348, art. 1.

[161] Only a minority of the cahiers (though more often of the nobles than of clergy or third estate) asked specifically for a declaration of rights. The overwhelming majority enumerated the rights without asking that they be set apart in a special document.

nificance lay in the individual rights that were advocated or defended.

The keynote of all declarations of rights in the cahiers was *liberty*. According to the nobles of Blois, liberty was a right possessed by all, equally, irrespective of class.[162] Liberty, as conceived in the cahiers, meant security from arbitrary power, and not license. According to the nobles of Artois, a declaration should be made "that the French nation is a free people, that is to say, that every Frenchman is free to do what does not harm another, and which is not forbidden by the law; the law alone can deprive a citizen of the liberty of his person."[163] The phrase that liberty allowed the individual to do anything that did not infringe upon the rights of others (*nuire aux droits d'autrui*) recurred frequently.[164] The cahiers did not stop, however, at the vague assertion of a principle, but applied the principle to particular matters.

The most frequent assertion of individual rights in the cahiers involved guarantees of personal security—liberty from arbitrary power. The overwhelming majority of cahiers regarded freedom from arbitrary arrest as a cardinal principle of individual rights. The relationship between liberty and security in this respect was well illustrated by the wording of the cahiers of the third estate of Angers: "The liberty of each citizen shall be assured against all arbitrary orders in such manner that no one may be deprived of it without the most exact observance of judicial and legal reforms."[165] The protection of this right involved a denunciation of *lettres de cachet*, which were almost universally condemned though seldom, curiously enough, on the ground of individual rights.[166] Not only was the individual to be free from arbitrary arrest, but no individual should be imprisoned or punished without due trial. In the words of the nobles of Orléans, "Personal liberty

[162] Cauchie and Lesueur, *D.I., op. cit.*, Vol. II, p. 415, art. 1.

[163] AP, Vol. II, p. 348, art. 1.

[164] This phrase had appeared in the writings of Siéyès, but it was the logical formula to express the thought. Evidence is insufficient to prove that each case was a direct borrowing from his writings.

[165] AP, Vol. II, p. 38, art. 6.

[166] On the variations in the demands relative to the abolition of *lettres de cachet*, *cf.* Seligman, E., *op. cit.*, Vol. I, ch. iii, *passim*, and the index volume of the *Archives Parlementaires*, under the phrase.

of citizens shall be assured, and no one may be arrested by virtue of ministerial orders, without being brought before competent judges within twenty-four hours."[167] The third estate of Paris *hors-les-murs* gave the most comprehensive declaration of rights. This cahier not only stated that no citizen could be arrested except for a crime against another citizen, as defined by law, but said also, "It is a natural right that no citizen may be condemned in criminal matters except by decision of his equals."[168] Many legal reforms asked by the cahiers were designed to safeguard the individual,[169] but their inclusion in a declaration of individual rights was less frequently specified. Personal liberty also implied freedom from forced military service,[170] but this was seldom expressed as a formal individual right.

Freedom of thought, and hence of religion, was sometimes included among the rights of citizens.[171] The right of free speech with the corollary of liberty of the press, was frequently asserted. In a section devoted to liberty, the nobles of Blois declared: "From personal liberty derives that of writing, thinking, the right to print and publish. . . ."[172] Corollaries less often expressed, were the right of free assembly, and of petition.[173] Twenty-four cahiers mentioned freedom of movement as an essential right of the individual.[174] The words of the nobles of Briey were typical: "There shall be understood, under the title of liberty, the right of every Frenchman to go and come, to establish himself where he prefers, within or outside the kingdom, without need of permis-

[167] Bloch, C., *D.I., Cahiers de doléances . . . d' Orléans* (Orléans, 1906-7), Vol. II, p. 424, art. 7.

[168] AP, Vol. V, p. 238, art. 9.

[169] *Cf.* discussion of legal reforms, Seligman, *op. cit., passim.*

[170] For example, T. La Rochelle, AP, Vol. III, p. 481, art. 37. *Cf.* also *infra,* p. 120.

[171] Freedom of conscience as an individual right was expressed in only eleven cahiers: 3 N, 8 T; N—Blois, Bourges, La Rochelle; T—Bar-sur-Seine, Dijon, La Rochelle, Nemours, Nîmes, Paris *hors-les-murs,* Paris *intra-muros,* Ustaritz. The principle of religious freedom was more often expressed in other ways. *Cf. supra,* pp. 45 *et seq.*

[172] Cauchie and Lesueur, *D.I., op. cit.,* Vol. II, p. 415, paragraph 2.

[173] For example, T. Paris *hors-les-murs,* AP, Vol. V, p. 239, art. 27. Only a few cahiers made a similar request. The cahiers did not assert the right to form associations.

[174] 16 N, 7 T, 1 U. N.—Alençon, Aval, Bar-le-duc, Briey, Chatellerault, Châteauneuf-en-Thimerais, Châtillon-sur-Seine, Comminges, Dourdan, Etain, Lyon, Longwy, Montreuil, Nemours, Reims, Tours; T—Bigorre, Châteauneuf-en-Thimerais, Marseilles, Rennes, Strasbourg, St. Pierre-le-Moutier, Valenciennes; U—Montfort-l'Amaury.

sion. . ."[175] The free choice of a trade or profession was recognized by a few cahiers as a fundamental right of man.[176] Slavery was occasionally denounced as a violation of personal liberty.[177] The declaration of the third estate of Paris *hors-les-murs* contained one item that appeared nowhere else—liberty of marriage, irrespective of religion.[178] Few cahiers of 1789 included all the foregoing applications of personal liberty.

Personal liberty and security were the major articles of the declaration of individual rights in the cahiers of 1789, but security of property was a close second. The united orders of Amont said that all property, "from the throne to the most wretched hut," should be protected.[179] According to the nobles of Senlis, "All property will be inviolable. No one may be deprived of it, even for public interest, without indemnification at the highest price and without delay."[180] The privileged orders might appeal to inviolability of property for the maintenance of *dîmes,* or of feudal dues,[181] but the third estate appealed to the same principle to justify their extinction.[182] The conservatism of the third estate in 1789 was shown, however, by the large number of cahiers that affirmed protection of property rights.[183] All three orders desired the inviolability of property.[184]

The second of the great passwords of the Revolution, equality, did not play the same prominent rôle in the articles of a proposed declaration of rights as did liberty and security. We have noted

[175] AP, Vol. II, pp. 201-2.

[176] This demand was made by eight cahiers: C, Autun, N, Mantes, T—Forcalquier, Mantes, Nemours, Paris *hors-les-murs,* Paris *intra-muros,* Provins.

[177] For example, T. Paris *hors-les-murs,* AP, Vol. V, p. 238, art. 16. Slavery was often denounced without reference to a declaration of rights. *Cf. infra,* p. 142.

[178] AP, Vol. V, pp. 238-39, art. 17.

[179] AP, Vol. I, p. 773, art. 2.

[180] AP, Vol. V, pp. 734, art. 9.

[181] The nobles of Montargis, for example, affirmed inviolability of property, and then said that their privileges were property. (AP, Vol. IV, p. 21, arts. 1, 2.)

[182] The third estate of Paris *hors-les-murs* followed the article on security of property by the statement that violations of natural right should cease.

[183] Two hundred and thirty-eight cahiers declared for inviolability of private property: 56, C, 89 N, 84 T, 1 CN, 1 CT, 1 NT, approximately half of all the general cahiers.

[184] The figures in note 183 do not include cahiers of the clergy and nobles whose general attitude was a mere conservation of privileges, but only those which specifically asked for inviolability of property.

that egalitarianism was relative rather than absolute in the cahiers of 1789.[185] Furthermore, equality was seldom voiced as an abstract right of the individual.[186] Even the demand for equality before the law which appeared in about a fifth of the general cahiers was seldom stated as a fundamental right of the individual but rather as a desirable legal reform.[187] The demand for a declaration of rights rested upon the assumption that its terms should apply equally to all Frenchmen, but other than this, equality was not considered an imprescriptible right of the individual.

The third of the revolutionary passwords, fraternity, did not play a part in any proposed declaration of rights. The desire for such a declaration arose from individualism, and not from social motives. Fraternity, as expressed in the cahiers,[188] involved social relationships and the unity of the French nation.

The three outstanding items to be embodied in a declaration of rights—liberty, security, and property—appeared in many

[185] *Cf. supra*, pp. 83 *et seq.*

[186] It is probable, however, that many conservatives in 1789 looked upon some of the demands and statements in the cahiers as radical and aiming at absolute equality, whereas today these same articles have lost their alarming import. The British ambassador wrote on March 19, 1789 (Browning, Oscar, *Despatches from Paris*, London, 1909-10, Vol. II, p. 174, Letter from Dorset to Carmarthen), "The elections in general are more quiet than expected, although the demands of the third estate are extraordinary, not to say ridiculous," after which he claimed that the third estate of Tours desired an equal division of property. The original of this cahier has been lost, but the following article appears in the summary of the cahier that has come down to us—"Suppression of all privileges, and the division shall be made indiscriminately on all classes." (AP, Vol. VI, p. 52, art. 12.) This was undoubtedly the article to which Dorset referred. It is an illustration of the ambiguity of the cahiers because of their brevity. Today, this statement appears as an attack upon the class system, to be sure, but not at all as an effort to establish an equality of all property. Only one other cahier has come to the author's attention where a phrase might be similarly misinterpreted. The third estate of Longuyon declared: "The third estate has no sacrifice to make . . . thus, no more discrimination in property; for it is all plebeian (*roturier*) as it has been ever since chaos." (MS, *Arch. Moselle* or reprint in *Guide.*) It is, however, easier to understand how statements against class discrimination might be interpreted by the conservatives of 1789 as aimed at establishing absolute equality.

[187] The wording of the cahier of the clergy of Dijon (AP, Vol. III, pp. 123 *et seq.*), where the phrase "the right of all citizens to be equal in . . ." recurs for each statement of rights, is misleading. When this cahier is analyzed, one discovers that qualifying demands neutralize the more extreme formula, and that the cahier is no more egalitarian than the majority, and less so than the few democratic ones. This was, however, the cahier whose phraseology laid the most emphasis upon equality.

[188] *Cf. infra*, pp. 158-59.

cahiers, while equality played a secondary rôle. The declaration of rights as conceived by the majority did not coincide exactly with the rights of individuals embodied in the constitution of 1791, the first theoretical offspring of the Revolution. All seventeen articles of the latter appeared in some of the cahiers with the notable exception of the right to resist oppression.[189] This right had been defended during the period of the French Civil Wars, was inherent in the contract theory, and was implied by the very composition of the cahiers, but there was no statement of it as one of the natural rights of Frenchmen. Its rebirth in the Constitution of 1791, together with an emphasis upon rights that had received infrequent assertion in the cahiers,[190] indicated the progress of radicalism during the first two years of the Revolution.[191]

The demand of the cahiers for affirmation of individual rights has a double significance. It was the only evidence of individualism in the cahiers,[192] and it laid the foundations of a future French tradition. Every constitutional debate thereafter involved discussion of the contents of a declaration of rights, and each time "the principles of eighty-nine," of which the cahiers were the gauge, were revived and discussed. The rights of man, irrespective of their varying content, became the rallying cry of liberals not only

[189] This was the last of the items under article 2. For the text of the constitutions, see Duvergier, *Collection Duvergier* (Paris, 1825), and for easy comparison, Anderson, F. M., *The Constitutions and Other Select Documents Illustrative of the History of France* (Minneapolis, 1908), pp. 58 *et seq.* The right to petition for redress was recognized. *Cf. supra,* p. 93, note 173.

[190] For example, freedom of conscience, of work, etc.

[191] The discussion of rights in the National Assembly early escaped the bounds of the cahiers. The draft of the declaration submitted by Mounier on the same day as Clermont-Tonnerre's summary of the cahiers, showed three essential differences. (*Cf.* text, *Procès-verbal de l'Assemblée nationale constituante,* Vol. II.) Mounier spoke of reciprocal rights and duties, whereas only a handful of cahiers had been concerned with duties. He also voiced the right of resistance, and the right of a citizen to emigrate and choose another *patrie* (art. 22 of Mounier's draft). The right of free movement mentioned in the cahiers was a phase of liberty, but it never implied for a moment that any French citizen might wish to renounce his citizenship. The pride of most cahiers in French nationality and the interest in population were contrary attitudes.

The declaration of rights actually incorporated into the constitution of 1791 was closer to the cahiers in tone than Mounier's draft, presented July 27, 1789. It was perhaps natural that the conflict for the union of the orders, and the transformation of the States-General into the National Assembly, should have brought resistance to the court to the fore.

[192] *Cf.* Table XV, Appendix, p. 261.

in France, but, through the extension of her influence, throughout Europe in the nineteenth century. When France entered upon foreign war in 1792, a part of the public believed that it was the mission of France to help oppressed peoples of other lands to acquire the rights which Frenchmen then enjoyed. The ideas, loosely spoken of as the principles of 1789, became the watchwords of nineteenth-century revolutions in all the states of Europe, and have become a very essential part of French national traditions.

SUMMARY OF DEMOCRACY

Various indications of the later development of democracy in France were widely distributed among the general cahiers, but were frequently accompanied by counter tendencies in individual cahiers. Only a small minority of cahiers were consistently democratic. Whereas there was widespread assertion of the sovereignty of the nation versus the king, the clergy were divided between those defining the nation as an aristocracy and those that would make it a democracy; the nobles clung to the aristocratic interpretation, while the third estate took a universal stand in favor of popular sovereignty. Only a very few expressed the radical attitude that the third estate alone was sovereign.

There was a widespread demand for the application of an elective principle to various administrative agencies; there were certain embryonic foreshadowings of the machinery of democratic government, and some expression of a desire for the application of equality to the administrative units.

The conservatism of the cahiers on the question of class divisions is patent. The attacks on the class system as such were negligible. The third estate were more insistent than the clergy or nobles upon establishing political and social equality between the three classes. The upper classes showed a semblance of democratic regard in their widespread renunciation of privileges and in their assertions of equal tax liability, both of which were, however, often accompanied by other statements showing aristocratic tendencies. The lines along which an elimination of classes would proceed were all indicated somewhere in the cahiers of 1789, and yet only a minority of these cahiers were consistently democratic.

The fundamental philosophy of democracy, individualism, was widely evidenced in the cahiers of 1789, but the individual was always subordinated to the nation. An individual possessed rights by virtue of his being a member of society, and also because he was a member of the French nation. The individualism of the cahiers of 1789 was within the framework of the national life, and neither against the sovereignty of the nation, nor antisocial. According to the cahiers, liberty was a social attribute.

What light does a comparison of the cahiers of 1789 with those of previous States-Generals throw upon the progress of democratic ideas since 1614? Claims for the power of the States-General, for popular sovereignty, and for the extension of the elective principle were much more marked in 1789, while the previous cahiers contained no demand whatsoever for equalization of the provinces. Suggestions for democratic machinery of government were a new development since 1614.

In respect to the classes, the early cahiers had shown a marked desire for the maintenance of class privileges,[193] and no challenge at all to division into classes. In view of this, the renunciation of privileges by the overwhelming majority of both the upper classes in 1789 assumes new significance. The same is true of statements for equal liability to taxes. Cahiers before 1789 had expressed the idea of ennoblement for merit only,[194] and the nobles of 1614 had asked that commerce be allowed to nobles without loss of caste.[195] The other expressions of egalitarianism noted in the cahiers of 1789 were new: the opening of opportunity to all irrespective of class, equality before the law, the removal of distinctions prejudicial to the third estate, and democratization within the orders. Thus, the wind was blowing in the direction of greater political and social democracy.

The claim of individual rights was also a new development.

[193] In 1483 the three orders had concurred in the demand for the confirmation of privileges of each order (Mayer, *op cit., Vol.* IX, pp. 314, 345). The cahiers of the nobles had frequently emphasized their historic rôle (*e.g.*, N, 1588, Lalourcé and Duval, *op. cit.*, Vol. III, p. 135; 1614—*loc. cit.*, Vol. IV, pp. 167, 188). Even the third estate had approved the maintenance of orders (1614, *loc. cit.*, Vol. IV, p. 305).

[194] C. 1560, Lalourcé and Duval, *op. cit.*, Vol. I, p. 48; C, N, 1614, *loc cit.*, Vol. IV, p. 97, arts. 168, 169, and pp. 167, 188.

[195] *Loc. cit.*, Vol. IV, p. 198.

One would scarcely expect to find it in the early cahiers, which had been composed before the development of a doctrine of rights by English philosophers of the seventeenth century. There had been some demand for security of persons and of property in the early cahiers,[196] but "individual liberty" in general and "individual rights" in particular had not entered into the popular consciousness until after 1614.

Thus, although democratic demands took but little space in the majority of cahiers in 1789, various expressions showed a marked trend toward democracy since the last States-General. The most consistent democracy appeared in fifty-five cahiers, the majority of which were cahiers of the third estate.[197] The *generalities* of Paris, Alençon, Rennes, and Aix were slightly more democratic than the other *generalities*.[198] The fifty-five cahiers were democratic in respect to the three elements of democracy which we have discussed: democracy in government, in regard to classes, and individualism. Although the Revolution carried out some of the democratic recommendations of the cahiers, it remained for the liberals of the nineteenth century to bring to full fruition the democratic seeds in the cahiers of 1789.

[196] *Cf.* U. 1483, Mayer, *op. cit.*, Vol. IX, p. 373; C. 1614, Lalourcé and Duval, *op. cit.*, Vol. IV, p. 118, art. 222; N. 1614—*loc. cit.*, Vol. IV, p. 225; T. 1614, *loc. cit.*, Vol. IV, pp. 323-31.

[197] *Cf.* Table XIV, Appendix, p. 261.

[198] This applies to the third estate only of Rennes and Aix.

CHAPTER V

ETATISME AND THE GENERAL CAHIERS

Under the old régime in France, sovereignty had been distributive. The state had shared its power with church, privileged classes, gilds, provinces, and even cities. The successful control of all these agencies by Louis XIV had weakened their independence of a central authority, but did not destroy the feudal or distributive theory. Political philosophy and practice in France of the seventeenth century was only *étatist* in so far as the king was sovereign and applied *étatisme* to many separate items of government.[1] Some cahiers in 1789 desired a continuance of the old régime, by the preservation of class privileges,[2] and regional prerogatives,[3] but public opinion was moving in the direction of one supreme authority—the state.

The principle of state sovereignty was seldom expressed in specific terms in the cahiers. According to the third estate of Angers, "The public authority belongs to the State, and resides actually in the person of the sovereign which represents it. . ."[4] In discussing tax exemptions, the third estate of Digne said that "there can exist no persons independent of the sovereign laws."[5] The most forceful statement of the fundamental principle of *étatisme* came from the third estate of Nemours, upon whose cahier Dupont de Nemours exerted such a strong influence. In one place this cahier said that hitherto anyone who tried to put the thought into words had been considered a dreamer, too impractical to administer government,[6] and then, later on, declared,

[1] Henri Michel, in his able thesis, *L'Idée de l'état* (Paris, 1895), said that there were three elements in the seventeenth-century idea of the state: the Roman element (sovereignty of the prince), the Christian element (the prince represents God), and the feudal element (the idea that the prince is suzerain). The first is *étatist*, while the second and third are anti-*étatist*.

[2] *Cf. infra,* pp. 191 *et seq.*

[3] *Cf. infra,* pp. 183 *et seq.*

[4] AP, Vol. II, p. 42, art. 13.

[5] AP, Vol. III, p. 348, art. 12.

[6] AP, Vol. IV, p. 139, col. 2.

It is necessary that there be no state within a state, no corps which can cause trouble or raise money by an authority independent of that of the *patrie,* and without accountability to the people itself.[7]

Not many of the cahiers actually stated the underlying principle, nor were they, in general, clear upon what constituted the State. The word *état* occurred frequently in the cahiers, but its use throws light rather on what the state was not than upon what it was. Certainly, the authors of the cahiers did not believe the doctrine ascribed to Louis XIV, "L'Etat, c'est moi." We find the king and the state mentioned together,[8] the king and the *patrie,*[9] the king, state, and *patrie,*[10] and the state and the *patrie.*[11] The relation of the state to the French nationality was equally ambiguous. For the majority, perhaps, the state meant the popular or national sovereign, with a decreasing emphasis upon the Christian element[12] and the element of suzerainty. For a minority, the last two elements were completely eliminated.

The independent sovereignty of France *vis-à-vis* other European states or potentates was also voiced in a few cahiers. This was usually expressed in terms similar to those of the third estate of Vitry-le-françois, which declared that the "king was independent of all foreign power, lay or ecclesiastic."[13]

Let us see by what means the cahiers proposed to increase the rôle of the state.

ETATISME AND THE CHURCH

Gallicanism in the cahiers of 1789 had its *étatist* as well as its patriotic implications.[14] As *étatist,* it worked toward the elimination of the Christian element in the theory of the state. In the cahiers, this involved demands for independence from papal power, and for an increase in state power over religious matters, made possible by the growth of a secular spirit.

[7] *Ibid.,* pp. 213-14.

[8] For example, N. Meaux, AP, Vol. III, p. 726, art. 1.

[9] For example, C. Vitry, AP, Vol. VI, p. 206.

[10] For example, T. Draguignan, AP, Vol. III, p. 261, col. 1.

[11] *Cf. infra,* p. 174, note 154.

[12] *Cf.* p. 100, note 1.

[13] AP, Vol. VI, p. 211, art. 2.

[14] Georges Weill (*Histoire de l'idée laique en France au dix-neuvième siècle,* Paris, 1925), distinguishes three phases of Gallicanism—ecclesiastical, royal, and parliamentary. The first and second were both *étatist* and patriotic, while the third was *étatist.*

The general relationship of the French church to the Papacy had been regulated by the Concordat of 1516, between Francis I and Pope Leo X. This was still in force. Over fifty of the general cahiers[15] registered opposition to the arrangement, either by direct denunciation of the Concordat,[16] or by approval of the Pragmatic Sanction which had preceded the Concordat.[17] According to the nobles of Bar-le-duc,

> Leo X and Francis I, in making the Concordat, gave to each other what did not belong to them; it is time that the nation reënter into its imprescriptible rights.[18]

The third estate of Belley expressed the general principle of French independence of papal power in the following terms:

> Make it a law, as a principle of the French constitution, that the Gallican church is independent, as to temporal affairs, of all powers and authorities, under whatever form they be.[19]

Such statements were not denials of the power of the French state over the church, but were aimed primarily at the pope.

An indirect attack upon papal power was also made by the cahiers that opposed papal appointments to French ecclesiastical officers, and payment of various papal dues. The third estate of Amiens summarized clearly the reasons for the opposition:

> Considering that the court of Rome does not and cannot know the individuals on whom it confers benefices, or accords dispensations, which renders the practice abusive and purely fiscal; that the graces and favors which emanate from the spiritual authority cannot be paid for with money without a sort of profanation; that the subjects of a State ought not to pay tribute to a foreign prince; and finally, that it is a matter of good administration not to allow currency to leave the kingdom except by exchange in an equivalent value . . . [hence the abolition of dispensations, annates, and other payments to the Pope].[20]

The fact that nearly half of the cahiers of all classes, but more

[15] *Cf.* Table XVI, Appendix, p. 262.
[16] For example, T. Gien, AP, Vol. III, p. 407, art. 1.
[17] For example, T. Beauvais, AP, Vol. II, p. 299, art. 10.
[18] *Cf.* reprinted text, *La Révolution française,* Vol. XXXII (1897), pp. 175-76, art. 38.
[19] *Cf.* reprinted text, Recamier, *Les Députés des communes de Bugey en 1789 et en 1876* (Paris, 1876), p. 10.
[20] AP, Vol. I, p. 745, art. 2.

especially the lay orders,[21] denounced payments to the papacy[22] was a strong indication that the French wanted the Gallican church controlled by France and not by the pope.

Was this control to be exercised by the French clergy, or by the French state? As Denys-Buirette has affirmed,[23] there was general acceptance of the right of the state to reform the church and to legislate concerning it. The broad principle was nowhere better expressed than by the third estate of Paris *intra-muros:*

> Ecclesiastical jurisdiction does not extend in any manner over temporal affairs; its external exercise is regulated by the laws of the State.[24]

The cahiers of 1789, even those of the clergy, contemplated a larger rôle for the state by their inclusion of detailed reforms which should be carried out by the States-General and not by the governing body of the French church—the general assembly. To be sure, many cahiers asked for the resuscitation of the General Assembly,[25] and especially for the re-creation of provincial councils.[26] Although this meant a democratization within the church government,[27] the same cahiers did not hesitate to enumerate reforms which the States-General should inaugurate.

The complete subordination of the church to the state subsequently effected by the Civil Constitution of the Clergy was only vaguely foreshadowed in the cahiers of 1789. When the clergy altruistically renounced their privileges, they did not mean that the church should become a mere instrument of the state. Carried to its legal limits, the abolition of clerical privileges meant an end of the ecclesiastical courts as well as of tax privileges, but the cahiers of the clergy had no such idea in view. The privileges renounced were exemptions or immunities prejudicial to the lay

[21] 224 cahiers: 49 C, 63 N, 106 T, 4 U, 1 CT, 1 NT.

[22] Even cahiers of the clergy opposed papal dues. They sometimes asked that such money be applied to pay off the church debt. For example, C. Chaumont-en-Bassigny, AP, Vol. II, p. 723, art. 31.

[23] Denys-Buirette, A., *Les Questions religieuses dans les cahiers de 1789* (Paris, 1919), p. 484.

[24] AP, Vol. V, p. 286, art. 8.

[25] For example, T. Rennes, Sée and Lessort, *D.I., op. cit.,* Vol. IV, p. 261, art. 113.

[26] For example, C. Meaux, AP, Vol. III, p. 723, art. 4.

[27] The lower clergy had a larger voice in the provincial assemblies than in the general assembly, and would gain power against the bishops by the re-creation of the former.

orders and not those inherent in the corporate existence of the Gallican Church. In fact, sixty-three cahiers of the clergy urged the retention of church privileges.[28]

The cahiers of 1789 did contain, however, four hints of the action taken by the National Assembly in 1791. The first of these concerned the personnel of the church offices. Six cahiers of the third estate spoke of the election of the clergy in such a way as to suggest choice by the parish.[29] The clergy made no such suggestion and expressed, furthermore, the desire to strengthen their own control of the Gallican priesthood, by occasional complaints against interference by pope, feudal laymen,[30] and non-Catholics.[31] One cahier of the clergy and three of the third estate suggested state payment of the clergy.[32] In view of the large number of general cahiers, it is obvious that little change in the method of ecclesiastical appointments was contemplated.

A more frequent foreshadowing of the Civil Constitution of the Clergy was indicated by statements about church property. The *étatist* point of view was rarely so forcefully expressed as by the third estate of Blois: "all ecclesiastical properties belong to the nation, and only the use thereof to the clergy."[33] The question of church property was complicated by that of the church debt. The clergy often made their renunciation of tax privileges conditional upon the state's assumption of the church debt, in part or in whole.[34] A number of cahiers of the lay orders distinguished two parts of the debt—that acquired for the state, and that acquired for the church—and conceded the assumption of the former by the state.[35] The third estate of Condom made the unique suggestion that the state utilize precious stones, silver, and

[28] These sixty-three cahiers came from all *generalities* of France except Strasbourg, which was under a separate ecclesiastical régime.

[29] T—Brest, Castelmoron-d'Albret, Nantes, Paris *hors-les-murs,* Rennes. It is noticeable that three of these came from Brittany.

[30] For example, C. Saumur, AP, Vol. V, p. 720, art. 17; C. Poitiers, AP, Vol. V, p. 390, art. 10.

[31] For example, C. Gien, AP, Vol. III, p. 399, art. 11.

[32] C. Le Mans, T—Foix, Nantes, Nemours.

[33] Cauchie and Lesueur, *D.I., op. cit.,* Vol. I, p. 13, and Vol. II, p. 448, art. 9.

[34] For example, C. Soissons, AP, Vol. V, p. 772, col. 1.

[35] For example, N. Montargis, AP, Vol. IV, p. 23, cols. 1-2, art. 2.

gold belonging to the church, which "did not serve for divine service, or was indifferent" to the church.[36] The curious feature of this suggestion was the implication that the government had actually done this in past crises. Some cahiers advocated state utilization of funds to be derived from the suppression of small monasteries, or from the complete dissolution of the monastic orders.[37] By various suggestions, sixty-eight cahiers, chiefly of the lay orders, proposed the use of church revenues, lands or other resources by the state for public purposes.[38] The general attitude of the majority of cahiers was, however, that the church should continue to administer its property, pay taxes as did laymen, but that the same guarantees against confiscation should exist for ecclesiastical property as for lay property. The principle of the inviolability of property was strongly respected in the cahiers. Only a small minority would sacrifice church properties to *étatisme*.

With respect to the monastic system, the cahiers did not desire wholesale suppression, but rather a complete reorganization on a utilitarian basis.[39] Wherever mentioned, the mendicant orders were denounced,[40] and many cahiers approved of the closing of small monasteries.[41] The majority of cahiers, however, recommended the retention of monastic orders, with reforms to render them more useful to the public.[42] Wherever the existence of monasteries was discussed, the right of the state to legislate concerning them was assumed.

The chief foreshadowing of the Civil Constitution of the Clergy was the evidence which the cahiers of 1789 supplied of a general

[36] AP, Vol. III, p. 40, art. 54.

[37] *Cf. infra,* pp. 136 *et seq.*

[38] 6 C, 21 N, 39 T, 1 U, 1 NT.

[39] Whereas 235 cahiers spoke for maintenance or reform of the monastic orders (104 C, 40 N, 86 T, 4 U, 1 NT), only 22 cahiers asked for outright suppression (2 C, 6 N, 14 T). C—Montargis, Sisteron; N—Calais, Guéret, Montargis, Moulins, Paris *intra-muros,* Villeneuve-de-Berg; T—Amiens, Annonay, Auray, Blois, Calais, Castelmoron-d'Albret, Chartres, Clermont-en-Beauvoisis, Foix, Guéret, Moulins, Périgord, Quimper, Tulle.

[40] Only one cahier, that of the clergy of Limoux, defended the mendicant orders. (See the text in Dom de Vic, *Histoire de Languedoc,* Toulouse, 1872-92, Vol. XIV, p. 2615, art. 12.) All other cahiers that mentioned them at all, condemned them.

[41] For example, U. Montfort l'Amaury, AP, Vol. IV, p. 42, col. 2.

[42] For example, C. Metz, AP, Vol. III, p. 762, art. 12. *Cf.* also *infra,* p. 137.

growth of secular spirit. In the first place, there was widespread concern for *moeurs* and ethics rather than for church doctrine. According to the nobles of Montpellier,

> The regeneration of the State cannot, Sire, be effected without the reformation of the *moeurs;* your Majesty is asked to give particular attention to an object so important; religion, whose influence on *moeurs,* be they national or private, cannot be unknown, will be, under the protection of your Majesty, the principle of public well-being.[43]

Religion and *moeurs* were frequently coupled together, but it is significant that one hundred and nineteen cahiers, chiefly of the clergy, evinced an anxiety for improving standards of public morality.[44]

A second evidence of secularism was the development of utilitarian ideas in connection with the church. Denys-Buirette has made a point of the practical bent of the majority of reforms advocated by the cahiers.[45] The retention of the monastic orders was upon condition that they be made useful,[46] or, on the other hand, their suppression was asked in order to liberate funds for more necessary enterprises.[47] The chief motive advanced for the demand that the number of religious holidays be decreased was that laborers might not be withdrawn from productive activity.[48]

Utilitarianism was not only apparent in such demands, but was sometimes expressed with respect to the rôle of the secular clergy. The third estate of Nemours said "that curates ought to be regarded as performing a public and a religious service, useful to the whole of society."[49] The clergy themselves sometimes recognized that they were not only churchmen, but also citizens with duties to the state.[50] Utilitarianism was one strong manifestation of the secular spirit, and it appeared in cahiers of all three orders, but more especially those of the lay orders.[51]

[43] AP, Vol. IV, p. 47, art. 17.
[44] *Cf.* Table XVII, Appendix, p. 263.
[45] Denys-Buirette, *op. cit.,* p. 487.
[46] For example, *cf.* p. 137, note 250.
[47] For example, N. Dôle, AP, Vol. III, p. 159, arts. 78, 83.
[48] For example, T. Château-Thierry, AP, Vol. II, p. 674, art. 28. Of the cahiers discussing church holidays, the lay orders (except T. Libourne, T. Lesneven), asked for their decrease, while twice as many cahiers of the clergy asked for their strict observance.
[49] AP, Vol. IV, p. 193, col. 2.
[50] *Cf. infra,* p. 161.
[51] *Cf. infra,* pp. 136 *et seq.*

Some cahiers of the lay orders went further in their secularism and showed an anticlerical attitude. This displayed itself in hostility to the privileges of the church, to the clergy as an order, or to the exercise of power by the church. Some denied the right of the clergy to vote the *don gratuit*.[52] According to the third estate of Montargis, the States-General should enact,

> That the clergy of the kingdom will no longer have the right to assemble in a body for other reasons than for the regulation and maintenance of the hierarchical order, without power to tax their members, or to deal with administration outside the States-General of which the clergy form a part.[53]

Certain cahiers opposed the judicial privileges of the clergy.[54] An anticlerical attitude was particularly vehemently expressed in the cahier of the third estate of Aix, which declared that "The clergy ought not to form an order in the state," and demanded a "Reduction of the number of ecclesiastics to what is absolutely necessary for divine service."[55] The lay cahiers from the *generalities* of Paris, Orléans, Aix, and Rennes were marked by anticlericalism.

The right of the state to control and reform, while protecting, the Gallican church was universally accepted, and similarly, the right of the state to regulate the status of non-Catholics was unquestioned.[56] There was antipapal sentiment, and there were foreshadowings of the Civil Constitution of the Clergy. Although the hold of religion still appeared basic, a secular spirit had gained acceptance among the lay orders. Over one-third of the cahiers displayed some degree of secularism, while thirty-six showed a marked tendency in that direction.[57] Despite scattered hints in a great many cahiers, only a minority were *étatist* in respect of the church.[58] Public opinion, as manifested in the general cahiers, was not ready in 1789 for the Civil Constitution of the Clergy. It was the *generalities* of Paris, Orléans, Aix, and Rennes which gave the chief indication that the state might assail and subdue the church.

[52] On the status of the clergy in 1789, see Denys-Buirette, *op. cit.* The *don gratuit* is described pp. 79 *et seq.*
[53] AP, Vol. IV, p. 29, art. 1.
[54] *Cf. infra,* pp. 114, 116.
[55] AP, Vol. I, p. 697, under *Clergé.*
[56] *Cf. supra,* pp. 45 *et seq.*
[57] *Cf.* Table XVIII, Appendix, p. 263.
[58] *Cf.* Table XIX, Appendix, p. 264.

ETATISME AND EDUCATION

Under the old régime in France, education had been generally supervised by the church and carried on largely by the regular clergy. However, some communal schools, and institutions under local lay supervision had functioned for several centuries. During the eighteenth century, educational reformers began to advocate state direction and control. Educational *étatisme,* which bore fruit in all the debates on education in the revolutionary assemblies, appeared to a very limited degree in the general cahiers of 1789.

The cahiers were conservative in respect of the supervision of education. The clergy generally advocated church supervision,[59] and a large number of cahiers of that order requested a fuller utilization of the monastic orders for education.[60] Several cahiers specifically recommended the Christian Brothers,[61] while the clergy of Beziers endorsed the Benedictines of St. Maur,[62] and the clergy of Dax even suggested the recall of the Jesuits.[63] With rare exceptions, the clergy desired no weakening of their control of education.

The cahiers of the lay orders asked for many educational reforms, but rarely discussed the question of supervision. Their silence was a tacit acceptance of the existing régime. Even where the cahiers did discuss supervision, they were scarcely more radical than the clergy. The majority approved of church supervision and the utilization of the monastic orders for instruction of the young.[64] A few contemplated joint supervision by church and state,[65] while several mentioned the power which the Provincial-Estates should exercise over education.[66] The cahier of the third

[59] One hundred and one cahiers approved church supervision: 62 C, 12 N, 25 T, 2 U. In addition, many cahiers of the clergy tacitly implied church control.

[60] Wherever the maintenance of monasteries was approved, the majority favored some such condition. Over one hundred cahiers of the clergy were of this opinion.

[61] For example, C. Toulouse, AP, Vol. VI, p. 29, art. 5.

[62] AP, Vol. II, p. 346, art. 1.

[63] AP, Vol. III, p. 88, art. 5.

[64] *Cf. supra,* note 59. Only nine cahiers would give supervision exclusively to the state: C—Dôle, Paris *hors-les-murs,* Puy-en-Velay; N—Amiens, Château-Thierry, Lyon; T—Digne, La Rochelle, Nemours.

[65] For example, T. Soissons, AP, Vol. VI, p. 699, art. 89.

[66] For example, N. Quesnoy, AP, Vol. V, p. 505, col. 1.

estate of Digne, which was generally anticlerical, furnished the clearest statement of the principle of secular education:

> It is of the greatest interest to the National Assembly to consider the education and the *moeurs* of the young. It is for the civil magistrate to supervise this; this right and this duty belong to him. As children will later become citizens in all classes of society, it is for the magistrates to have them raised in the manner best suited to give them energy of spirit, to show them the unity of the general interest with that of the individual, and to banish all idea of superstition which has cramped and distorted peoples and kings for many centuries.[67]

In view of the general conservatism of the cahiers on education and the very limited demand for universal education, one should not expect to find any discussion of compulsory education. Only three cahiers suggested this indirectly. The cahier of the third estate of Marseille, after asking for the extension of educational opportunities, and the use of uniform textbooks, asked that the patriotic views of M. Philipon de la Madeleine be adopted.[68] Inasmuch as compulsory education was one of his tenets,[69] we may assume that the makers of the cahier were of the same opinion. The nobles of Clermont-en-Beauvoisis vaguely hinted at compulsion when they said "that some powerful means of legislation determine fathers to make their children profit by the schools."[70] According to the nobles of Dourdan, no one should hold a civil or military position before the age of twenty, "since until that age, the efforts of each ought to be devoted to education."[71] Aside from these three cahiers, a superior rôle of the state was implicit in the cahiers that asked for a national plan of education or for the national issuance of textbooks, or that voiced a desire for education in citizenship.[72]

Over one-fifth of the general cahiers of 1789[73] championed some degree of *étatisme* in education, and as might be expected the lay

[67] AP, Vol. III, p. 350, art. 36.

[68] Fournier, J. J., *D.I., Cahiers de doléances . . . de Marseille* (Marseille, 1908), p. 367, art. 19.

[69] See the analysis of the principles of Philipon de la Madeleine by Buisson, F., *Dictionnaire de pédagogie et d'instruction primaire* (Paris, 1882-87).

[70] AP, Vol. II, p. 749, art. 16.

[71] AP, Vol. III, p. 248, col. 1.

[72] *Cf. infra*, p. 179.

[73] *Cf.* Table XX, Appendix, p. 265.

orders evinced a stronger secularism and utilitarianism than the clergy. *Etatisme* in education found more frequent advocates in the *generalities* of Paris, Bordeaux, Amiens, and Aix.

ETATISME AND PUBLICITY

In *The Marriage of Figaro,* the popular play by Beaumarchais, first given in 1784, the hero was made to say (Act V, Scene 3):

> They tell me that during my absence in order to economize, a system of liberty of the sale of productions, which extends even to those of the press, has been established in Madrid; and provided that I do not speak in my writings either of the authorities, or of religion, or of politics, or of morality, or of men in office, or of the group in power, or of the Opera, or of other dramatic performances, or of anyone who possesses a definite opinion, I may print everything freely, under the inspection of two or three censors.

It is small wonder that the play was permitted to appear only after innumerable delays, and then, through the intercession of influential members of the court. As time passed, the censorship of the press was relaxed, and on the eve of the Revolution, a flood of pamphlets appeared,[74] but a board of censors continued to exist and to exercise a curb on publication by occasional arbitrary condemnations. Many general cahiers of 1789 were desirous of abolishing this censorship.

A very large number of the cahiers of the nobles and of the third estate asked for freedom of the press.[75] Most of these added that the author or printer, or both, should be held responsible for writings contrary to religion, morality, or the state. A great many cahiers spoke of liberty of the press as proceeding from individual liberty.[76] According to the third estate of St. Pierre-le-Moutier,

> Since liberty to publish one's opinions is a part of individual liberty, since man cannot be free while his thoughts are enslaved, liberty of the press should be accorded indefinitely, except for such reservations as the States-General may adopt.[77]

Several special arguments were advanced in support of the free-

[74] *Cf. supra,* p. 4 and note 5.
[75] *Cf.* Table XXII, Appendix, p. 267.
[76] Only a few included this in any proposed declaration of rights. *Cf. supra,* p. 93.
[77] AP, Vol. V, p. 640, art. 59. This was not the only cahier to speak of the enslavement of men's thought under a censorship.

dom of the press, such as the spread of enlightenment,[78] and the checking of arbitrary government.[79] In the words of the third estate of Bar-sur-Seine,

> It is by means of the continuous communication of men's thoughts that philosophy, letters, science and all the arts make new developments, and that they can achieve perfection, which makes people happy, and empires flourishing.[80]

The third estate of Carcassonne was not only optimistic about human taste, but also appreciated the psychology of prohibition;

> The most certain effect of prohibition is to give vogue to the works forbidden; the sure result of liberty of the press is to make the public indifferent to the works that are mediocre or bad. Liberty of the press will have the added result of regaining for France an important branch of commerce which our neighbors have seized.[81]

As was so often true with other liberalizing topics under discussion, the keenest appreciation of the value of freedom of the press came from the third estate of Nemours. According to it, freedom of the press was bound to develop

> in the household of each father of a family, a multitude of persons coöperating for the public good, animated with a veritable zeal, an immense number of good councillors for the nation, . . . who will constitute, in public opinion, an invincible barrier to any ignorant or guilty administration.[82]

The clergy were less desirous than apprehensive of liberty of the press.[83] They feared that irreligion would result from freedom, and requested a reasonable censorship,[84] which would be administered by the church or by the state, or by a joint board of the two. The clergy of Soissons looked upon the demand for liberty of the press as a pernicious result of eighteenth-century philosophy,[85] while the cautious attitude of the clergy of the town of Arles was betrayed in their concession that a progressive freeing of the press might accompany the advance of education.[86] In

[78] For example, *cf.* note 80.
[79] For example, T. Villefranche-de-Beaujolais, AP, Vol. II, p. 285, art. 27.
[80] AP, Vol. II, p. 258, art. 35.
[81] AP, Vol. II, p. 529, col. 1.
[82] AP, Vol. IV, p. 164, col. 1.
[83] *Cf.* Tables XXII and XXIII.
[84] For example, C. Melun, AP, Vol. V, p. 734, art. 9.
[85] AP, Vol. V, p. 768, col. 1.
[86] AP, Vol. II, p. 54, art. 2.

general, the clergy's prime interest in religion led them to desire censorship and control rather than freedom of the press.

At first thought, freedom of the press would seem to be opposed to *étatisme,* but one must remember the existing conditions and the lack of press development. The stimulation of the press was a necessary step, along with wider democracy and governmental control of education, toward conscious development of nationalist sentiment and action. A few cahiers asked for direct governmental encouragement of the printing trade.[87] The third estate of Vézelise went so far as to suggest a commission which should publish a list of good books.[88] This would be neither a complement to the Papal Index, nor a list of best sellers, but might be used by the government (through the commission) to attract attention to the publications that it deemed desirable.

A second type of demand concerning publicity arose from the desire to know what the government was doing. Various suggestions for publicity of governmental action were advanced. The nobles of Paris *intra-muros* asked that the sessions of the States-General be public.[89] Although other cahiers dealing with the question were opposed to this because of fear of perversion or of court pressure,[90] it may be remembered that the policy of opening its doors to the public, pursued by the Third Estate and by the National Assembly had a profound effect upon the course of the Revolution.[91] A demand more significant for persons at a distance from Paris, was that of twenty-four cahiers for the publication of the minutes of the States-General.[92] According to the nobles of Angoulême,

> The aforesaid deputies invite the States-General to authorize the daily publication, by printing, of the work and deliberations of the National

[87] For example, T. Tulle (AP, Vol. III, p. 542, art. 56), which asked that a printing press be set up in the chief town of each *bailliage.*

[88] Etienne, *D.I., Cahiers de doléances . . . de Vézelise* (Nancy, 1930), p. 397.

[89] AP, Vol. V, p. 275, col. 1.

[90] Nine cahiers asked that all visitors be excluded: C—Alençon, Bellême; N—Nîmes, Pont-à-Mousson; T—Boulay, Digne, Draguignan, Forcalquier, Rennes.

[91] Consult any of the diaries of the time for influences upon the National Assembly itself, as well as on the populace of Paris.

[92] 3 C, 12 N, 7 T, 1 U, 1 NT. C—Châtillon-sur-Seine, Rodez, St. Mihiel; N—Angoulême, Artois, Belley, Forez, Orléans, Paris *intra-muros,* Ponthieu, St. Quentin, Saintes, Senlis, Villeneuve-de-Berg; T—Amiens, Angers, Alençon, Limoux, Paris *intra-muros,* Rennes, St. Brieuc, Senlis; U—Montfort l'Amaury, NT—Péronne.

Assembly. This publication is a right [*du droit*] since every citizen is interested in knowing about the affairs of the nation.[93]

The joint cahier of the nobles and third estate of Péronne hinted at the use of the press for the transmission of opinion to the States-General, "in order that the opinion and enlightenment of educated men who were not summoned among the representatives of the nation may be utilized. . . ."[94]

The aim of the demand for publicity about taxation,[95] about governmental expenditure,[96] and about ministerial action,[97] was partly to check arbitrary government, and partly to satisfy the general interest in national affairs. The strength of the latter motive was further shown by the demands for publicity concerning the French constitution. Publication of the new constitution and of a catechism of citizenship for use in the schools would provide means for instruction of future citizens in the ideals and practices of government.[98] Besides, the clergy of Annonay requested that a copy of the projected civil and criminal code be sent to each community,[99] while many cahiers asked for the publication of the laws to be enacted by the States-General.

A few cahiers asked for the establishment of national archives.[100] The idea expressed was that in the future there should be national, not royal, archives, and that they should be open to the public. This wish was fulfilled when the National Assembly chose Camus as archivist on August 14, 1789, and when he proceeded to organize the French National Archives. One cahier, that of the third estate of Paris *intra-muros*, asked that the royal library be made accessible to the public.[101] Both of these demands presupposed the desire and the right of the individual to consult public records.

Two hundred cahiers made one or more demands for some publicity of governmental action, and of this number, the demands

[93] *Cf.* mandate in p.v., MS, *Arch. Nat.* Ba 14.
[94] AP, Vol. V, p. 356, col. 2, art. 6.
[95] For example, C. Clermont Ferrand, AP, Vol. II, p. 764, art. 34.
[96] For example, T. Dax, AP, Vol. III, p. 96, col. 2, art. 18.
[97] For example, T. Rennes, Sée and Lessort, *D.I., op. cit.*, Vol. IV, p. 246, art. 32.
[98] *Cf. infra*, p. 180.
[99] AP, Vol. II, p. 46, art. 14.
[100] For example, NT, Péronne, AP, Vol. V, p. 357, col. 2, art. 1.
[101] AP, Vol. V, p. 290, art. 37. According to Arthur Young, the royal library was already open two days a week, and was very useful. (*Voyages,* Vol. I, pp. 280-81.)

of fifteen were particularly strong.[102] The desire for national publicity was manifested in all parts of France and among all classes.

Aside from the demands in the cahiers, these documents themselves were tremendously significant because of their publication and subsequent influence on the course of events.[103] The whole electoral campaign was a great educative process. Although the censorship was formally reëstablished on May 6,[104] newspapers sprang into circulation; and subterfuge, evasion and finally the *laissez-faire* attitude of the National Assembly itself soon permitted the rise of an active and influential press.

The constitutions of 1791 and 1793 both included liberty to print opinions among the fundamental rights of the individual, but it was not reaffirmed in the constitution of 1795. Napoleon, as we know, restored the censorship.

ETATISME AND JUSTICE

The exclusive exercise of judicial power by the state has nowadays becomes so inherent in the theory and practice of government, that one is inclined to overlook judicial survivals of plural sovereignty in eighteenth-century France. As a matter of fact, the Catholic Church then had certain privileges of jurisdiction, and the nobility still retained important remnants of feudal justice. When the cahiers asserted the general sovereignty of the national government, they implied that it covered all fields, but numerous cahiers went further and attributed exclusively to the national government the exercise of judicial functions. According to the third estate of Bar-sur-Seine,

> The right to administer justice belongs to the sovereign, and may not, without running counter to all principle, reside in the person of a subject.[105]

Quite naturally, opinion in the cahiers was not unanimous on the abolition of seignorial jurisdiction.[106] To begin with, the majority

[102] *Cf.* Table XXI, Appendix, p. 266.

[103] *Cf. supra,* pp. 16 *et seq.,* and *infra,* pp. 228 *et seq.*

[104] See Brette, *op. cit.,* Vol. I, p. 51.

[105] Vernier, J. J., *D.I., Cahiers de doléances . . . et de Bar-sur-Seine* (Troyes, 1911), Vol. III, p. 487, art. 42, or AP, Vol. II, p. 259, art. 42.

[106] The privilege of exercising high, medium, or low justice was attached to a fief. The classification depended upon the case.

of cahiers did not discuss the question at all. This probably meant acquiescence in the *status quo*. Of those that did discuss the problem, three shades of opinion may be noted: reform, reduction, abolition. The cahiers of the two privileged orders were generally silent on the subject, with rare demands for abolition, some for maintenance,[107] and a few for reform.[108] Many more cahiers of the third estate were concerned about the feudal régime, and were chiefly divided between a desire for reduction of feudal jurisdiction and a desire for its abolition.[109] The third estate of Angers was explicit:

> Public power belongs to the state and resides essentially in the person of the sovereign which represents it; this power ought not to be confided to lords, nor to their officers, who are so often tempted to consider its exercise as a property.[110]

It was, however, the minority of cahiers that were as outspoken as this cahier. There was no widespread denunciation of the exceptions to national justice. The abuses of the system were to be eliminated, but only sixty-three cahiers would eradicate all private jurisdiction, and build in its place one sovereign justice.[111] The cahiers of the *generalities* of Paris, Orléans, Aix, and Rennes showed the most frequent demand for abolition.

The payment of feudal dues was discussed and denounced more frequently than seignorial jurisdiction. No cahiers of the clergy defended seignorial dues, and several denounced them. While a few cahiers of the nobles asked directly for their maintenance,[112] it is probable that a much larger number included them tacitly

[107] The cahiers listed in table XXXI, are only those expressly asking for maintenance.

[108] *Cf.* Table XXXI, Appendix, p. 273.

[109] *Idem.*

[110] AP, Vol. II, p. 42, art. 13.

[111] 14 C, 4 N, 43 T, 2 U. C—Angers, Belfort, Bellême, Boulogne-sur-mer, Châtillon-sur-Seine, Chaumont-en-Bassigny, Coutances, Mantes, Nérac, Poitiers, Rodez, Rouen, Sézanne, Vermandois; N—Angoulême, Bellême, Lyon, Rodez; T—Aix, Amont, Angers, Angoulême, Annonay, Artois, Bar-sur-Seine, Bellême, Blois, Brest, Caen, Charolles, Chartres, Castelnaudary, Coutances, Dôle, Draguignan, Forcalquier, La Rochelle, Lannion, Longwy, Mâcon, Mans (le), Mantes, Montreuil, Nantes, Orléans, Ploërmel, Poitiers, Reims, Rennes, St. Brieuc, St. Flour, St. Pierre-le-Moutier, Saumur, Toul, Tours, Vézelise, Vannes, Vendôme, Verdun, Vitry-le-françois; V—Rouen; U—Bourg-en-Bresse, Mohon.

[112] Seventeen cahiers approved such maintenance: 16 N, 1 CN. N—Agen, Artois, Autun, Bar-sur-Seine, Beziers, Colmar, Dieuze, Etain, Evreux, Limoges, Mâcon, Mirecourt, Montpellier, Orléans, Troyes, Vermandois; CN—Sarrelouis.

in the reserves to their renunciation of privileges.[113] Eleven cahiers of the nobles were altruistic enough to ask for abolition of seignorial dues.[114] The third estate were sometimes silent, sometimes asked for reduction, but more frequently for abolition.[115] A reduction of feudal dues would in turn reduce feudal justice, since cases involving their payment formed the chief roster of feudal courts. By direct and indirect means, the third estate showed a marked hostility to feudal justice.

An unfavorable attitude toward feudal justice was also implied in the expressed desire for the increase of royal justice by a clarification of jurisdictions,[116] the establishment of more presidial courts,[117] and the institution of justices of the peace.[118]

Ecclesiastical jurisdiction elicited less frequent attention in the cahiers than feudal justice. The cahiers of the clergy that discussed church courts were either for their maintenance, or for their reform.[119] According to the clergy of Montargis,

> The church courts (*officialités*) should be conserved in all their rights and authority, chiefly in criminal matters; a privilege which is no stranger than that of the nobles to take capital cases, even in the first degree, to the great chamber of Parlement; a privilege derived, without doubt, from the same principle, to wit, the desire to safeguard the accused from the envy and jealousy which might be provoked against the two orders.[120]

The nobles, perhaps with thought of their own judicial privileges, were for reform only, while the third estate was almost evenly divided between reduction and abolition.[121] An extreme position

[113] *Cf. supra,* p. 85.

[114] *Cf.* note. 112.

[115] *Idem.* The parish cahiers were not so silent.

[116] This was a widespread demand. *Cf.* for example, T. Villefranche-en-Rouergue, AP, Vol. VI, p. 167, art. 21. Some cahiers made no mention of seignorial justice, but merely asked for increase in royal (*i.e.* state), justice. For example, T. Etampes, AP, Vol. III, p. 284, art. 4.

Many cahiers spoke for a reduction in the degrees of justice, and of eliminating the distance between judge and judged. For example, T. Montargis, AP, Vol. IV, p. 28, art. 2; C. Armagnac, AP, Vol. II, p. 67, art. 5.

[117] For example, T. Carcassonne, AP, Vol. II, p. 533, art. 26.

[118] *Cf. supra,* p. 82.

[119] *Cf.* note 121.

[120] AP, Vol. IV, p. 19, art. 10.

[121] For maintenance: 30 C, 2 N, 1 T. C—Amiens, Armagnac, Artois, Auch, Auxerre, Avesnes, Bigorre, Boulogne, Bourg-en-Bresse, Charolles, Chaumont-en-Bassigny, Clermont Ferrand, Draguignan, Evreux, Forcalquier, Guéret, Libourne, Limoges, Longwy, Montargis, Nemours, Nivernais, Paris *intra-muros,* Puy-en-Velay, Riom, Rivière-Verdun, Soissons, Toulouse, Villeneuve-de-Berg, Ustaritz; N—Mantes,

was taken by the third estate of Annonay, which demanded in respect of both seignorial and ecclesiastical justice:

Art. 28. That the seignorial justices may be suppressed, and that the king may be asked to provide substitutes according to his wisdom.

Art. 31. That all courts of exceptional jurisdiction and ecclesiastical courts may be suppressed, and there shall be in France only one order of courts and of judges.[122]

The third estate of Reims stated that ecclesiastics should henceforth be subject to ordinary justice both for civil and for criminal cases.[123] The strongest opposition to the judicial privileges of the Catholic church came from Provence. The demand of the third estate of Digne recalls the investiture debates of the middle ages;

. . . that the jurisdiction of the archbishops and bishops, and of their officers, be limited definitely to spiritual matters, and they may not take jurisdiction in civil and criminal cases between ecclesiastics or laymen. Without this restriction, the church power presents a mixture of spiritual and temporal, pernicious in all its results on the religion and tranquility of the people. The clergy, by the spirit of empire and domination, have always sought to confound the real and obvious distinction between the two powers.[124]

The reason assigned for opposition to both seignorial and ecclesiastical justice was the exception to state justice which this constituted, rather than the burden of its administration or the inefficiency of its application. The demand for exclusively state justice was especially strong in about sixty cahiers, chiefly of the third estate, and especially in those of the *generality* of Rennes.[125]

Lille; T—Riom. For reform or reduction: 5 N, 8 T. N—Bar-le-duc, Castres, Dourdan Mende, Vermandois; T—Brest, Châlon-sur-Saône, Draguignan, Mans(le), Mont-de-Marsan, Paris *intra-muros,* Ploërmel, Toul. For abolition: 1N, 8 T. N—Bourg-en-Bresse; T—Amiens, Annonay, Artois, Aix, Bourg-en-Bresse, Digne, Montargis, Reims.

[122] AP, Vol. II, p. 52, arts. 28 and 31.

[123] AP, Vol. V, p. 531, art. 33.

[124] AP, Vol. III, p. 350, art. 29.

[125] 64 cahiers: 14 C, 4 N, 44 T, 2 U. C—Angers, Belfort, Bellême, Boulogne-sur-mer, Châtillon-sur-Seine, Chaumont-en-Bassigny, Coutances, Mantes, Nérac, Poitiers, Rodez, Rouen, Sézanne, Vermandois; N—Angoulême, Bellême, Lyon, Rodez; T—Aix, Amont, Angoulême, Annonay, Artois, Bar-sur-Seine, Blois, Brest, Caen, Castelnaudary, Charolles, Chartres, Coutances, Dôle, Draguignan, Forcalquier, Lannion, La Rochelle, Longwy, Mâcon, Mans(le), Mantes, Montreuil, Nantes, Orléans, Ploërmel, Poitiers, St. Brieuc, St. Flour, St. Pierre-le-Moutier, Saumur, Reims, Rennes, Rouen (ville), Senlis, Soissons, Toul, Tours, Vannes, Vendôme, Verdun, Vézelise, Villeneuve-de-Berg, Vitry-le-françois; U—Bourg-en-Bress, Mohon.

ETATISME AND NATIONAL DEFENSE

Land defense has always played a greater part in French history than naval defense, and this fact is reflected in the cahiers of 1789, which gave major attention to the army.

LAND DEFENSE.—Land defense in the eighteenth century included three branches—the standing army, the militia, and the *marechaussée,* or mounted police. Since the cahiers did not contemplate a complete reorganization of the existing system, the underlying principles are apparent only if the reforms advocated for each of the three branches are treated separately.

The Standing Army.—The most important reform advocated by numerous cahiers, chiefly of the nobility, was that the standing army should become a national instrument, controlled by the king and the States-General, or by the latter alone. This was indicated by demands for an oath of allegiance to the nation, or to the king and the States-General,[126] by demand for safe-guards against the use of the army for arbitrary purposes,[127] and by direct statement that the army should be made national.[128]

Various cahiers asked for the abolition of foreign corps, which would diminish the personal relationship of the army to the king. The reasons for such a demand were well summarized by the clergy of Melun:

> Finally, foreign troops on the one hand are more expensive than the national troops, and on the other hand, they deprive a large number of families, in all classes, of incomes which service to the state would bring them. . . .[129]

The motives of the nobles of Limoges were more patriotic; they asked that

> Foreign troops, as extra-national, should be diminished, because the French have, and ought to have, confidence in their fellow countrymen.[130]

Exception in favor of the Swiss guards was sometimes made,[131] but the third estate of Angers asked that henceforth the person

[126] For example, N. Blois, Cauchie and Lesueur, *D.I., op. cit.,* Vol. II, p. 432.
[127] For example, N. Etain, AP, Vol. II, p. 218, col. 1.
[128] For example, T. Senlis, AP, Vol. V, p. 742, col. 2.
[129] AP, Vol. III, p. 735, cols. 1-2.
[130] AP, Vol. III, p. 569, art. 4.
[131] For example, N. Douai, AP, Vol. III, pp. 178-79, art. 70.

of the king be safeguarded by French soldiers only.[132] Although only ten cahiers expressed hostility to foreign corps in the army,[133] the demand was indicative of a changing conception of the relationship between monarch and army. It is also worthy of note that three of the ten cahiers came from the *generality* of Tours, not a frontier territory, menaced by foreign aggression, but one where large royal domains existed.[134] A demand for the appointment of only Frenchmen to military office was dictated by similar motives.[135]

The question of conscription versus voluntary service did not arise with regard to the regular army. In 1789, recruiting was by voluntary enlistment and the cahiers did not ask for any change. Formerly, enlistment had involved a contract between the soldier and the king. Some cahiers now asked that the king and the nation together be a party to this contract. Many cahiers offered programs of reform for the organization and discipline of the army without any particular bearing on *étatisme*.[136] There was, however, one contrast between the attitude of the nobles and that of the third estate; the nobility deemed appointment to army leadership to be one of their privileges, while the latter wished to share it.[137]

A few cahiers desired to eliminate the army as an independent corps in the state. According to the nobles of Carcassonne, all corps, both civil and military, should be responsible to the States-General.[138] There was also some sentiment for the elimination of distinctions between soldier and civilian.[139]

Only twenty-nine cahiers, chiefly of the nobility, asked that the standing army be made an instrument of the national state, with a national organization.[140] The same national motives were, however, a force behind the reforms asked for the militia.

[132] AP, Vol. II, p. 40, arts. 31-32.

[133] C—Melun; N—Douai, Limoges, Tours, Villeneuve-de-Berg; T—Angers, Calais, Mans(le), Rennes, Villefranche-de-Beaujolais.

[134] N. Tours; T—Angers, Mans(le).

[135] For example, N. Foix, AP, Vol. IV, p. 281, col. 2, art. 5.

[136] For an example of a detailed program of military reform, *cf.* N. Vermandois, AP, Vol. VI, pp. 143 *et seq.*

[137] *Cf. supra*, p. 88. Compare N. Lyon, AP, Vol. III, p. 606, art. 3 with T. Provins, AP, Vol. V, p. 453, art. 23.

[138] AP, Vol. II, p. 529, art. 21.

[139] For example, C. Bouzonville, AP, Vol. V, p. 697, art. 42.

[140] *Cf.* Table XXIV, Appendix, p. 268.

The Militia.—The second branch of the national land defense, the militia, was an institution of long standing, and had received a definite constitution as a permanent reserve force by a royal ordinance of 1726. The militia was recruited by obligatory drawing of lots among members of the third estate, with certain exemptions recognized and defined by an ordinance in 1765.[141] In the execution of these ordinances, however, there were inequalities in the apportionment of the quotas among provinces, and injustices in the drawing of lots and in regimental assignments. During the reign of Louis XVI, the militia had been improved, and some abuses corrected. Nevertheless, every effort had been made to avoid militia service, for it rested upon arbitrary authority fully as much as any other branch of the government. In 1788, and again in 1789, the drawing of lots for service was suspended, to the great joy of the rural population. This did not, however, prevent the cahiers from voicing disapproval of the institution.

The majority of cahiers opposed the form of compulsory service which the militia represented, and therefore evinced approval of voluntary service. This opinion was expressed in a variety of demands. In the first place, there was a widespread demand, especially in cahiers of the third estate, for abolition of the drawing of lots,[142] and if not its abolition, for at least some modification. The chief motive was egalitarian, to get rid of an injustice to the third estate. Other reasons for its abolition were also advanced, as for example, the disadvantage to agriculture of taking workers away from their farms.[143] Some cahiers asked for abolition of exemptions enjoyed by the nobility,[144] or by domestic servants.[145] Some asked for extension of exemptions in favor of persons whose service would be prejudicial to family life.[146] The suggestion was made by numerous cahiers that a tax should be levied upon all citizens to pay a militia force recruited by voluntary enlistment.[147] The

[141] For a concise list of these exemptions, see Duruy, *L'Armée royale en 1789* (Paris, 1888), p. 39.

[142] For example, T. Provins, AP, Vol. V, p. 453, art. 24.

[143] For example, T. Chaumont-en-Vexin, AP, Vol. II, p. 741, art. 8.

[144] For example, T. La Rochelle, AP, Vol. III, p. 489, art. 11.

[145] For example, T. Castres, AP, Vol. II, p. 570, col. 1.

[146] For example, T. Bellême, AP, Vol. V, p. 326, art. 19.

[147] For example, T. Bourmont, AP, Vol. II, p. 200, art. 43.

third estate of Château-Thierry mentioned several of these reasons for the abolition of drawing of lots, and added: "justice requires that one not leave to chance what ought to be confided to reason."[148] The aim of all of these statements was elimination of an unfair humiliation of the third estate and of privileges enjoyed by the nobles. By inference, therefore, opposition to the drawing of lots was approval of universal liability for service.

There was also a demand for the abolition of the militia with little or no explanation. This was a more direct way of advocating voluntary enlistment for army service.[149] If the militia were abolished, then the standing army alone would remain, and it was based upon voluntary service. In one form or another, one hundred and eighty-seven cahiers advocated voluntary enlistment.[150]

The principle of equality was the basis of most of the demands relative to the militia. The aim was not universal service, but universal liability for either service or a militia tax. None of the cahiers favoring voluntary enlistment denied the duty of defense of the state in time of danger, but the third estate in particular were unwilling that this duty devolve upon their class alone. The cahiers afforded numerous statements to this effect. According to the third estate of Castelmoron-d'Albret, "Every citizen is a soldier in time of need,"[151] while the third estate of Château-Thierry proclaimed that "without doubt, all citizens ought to carry arms and serve in the defense of the *patrie*. . . ."[152] It had become a reproach not to serve in the army, according to the third estate of Ponthieu.[153] Such statements were further proof that the third estate was not opposed to military service as such, but to the unfair system then in use.

Compulsory, universal service was nowhere advocated in the cahiers of 1789. The cahier of the third estate of Auxerre came the nearest to an approval of compulsory service;

> The militia; one can hardly consider it as other than a tax; it causes expense and considerable loss of time. . . . The duty to defend the

[148] AP, Vol. II, p. 676, art. 44.
[149] For example, C. Etampes, AP, Vol. III, p. 282, art. 53.
[150] 34 C, 26 N, 122 T, 4 U, 1 NT.
[151] AP, Vol. II, p. 545, art. 12.
[152] AP, Vol. II, p. 676, art. 44.
[153] AP, Vol. V, p. 441, col. 1.

patrie being obligatory for all, it is just that all contribute to the expenditures for the formation of military corps.[154]

This did not mean necessarily obligatory service, but at least obligatory payment of the tax. On the other hand, the third estate of the Ten Imperial Cities of Alsace clearly condemned compulsory service, "His Majesty should be informed that a man forced to military service does not make a good soldier [*homme de guerre*]."[155]

Majority sentiment in the cahiers was for voluntary service, while a minority emphasized universal liability either for service or for military taxation.[156] The latter attitude appeared chiefly in cahiers of the third estate but from many different parts of France.

A few cahiers seem to have looked further into the future toward a union of army and militia into one national force, based upon voluntary enlistment, with privilege and favoritism eliminated. The third estate of Verdun asked that voluntary enlistment be adopted in place of the compulsory drawing of lots, and that those who volunteered for this service be constituted a corps apart, called the *Volontaires français*.[157] According to the third estate of Angers,[158] and the nobles of Belley,[159] national troops supported by each province should be substituted for the existing system. These few cahiers forecast the formation of the National Guard.

Events during the Revolution bore out the sentiment of the cahiers. The militia was abolished in principle, August 4, 1789, and by law March 4, 1791. Soon after the beginning of the Revolution, the voluntary organization of the National Guard sprang up and gradually superseded the old standing army. The principle of requisition for military service was adopted in 1793, while conscription was not really inaugurated until 1798.

The Mounted Police.—The purpose of the mounted police in 1789 was to maintain order within France. Where there was occasion to mention them at all, the cahiers asked for their in-

[154] AP, Vol. II, p. 125, col. 1.
[155] German text, printed edition, *Bib. Colmar; cf.* French translation in *Guide.*
[156] *Cf.* Table XXV, Appendix, p. 269.
[157] Text in *La Révolution française,* 1897, Vol. XXXII, pp. 450-51.
[158] AP, Vol. II, p. 40, art. 33.
[159] AP, Vol. II, p. 484, art. 46.

crease.[160] Their functions were subsequently taken over by the National Guard.

During the Revolution the close personal relationship of the army to the monarch ceased and the army became national. This change was not dependent upon the fall of the monarch alone, but was part of a general movement for national unity and control. The demands of the cahiers for nationalization of the standing army, and for universal liability for service were evidences of this movement, as were also the expressions of the general duty of military service.

NAVAL DEFENSE.—The French navy has always played a secondary rôle in French history. Its activities during the American Revolution were less inglorious than at other periods, and according to Trousset, it stood in 1789 second only to that of England.[161] The electorate was not navy-conscious, however, for the cahiers included few demands relative to the navy. Except for two or three references to donations of money for ships,[162] the demands had to do only with recruiting and with coastal fortification. There was no suggestion of a national program as was the case with land defense. Much more attention was paid to commercial shipping than to naval armament.

The method of recruiting sailors was the same as for the militia, that is, by a drawing of lots in the coastal towns. Objection to this method was made whenever the subject was mentioned,[163] and the motives were the same as in the case of the militia—opposition to privilege, to unfair exemption, and to the burden upon the poorer members of the third estate. Equal liability for service should be substituted and, in addition, equal accessibility to the grade of officer should be enacted.[164] There was an occasional appeal for encouragement of naval service by the grant of pensions.[165]

A few cahiers were concerned with the fortification of the coast.

[160] Eighty-four cahiers (9 C, 22 N, 51 T, 1 U, 1 NT) asked for an increase of the mounted police.

[161] Trousset, J., *Histoire nationale de la marine et des marins français* (Paris, s. d.), p. 623.

[162] For example, C. Dijon, AP, Vol. III, p. 127, col. 2.

[163] For example, N. Marseille, Fournier, *D.I., Cahiers de doléances . . . de Marseille* (Marseille, 1918), p. 412, art. 22.

[164] For example, T. Caudebec, AP, Vol. II, p. 580, art. 80.

[165] For example, T. Nérac, AP, Vol. IV, p. 234, art. 39.

The third estate of Caudebec-en-Caux approved of the fortification of Le Havre,[166] while, on the other hand, the nobles of Coutances questioned the desirability of fortifying and developing Cherbourg.[167] Several others asked for the fortification of some particular port, such as Brest, Quimper, Boulogne, Toulon, but there was no general national program.

Of the fifty cahiers that mentioned reforms relative to the navy,[168] only ten can be said to have shown any appreciation of the service which the navy might render to national defense.[169] For most of these cahiers, the navy was merely another branch of the public service in need of reform.

War and Peace.—Under the old régime, the making of war and peace, with the concomitant direction of national defense, was a prerogative of the king. Parallel with nationalization of the army, a number of cahiers of 1789 were careful to stipulate that war, for the future, should be a national concern, and not merely dynastic. These cahiers stated that at the outbreak of war, the States-General should be summoned.[170] The nobles of Villeneuve-de-Berg were specific about placing control of national defense in the States-General:

> The king, aided by a council of war, will dispose as he wishes of the troops for external defense; he is, however, requested to make his intentions known in this respect in a precise manner. The States-General will decide according to fixed and invariable rules in what manner the military force shall be used to enforce the law and public security.[171]

No longer was entry into war to be undertaken and financed by extra-legal measures initiated by the king alone. These cahiers were none the less desirous that France should uphold her honor and prestige, but the agency of the national will should henceforth control the matter. The nobles of Etain went further and denied the right of the king to wage aggressive warfare without the approval of the States-General,[172] while the nobles of Douai asked

[166] AP, Vol. II, p. 580, art. 67.
[167] Bridrey, E., *D.I.*, *op. cit.*, Vol. III, p. 523, art. 16.
[168] *Cf.* Table XXVI, Appendix, p. 269.
[169] N—La Rochelle, Montpellier, Saintes, Tours, Ustaritz; T—Auray, Nantes, Rennes, Vannes.
[170] For example, N. Sarrebourg, MS, *Arch. Meurthe et Moselle,* art. 43.
[171] AP, Vol. VI, p. 179, art. 10.
[172] AP, Vol. II, p. 218, art. 7. The T. Mâcon took a similar view.

that a special council of war be established, which, in reality, would be a ministry of national defense.[173]

The demands in respect of national defense which showed an *étatist* tendency were the nationalization of the army, universal liability for military service, increase of the navy, and state control of the making of war and peace. Although many cahiers asked for reforms in national defense, only seventy-eight may be said to have been clearly *étatist.*[174] These came from various parts of France, chiefly from the nobles and the third estate, and not exclusively or even chiefly from the frontier districts. One fact is striking; greater concern was evinced along the Flemish frontier and the seacoast facing England than on the German, Swiss, Italian, or Spanish borders. Austria (which controlled the Flemish provinces) and England were to be the great opponents of revolutionary France, and there would seem to have been some anticipation of this in the cahiers of 1789.

ETATISME AND ECONOMIC ACTIVITY

In the field of economic activity, the problem in 1789 was whether the mercantilism of Colbert should be strengthened and extended, or whether governmental and other restrictions should be removed. Under a régime of economic liberalism, the functions of the government would normally be reduced—a tendency away from *étatisme.* The cahiers of 1789 throw some light upon the state of public opinion in this matter. The issue will be clearer if we first analyze in turn the expressions of mercantilism and of liberalism, and then compare them.

MERCANTILISM.—Mercantilism had existed in France long before Colbert,[175] but it was Colbert who developed it most fully

[173] AP, Vol. III, p. 179, art. 71. The N. Lyon made a similar demand.

[174] The distribution of cahiers by *generalities* was as follows: Paris, 9; Orléans, 3; Moulins, 2; Lyon, 3; Riom, 2; Montpellier, 2; Toulouse, 1; Bordeaux, 5; Limoges, 5; La Rochelle, 2; Poitiers, 1; Tours, 4; Alençon, 1; Rouen, 1; Amiens, 5; Lille, 3; Soissons, 1; Châlons, 6; Dijon, 3; Besançon, 2; Aix, 1; Rennes, 8; Valenciennes, 1; Nancy, 4; Metz, 3.

[175] A good analysis of mercantilism has been made by Charles Cole, *French Mercantilist Doctrines before Colbert* (New York, 1931), *passim.* See also, Palm, F.C.. *The Economic Policies of Richilieu* (Urbana, 1922).

under the national state. Thereafter, until 1789, the economic system of the old régime continued to be based upon mercantilism, upon protective tariffs, limitations of exports and of imports, governmental regulation of agriculture, industry and commerce, prohibition of the export of gold, taxes on manufactures, etc. In what ways did the cahiers ask for a continuance of this régime?

France remains today, despite the post-war industrial development, primarily an agricultural nation. Before the comparatively late penetration of the industrial revolution, this was even truer. It is, therefore, not surprising that the cahiers of 1789 often remarked on the basic rôle of agriculture in French economy.[176] This was undoubtedly due in part to the spread of physiocratic doctrines, but the theory fitted the facts. Many demands for the stimulation and protection of agriculture were expressed in 1789. Numerous cahiers asked for agricultural premiums. The clergy of Auch expressed with some fullness what many indicated briefly:

> that in order to encourage agriculture, which has been justly called the nerve of the state, there should be accorded to those who devote themselves to such labors, which are as hard as they are useful and necessary, some prerogatives such as exemption from the militia, from sequestration, etc.; and a national prize should be established in each community, or in certain districts, composed of funds provided by the Provincial-Estates, for an award to the cultivator who shall be judged the hardest worker, the most careful, and the best versed in his art. . . .[177]

Furthermore, this same cahier urged diminution of taxes for the agricultural population, and even asked for the establishment of dowries for daughters of farmers.

Aside from measures to stimulate agriculture, many cahiers asked for governmental regulation of the grain supply. Sometimes, a cahier asked for prohibition or limitation of grain exports.[178] Numerous cahiers asked for the construction of granaries for the better control of distribution.[179] Hitherto, the provincial governments had controlled the circulation of grain, with detrimental effects. While one province might have a large surplus, a neighbor-

[176] For example, T. Bordeaux, AP, Vol. II, p. 402, col. 2.
[177] AP, Vol. II, p. 93, art. 27.
[178] For example, T. Provins, AP, Vol. V, p. 454, art. 56.
[179] For example, T. Le Mans, AP, Vol. III, p. 647, art. 9.

ing province might suffer from famine. A few cahiers asked directly for supervision of the grain supply by the central government.[180] Such an attitude suggests the law of the maximum of 1793.

In the field of industry, there were two mercantilist issues, the maintenance of the gild system, and direct state regulation or stimulation. The gilds had declined markedly in the eighteenth century, and especially after the unsuccessful reforms of Turgot. Their partial reëstablishment in 1777 had led to a confused situation in which some gilds continued in the old way, some adopted the new régime, and certain industries carried on without gild organization. The gilds were no longer fully independent economic units, and by governmental interference and regulation, they had become one of the agencies of national control over industry. There was often a double supervision of industry, by the gilds and by the state.

The desire for the maintenance of the gild system was manifested in various ways. Frequently, the reforms advocated implied a continuance of gild organization. For example, numerous cahiers asked that sons and wives of masters might enjoy special preferment in becoming masters.[181] Some cahiers asked for the abolition of mastership by purchase or by royal grant (*lettres de maîtrise*), thereby implying that the regular requirements of the gilds be fulfilled,[182] while some asked for a reduction of the fees for joining a giid.[183] Some cahiers commended the edict of 1777 reconstituting the gilds.[184] The strongest support of the gilds came from the third estate of Brest:

> It is to be observed that the general wish of the inhabitants of this town, expressed in the cahiers, is not only for the maintenance of the existing gilds [*jurandes*] but for their extension to all arts and crafts which do not have such an organization.[185]

In one way or another, forty-six cahiers approved the continuance

[180] For example, T. Mantes, AP, Vol. III, p. 672, art. 1.

[181] For example, T. Etampes, AP, Vol. III, p. 288, ch. viii, art. 6.

[182] The gilds required a period of apprenticeship, a masterpiece, and the initiation. For example of a cahier denouncing *lettres de maîtrise,* NT Péronne, AP, Vol. V, p. 360, art. 39.

[183] For example, T. Chatellerault, AP, Vol. II, p. 698, ch. 7.

[184] For example, U. Fénestrange, AP, Vol. V, p. 712, art. 9.

[185] AP, Vol. II, p. 473, col. 1.

of gilds,[186] and by implication, therefore, approved a form of mercantilism.

Direct stimulation of industry by the state was also recommended. In some cases it took the form of demands for industrial premiums and bounties, and in other cases, the cahiers made the bald statement that the government should regulate industry.[187]

One way in which the government could subsidize national industry was by tariff protectionism. Many cahiers were decidedly protectionist. The nobles of Lyon asked for a general tariff designed to promote national industry,[188] while the nobles of Château-Thierry were willing to leave to the States-General any further rise in the existing tariffs.[189] According to the third estate of Comminges, a district of southwest France, the best means of encouraging national manufactures would be to levy an import duty upon foreign goods, "which would make them much more expensive than articles made in France."[190] The most highly protectionist opinion was expressed by the third estate of Amiens, who would have the tariffs reckoned "at the highest rate possible."[191] Several cahiers endorsed the mercantilist policy of preventing the export of gold.[192]

There were several ways in which the cahiers of 1789 espoused mercantilism in matters of commerce and shipping. The third estate of Forcalquier declared: "The national commerce, one of the principal sources of prosperity of the State, merits in every respect the protection of the government.[193] According to many cahiers, an important measure for the encouragement of French industry and commerce alike would be the termination of the commercial treaty made with England in 1786. Whenever referred to, with two exceptions,[194] this treaty was denounced. In the south,

[186] *Cf.* Table XXVII, Appendix, p. 270.

[187] For example, T. Caudebec-en-Caux, AP, Vol. II, p. 579, art. 57.

[188] AP, Vol. III, p. 606, col. 1.

[189] AP, Vol. II, p. 663, art. 8.

[190] AP, Vol. III, p. 27, art. 28.

[191] AP, Vol. I, p. 751, art. 10.

[192] For example, T. St. Pierre-le-Moutier, AP, Vol. V, p. 637, art. 17.

[193] AP, Vol. III, p. 333, col. 2 under *Commerce.* This was the reason given for the suppression of the gilds, but it shows the protective rôle of the state.

[194] The two exceptions were N. Tours and N. St. Mihiel. The reasons in the second case are interesting. The nobles of St. Mihiel cited the danger of war

the cahiers were willing to leave the abrogation or modification of the treaty to the States-General or to a national committee,[195] while in the north, where French industry was more developed, and where the consequences of the treaty had been more unfavorable, the cahiers were for immediate abrogation of the treaty.[196] The supposition seemed to be that a régime more protective of French wines and industry, and more favorable to French shipping, would be devised.

The cahiers were not only concerned with the theory of a favorable balance of trade, but with practical stimulation of French shipping. The third estate of Bailleul asked that the shipbuilding trade employ only French workmen, and that only French ships be used for French commerce, although they were willing that ships constructed in France be sold abroad.[197] The cahiers of Brittany and of Provence were naturally more solicitous in shipping matters than other districts of France. They especially desired the protection and fostering of fisheries,[198] and recorded their value as a training school for seamen.[199] The third estate of Nantes asked for the separation of the royal navy from the merchant marine as a means of building up the latter,[200] while the third estate of Rennes asked that the coastal trade be reserved for French ships.[201] A few cahiers asked for schools of hydrography in seaport towns.[202] Two cahiers of the north of France asked that a separate ministry of commerce be established.[203] All of these demands had in view the welfare and promotion of French commerce.

---

in case of a broken treaty, and counseled that, by granting premiums to Frenchmen who would use machines and make hand industry less expensive, the disadvantages of the treaty could be avoided (AP, Vol. II, p. 242, art. 4). Over fifty cahiers denounced the treaty.

[195] For example, T. Montpellier, AP, Vol. IV, p. 57, col. 1, art. 7.

[196] For example, T. Beauvais, AP, Vol. II, p. 306, art. 1.

[197] AP, Vol. II, p. 178, art. 12.

[198] Cahiers interested in fisheries were: C—Dôle, Mans; T—Aix, Alençon, Auray, Bellême, Castelmoron, Dinan, Dôle, Grasse, Mans(le), Marseille, Montargis, Nantes, Ploërmel, Ponthieu, Rennes, St. Brieuc, Tartas, Toulon, Rouen(ville).

[199] For example, T. Rennes, Sée and Lessort, *D.I., op. cit.*, Vol. IV, p. 273, art. 184.

[200] AP, Vol. IV, p. 97, arts. 101-2.

[201] Sée and Lessort, *D.I., op. cit.*, Vol. IV, p. 274, art. 188.

[202] T—Nantes, St. Brieuc, Grasse.

[203] T—Beauvais, Caudebec-en-Caux.

The French colonies were referred to in the cahiers of 1789 largely in relation to French commerce and shipping. Aside from the demand for representation of the colonies in the States-General,[204] recommendations concerning them were mercantilist. The main interest was the welfare of the mother country. The one demand which appeared with any degree of frequency[205] was for the abrogation of the order in council of August 30, 1784, which had opened colonial trade to foreign ships.[206] According to the cahiers of Brittany, the results had been ruinous to French trade. The third estate of Amiens went further and said that it had been detrimental also to the maritime provinces.[207] It seems to be a warrantable assumption that these cahiers favored the exclusion of all foreign trade from the French colonies. A few cahiers favored the adoption of Navigation Acts, on the model of the English Acts.[208] The majority of the cahiers of 1789 were, however, indifferent to the French colonies and to colonial trade.

Two demands of the cahiers had a significantly *étatist* bearing on French internal commerce. With the establishment of a uniform system of weights and measurements, requested by a large number of cahiers,[209] greater emphasis would be put on a national act of the central government. When the demand for the abolition of internal customs duties was accompanied by a protectionist attitude, this too would place more regulative power in the hands of the central authorities.[210]

The foregoing measures for state stimulation of agriculture, industry, and commerce all pointed to the maintenance, and sometimes to the elaboration of the mercantile system. They looked upon governmental regulations of economic activity as a means of achieving national well being.

ECONOMIC LIBERALISM.—The cahiers were less specific in their

[204] *Cf. supra,* p. 36.

[205] Twenty-two cahiers of the third estate made this demand. T—Amiens, Bailleul, Brest, Bordeaux, Caen, Cahors, Caudebec, Coutances, Dinan, Grasse, Lille, La Rochelle, Mans (le), Marseille, Nantes, Ploërmel, Rennes, Rouen (ville), St. Brieuc, Troyes, Toulon, Vannes.

[206] *Cf.* text in Isambert, *op. cit.,* Vol. XXVII, pp. 459-64.

[207] AP, Vol. I, p. 753, art. 8.

[208] For example, T. Calais, AP, Vol. II, p. 515, col. 2.

[209] *Cf. supra,* p. 56.

[210] *Cf. supra,* pp. 56 *et seq.*

demands for economic liberalism than in those favoring mercantilism. Economic freedom involved the general principle of liberty, and the elimination of local privilege, but in no case did the cahiers deny the right of the state to make regulations. If the state abstained from the exercise of its right, it should be for patriotic purposes, for the greater prosperity of France. Economic liberty, it was suggested, would allow more individual initiative with a consequent increase in national prosperity.

The simple phrase *liberté de commerce* found frequent expression in the cahiers of 1789.[211] It appeared more often in cahiers of the third estate, whose demands in the economic sphere were more frequent than those of the clergy or nobles. A phrase that was equally vague, but which was also some indication of economic liberalism, was the request for the removal of hindrances to commerce.[212] In many such cases, no detailed recommendations were made.

Sometimes the vague phrases of liberalism were accompanied by specific explanations. According to the third estate of Cahors, liberty of commerce meant the abolition of all taxes levied by provinces or towns upon the entrance or exit of produce and of all tolls and special privileges of manufacture and marketing.[213] The third estate of Château-Thierry, after denunciation of existing river and bridge tolls and storage charges, added the inclusive expression, "public servitudes."[214]

There were demands for the abolition of "exclusive economic privileges,"[215] often without any specification as to what these were. The cahier of the third estate of Toulouse recommended the suppression of "every kind of exclusive privilege, in order to give free rein both to commerce and to industry."[216] One article of the nobles of Nemours was,

> That agriculture, industry, the crafts, and commerce should enjoy

[211] One hundred and sixteen cahiers; 17 C, 31 N, 65 T, 2 U, 1 NT.

[212] As examples of these two general phases, *cf.* N. Paris *intra-muros,* AP, Vol. V, p. 274, col. 1, and T. Douai, AP, Vol. III, p. 181, art. 42.

[213] AP, Vol. V, p. 492, art. 18.

[214] AP, Vol. II, p. 672, art. 14.

[215] One hundred and fifty-nine cahiers made this demand: 17 C, 53 N, 86 T, 1 U, 1 CN, 1 NT.

[216] AP, Vol. VI, p. 36, art. 19.

the widest liberty, and should be freed from the monopoly which exclusive privileges entail.[217]

The clergy of Castelmoron d'Albret were slightly more definite in asking for

> The freedom of commerce as much within as outside of the kingdom, the destruction of monopoly and speculation, the suppression of the privileges of cities.[218]

More specific requests looking toward commercial liberty were those for the abolition of internal customs barriers,[219] the negotiation of reciprocal treaties,[220] and the abolition of export tariffs.[221]

There were similar generalizations about freeing agriculture and removing hindrances to its development. Besides statements of the broad principle, the cahiers also asked for certain reforms the ultimate result of which would be a freeing of agriculture. It is probable that abuses in the existing restrictions, rather than a conscious sponsoring of liberal theory, prompted many of these demands. One such reform solicited was the abolition of feudal dues. Complaints against particular payments were more frequent than wholesale denunciations of all feudal dues.[222] Reform in taxation was a second method of liberating agriculture. The belief was often expressed that by making taxation proportionate to the ability to pay, irrespective of class,[223] the heavy burden on agriculture would be decreased. A third reform was the removal of restrictions, chiefly of a local nature, on the sale and distribution of farm products. The cahiers contained many requests for free circulation of grain,[224] for the abolition of tolls and taxes levied for the profit of special towns or individuals,[225] and for the facilitation of marketing by improvement of roads and canals.[226]

[217] AP, Vol. IV, p. 110, art. 15.

[218] AP, Vol. II, p. 542, art. 19.

[219] *Cf. supra,* pp. 56 *et seq.*

[220] For example, T. Vannes, AP, Vol. VI, p. 109, art. 97.

[221] For example, T. Paris *intra-muros,* AP, Vol. V, p. 285, art. 3.

[222] For a blanket demand of this kind, see N. Dourdan, AP, Vol. II, p. 247, col. 2. In behalf of the abolition of particular dues, see T. Montpellier, AP, Vol. IV, pp. 57-58. *Cf.* also *supra,* pp. 115-16.

[223] *Cf. supra,* pp. 84-85.

[224] For example, T. Castres, AP, Vol. II, p. 570, col. 1.

[225] For example, T. Bordeaux, AP, Vol. II, p. 402, col. 2.

[226] For example, T. Dinan, AP, Vol. III, p. 149, art. 20.

Directly or indirectly, many cahiers requested a greater degree of freedom for agriculture.[227]

In the industrial sphere, economic liberalism took the form of opposition to the gilds, or to other monopolistic enterprises, and to state taxes on manufactures. Opposition to the gilds was shown in various ways. A small number of cahiers came out with a direct demand for their suppression,[228] although even these frequently made exceptions in favor of large towns or particular industries.[229] Other cahiers asked for abolition of mastership,[230] or of the *jurandes,*[231] both of which were tantamount to abolition of the gild organization. Eighty-two cahiers, almost double the number of those favoring the maintenance of gilds, asked for their abolition in one way or another.[232] Many cahiers offered a compromise by asking for the elimination of certain abuses in the gild system without demanding its outright suppression.[233] In these latter cases, economic liberalism involved a lessened degree of regulation by agencies independent of the government, rather than the removal of all organization from industry.

The demand for removal of taxes upon manufactured articles was, to a degree, *anti-étatist.* There were governmental taxes on leather, gold and silver products, the general *droit d'industrie,* and the *droit de contrôle.*[234] These were frequently denounced as ruinously high,[235] while the inquisitorial method of collection was also arraigned.[236] The motives for opposition to these taxes were partly

[227] These various demands have been put together in tables summarizing mercantile and liberal ideas respectively. *Cf.* Tables XXVIII and XIX.

[228] For example, C. Auxerre, AP, Vol. II, p. 111, art. 88.

[229] Some cahiers expressly excepted from general suppression, gilds of printers, apothecaries, goldsmiths, etc. For example, T. La Rochelle, AP, Vol. III, p. 489, art. 12. The nobles of Coutances would except the gilds in large cities (Bridrey, E., *D.I., Cahiers de doléances . . . de Coutances,* Paris, 1907-12, Vol. III, p. 522, art. 10).

[230] For example, N. Auxerre, AP, Vol. II, p. 118, art. 71.

[231] For example, N. Lyon, AP, Vol. III, p. 606, col. 1.

[232] *Cf.* Table XXVII, Appendix, p. 270.

[233] For example, T. La Rochelle, AP, Vol. III, p. 483, arts. 76 *et seq.*

[234] On these taxes, see Boursin and Challamel, *Dictionaire de la Révolution française* (Paris, 1893), under the various taxes.

[235] Under each tax, the index volume (VII) of the *Archives Parlementaires* gives numerous examples. The index does not attempt to list all cahiers making each demand.

[236] For example, T. Charolles, AP, Vol. II, p. 619, art. 5, or T. Bordeaux, AP. Vol. II, p. 398, col. 1.

egalitarian, partly the desire for uniformity, but more often a desire for economic liberty. Numerous cahiers suggested exemption of laborers from taxation as a measure that would contribute to general prosperity.[237]

Many cahiers displayed economic liberalism by general statements in behalf of liberty of commerce, agriculture, and industry, and by more specific opposition to particular hindrances. The power of the state was not questioned, but a lessening of regulation both by agencies within the state and by the state itself was represented as advantageous to France and to the individual.

SUMMARY OF ETATISME AND ECONOMIC AFFAIRS.—We have seen the chief forms that economic demands, whether mercantilist or liberal, took in the cahiers of 1789. Were the cahiers preponderantly one or the other?

A comparison of the statements on economic reform in each general cahier shows that the majority of cahiers in 1789 were neither mercantilist nor liberal.[238] The majority included statements of both kinds. These cahiers combined economic liberalism as regards internal commerce with protectionism as regards external commerce, and either or both of these, with freedom and yet government stimulation of agriculture and industry. Moreover, the question of governmental regulation versus *laissez faire* was complicated by two other considerations, the needs of local economic development, and the desire for egalitarianism. On the whole, however, the weight of opinion was on the side of economic liberalism. Nearly four times as many cahiers advocated economic liberalism alone as mercantilism alone.[239] And yet, while the statements in favor of liberalism were more frequent, they were more vague. One gets the impression that the liberal cahiers were not so much *anti-étatist,* as they were nationalist in seeking the welfare of all French economy. It is noteworthy that the privileged orders were relatively more devoted to economic liberalism than was the third estate.[240]

[237] For example, C. Nîmes, Bligny-Bondurand, *D.I., op. cit.,* Vol. II, p. 577, art. 6.

[238] *Cf.* Table XXVIII, Appendix, p. 271.

[239] *Cf.* Tables XXIX and XXX.

[240] Compare the figures for all three classes in Tables XXIX and XXX.

Another fact is significant. Although the cahiers from *bailliages* where the larger towns were situated, nearly always combined mercantilism and liberalism, actually more stress was laid upon state regulation.[241] With a few exceptions, the big industrial centers of eighteenth-century France favored mercantilism.

We must conclude from these facts that, although more cahiers in general expressed economic liberalism than mercantilism, the centers whose interests were most important for economic development were economically conservative. It is small wonder, therefore, that economic liberalism progressed less rapidly in France than in England, and chiefly entailed elimination of non-governmental regulation rather than any lessening of state regulation. During the Revolution, competition with England and the exigencies of foreign war led to intensified state control of French economic life.

ETATISME AND PUBLIC WELFARE

One of the bases of eighteenth-century enlightenment, differentiating it from the philosophical developments of preceding centuries, was a belief in the perfectibility of human nature. From this concept a number of philosophical corollaries were derived. Utilitarianism, with its emphasis upon "utility" for the progress of mankind, was one. Another was humanitarianism, the recognition of the unity of the human species and of the need of a large number of reforms to promote its social betterment. According to the *Dictionnaire* of the Encyclopedists, humanitarianism was "a sentiment of benevolence for all men, which is hardly ever felt

[241] Some idea may be gained of the important towns in 1789 from the lists of towns allowed specially large representation in the *bailliage* assemblies (*cf.* Brette, *op. cit.*, Vol. I, pp. 101 *et seq.*, and after p. 162, under each province). Thirty-one of the towns of these lists were obviously important centers (they were allowed more than 20 delegates in the *bailliage* assembly). Opinion of the corresponding *bailliage* assemblies was as follows:

2, mercantilism only (Metz, Strasbourg).

3, liberalism only (Limoges, Orléans, Artois [town of Arras]).

24, both opinions, but favoring mercantilism (Aix, Amiens, Angers, Bailleul [town of Dunkirk], Bordeaux, Brest, Caen, Cahors [town of Montauban], Clermont Ferrand, Dijon, Caudebec-en-Caux [town of Havre], Lille, Marseille, Nancy, Nîmes, Nantes, Paris *hors-les-murs*, Paris *intra-muros*, Reims, Rouen (ville), Toulon, Toulouse, Troyes, Valenciennes).

2, both opinions, but favoring liberalism (Lyons, Tours).

except in great and sensitive persons."[242] Still a third corollary from perfectibility was a generic socialism—the subordination of the individual to the welfare of human society as a whole. These three ideas were not dissociated in eighteenth-century philosophy as they tended to be in the next century. They were overlapping phases of the "progress of mankind." For an analysis of the cahiers in respect of public welfare, however, it will be convenient to disentangle and separate them, even if somewhat arbitrarily. The cahiers seldom included statements of abstract social theory, with the result that we can appraise their social concepts only from their tangible suggestions for reform. The cahiers, by such evidences of utilitarianism, humanitarianism, and "socialism," showed not only the spread of eighteenth-century enlightenment, but also foreshadowed more special developments of the following century.

UTILITARIANISM.—Utilitarianism in France did not suddenly arise in 1789. Helvetius had been the spokesman of the doctrine in France two decades before Bentham stressed "the greatest good of the greatest number."[243] Furthermore, many ideas of the physiocrats harmonized with this general philosophy. It is not surprising, therefore, that cahiers of 1789 assumed an utilitarian philosophy.

A few cahiers contained direct references to the idea. The clergy of Alençon asked that the government "direct the national genius toward useful objects,"[244] while the lower clergy of Rennes employed the very words which became the catch-phrase of nineteenth-century utilitarianism, "the happiness of the greatest number."[245]

The brevity and direct phraseology of most cahiers explains why they expressed utilitarianism in relation to specific reforms rather than as pure theory. "Utility" was the criterion for the maintenance, modification, or abolition of many an institution of the old régime. Some mention has already been made of utilitarian con-

[242] *Encyclopédie ou dictionnaire . . .* (Neufchâtel, 1765), under *humanité.*

[243] Helvetius published *De l'esprit* in 1758 and *De l'homme* in 1772. Bentham's *The Principles of Morals and Legislation* appeared in the very year of the French Revolution.

[244] AP, Vol. I, p. 709, art. 17.

[245] Sée and Lessort, *D.I., op. cit.,* Vol. IV, p. 296.

siderations in connection with the clergy.[246] Although applied to the rôle of the clergy in general, the chief application of utilitarianism to the church was in connection with the monastic orders. The argument, both for the retention and for the suppression of the monasteries, was often frankly utilitarian. According to the clergy of Metz, "public utility requires the conservation of the religious orders. . . . "[247] The clergy of Soissons recommended that the religious orders devote themselves to education in order that they might be "as useful to the state" as they had been to the church.[248] The nobles of Dôle made a thrust at the monasteries, when, after asking for the union of small ones and the use of funds thereby liberated for larger salaries to bishops and curates, for hospitals and charity, they declared "that the administrators of these houses should not employ the surplus of revenues for buildings which are more luxurious than useful."[249] The third estate of Tulle was obviously actuated by utilitarian motives in asserting

> That all the monastic and religious houses, whose existence should be recognized by the States-General as useless, shall be suppressed, and their property employed for the state debts, or any other use that the nation considers desirable; and that those that are kept, shall be required to make themselves useful to the state.[250]

Many similar statements could be quoted. Approximately one-third of the general cahiers evinced an utilitarian philosophy in respect to the rôle of the clergy, church property, or the monastic orders.[251]

Utilitarianism was applied to education in certain cahiers, with respect both to the supervision of education and to the aims of instruction. A wider curriculum was suggested. In the words of the third estate of Bordeaux,

> There shall be formulated by the States-General a new plan for national education; instead of the old method practiced in our colleges,

[246] *Cf. supra*, pp. 105 *et seq.*
[247] AP, Vol. III, p. 762, art. 12.
[248] AP, Vol. V, p. 769, col. 1.
[249] AP, Vol. III, pp. 159-60, arts. 83-86.
[250] AP, Vol. III, p. 541, art. 48.
[251] About one hundred and fifty cahiers evinced this attitude. A third of this number were cahiers of the clergy, which may be explained by the fact that the clergy always dealt with ecclesiastical items, whereas the lay orders often gave very little or no space to church problems.

which consumed the first years of manhood in the arid study of a dead language, there shall be established houses of instruction where religion, ethics, liberal arts, languages, sciences, history, international law and natural law, will be given the instruction which accords with present times, with public interest, and with the subjects of a large and rich empire.[252]

Although religion was still considered basic, many cahiers displayed utilitarian aims by requests for training for citizenship.[253] Various additions to the curriculum were suggested, the most comprehensive being that of the third estate of Bordeaux just cited. Some cahiers specifically recommended the study of politics,[254] and others, medicine.[255] The clergy of Montargis desired instruction in better methods of agriculture,[256] while the nobles of Riom endorsed training in trades.[257] The third estate of Château-Thierry asked that "some agreeable arts" be taught.[258] The fundamental principle of modern progressive education, of developing the talents of the individual, was expressed by the third estate of Rochefort-sur-Mer, which asked for the development "of the physical and moral faculties which man and woman receive from nature."[259] About seventy cahiers, chiefly of the lay orders, revealed a utilitarian sentiment toward the educational curriculum.[260]

Utilitarianism was displayed in a variety of other demands. Many cahiers asked that the army be employed in peace times on the construction of roads, or other public works.[261] The aim was sometimes to avoid idleness, which was considered conducive to vice, sometimes to provide labor for much needed public works.[262] The same motives dictated the widespread request for suppression of beggary, for even beggars should be made useful to society, in-

[252] AP, Vol. II, p. 405, col. 2.
[253] *Cf. infra,* p. 179.
[254] For example, T. Melun, AP, Vol. III, p. 748, art. 21.
[255] For example, T. Cambrésis, AP, Vol. II, p. 522, art. 92.
[256] AP, Vol. IV, pp. 17-18, art. 4.
[257] AP, Vol. V, p. 566, art. 1, sec. 6.
[258] AP, Vol. II, pp. 665-66.
[259] AP, Vol. III, p. 487, art. 2.
[260] These cahiers appear in the general tables of utilitarianism, Table XXXIII, p. 275. 9 C, 22 N, 37 T, 1 CT, 1 CN, 1 NT.
[261] For example, N. Limoges, AP, Vol. III, p. 569, art. 8.
[262] The widespread denunciation of the *corvée* showed the hostility to such work among the third estate.

stead of a burden.[263] The third estate of Neufchâteau suggested the transfer of criminals from galley service to public works,[264] and the third estate of Auray also asked that criminals be made useful.[265] Many cahiers recommended the establishment of workshops where beggars, the indigent, and, in a few cases, criminals might be put to work.

Utility was also the aim in several cahiers dealing with the care and education of foundlings. The third estate of Lyon asked "that foundlings be raised at the expense of the nation, to be made into useful citizens and good soldiers."[266] The nobles of Semur-en-Auxois suggested that boy foundlings be raised in the maritime service and called "children of the state," and that girl foundlings be employed in manufacture, weaving, and so forth.[267] A similar attitude, the desire to make useful citizens, was apparent in several cahiers dealing with the subject of bastards.[268]

Other miscellaneous projects with a utilitarian flavor were suggested. The nobles of Rouen advanced as a reason for reforms in the royal domains the greater agricultural value that would result.[269] The cahier of the third estate of Nemours, always exceptional, made constant appeal to utility.[270] If the different expressions of utilitarianism are taken together, a total of two hundred and fifty-two cahiers revealed such a philosophy behind one or more of their demands, but only sixty-seven made it an important feature.[271] The state was to be, according to these cahiers, the directing force to make the individual useful for the benefit of all. The third estate was more frequently utilitarian than the privileged orders, while the frontier provinces showed less utilitarianism than the rest of France.

HUMANITARIANISM.—Cahiers of 1789 ascribed to the state not only the goal of fostering the good of the greatest number of its citizens, but also the promotion of humanitarianism. Institutions

[263] For example, T. Provins, AP, Vol. V, p. 453, art. 29.
[264] Duhamel, *op. cit.*, Vol. II, p. 336.
[265] AP, Vol. VI, p. 113, art. 21.
[266] AP, Vol. III, p. 611, col. 2.
[267] AP, Vol. II, p. 131, art. 22.
[268] For example, T. Dijon, AP, Vol. III, p. 135, art. 87.
[269] AP, Vol. V, p. 595, art. 22.
[270] AP, Vol. IV, pp. 112-215, *passim*.
[271] *Cf.* Table XXXIII, Appendix, p. 275.

and practices must be humane, as well as useful. The state should be the chief agency for amelioration of the lot of its citizens. Although the Catholic Church had carried on humanitarian work under the old régime, the cahiers were asking for state institutions.[272] Many cahiers ascribed specific powers in welfare work to the Provincial-Estates.[273]

One evidence of humanitarianism was concern for poor relief. Beggary was denounced,[274] and should be eliminated for the future by the establishment of workshops and bureaus of charity, usually under provincial supervision.[275]

A second humanitarian concern was for health and sanitation. According to the third estate of Château-Thierry, "Birth is a first boon (*bien*), health is a second."[276] Mention has already been made of the anxiety of many cahiers for better surgeons and midwives for the country districts.[277] Many districts asked for improvement of the hospitals or for an increase in their number,[278] while institutions for the insane,[279] for the deaf and dumb,[280] juvenile reformatories,[281] and homes for the aged and infirm[282] were also requested.

Cahiers also applied humanitarianism to the treatment of criminals. There was no suggestion of the sociological theory of the responsibility of society for the criminal, but several demands pointed toward improvement in the treatment of crime. Many cahiers asked for prison reform, although few gave detailed programs. The third estate of St. Pierre-le-Moutier significantly requested:

> That the prisons, which ought to be considered only as a means of security for society, and not as a penalty, be made more sanitary, in order not to alter the health of the persons detained.[283]

Moved partly by a desire for justice, and partly from humani-

[272] One cahier, T. Montreuil, specifically denied the Catholic church a share in future welfare work (AP, Vol. IV, p. 69, art. 25).

[273] For example, N. La Rochelle, AP, Vol. III, p. 473, art. 7, and pp. 477-78.

[274] *Cf. supra,* p. 138.

[275] For example, N. Caen, AP, Vol. II, p. 491, arts. 6, 7.

[276] AP, Vol. II, p. 675, col. 1.

[277] *Cf. supra,* p. 37. About one-fifth of the cahiers made this demand.

[278] For example, N. Agen, AP, Vol. I, p. 684, art. 13.

[279] For example, T. Troyes, Vernier, J. J., *D.I., op. cit.,* Vol. III, p. 205, art. 171.

[280] For example, N. Reims, AP, Vol. V, p. 527, art. 43.

[281] For example, T. Nantes, AP, Vol. IV, p. 98, art. 130.

[282] For example, NT Péronne, AP, Vol. V, p. 361, art. 47.

[283] AP, Vol. V. p. 641, art. 91.

tarian motives, certain cahiers wished to lighten the punishment of criminals. The assemblies sponsoring such reforms must have been familiar with the works of Voltaire, Beccaria, Dupaty, and others. Mention has been made already of the widespread demand that punishment be the same for all classes.[284] For egalitarian as well as humanitarian reasons, several cahiers would substitute beheading, in cases of the death penalty, for hanging.[285] A great many cahiers asked that punishment be proportionate to the crime. This principle was well stated by the clergy of Toulouse, who asked that the criminal code "apportion the penalty to the crime, without distinction of persons; conciliate the severity with which one ought to arm oneself against crime, with the sentiments of humanity which ought never to be waived, even with criminals. . . . "[286] Charity for the condemned was desired by many cahiers[287] but many more were concerned about justice for the accused. Counsel for the defense and motivation of judgments were asked by a majority of cahiers in 1789.[288] Torture, both that used to force confession of a crime (*préparatoire*), and that employed before execution (*préalable*), was condemned.[289] Approximately forty cahiers, chiefly of the third estate, denounced capital punishment or stipulated that its use be restricted to a few very serious crimes.[290]

Humanitarianism prompted a number of requests for the aboli-

[284] *Cf. supra,* p. 86.

[285] For example, T. Autun, Charmasse, *op. cit.,* p. 332, art. 30. Hitherto only criminals of the third estate had been hanged.

[286] AP, Vol. VI, p. 30, sec. 2, art. 4.

[287] This was implied chiefly in the demand that crime be considered personal, and that no stigma be attached to the family of the condemned. For example, N. Senlis, AP, Vol. V, p. 735, art. 25.

[288] For example, T. Forez, AP, Vol. III, p. 386, art. 16.

[289] For example, T. Meaux, AP, Vol. III, p. 730, art. 15. The edicts of May, 1788 on judicial reform had abolished torture before execution, but these edicts were never put into force, because of opposition by the Parlements. Torture for confession or for evidence had presumably been abolished in 1780, but the fact that some cahiers included its abolition in their demands showed that it must still have been in use. The *sellette,* an oath before trial, which was looked upon as a form of torture, was also widely condemned in the cahiers. For example, T. Meaux, *loc. cit.*

[290] Cahiers condemning or limiting the death penalty numbered 40: 2 C, 6 N, 27 T, 2 U, 1 CN. C—Mantes, Limoges; N—Dourdan, Lille, Gien, Montargis, Paris *intra-muros,* Saintes; T—Angers, Auray, Autun, Bourmont, Chartres, Chaumont-en-Vexin, Château-Salins, Corsica, Dôle, Draguignan, Etampes, Forcalquier, Gien, La Rochelle, Lyon, Mâcon, Meaux, Montpellier, Neufchâteau, Nivernais, Orléans, Paris *hors-les-murs,* Paris *intra-muros,* Ponthieu, St. Pierre-le-Moutier, Senlis, Vannes; U—Montfort-l'Amaury, Rustaing; CN—Lixheim.

tion of serfdom and of slavery. The third estate of Dôle asked that all personal servitudes, as well as all dues for feudal services, either lay or ecclesiastical, be abolished.[291] Not very many cahiers directly condemned serfdom,[292] but many discussed the condition of the *mainmortables,* who held the lowest position in the social scale, and asked its amelioration.[293]

The propaganda of the *Société des Amis des Noirs* bore fruit, despite opposing efforts by colonial committees,[294] in the demand for the abolition of the slave trade, or of slavery. The third estate of Amiens put such a demand in the following words:

> The assembly, having taken into consideration the commerce with the African coast and our colonies, remain agreed that the negro trade is the origin of the most atrocious crimes; that one man cannot, by any claim, become the property of another man; that justice and humanity are equally opposed to slavery.[295]

The clergy of Péronne referred to the Negroes as "their unfortunate brothers."[296] Forty-nine cahiers asked for abolition of slavery, or of the slave trade.[297]

By their interest in the poor, in health, in better treatment of criminals, in justice for the accused, and in the demand for abolition of personal servitude, the cahiers showed a widespread humanitarianism. These cahiers made either tacit or explicit reference to universal principles of law and justice, and to mankind, but the immediate application was national. While one cahier cited "humanity and equity,"[298] another mentioned "humanity and reason,"[299] and another coupled "humanity, reason and good policy" together.[300] It was, however, French prisons, French poverty, French criminal law, and slavery and serfdom within French dominion which interested the authors of cahiers. Humanitarian-

291 AP, Vol. III, p. 164, arts. 1, 2.

292 *Cf.* Table XXXIV, Appendix, p. 276.

293 For example, T. Charolles, AP, Vol. II, p. 620, col. 2, art. 12.

294 The Society, under the leadership of Brissot, Condorcet and others, sent out propaganda against personal servitudes. The colonial agents, especially of St. Domingue under the leadership of Gouy d'Arsy, tried to prevent discussion of slavery.

295 AP, Vol. I, p. 754, art. 11.

296 AP, Vol. V, p. 347, col. 2.

297 *Cf.* Table XXXV, Appendix, p. 276.

298 For example, T. Ploërmel, AP, Vol. V, 381, col. 2.

299 For example, T. Ponthieu, AP, Vol. V, p. 440, art. 12.

300 For example, N. Montreuil, AP, Vol. IV, p. 66, col. 1.

ism, as it appeared in the cahiers, drew upon the experience of mankind for the amelioration of life in France.

Three hundred and forty-one general cahiers out of the available total of five hundred and twenty-two showed some degree of humanitarianism in phrase or recommendation, but only seventy-six of this number were markedly humanitarian in the ensemble of their demands.[301] Humanitarianism came from all classes and from all parts of France, but more especially from the clergy and the third estate. The *generalities* of Paris, Orléans, and Amiens gave the strongest expressions of humanitarianism.

Socialist Tendencies.—The fundamental proposition that man is a social being was at the basis of reforms advocated by the cahiers. Nevertheless, "socialism" as opposed to "individualism," was not expounded in the cahiers. Individualism was too strong at the time. The cahiers did, however, give hints of a socializing tendency, and occasionally of sympathy with what may be called "state socialism." The hints were less in the form of philosophical expressions than in concrete demands for particular reforms.

One demand pointing toward a kind of "state socialism" (or, at any rate, "paternalism") was for national insurance. Agricultural insurance was the form most frequently advocated. The clergy of Dôle stated: "A sum will be determined each year for pressing needs in case of hail, fire, floods, etc. . . . "[302] According to the nobles of Quesnoy,

> There will be fixed an annual fund at the disposition of the Provincial-Estates, to grant aid in case of unfortunate events, and they will render account thereof to the States-General.[303]

The third estate of Longuyon asked that loans at 2½ per cent be made to farmers in times of need.[304] A national company for insurance with headquarters in Paris was proposed by the third estate of Calais.[305] While the third estate of Nemours asked for accident insurance,[306] several cahiers suggested pensions for wid-

[301] Cf. Table XXXVI, Appendix, p. 277.
[302] AP, Vol. III, p. 154, art. 69.
[303] AP, Vol. V, p. 504, art. 10.
[304] MS, *Arch. Meurthe-et-Moselle,* or reprint in *Guide.*
[305] AP, Vol. II, p. 515, col. 2.
[306] AP, Vol. IV, pp. 203-4.

ows,[307] aid for minor children or foundling homes,[308] and in one case, for the appointment of a surgeon to be paid by the state and to attend the poor, without charge to them.[309] Inherent in all these demands was an increase in the functions of the state, and a protective attitude toward those unable to care for themselves.

Another "socialist" idea appearing in a few cahiers of 1789 was clearly stated by the third estate of Château-Thierry: "The means of assuring food to its citizens should be considered by a wise government."[310] This did not signify a desire to revive the old Roman practice of *panem et circenses,* but a belief, as the third estate of Mantes expressed it, that "the *patrie* owes food to him who has given it his labor (*bras*) and his life."[311] Demands for price fixing of grain, for public granaries, for national regulation of grain circulation, were all based upon this idea.[312]

The subject of employment was discussed by several cahiers. A few mentioned the right of every man to work.[313] The third estate of Metz revealed a large measure of socialistic thought in the requests:

> That there be established public works, where all who are in a condition to work, may find work and a salary proportioned to the common price of primary necessities. That in regard to the poor who are not yet able or can no longer work, there be furnished to them, at the expense of the state, the means of subsistence, out of funds first set aside for charity. That there be established, in the same way, assistance to prevent the spread of fires; to help unfortunate persons who have suffered from fires, an indemnity to those who have suffered grave losses, whether by reason of epidemics of epizooties, floods, or other accidents.[314]

In general, however, unemployment was looked upon as willful idleness. Except for the demand that all citizens be made useful to the state, no cahiers hinted that the state should provide work to supplement a shortage in private employment. The industrial revolution had barely begun in France, and technological unem-

[307] For example, T. Lesneven, AP, Vol. III, p. 498, art. 74.
[308] *Cf. supra,* p. 139.
[309] T. Neufchâteau, Duhamel, *op. cit.,* Vol. II, p. 346.
[310] AP, Vol. II, p. 675, art. 36.
[311] AP, Vol. III, p. 673, col. 2, art. 2.
[312] *Cf. supra,* pp. 126-27.
[313] *Cf. supra,* p. 94.
[314] AP, Vol. III, p. 770, arts. 79-80.

ployment was still far in the future. The third estate of Rennes did, however, suggest government regulation of wages.[315]

Some of the conservatives in 1789 accused the third estate of an egalitarianism tantamount to communism.[316] It is difficult for us today to read communism into any of the cahiers of 1789. Only one statement might be so construed, but as that appeared in a cahier of the nobles, and one which also defended private property, it is quite unlikely that these nobles would have offered some of their own land for distribution. The statement was from the nobles of Dax and read as follows:

> That the law has an essential object, to try to place some landed property in the hands of every citizen, either by the partition of communal lands, or by other means.[317]

Other than this, there was some opposition of the third estate to enclosures,[318] and an occasional demand for return of communal land to the parishes.[319] On the other hand, private property was widely defended.[320]

The enumeration of "socialistic" demands and the citation of statements from various cahiers may lead the reader to the erroneous conclusion that the tendency toward "state socialism" was strong and widespread. It was not. Forecast of it appeared in only twenty-six cahiers, more often of the third estate, and more frequently of the *generality* of Rennes.[321]

SUMMARY OF ETATISME

In the cahiers of 1789, the absolute and sole sovereignty of the state was affirmed both directly and indirectly. The desire for a single state system of justice was especially marked. The growth of a secular spirit was paving the way for the Civil Constitution of the Clergy, while suggestions later embodied in it were advanced by scattered cahiers. The cahiers also expressed some desire for secular education, but more often in respect of the aims

315 Sée and Lessort, *D.I., op. cit.*, Vol. IV, p. 265, art. 138.
316 *Cf.* p. 95, note 186.
317 AP, Vol. III, p. 94, art. 35.
318 For example, T. Poitiers, AP, Vol. V, p. 414, col. 2.
319 For example, T. Dax, AP, Vol. III, p. 108, col. 1.
320 *Cf. supra,* p. 94.
321 *Cf. Table* XXXVII, Appendix, p. 278.

of education than of its state management. The majority of cahiers, especially of the lay orders, recommended freedom of the press with a minimum of interference by the state. This *anti-étatist* request represented a natural reaction against the existing arbitrary régime, but the demands for publicity of governmental action were especially significant in promoting the very agencies which later were used for national propaganda. The publicity of the cahiers themselves was one great force in the formation of public opinion during the early months of the Revolution. National defense was a less important concern, except for the nobles, whose past rôle led them to demand military reforms. Significant demands relative to the army were those pointing toward the transformation of defense into a national affair, and voluntary enlistment. In economic matters opinion, especially among the clergy and nobles, was moving in the direction of liberalism, but most cahiers showed a compromise between state regulation and economic freedom. Among the cahiers of the third estate, the big industrial centers were tenacious of mercantilism, while the lesser towns favored liberalism. The most marked advances in *étatisme* were in the field of public welfare and evinced a fundamental attitude of utilitarianism and humanitarianism, and, in a few instances, a "socializing" tendency.

A great many cahiers were *étatist* in one way or another, but the majority neutralized *étatisme* in one respect by *anti-étatisme* in another. Secularism in regard to the church might be offset by economic liberalism, or other similar contractions of state power. As a consequence, few cahiers were consistently *étatist* in several respects. A hint of future developments may be found in the cahiers of 1789, but only a small minority displayed a constantly *étatist* psychology.[322] The third estate was more *étatist* than the privileged orders, and *étatisme* was strongest in Brittany.

A comparison of the various opinions bearing on *étatisme* in the cahiers of 1789 with those of earlier cahiers accentuates some of the *étatist* developments of the later date. In the first place, the word "*état*" came into general usage sometime after the cahiers

[322] Sixteen cahiers: 2 N, 14 T; N—Lyon, Quesnoy; T—Amiens, Angers, Brest, Artois, Forcalquier, Mans(le), Mantes, Nantes, Nemours, Rennes, Paris *intra-muros*, Vannes, Vendôme, Vitry-le-françois.

of former States-Generals. In these, references were to the king, his Majesty, or to the state represented in the person of the king. Gallicanism had made advances, likewise, in the hundred and fifty years that elapsed between 1614 and 1789. The clergy of early States-Generals had affirmed the royal title of the king of France as *très chrétien, et de fils ainé de l'église,*[323] but the nobles and the third estate had denounced annates on several occasions.[324] The first article of the cahier of the third estate in 1614, claiming that the French church was independent of all temporal authority,[325] was looked upon as heretical by the clergy, and led to a quarrel between the two orders, and ultimately to the failure of the States-General of that year. In 1789, similar claims were made without counter charges of heresy, and appeared even among cahiers of the clergy.[326] Thus, antipapal sentiment had increased among all classes between 1614 and the Revolution. The secularism of the lay orders was also a new development since the early States-Generals. The early cahiers contained no suggestion of lay supervision of education,, and no intimation of changes in the curriculum. Similarly, the early cahiers showed no consciousness of the value of publicity. There was no demand for publicity of government action,[327] and in 1614, the clergy and the third estate both asked for a closer censorship of the press.[328] This attitude in 1614 added significance to the widespread demand for publicity in 1789. Exclusive state control of justice had not been imagined by the makers of the early cahiers. The attitude in 1789 that national defense was a national problem, and not one of the king and feudal lords, was also an advance over previous centuries.

[323] For example, C. 1576, Lalourcé and Duval, *op. cit.*, Vol. II, pp. 2-3. The clergy in 1614 used the same phrase and referred to the favorable results of close unity between France and the Papacy (*loc. cit.*, Vol. IV, p. 5, art. 5).

[324] T. 1560, Lalourcé and Duval, *op. cit.*, Vol. I, pp. 297-98; N, T, 1576—*ibid.*, Vol. II, p. 128, art. 15, and p. 220, art. 93; N, T, 1588, *ibid.*, Vol. III, p. 94, art. 9; p. 196, art. 47; N.1614—*ibid.*, Vol. IV, p. 179.

[325] The first article was adopted from the cahier of Paris, and was not reprinted by Lalourcé and Duval. It may be found, however, in Danjou and Cimber, *Archives curieuses de l'histoire de France de Louis XI à Louis XVIII* (Paris, 1837), Vol. I, p. 95.

[326] For example, C. St. Quentin, AP, Vol. V, p. 647, col. 2, art. 1.

[327] Printing had been too expensive for widespread use in connection with former States-Generals.

[328] Lalourcé and Duval, *op. cit.*, Vol. IV, p. 81, arts. 129-30, and p. 303.

The united orders of 1484 had asked for freedom of commerce,[329] but otherwise the early cahiers had been strongly mercantilist.[330] The appearance of the demand for abolition of internal customs barriers and for uniform weights and measures in the early cahiers shows that these two demands were not necessarily a part of economic liberal philosophy, but rather a reaction to the existing diversity.[331] Consequently, the vague statements of economic liberalism in many cahiers of 1789 indicated opposition to the existing mercantilism, and a gradual conversion of some Frenchmen to the philosophy of the liberal economists.

The marked humanitarian interest of the eighteenth century stands out in clearer relief when we consider the absence of humanitarian demands and expressions in the early cahiers, and the presence of counter-tendencies. In 1576, the clergy had asked that vagabonds be used on the roads,[332] while in 1614, the nobles would send them to the galleys.[333] Although the third estate of the same year asked to have vagabonds branded and then either sent to the galleys or hanged, they did devote some space to the care of the honest poor.[334] The early cahiers generally approved of harsh treatment of criminals.[335] Besides these counter-tendencies, the early cahiers betrayed no "socialist" tendency.

The contrast between the cahiers of early States-Generals and those of 1789 accentuates the rise of *étatisme* on the eve of the Revolution in respect of the church, education, justice, national defense, and public welfare. At the same time, the *anti-étatist* demands for freedom of the press and for economic liberalism assume special significance.

The French public was not, however, essentially *étatist* in 1789. One must not forget the widespread individualism manifested in the general cahiers. Individualism and *étatisme* are antithetical

[329] Mayer, *op. cit.*, Vol. IX, p. 376.

[330] Governmental regulation and protection were constantly asked, especially in 1614.

[331] *Cf. supra*, pp. 56 *et seq.*

[332] Lalourcé and Duval, *op. cit.*, Vol. II, p. 81, art. 242.

[333] *Ibid.*, Vol. IV, p. 242.

[334] *Ibid.*, Vol. IV, pp. 365-66, and p. 294. The care of the poor was, however, to be left in ecclesiastical hands.

[335] For example, T. 1614, *ibid.*, Vol. IV, pp. 355 *et seq.*, and p. 365.

philosophies. The former, as expressed in the cahiers, was a reaction against the régime of Louis XIV and against absolutist principles carried forward in the eighteenth century by supporters of enlightened despotism. The feeling for individualism was actually far stronger than *étatisme* in the general cahiers. It is significant, nevertheless, that at this very time many ways of increasing secular control should have been proposed. During the Revolution, the king was temporarily eliminated from the state, and for a period at least, the individual was subordinated to the controlling power of the state.

CHAPTER VI

PATRIOTISM IN THE GENERAL CAHIERS

In the introduction to their volume on French patriotism in the nineteenth century,[1] Stewart and Desjardins have given an excellent historical survey of French patriotism. A good many of their generalizations[2] apply to the cahiers, but they have failed to distinguish certain elements both in recent French patriotism and in that manifested in 1789. In the first place, their study ignores the distinction made by present-day Frenchmen between the *patrie* and the *state*. It is not the state that has been substituted for the person of the king as the central object of patriotism but rather a compound of French nationality, institutions, and soil.

Again, Stewart and Desjardins have erred in treating the whole period from 1715 to 1800 as a unit, and in regarding the Napoleonic period as the source of the essential changes in French patriotism. This overlooks the all-important rôle of the French Revolution in arraying new loyalties against old, and in paving the way for the characteristic patriotism of the Napoleonic régime. The actual crisis for French patriotism came in 1792 with the beginning of foreign war, but its divergent tendencies were already displayed at the very beginning of the Revolution in 1789.

Although 1789 was not a sharp turning point in French patriotism, the cahiers of that date provide us with an especially valuable means of gauging its nature and intensity on the eve of the Revolution. What, precisely, did the electors of 1789 mean by patriotism?

PATRIOTISM, THE KING, AND THE NATION

In his small, but thoughtful, study of French patriotism, Aulard devoted one chapter to the cahiers of 1789.[3] In these documents

[1] Stewart, H. F., and P. Desjardins, *French Patriotism in the Nineteenth Century* (Cambridge, 1923).

[2] *Cf. infra*, p. 193.

[3] Aulard, A., *Le Patriotisme français de la Renaissance à la Révolution* (Paris

he recognized three different types of patriotic loyalty: to the king, to the king and the nation together, and to the nation alone. Although the validity of his analysis has been confirmed by the present study, the method herein applied has made possible a fuller analysis. Aulard made no attempt to distinguish between the two general classes of cahiers, nor did he pretend to consult the complete number of available cahiers. We have, therefore, the advantage of a class and regional analysis and have observed various aspects of patriotism overlooked by Aulard.

The most outstanding characteristic of French patriotism as manifested in the general cahiers of 1789 was its close association with the Bourbon monarchy. The cahiers almost invariably began or ended, or both, with statements of devotion to Louis XVI. For example, the third estate of Villefranche-en-Rouergue began their cahier by offering to the king:

> the homage of their submission to his will, of their love for his sacred person, and of their gratitude for the beneficent act of justice which his Majesty has just exercised for his peoples, in recalling for France the States-General, in restoring the nation to its imprescriptible rights; and desiring to cooperate as much as possible in the happy revolution which is preparing, they make the present cahier . . .[4]

The same cahier closes with still more ardent phrases promising the unity of the orders, "their zeal and fidelity," and declaring that Louis XVI would "break the fetters of the nation."[5] But in addition to the introductory and concluding portions of the cahiers, where expressions of loyalty might be perfunctory, patriotic utterances frequently occurred in connection with the reforms requested in the body of a cahier. Some expression of patriotism was well-nigh universal, and by direct statement in the majority of cahiers. In only a small minority, the patriotism was independent of the monarch. Most frequently, it combined a loyalty to the king with a loyalty to the nation. It was also a minority whose patriotism was identical with loyalty to the monarch alone. The king, in such cases, was usually given one of two rôles, paternalistic or symbolical.

1921), ch. iv. In order to avoid confusion and to make the present presentation complete, there will be no attempt to repeat the conclusions of Aulard.

[4] AP, Vol. VI, p. 169.

[5] AP, Vol VI, p. 171.

The paternalistic rôle of the monarch was that of a benevolent despot, and patriotism then meant coöperation with and obedience to his wishes. According to the third estate of Meaux:

> The third estate attributed the greatness of their evils to remoteness from the presence of the monarch. . . . The unique way to cut at the root of abuse is to recall principles, to sanction anew, and reëstablish the communication which ought always to exist between the nation and the monarch.[6]

The nobles of Sens enjoined upon their deputy that nothing be done contrary to the monarchy, "and to the conservation of filial respect which every Frenchman, by gratitude and by hereditary sentiments, has vowed to the ancient race of their kings."[7] Furthermore, the nobles of Rouen recognized that love of their king had made heroes out of Frenchmen.[8] According to the third estate of Vannes, the title of "father of the people" should be bestowed upon Louis XVI for his benevolence.[9] The nobles of Belley spoke of Frenchmen as brothers with a common father, the king.[10] Demand for a revival of royal audiences,[11] emphasis upon the pardoning power of the kings,[12] and the demand for a general amnesty at the opening of the States-General[13] were signs of a paternalistic patriotism. Monarchy was a French tradition, not merely as a form of government, but for some, at least, as the object of French patriotism.[14]

The monarchy fell three years later, and one is tempted to question the profundity of the paternalistic patriotism expressed in 1789. As a matter of fact, a great many statements and demands in the cahiers indicated that the sentiment of filial obedience toward the king was losing its hold, and that the king was then honored rather as a symbol of national unity.

One hint of a changing attitude toward the kingship is afforded

[6] AP, Vol. III, p. 728, col. 1.
[7] AP, Vol. V, p. 757, col. 1.
[8] AP, Vol. V, p. 594, col. 1.
[9] AP, Vol. VI, p. 107, col. 1.
[10] AP, Vol. II, p. 481, col. 2.
[11] For example, T. Le Mans, AP, Vol. III, p. 644, art. 16.
[12] For example, N. St. Jean d'Angely, Mesnard, *St. Jean d'Angely sous la Révolution* (Paris, 1910), art. 63.
[13] For example, T. Trévoux, AP, Vol. VI, p. 70, col. 2.
[14] *Cf.* Table XLIV, Appendix, p. 282.

by references to the coronation oath, which was looked upon as a solemnization of the contract between each new king and France. The oath, as administered to Louis XVI in 1774,[15] comprised four parts: a pledge to maintain Catholicism, another to administer the government, a special oath as head of the order of St. Louis, and a special oath to suppress duelling. The formula was in accordance with the theory of absolute monarchy, although a semblance of election had been retained in the ceremony of administering the oath.[16] Ten of the general cahiers of 1789 asked for a change in the ceremony or the oath, in order to emphasize the union of king and nation, and in six of these cahiers the further request was made that the altered oath should include a promise to uphold the new constitution of France.[17] The nobles of Dourdan devoted an entire paragraph to the subject:

> Finally, in order to make French law more imposing, let a uniform, unchangeable formula of oath be drawn up which the kings must swear in the presence of the States-General to observe; the declaratory act, of which a duplicate will be deposited in the treasury of the church of St. Rémy of Reims, will be presented to them with as much solemnity as the sacred oil. By this oath the monarch will be formally pledged to protect the Christian religion, catholic, apostolic and Roman, to employ all his power and all means to maintain it in all its purity, and finally by this oath the constitution of the kingdom ought to be firmly guaranteed.[18]

Such a royal oath would bear witness to the transformation of France into a constitutional monarchy,[19] and would be a memorial of the union of king and nation.

[15] For the text of the oath, see Pichon et Gobet, *Le Sacre et couronnement de Louis XVI . . .* (Paris, 1775), pp. 52 *et seq.*

[16] The theory of absolute monarchy was implicit in these words: "I promise in the name of Jesus Christ to the Christian people who are subject to me . . ." The semblance of elective monarchy appeared in the part of the ceremony where the Grand Chamberlain twice refused to name the king to the Archbishop of Laon, and the third time said, "we ask for Louis XVI whom God has given us as king." (Pichon et Gobet, *op. cit.,* p. 38.)

[17] *Cf. supra,* p. 71, note 39. The six were: C—Aval, Besançon; N—Artois, Dourdan; T—Paris *hors-les-murs,* Perpignan.

[18] AP, Vol. III, p. 247, col. 1.

[19] When Charles X was crowned in 1825, the old ceremony of coronation was revived, but with modifications. The peculiar circumstances attending the accession of Louis XVIII offered no occasion for a coronation ceremony in his case, with the result that the coronation of Charles X was the first since 1774. It was performed at Reims, with some of the original sacred oil which it was claimed had

A similar tendency was indicated in the demand of thirty-five cahiers for a new formula of law.[20] The formula in use prior to the Revolution may be explained by reference to the opening phrases of the royal regulation for convocation of the States-General. There were two parts: a *Lettre du Roi,* and a *Règlement fait par le Roi.* The former began:

> *De par le Roi.*
>
> Notre amé et féal, We have need of the coöperation of our faithful subjects to aid Us to surmount all the difficulties in which We find Ourselves . . .[21];

while the *Règlement* opened as follows:

> The King, in addressing to the different provinces subjected to his dominion letters of convocation for the States-General, has wished . . .[22]

and ended:

> Made and voted by the King, in his council, held at Versailles the 24th of January, 1789. Signed: Louis. And lower: Laurent de Villedueil.[23]

French laws of the old régime implied the divine right of the king in their simple introductory clause, and again in their concluding phrases. The cahiers of 1789 which asked for a new formula wished to record in the laws the fact that they represented the will of the nation. On this point the nobles of Dourdan said:

---

been preserved. Charles was interested in the legitimacy of the monarchy, and only at the last moment did he consent to a modification of the oath to include a promise to maintain the constitutional charter of 1814. The oath as actually administered (see text in *Le Moniteur universel,* 1825, no. 151, May 31, 1825), might appear on the surface to have fulfilled the demands of the cahiers of 1789, but it did not in two respects. The constitution which Charles X promised to uphold was not one made by the representative body of the French nation, but one issued by the grace of Louis XVIII. Secondly, although the members of the Senate and Chamber were present at the coronation, the revival of the old rites and the rôle assigned to the immediate followers of Charles X made the ceremony symbolic of Bourbon court splendor rather than of oath-taking to the representatives of the nation.

[20] 2 C, 23 N, 10 T. C—Blamont, Colmar; N—Amiens, Beauvais, Carcassonne, Crépy-en-Valois, Dijon, Dourdan, Lille, Limoux, Mantes, Melun, Moulins, Nomény, Perpignan, Ponthieu, Quesnoy, Rodez, Saintes, Semur-en-Auxois, Toulouse, Troyes, Tulle, Villeneuve-de-Berg, Villers-Cotterets; T—Crépy-en-Valois, Briey, Metz, Montpellier, Rennes, Saumur, St. Dié, Villers-Cotterets; V—Metz, Rouen.

[21] *Cf.* Brette, *op. cit.,* Vol. I, p. 64.

[22] *Ibid.,* Vol. I, p. 66.

[23] *Ibid.,* Vol. I, p. 87.

Let a formula be established, as much for the publication as for the formulation of the law, and let it express the right of the nation as well as that of the king, by the following words or similar ones: The Estates, free and general of France, declare that the general will is . . . We, King of France, on the request made to us by the States-General assembled . . . have published and do publish . . . etc., [and ending] For such is the result of the national will which has received the seal of our authority.[24]

This would be a recognition that the king alone was no longer the source of law, but the king and the nation together. It would likewise imply an association of king and nation in the supreme object of patriotism. Changes in the preambles of the laws issued during the Revolution reflected the modifications in popular theory.

A similar implication was conveyed in the demand of certain cahiers for an oath by all public officials, civil,[25] or military,[26] to the king and the constitution, or to the king and the nation.

Still another indication of a changing attitude toward the monarchy was inherent in demands relative to the royal domain. The early unification of France had been achieved, step by step, by the increase of this domain. By inheritance, marriage, escheat, purchase, and conquest, feudal lands had come gradually under the direct suzerainty of the French king. With the decline of the feudal system, and with the centralization achieved by Louis XIV, all of France was considered the patrimony of the king. He reserved from the whole certain lands and the right of particular tax collections for himself, and these reservations comprised the technical "royal domain." In 1789, this domain was very extensive, and its revenues were quite separate from the public finances. The early States-Generals had declared the domain inalienable,[27] but the cahiers of 1789 were divided upon the question, with a larger number recommending alienation.[28] In the words of the third estate of Paris *hors-les-murs:*

The alienation of the domains is an incontestable right of the nation

[24] AP, Vol. III, p. 246, cols. 1-2.

[25] For example, T. Rennes, Sée and Lessort, *op. cit.,* Vol. IV, p. 251, art. 58.

[26] For example, NT Péronne, AP, Vol. V, p. 356, art. 12.

[27] *Cf.* T. 1614, Lalourcé and Duval, *op. cit.,* Vol. IV, p. 373.

[28] Fifty-six cahiers reaffirmed the inalienability of the royal domain (17 C, 15 N, 22 T, 1 U, 1 CN). One hundred and eighty-six cahiers approved partial or total alienation (20 C, 68 N, 91 T, 5 U, 2 NT).

represented by the States-General, and the revenues coming from them ought to be employed for the payment of public expenses and the debt, and for the reimbursement of the undesirable and useless offices that will be abolished.[29]

The underlying political theory was seldom explained in the brief article devoted to the subject, but must certainly have been appreciated. The nobles of Gien gave a fleeting indication; after they had spoken of the king as formerly only the head of a "confederation of sovereigns," they ended with the statement: "The constitutional principle in the public law of a French duke is no longer the principle of a king of France."[30] The implication was that the domains belonged to the nation, which loaned them to the monarch, and therefore, that the ownership was not personal to the king. The nobles of Angers went a step further, and asked that an allowance for the king be established.[31] In other words, the king should be, according to such a cahier, a public official paid by the state, and no longer a ruler with divine-right prerogatives. In such an attitude, national patriotism was superseding feudal suzerainty.

At this point, the question may be asked whether the cahiers indicated either *Orléanisme* or Republicanism? Despite the extensive electoral propaganda and activities of the Duke of Orléans,[32] cousin of Louis XVI, the cahiers gave evidence neither of the popularity which he enjoyed during the early days of the Revolution, nor of any unfavorable comparison of Louis XVI with him. If there was any idea of substituting the Duke for Louis XVI, the cahiers failed to reveal it. Furthermore, the cahiers gave absolutely no indication of republicanism. Though they sometimes advocated an elective monarchy,[33] a reduction of the king's expenses, a reform of the royal appanages,[34] and frequently demanded re-

[29] AP, Vol. V, p. 239, col. 2, art. 20.

[30] AP, Vol. III, p. 403, col. 1.

[31] AP, Vol. II, p. 35, art. 8.

[32] *Cf. Guide* on the influence of the Duke of Orléans. Although his propaganda undoubtedly influenced the cahiers, there were only three definite acknowledgments of it (N. Chartres; T—Marseille, Villefranche-de-Beaujolais, *cf.* these cahiers). If *Orléanisme* meant support of a constitutional monarchy, the cahiers were full of it, but if it meant the substitution of the Orleans for the reigning line of Bourbon monarchs, the cahiers offered no evidence of it.

[33] *Cf. supra*, p. 71.

[34] For example, N. Beauvais, AP, Vol. II, p. 297, col. 1.

sponsibility of ministers,[35] and though they betrayed a changing attitude toward the king, they had in view merely a constitutional monarchy and not at all a republic. We have already noted how strong was the tradition of monarchy.[36]

A further argument for the hypothesis that the king continued to be an essential object of French patriotism lies in the identification of the king with the reform movement. Louis XVI was looked upon as the "regenerator of France." He was the symbol of a new France at the same time that he was linked with great kings of the past, especially with Louis XII and Henry IV. Both of these were regarded as reforming monarchs, who had represented the will of the French people of their times. The States-General of 1506 had voted to call Louis XII the "father of the people."[37] Henry IV had been styled the pacifier of France, the great reformer, and the embodiment of patriotism. Numerous cahiers of 1789 linked the names of both these kings with that of Louis XVI.[38] An approach to religious fervor in the matter was made by the third estate of Barcelonnette:

> If Louis XII, if Henry IV are still to-day the idols of Frenchmen because of their good deeds (*bonté*), Louis XVI the beneficent, is the God of Frenchmen; history will propose him as the model of kings in all countries and in all centuries.[39]

These citizens of the southeast may have been sorely disillusioned later, but that does not detract from the strength of the above statement when it was made.

The symbolical rôle of Louis XVI and the identification of him with national reform were indicated by a number of cahiers asking for the erection of a monument to the king. The suggested inscriptions were various: "Louis XVI, *le français*,"[40] "Louis, the restorer of liberty,"[41] "Louis, the restorer of the rights and liberties of the nation."[42] The united orders of Montfort l'Amaury asked for

[35] For example, C. Auch, AP, Vol. II, p. 92, art. 6.
[36] *Cf. supra,* p. 40.
[37] See Picot, G., *Histoire des Etats-généraux,* Vol. II, pp. 141 *et seq.*
[38] For example; with Louis XII, V. Rouen (AP, Vol. V, p. 602); with Henry IV, T. Puy-en-Velay (AP, Vol. V, p. 469, col. 1).
[39] AP, Vol. III, p. 366, col. 2.
[40] N. Mantes, AP, Vol. III, p. 665, art. 14.
[41] T. Paris *hors-les-murs,* AP, Vol. V, p. 244, col. 2.
[42] V. Lyon, AP, Vol. III, p. 618, col. 1.

a monument with the inscription: "To public liberty and the fame of Louis XVI."[43]

Any pessimism in the general cahiers[44] was overbalanced by repeated assurances of confidence and faith in the king as agent of regeneration. One need only recall the opening and closing words of the cahier of the third estate of Villefranche-en-Rouergue already quoted, and which were typical of the overwhelming majority of cahiers, to find ready proof of the widespread identification of Louis XVI with national regeneration. The keynote of the general cahiers was not pessimism and selfish complaint but rather optimism about a restoration of France.

The majority of the general cahiers expressed patriotism toward the king and the nation, but some cahiers foreshadowed the substitution of the nation for the king as an object of patriotism. Such cahiers were prone to appeal to the sentiment of fraternity. The word "fraternity" was seldom used, but the idea of a national brotherhood of Frenchmen was fairly frequently expressed. An especially clear expression came from the nobles of Caen:

> Full of this hope [the peace and happiness of France] we see the three orders unite in spirit and in sentiment, and by all the resources of genius and virtue transform this disturbed nation into a gentle society of brothers, all guided by the same principles . . .; a spectacle which presents a state, issuing from a crisis which presaged ruin, and raising itself to the pinnacle of fame and prosperity, by the conquest which it has made over itself in submitting all passions to the salvation of the *patrie*.[45]

According to the clergy of Meaux, "love of the public well-being ought to inspire all classes with a single will, that of the general prosperity of the nation and the glory of the state. . . ."[46] Fraternity was most often expressed in connection with the renunciation of privileges by clergy and nobles. Within *bailliages* deputations between the electoral assemblies were exchanged and such occasions were utilized for fraternal, as well as flowery, speeches.[47]

[43] AP, Vol. IV, p. 40, col. 2.

[44] *Cf. supra*, pp. 13-14.

[45] AP, Vol. II, pp. 491-92.

[46] AP, Vol. III, p. 721, col. 1.

[47] Expressions of interclass fraternity appeared more frequently in the *procès-verbaux* of the electoral assemblies than in the cahiers proper. Champion has called

The speeches were not insincere, but rather an evidence of the common aspiration of the period.

Reconnaissance, the word most often employed to express fraternity, was used widely by all classes.[48] In referring to interior customs duties, the clergy of Melun spoke of "all citizens being brothers, all provinces being sisters and integral parts of one empire. . . ."[49] The nobles of Castres contrasted the classes in France with those in other European states; whereas in the latter, the classes were separate with the nobles superior to the others, in France "the one and the other, Sire, unite and are brought together in your empire."[50] The third estate of Forez concluded its cahier with cheers:

> Long live the king! Long live the clergy! Long live the nobles! Long live the reunion of the three orders, for the welfare of France![51]

Two special demands of a minority of cahiers indicated more clearly than general fraternal expressions the national character of patriotism. Seventy-eight cahiers asked for a declaration of the inviolability of the deputies to the States-General.[52] The motives for this were twofold—protection of the deputies against arbitrary action or violence, and a guarantee of the constitution. In either case, however, the deputies would henceforth share a sanctity which had hitherto been the prerogative of the monarch alone.

The discussion of treason in some of the cahiers of 1789 also implied the sanctity of the nation rather than of the king. The traditional term for treason was *lèse-majesté.* The changing psychology and sentiments were illustrated by the use of five other terms in the cahiers of 1789: *crime d'état, lèse-nation, lèse-patrie, lèse-liberté,* and *lèse-humanité.* Of the thirty-six cahiers discussing

---

attention to fraternal phrases in the minutes of the assemblies, and to the fact that they are likely to be obscured by the subsequent conflict between the orders in the States-General. This conflict did not carry with it, in the beginning at least, class hatred so much as a political quarrel for power. (*Cf.* Champion, E., *La France d'après les cahiers,* p. 241 and footnote.)

[48] For example, T. Nemours, AP, Vol. IV, p. 204, col. 2.

[49] AP, Vol. III, p. 735, col. 2.

[50] AP, Vol. II, p. 566, col. 1.

[51] AP, Vol. III, p. 387.

[52] 7 C, 39 N, 28 T, 3 U, 1 NT. For example, T. Aix, Vol. 1, p. 695, cols. 1-2.

treason,[53] nearly all of them thought of it as action against constitutional government or against the rights of citizens. Obstruction of the States-General,[54] ministerial misdeeds,[55] illegal taxation,[56] or action contrary to the constitution[57] were treason against the French people collectively, while abuse of the inviolability of letters,[58] and of *lettres de cachet*[59] were treasonable violations of the individual rights of citizens. In all of these cases, treason was no longer action against the monarch, but against the rights and interests of the French people. For such cahiers, patriotism clearly was loyalty to the nation.

The relative importance of the nation as the object of patriotism was occasionally increased by the absence of expressions of patriotism toward the king. We have noted that most cahiers began or ended with praise and loyalty to Louis XVI. In the rare cases where no such statements appeared, and where, in their place, were evidences of patriotism toward the nation, the new type of patriotism was more noticeable.[60] Patriotism primarily toward the nation was shown by one hundred and four cahiers,[61] chiefly of the lay orders, and noticeably prevalent in the *generalities* of Paris and Amiens.

OTHER ELEMENTS IN THE PATRIOTISM OF THE CAHIERS

The person of the king, the symbolic unity of monarch and nation, or the nation alone were not the only elements in the patriot-

[53] 5 C, 14 N, 16 T, 1 U. C—Beauvais, Limoges, Mans(le), Mantes, Melun; N—Auxerre, Blois, Bourmont, Carcassonne, Châteauneuf-en-Thimerais, Comminges, Dourdain, Etain, Limoges, Mantes, Moulins, Provins, Toulouse, Tours; T—Château-Thierry, Corsica, Dourdan, Lyon, Mans(le), Mantes, Nemours, Neufchâteau, Nivernais, Nomény, Paris *intra-muros,* Rennes, Semur-en-Auxois, Thiaucourt, Vézelise, Ustaritz; U—Montfort l'Amaury.

[54] For examples, *cf.* T. Paris *intra-muros,* AP, Vol. V, p. 282; T. Nivernais, AP, Vol. IV, p. 261; N. Bourmont, MS, *Arch. Haute-Marne,* art. 34, or reprint in *Guide.*

[55] T. Vézelise, Etienne, *D.I., Cahiers de doléances . . . de Vézelise* (Nancy, 1930), p. 391, art. 45.

[56] For example, N. Limoges, AP, Vol. III, p. 567, art. 6.

[57] *Cf.* N. Toulouse, AP, Vol. VI, p. 32, col. 2; T. Mans, AP, Vol. III, p. 643, art. 4, secs. 1-2.

[58] C. Melun, AP, Vol. III, p. 734, art. 9.

[59] C. Beauvais, AP, Vol. II, p. 290, art. 2.

[60] *Cf.* for example, T. Paris *intra-muros,* AP, Vol. V, pp. 281-90.

[61] *Cf.* Table XLV, Appendix, p. 283.

ism of the cahiers of 1789. There were many other elements which assumed a varying importance *vis-à-vis* the two outstanding factors of nation and monarch. When the monarchy fell, these elements gradually strengthened national patriotism.

GALLICANISM.—As has already been noted, Gallicanism had both *étatist* and patriotic significance. Emphasis upon the rights of the Gallican Church against papal encroachment and upon the coöperation of the French clergy for national welfare were patriotic phases. Both clergy and laity desired greater independence of the Pope,[62] while many cahiers of the clergy affirmed that they were French citizens quite as much as they were priests. In the words of the clergy of Paris *intra-muros,*

> The ministers of the altars are at the same time citizens, and their patriotic zeal, animated and made more perfect by the religion that they profess, does not permit them to be indifferent to the condition of the state, of which they have the fortune to form a part.[63]

Furthermore, the frequent assertions that Catholicism was a French tradition implied a patriotic rôle for the French church. Over a third of the general cahiers of 1789 manifested Gallicanism in their concept of patriotism.[64] The more patriotic statements came from the clergy although more cahiers of the third estate showed Gallicanism.

MILITARISM.—Patriotism has seldom attained a high degree of intensity without becoming militant. It is an evidence of the cosmopolitanism of the eighteenth century, that the patriotism evinced in the cahiers was not militaristic. The majority of cahiers ignored military questions or looked upon military reform merely as a routine matter. Among a minority appeared some antimilitaristic statements, and among another minority some patriotic emphasis was put upon national defense.

A variety of attitudes denoted antimiltarism. We may call antimilitaristic the tendency to ignore or belittle the professional character of the army, to deplore military *esprit de corps,* and to discredit war. The cahiers contained an occasional denunciation of

[62] *Cf. supra,* p. 101.
[63] AP, Vol. V, p. 265, col. 2.
[64] *Cf.* Table XXXVIII, Appendix, p. 278.

aggressive warfare,[65] and voiced some agitation for "disarmament." According to the third estate of Senlis,

> The army shall be reduced in peace times to the number of soldiers strictly necessary for the defense of frontiers and fortified places, for the maintenance of internal orders, and for service in the colonies.[66]

The united nobles and third estate of the town of Arles set as the standard for national defense a "number of men of war exactly proportioned to the requirements of security and defense of the state."[67] Numerous cahiers asked for the reduction of the army in peace times,[68] for its employment on public works,[69] or for a reduction in military expenditures.[70] An antimilitary spirit was also shown, chiefly by the third estate, in an expressed preference for voluntary enlistment, and in active opposition to the drawing of lots for the militia. According to the third estate of Etampes, the people openly defied the law in their efforts to escape militia service.[71] This opposition, however, was not unpatriotic;[72] it denoted, nevertheless, an absence of any aggressive military spirit.

The confusion of many cahiers about the purpose of an army also indicated a lack of military spirit. So long as the army was a corps subservient to the king, its object was not purely national defense. The army had been used by French monarchs not only for foreign wars but also to enforce arbitrary orders within France. Misuse of the army in this way was looked upon by a few cahiers as violation of the rights of citizens,[73] but many more cahiers did not distinguish between the use of the army for external defense and its use for internal security.[74] All such attitudes signified a lack of militarism.

On the other hand, certain factors showed some degree of militarism. There was nowhere a rampantly aggressive militarism such as the twentieth century has witnessed, but about one-seventh

[65] *Cf.* T. Mâcon, N. Etain.
[66] AP, Vol. V, p. 742, col. 2.
[67] AP, Vol. II, p. 173, art. 57.
[68] For example, T. Senlis, cited in note 66.
[69] *Cf. supra,* p. 138.
[70] For example, N. Trévoux, AP, Vol. VI, p. 67, art. 43.
[71] AP, Vol. III, p. 288, col. 2, art. 1.
[72] *Cf. supra,* pp. 120-22.
[73] For example, N. Villeneuve-de-Berg, AP, Vol. VI, p. 179, art. 10.
[74] For example, N. Tours, AP, Vol. VI, p. 40, art. 8.

of the general cahiers expressed some anxiety for national defense and security, or for a military *esprit de corps*.[75] Such anxiety was manifested in a variety of demands or statements.

Security for France was a matter of concern for a handful of cahiers. The nobles of Bailleul recognized the importance of frontier fortification for the national security.[76] When a cahier asked for the automatic convocation of the States-General in case of war, it implied an anxiety to provide money, through legal channels, for adequate defense.[77] According to the nobles of Montargis, the French army should be large enough to protect France, help her allies, and attack her enemies.[78] The elimination of foreign corps from the army would assure its patriotism and at the same time increase the active rôle of French citizens in their national defense.[79] The chief manifestation of military spirit in the cahiers was, however, relative to army discipline, and appeared especially among the nobility. Nearly one-fifth of the cahiers considered the Prussian disciplinary measures which had been introduced into the French army to be contrary to French honor and destructive of patriotic service.[80] Similarly, there was opposition to the arbitrary and vacillating administration of the army. A few phrases from the cahier of the nobles of Bruyères suggested the chagrin of patriotic Frenchmen;

> We have seen assigned, successively, green uniforms, large uniforms, small hats, large hats, with two, three, or four corners, helmets of an absurdity revolting to French character; the proposal to make jockeys of unconquerable infantry by obliging each individual to cut his hair according to the English fashion. . . .[81]

Obviously, a single paragraph devoted to military discipline or security among the many devoted to other matters hardly evidenced a strong military spirit. For the majority of cahiers, liberty, equality, and patriotism were interlocking interests, and the desire for the first two prevailed over any patriotic militarism. The true

[75] *Cf.* Table XLI, Appendix, p. 281.
[76] AP, Vol. II, p. 173, art. 57.
[77] *Cf. supra*, p. 124.
[78] AP, Vol. IV, p. 24, col. 1, art. 2.
[79] *Cf. supra*, p. 118.
[80] *Cf. supra*, p. 32. The sword-blow as a method of discipline was particularly unpopular. *Cf.* Table XXXIX, Appendix, p. 279.
[81] *Cf.* MS, *Arch. Vosges*, and reprint in *Guide*.

tone of the greater number of general cahiers is well illustrated by a statement from the third estate of Briey:

When the States-General discusses military reform, the deputies will consider seriously that nothing should be sacrified to vain show [*éclat*] which indisposes neighboring powers, but it is necessary to give the State a great stability [*consistance*]; they will advocate a small army, but patriotic and well composed, in which honor, rather than money, will be the reward for service, and which will make France forever the first power of Europe; an army which is too large only gives warning to the enemy, endangers liberty, and keeps the people under the yoke of despotism.[82]

Adequate defense and an army of which the French could be proud were the patriotic desire of most of the cahiers of 1789.[83] The later rôle of the average Frenchman in the armies of the Revolution and of Napoleon was proof of the essential patriotism of the masses, but conditions on the eve of the Revolution led many to distrust the army and the militia of the old régime. No wars had been fought on French soil for several generations, with the consequence that the majority of Frenchmen associated patriotism with national security but not with militarism. A military spirit was limited to a small number of cahiers, among which were notably cahiers from along the Flemish border.[84]

Navalism did not exist in 1789. The most that one could claim from the cahiers was a statement of pride in the recent achievements of the French navy,[85] and an occasional demand that France improve her navy.[86] The French electorate were not navy-conscious.

Imperialism.—The cahiers of 1789 were even less imperialistic than militaristic. Outside of the rare requests for representation for the colonies,[87] and the denunciation of the Act of 1784 on colonial trade,[88] the general cahiers ignored the French colonial empire. Only two cahiers hinted more directly at imperial consid-

[82] AP, Vol. II, pp. 211-12.

[83] This deduction follows from a comparison of all demands relative to defense with other patriotic expressions and with the general tone of the cahiers.

[84] *Cf.* cahiers of the *generalities* of Amiens and Lille, Table XLI, p. 281.

[85] N. Montpellier, AP, Vol. IV, p. 48, art. 24.

[86] N. Lyon, AP, Vol. III, p. 606, art. 6.

[87] *Cf. supra,* p. 36.

[88] *Cf. supra,* p. 130.

erations. The joint cahier of the clergy and nobles of Lixheim spoke of the French colonies as the best in the world,[89] while the nobles of Tours asked for a colonial administration "established on a stable basis, with consideration of their climate, their distance from France, and the nature of their produce."[90] Aside from these rare phrases or demands, France was not only not imperialist, but by omission of colonial references from the cahiers showed herself quite indifferent to the empire which she still possessed.

Was there danger that France might lose her colonies? Foreign war was not imminent, but what of the colonists themselves? Did they think of themselves as Frenchmen, and were they patriotic to France? Unfortunately, the omission of the colonies from the royal convocation,[91] the irregular elections, and the loss of documents leaves us with a very imperfect picture of colonial opinion. Even though the documents which are available[92] may not have been a true expression of colonial opinion,[93] the ensemble of electoral material affords us some evidence. The colonial cahiers were drawn up at different times after the Revolution had begun, with varying knowledge of events in France, and subject to the peculiar

[89] CN. Lixheim, AP, Vol. V, p. 715, art. 18.

[90] AP, Vol. VI, p. 40, art. 10.

[91] On the convocation of the colonies, see the *Guide*.

[92] Five out of a possible total of nine colonial cahiers have been lost. See Appendix, pp. 243-44. It is desirable to consult all of the following documents as representative of official opinion in the colonies:

St. Domingue—Exposition of the colonial demand for representation drawn up by the Paris committee (MS, *Arch. Nat.*, Ba 38).
Petition for admission to the National Assembly (MS, *Arch. Nat.*, C 86/15).
Criticism of the cahier of the northern section of the colony (*Bib. Nat.*, 8° LK 12.229; PR.).
Petition of the free Negroes of the St. Domingue—*Cahiers contenant les plaintes, doléances et reclamations des citoyens libres et proprietaires de couleur des îles et colonies françaises* (*Bib. Nat.* 8° Le 24.203; PR.).

Martinique—Letter authorizing action by the committee in Paris, and instructions by the committee (*Bib. Nat.* 8° Le 23.183; PR.).

Guadeloupe—instructions prepared in Guadeloupe (AP, Vol. VI, p. 235).

Pondichéry—The cahier (AP, Vol. VI, p. 235). Six *Mémoires* (MS, *Arch. Nat.* C 42/368). Malabre *Mémoire* (*Arch. Nat.* C 42/368).

All documents for the Iles de France et Bourbon have been lost.

[93] Actual opinion in the colonial documents was that of a relatively small minority. Suffrage in the colonies was restricted to white property owners. In addition, the colonists did not always approve of the action taken by their agents in France, although the latter were granted power to make the cahiers by some of the colonies.

conditions of each colony. In these circumstances, though the colonial documents are hardly comparable with the cahiers of the *bailliages* of France, they are susceptible of some comparisons among themselves.

The colonial documents agreed on four points.[94] First, they all affirmed their unity with France, and their right to representation in the States-General.[95] The cahier of Martinique actually used the expression "no taxation without representation."[96] Although both St. Domingue and Martinique made stronger statements of colonial rights than did Guadeloupe and Pondichéry, expressions of patriotism toward France were more ardent in the documents of St. Domingue and Pondichéry.[97]

Second, all expressed a desire for the stimulation of colonial trade, and supported the demand with reference to the value of the particular colonies for the commercial welfare of France. Pondichéry was insistent upon the abolition of the India company and the establishment of free trade, though with some reservations in behalf of French protectionism.[98] Martinique asked colonial preference.[99] St. Domingue and Guadeloupe were not explicit. The general idea of all the colonies was that improvement of colonial trade would benefit both the colony and France.

Third, all the colonies enjoined upon their representatives the

[94] The documents which we are using in the present comparison vary in date from the petition of admission by St. Domingue (June 8, 1789), to the cahier of Pondichéry (March, 1790).

[95] Guadeloupe, AP, Vol. VI, p. 235, arts. 1, 3. Martinique, see text reprinted in *Guide*. St. Domingue, *Arch. Nat.* B III 135, pp. 792 *et seq.* Pondichéry, AP, Vol. VI, p. 235, art. 1, and in the 2d *Mémoire (Mémoire pour demander des représentants à l'Assemblée Nationale de France),* where appeared: "Le droit de ne pouvoir être imposés que de leur consentement."

[96] Text reprinted in *Guide.*

[97] *Cf.* especially, 1st, 3d, and 5th *Mémoires,* for Pondichéry *(Exposé abrégé de la position dans laquelle au 26 fevrier 1790, se trouvaient les citoyens des Etablissements françaises dans l'Inde . . .; Mémoire sur les avantages et la nécessité du commerce dans l'Inde; Mémoire au sujet de l'évacuation de Pondichéry*). The idea was "Nous étions tous français" (1st *Mémoire*). The petition for admission to the States-General for St. Domingue was most ardent. Its language may have been largely due to Gouy d'Arsy, the active and fervent colonial propagandist.

[98] AP, Vol. VI, p. 235, art. 4. Compare also 3d, 4th, and 5th *Mémoires* (See note 97 for titles of 3d and 5th *Mémoires;* 4th, *Mémoire pour demander protection pour le commerce et une exemption dans le cas où le commerce de l'Inde serait exploité par une compagnie nationale ou autre*).

[99] *Loc. cit.*

duty of promoting the interests of the colony.[100] And fourth, all provided for some such means of keeping the colonists informed of what went on at Paris, as many districts in France had provided for in the "committee of correspondence."[101]

The three colonies of the New World were similar in that they took no cognizance of non-French inhabitants.[102] It was the French-born whites alone who carried on elections, and whose unity with France was affirmed. The blacks were to be excluded from any benefits which colonial reform might achieve. The Negro freemen of St. Domingue drew up a petition whose details implied: equality of treatment for free blacks, and retention of slavery.[103] In contrast with this was the patriotic petition of the Malabres of Pondichéry, accompanied by their plea for increased imperial control of French India.[104]

Aside from these general characteristics of colonial opinion, a few details for each colony are worthy of attention in a discussion of imperialism. The spirit of independence appeared to be much greater in St. Domingue and Martinique than in the other colonies. The former intimated the strength of colonial interests, the power of St. Domingue, and that, in case of a conflict between the interests of France and of the colony, loyalty to the latter might serve to weaken the former.[105] Various demands of Martinique pointed toward a very wide measure of self-government.[106] None of the colonies desired a firmer control by France, but they all solicited more efficacious protection. The benefit of French reform was desired, but also liberation from the arbitrary and monopolistic régime of the past.

[100] *Cf.* each of the documents.

[101] *Cf. infra,* p. 231.

[102] The activity of the Paris committee of St. Domingue was directly against the humanitarian movement in favor of Negroes. (*Cf. supra.* p. 142).

[103] The detailed regulations suggested for intermarriage, with differentiation between black freemen and black slaves, shows that there was no movement to abolish slavery by the Negroes themselves. (*Cf.* Cahier, arts. 1-3, arts. 7-9.)

[104] The *Mémoire* began thus: "The long experienced habit of living under the gentle dominion of France has transformed our hearts into those of Frenchmen. We consider the king of France our king." (*Arch. Nat.* C 42/368.)

[105] The exposition of the colonial position is calmer than the petition for admission to the National Assembly.

[106] The cahier of Martinique dealt at length with a proposed colonial referendum on legislation enacted in France (see art. 3).

From the colonial standpoint, therefore, the colonies were an essential part of the French empire. It was natural that they should emphasize the value of the colonial trade,[107] strategic location for imperial defense,[108] and a spiritual unity with the mother country. If Frenchmen at home were not imperialists, those who lived in the colonies or dealt with colonial interests in France were. The colonial representatives were admitted to the National Assembly, but imperial concerns were lost sight of in the pressure for a national constitution and for the internal reorganization of France. Napoleon displayed an ephemeral interest in colonial empire, but on the whole imperialism played a minor part in French nationalism until the late nineteenth century.

Economic Patriotism.—During the electoral period, Mirabeau wrote to the third estate of Marseille: "Every citizen can and ought to know his own country [*pays*]. The merchant alone knows the universe; and all laws for commerce react, today, on both hemispheres."[109] The cahiers were a long way from recognition of any such economic cosmopolitanism. Few of them directly stated that their aim was prosperity and wealth for France, but this was the implied aim of most of their economic discussion. Whether it could be best achieved by a continuation of mercantilism or by economic liberalism, all tacitly implied the welfare of France as their goal. According to the clergy of Auch, a balance between the commerce of France and of foreign powers should be sought.[110] The nobles of Lyon envisioned a régime that would bring France "equality, liberty, facility, security, and dignity."[111] The nobles of Angoulême believed that economic freedom would result ultimately in economic superiority for France,[112] while the third estate of Châlons-sur-Marne recognized that a prosperous commerce brings riches to a state.[113] While some thought that freedom of commerce, agriculture, and industry would stimulate natural economic forces, and lead to improvement of French

[107] See especially the *Mémoires* for Pondichéry.

[108] This was specifically mentioned by Pondichéry and Martinique.

[109] Mirabeau, *Mémoires* (Paris, 1834), Vol. V, p. 421. *Seconde réponse de Mirabeau au tiers état de Marseille,* 7 avril, 1789.

[110] AP, Vol. II, p. 68, art. 10.

[111] AP, Vol. III, p. 606, col. 1.

[112] Boissonade, P., *D.I., Cahiers de doléances . . . d'Angoulême* (Paris, 1907), p. 510, art. 60.

[113] Laurent, *D. I., op. cit.*, p. 849.

economy, others believed that limitation of foreign imports, restriction in the employment of foreigners in French industry, and navigation laws would yield economic benefit for France among the nations.

Economic patriotism was also shown directly in some cahiers of 1789. The third estate of Caen asked that the king and the royal family use only French products, "in order to influence the national spirit by their example,"[114] while the third estate of Douai made a similar appeal.[115] According to the third estate of Aix, French textiles should be preferred to foreign, and the national animal stock improved.[116] The third estate of Etampes was willing to risk the danger of war rather than to continue the disadvantageous treaty of commerce of 1786 with England.[117] The slogan "buy French" had not been invented in 1789, and yet some found in its essence a remedy for the existing depression. Self-sufficiency for France was desired by the nobles of Etain who asked that French mines be encouraged so that France might be independent of foreign fuel.[118] Even the third estate of Nemours, which was so often liberal and cosmopolitan, suggested that the government procure "by all possible means" the industrial secrets and processes of other countries.[119]

Although not a few of the economic demands were dictated by the needs of a particular industry or of a special locality,[120] and although not all the cahiers conceived of commerce, industry, and agriculture as interrelated factors in a national economy, nevertheless, the ultimate aim was the prosperity of France. There was never the slightest suggestion of altruism for British or Germanic rivals. Economic patriotism was an element in the patriotism of fifty-five cahiers, mostly of the third estate, and noticeably concentrated in the *generalities* of Rennes, Amiens, and Lille.[121]

COSMOPOLITANISM.—Cosmopolitanism generally connotes the

[114] AP, Vol. II, p. 494, art. 49.

[115] AP, Vol. III, p. 182, art. 44.

[116] AP, Vol. I, p. 696, col. 2.

[117] AP, Vol. III, p. 287, col. 2, art. 1.

[118] AP, Vol. II, p. 218, art. 8.

[119] AP, Vol. IV, p. 214, col. 1.

[120] For example, T. Châlons-sur-Marne, Laurent, *D.I.*, *op. cit.*, pp. 962 *et seq.* The third estate of Châlons-sur-Marne was quite as interested in the needs of the province of Champagne as in the prosperity for France as a whole.

[121] *Cf.* Table XLII, Appendix, p. 281.

antithesis of national patriotism, but in the cahiers of 1789 it was a phase of patriotism rather than a foe of it. Even in the writings of the chief French philosophers of the eighteenth century, cosmopolitanism usually involved the application of universal law to French conditions. Their tenets might apply equally to all men, all governments, all states, but Montesquieu, Rousseau, and Voltaire all aimed at reform in France. Similarly, the cosmopolitanism reflected by the cahiers was limited by a patriotic focus. The purpose of the cahiers and the international situation of 1789 must both be remembered. The cahiers were programs of reform deemed most necessary. The needs of farmer, merchant, poor noble, and curate, as well as the collective need of constitutional government, were too pressing for the French electorate to pay much attention to the welfare of mankind in general.

The cahiers of all three orders contained many implied and direct appeals to natural laws as justification for reforms in France. The third estate of Chatellerault affirmed that no property had been reckoned as noble, according to "the first notions of natural law and reason."[122] Liberty and property were rights of the individual "according to natural law," in the thought of the nobles of Angers.[123] Without calling it natural law, many cahiers referred to universal principles of justice, equity and reason. The third estate of Digne appealed to universal history as proof of the dominant rôle of agriculture in national prosperity,[124] while the clergy of Melun cited the spread of Christianity and its moral precepts as reason for the abolition of serfdom.[125] The third estate of Le Mans spoke of the rights of man and of the rights of society.[126] According to the nobles of Mantes, the principles of politics and of morality were both absolute, because both were based upon "reason."[127] The third estate of Agen believed that an era of reason, philosophy and humanity was about to open.[128] One might cite numerous similar appeals to natural law and prin-

[122] AP, Vol. II, p. 694, col. 1.
[123] AP, Vol. II, p. 32, art. 10.
[124] AP, Vol. III, p. 351, art. 40.
[125] AP, Vol. III, p. 736, art. 29.
[126] AP, Vol. III, p. 646, col. 1.
[127] AP, Vol. III, p. 663, col. 1, art. 5.
[128] AP, Vol. I, p. 686, *cf. supra*, pp. 142 *et seq.*

ciples, but these were almost invariably accompanied in the same cahier by appeals to French traditions. If a French institution violated principles of natural right, it should be reformed to harmonize with reason and justice. Such appeals implied an appreciation of a world movement and a lack of national insularity, but did not denote an absence of French patriotism.

Some degree of cosmopolitanism was indicated by the absence of expressions of hostility to other European nations, and by the willingness of some cahiers to adopt the good features of foreign institutions. Some hostility to England was inherent in the opposition to the commercial treaty with England,[129] while the denunciation of Prussian military discipline in the French army[130] also signified some disdain for that foreign state. Similarly, the third estate of Longwy referred to "national prejudices";[131] but only three cahiers of all those available suggested directly the existence of international enemies. These three were from the third estate of Brest, Château-Thierry, and Poitiers.[132] The strongest statement was that of Château-Thierry, which supported its plea for co-operation among social classes of France with the argument,

> Thus will be deceived the hopes of the nations that are jealous and enemies of France, who have thought that the irreparable evil of civil dissensions would be added to the temporary disorder of the finances.[133]

Other than a very few such phrases, the cahiers expressed no patriotic animosities against other European states.[134]

On the other hand, some cahiers evinced a readiness to borrow from foreign institutions. The Prussian system of justices of the peace was admired.[135] The English *habeas corpus* and jury system[136] and British Navigation Acts[137] elicited approval. One cahier

[129] *Cf. supra,* pp. 128-29.

[130] *Cf. supra,* p. 163.

[131] MS, *Arch. Moselle,* and reprint in *Guide.*

[132] *Cf.* T. Brest, AP, Vol. II, p. 473, col. 1, T. Poitiers, AP, Vol. V, 406, art. 29, T. Château-Thierry, see note 133.

[133] AP, Vol. II, p. 669, col. 2.

[134] It is remarkable that the cahiers contained no reference to Austria or to Austrian influence at court.

[135] For example, T. Poitiers, AP, Vol. V, pp. 410-11.

[136] For example, *cf.* C. Péronne, AP, Vol. V, p. 352, col. 1; T. Autun, Charmasse, *op. cit.,* p. 332, art. 27; N. Blois, Cauchie and Lesueur, *D.I., op. cit.,* Vol. II, p. 422.

[137] *Cf. supra,* p. 130. N. Bailleul admired the Bank of England (AP, Vol. II, p. 171, art. 14).

suggested the adoption of the policy in road construction pursued in Austrian Flanders.[138] The cahiers wanted France to build her institutions upon French foundations, but this would not prevent her from adapting to her own use the good in foreign institutions. Direct references to foreign institutions were, however, scattered and infrequent, by comparison with the total number of general cahiers.[139]

The limitation of cosmopolitanism by French patriotism was further indicated in the cahiers of 1789 by occasional expressions that France should be an example to the other nations of the world. A community of mankind was implied, with each nation ready to profit by the good example of others. Numerous cahiers hinted that the eyes of Europe were upon France. The third estate of Provins and Montereau said that the work of Louis XVI was finer than that of kings who added conquests, because it would afford "the people of Europe, attentive to our actions, the example of a constitution which they can imitate, and which will cause the happiness of our descendents."[140] The third estate of Castelmoron d'Albret spoke of Louis XVI as a monarch whose name would resound throughout all Europe, and to the extremities of this hemisphere, to the least hut of his kingdom,[141] while the third estate of Barcelonnette referred to him as a model for all countries and all centuries.[142]

The idea of the brotherhood of all men irrespective of nationality and patriotism, was not remote from a belief in a national mission in the world's evolution, and a desire to extend the blessings of the French régime to other less fortunate nations. Several cahiers expressed the superiority of French institutions or looked upon France as the foremost power in Europe, or even of the entire world.[143] A few cahiers combined statements of su-

[138] *Cf.* N. Bar-le-duc, AP, Vol. II, p. 252, col. 1.
[139] At most, not more than twenty cahiers referred directly to foreign institutions.
[140] AP, Vol. V, p. 452, Introduction.
[141] AP, Vol. II, p. 548, col. 2.
[142] *Cf.* quotation, p. 157.
[143] Among the cahiers that expressed superiority were: N—Calais, Clermont-en-Beauvoisis, Melun, Sens; T—Château-Thierry, Foix, Nemours, Paris *hors-les-murs,* Pont-à-Mousson; U—Rustaing.

periority with suggestions that France was an example to the world. Some hint of a missionary rôle in the world's amelioration was implied as the traditional rôle of France by the third estate of Château-Thierry, an extremely patriotic group,

> Considering that France has been during all times the sanctuary of kings, and the protector of oppressed nations; that the slave by merely breathing the air of her fortunate climate, finds anew his liberty . . . [let slavery be abolished.][144]

From a different corner of France came the following invocation: "Finally, let us dare to hope for the most from a good and just king, from the high destiny of our august race, and of the French empire."[145] The actual progress of ideas in the French popular mind from national fraternity to a world fraternity was well illustrated by the closing words of the cahier of Arches and Charleville, which was drawn up in December, 1789 (i.e., about eight months after most of the general cahiers).[146] The final words were an expression of patriotism to the king and the nation, extended to "fraternity of all the nations."[147] It was this messianic psychology which foreshadowed the Declaration of November, 1792, and ultimately a spirit of war, which proved to be antithetical to cosmopolitanism.

The foregoing illustrations support the assertion that cosmopolitanism was a phase of French patriotism in the cahiers rather than an antithetical movement. Either the revival of patriotism coincident with the convocation of the States-General caused philosophical cosmopolitanism to be temporarily eclipsed or else cosmopolitanism had never really penetrated the masses of the French nation. Patriotism in 1789 was neither militant nor imperialistic, nor was it subordinated to the welfare of mankind. One may say that less than one-fifth of the general cahiers showed a marked cosmopolitan bent in their patriotism,[148] but it is worthy of note that these cahiers were scattered among the three classes and among all districts of France.

[144] AP, Vol. II, p. 676, art. 46.
[145] N. Tartas, AP, Vol. I, p 700, col. 1.
[146] On the convocation and elections of Arches and Charleville, see the *Guide*.
[147] MS, *Arch. Nat.* C 33/280 and reprint in *Guide*.
[148] *Cf.* Table XLIII, Appendix, p. 282.

Ideal Patriotism.—Today French patriotism involves a very high degree of loyalty to the soil of France and a belief in the sanctity of the geographic area called France. In 1789, however, neither nationality nor patriotism was expressly associated with a defined physical territory. If such a sentiment was felt it did not receive expression in the cahiers of 1789. Only four cahiers of all those available made any statements whatsoever implying love for France as a geographic area. While two cahiers remarked the superior fertility of French soil,[149] the third estate of Pont-à-Mousson spoke of France as the most beautiful kingdom in Europe.[150] The strongest hint of devotion to French soil came, however, from that exceptional cahier—the cahier of the third estate of Nemours. According to it, some French powder-makers, who had moved to Astrakan and set up their industry there rather than submit to the arbitrariness of French regulation, "mingle with the waters of the Volga, on distant shores, tears of regret and patriotism."[151] Without doubt, the makers of the cahiers were conscious of a section of Europe called France, but expressions of patriotism, other than the few just noted were directed toward a person, a group, or an ideal, rather than toward the territory of France. It required the achievements of Napoleon to awaken in the popular mind ideas of the sanctity of French soil.

What, then, was the *patrie* of 1789? The word appeared many times, and was used in many ways. A noticeable number of cahiers referred to their province or locality as the *patrie*.[152] In some cases, the king and *patrie* were so closely linked as to appear synonymous.[153] In others, *état* and *patrie* were equivalent.[154] For the majority of cahiers using the term, the *patrie*, was not a geographic area but an ideal. It combined elements of a place called France, the nation, the king, the state, traditions—many elements. Let us quote from the nobles of Ponthieu:

[149] N. Blois (Cauchie and Lesueur, *D.I., op. cit.*, Vol. II, p. 427); T. Vézelise (Etienne, *D.I., op. cit.*, p. 403).

[150] AP, Vol. II, p. 230, col. 1.

[151] AP, Vol. IV, p. 132, col. 1.

[152] For example, *cf.* C. Caudebec, AP, Vol. II, p. 573, col. 1, N. Rivière-Verdun, AP, Vol. V, p. 584, col. 2, etc. *Cf.* also *infra*, pp. 185 *et seq.*

[153] For example, T. Briey, AP, Vol. II, p. 207, col. 1. *Cf. supra*, p. 101.

[154] For example, N. St. Mihiel, AP, Vol. II, p. 235, art. 1.

> The nation, enlightened by this generous and patriotic avowal [a statement by the Parlements], ought to watch over its rights and interests itself.
>
> It is in this spirit that the cahiers should be written. Dictated by the purest and most sincere patriotism, the least mixture of special interest, *esprit de corps,* or class spirit ought to be banished absolutely; the voice of the *patrie* alone should be heard.[155]

The majority took a similar view; national welfare was the goal of patriotism.

The use of the word "*patrie*" by the cahiers is not, however, a key to the chief object of their patriotism. It throws some light on the question, but one must take into account all patriotic statements. Was patriotism in the cahiers directed toward the institutions of the old régime symbolized in the monarchy, or toward a new reformed entity? Between 1789 and 1792, patriotism came to signify support of the Revolution, and, consequently, opposition to a return of the prerevolutionary régime. The more radical the Revolution became, the less the monarchy and its supporting institutions figured in patriotism. When foreign war came, patriotism was less a question of defense of French soil than defense of the revolutionary régime against its enemies, composed of both French *émigrés* and their foreign allies. The *émigrés,* however, believed that they were patriotic also, even when invading France.[156] Thus, in 1792, there were two opposite forms of patriotism—loyalty to a new régime which required the defense of the soil of France, and secondly, loyalty to the old régime, which entailed invasion of France. Did the cahiers of 1789 give any evidence of these two divergent types of patriotism on the threshold of the Revolution?

The answer to this question involves the majority concept of patriotism. Had it been a simple emotion directed toward a paternalistic king, or toward an aggressive nation, then patriotism on the eve of the Revolution would have shown a marked cleavage. When each cahier is examined for the various objects of patriotic

[155] AP, Vol. V, p. 431, col. 1.

[156] Babeau in *La Vie militaire sous l'ancien régime* (Paris, 1890), Vol. II, p. 285, said "*La patrie,* for the majority of *émigrés,* was not the soil where they were born; it was the ensemble of institutions and secular traditions under the shelter of which they and their fathers had been raised . . ."

devotion, we discover that patriotism, for the overwhelming majority of Frenchmen, was directed toward an ideal which king and people would coöperate to establish. National fraternity and collaboration between Louis XVI and the nation to bring about a regeneration were the passwords of the day. Reform, regeneration! In agreement with the nobles of Ponthieu, cited above, and as if the French electorate were well versed in the definition of patriotism given by the Encyclopedists, patriotism was love of law and of public welfare.[157] Law, according to the cahiers, required a constitutional monarchy, and public welfare meant a general interest in national happiness. In their oft-repeated loyalty to Louis XVI and to their monarch symbolized as the restorer of the nation, the cahiers avoided the divergence which characterized the Revolution.

Although the cahiers by and large showed no contradictory elements in their supreme patriotism, there were occasional hints of the future conflict. It was, of course, inherent in the essential conservatism or radicalism of individual cahiers. Some desired reforms so thoroughgoing that traditional foundations of French life would have been greatly weakened;[158] others desired only slight ameliorations. The future divergence was also foreshadowed in the contradictory demands that the army be used to enforce the constitution,[159] and that it never be used against citizens.[160] Not many months later, the National Guard was defending the Revolution against conservative opponents within France.

The word *patriote* was rarely used. Although *patriotisme* appeared in almost every cahier,[161] and the word *patrie* fairly widely, *patriote* was employed in only eight general cahiers.[162] The term

[157] *Cf.* under *patrie* and *patriotisme* in *Encyclopédie ou dictionnaire.* Curiously enough, these two articles were written by the Chevalier de Jaucourt.

[158] Even the most radical cahier was conservative along a few lines. See, for example, the regional implications of the cahier of the third estate of Rennes. which otherwise was one of the most revolutionary cahiers.

[159] *Cf. supra,* p. 162. For example, N. Artois, AP, Vol. II, p. 80, art. 16.

[160] For example, N. Villeneuve-de-Berg, AP, Vol. VI, p. 179, art. 10.

[161] Only about seventy-five cahiers omitted all patriotic sentiments. *Cf.* Table XLVI, Appendix, p. 284.

[162] It is curious that five of the eight were cahiers from Lorraine. The eight were: C. La Marche; N—Bruyères, Darney, Ponthieu; T—Briey, Boulay, Limoges, Orange.

patriote had already been in use to designate anyone active in the movement for reform,[163] but after the Revolution had begun, it signified a defender of the Revolution or a partisan of the dominant revolutionary faction. In all cases of its use in the cahiers, the *patriote* was a man who put the interest of the nation above private gain—the zealous citizens, enlightened, and championing any institution which upheld national interests. The implication was invariably that the administration of existing institutions was unpatriotic, but that it would be transformed for the better when *patriotes* took over the reins of government.[164] The rare appearances of *patriote* and the widespread association of king and nation in the cause of reform, justify the assertion that patriotism on the eve of the Revolution was loyalty, not to the old régime, but to a regenerated régime.

France as the object of patriotism, for most Frenchmen of 1789, was not a geographic area, but a combination of loyalty to the king, the king and the nation, or the nation, French traditions, Gallicanism, economic prosperity and cosmopolitanism, tempered by the absence of militarism and imperialism. Patriotism was devotion to this ideal, and patriotic action would realize it. Patriotism has occasionally become a religion. It became so for a part of the French people during the Revolution, and it was so foreshadowed in a few cahiers of 1789, in symbolic praise of Louise XVI, in ascription of sanctity to the French nation, or in the demands for the propagation of patriotism,[165] but in 1789 it was especially evident in two electoral districts.

The birthplace of Jeanne d'Arc, Domremy, lay within the jurisdiction of the *bailliage* of La Marche. The cahier of the third estate of this district devoted a special section to the needs of Domremy. Although the cahier made the fact of Jeanne's birth in that district a reason for maintaining the local privileges, its phrases

[163] See Jefferson, *Writings* (New York, 1859), Vol. II, p. 555, Letter to Jay, January 8, 1789.

[164] *Cf.* for example N. Ponthieu, AP, Vol. V, p. 435, col. 1; T. Boulay, *Annuaire,* Vol. XVI, p. 206; N. Bruyères, MS, *Arch. Vosges* or reprint in *Guide;* N. Darney, Duhamel, *op. cit.,* Vol. II, p. 365; T. Limoges, AP, Vol. III, p. 570, col. 2. Necker was considered a patriot.

[165] *Cf. infra,* pp. 178, *et seq.*

bespoke some special honor and even sanctity already associated with Jeanne d'Arc.[166]

A second illustration was from the electoral assembly of Château-Thierry. M. Hammond, the first choice of the third estate for deputy, was reported to have shed tears of patriotic joy upon his election.[167] The following day, patriotism reached a greater pitch. M. Lemaire, curate of a small parish, speaking in the closing assembly of the three orders,[168] declared that the renunciation of immunity from taxation enjoyed by the church was insufficient. "In this moment of crisis . . . there is need of an extraordinary contribution."[169] Whereupon he placed a gift of twenty-five *louis* on the table.[170] The enthusiasm of the assembly was so great, that, after the oath of the deputies and the *Te Deum,* members of the third estate crowded around the curate, put a "civic crown" on his forehead, and carried him on their shoulders to their own assembly room. Such ceremonies were a revival of classical scenes, and were suggestive of a ritual of patriotism. Civic crowns might be displacing saintly halos in popular consciousness.

A further proof of idealism in the patriotism of the cahiers is furnished by the attention given in many cahiers to means for the propagation of patriotism. These were not only an index of the ideas inherent in patriotism, but also a sign of its appreciation as a valuable force in national evolution.

THE PROPAGATION OF PATRIOTISM

The Abbé Coyer had claimed in 1755, that patriotism was out of vogue.[171] Whatever may have been true prior to the electoral

[166] *Cf.* text in Duhamel, *op. cit.*, Vol. II, p. 397, art. 7. Since translation of the particular passage might lead to ambiguities, the original French is given: *Son pays ou sa patrie se glorifie et jouit du bienfait de son origine, le seul lieu de sa naissance gémit d'en être privé! Quelle plus juste doléance?*

[167] *Cf.* p.v., MS, *Arch. Nat.*, C 17/52.

[168] *Cf.* p.v., of the three orders, *idem.*

[169] *Idem.*

[170] This sum would have bought about 1,200 pound-loaves of the cheapest grade of bread in Paris, in July, 1789. It would undoubtedly have bought much more in the provinces four months earlier. (See Boursin and Challamel, *op. cit.*, under *pain, mesures,* and parish cahier of Le Bourget (*bailliage* of Paris *hors-les-murs*), AP, Vol. IV, p. 371, art. 5.

[171] Anonymous [Abbé Coyer], *Dissertations pour être lues . . .* (La Haye, 1755).

period of 1789,[172] the convocation of the States-General resulted in a widespread patriotic revival. Voltaire had said in 1733, "If we learned what is the origin and the kindness of our government, patriotism would reanimate us."[173] A great many cahiers avowed the revival of patriotism that had resulted from the convocation of the States-General. The nobles of Nérac were convinced that, "the return of the national assemblies would revive true patriotism and tap immediately all the sources of public prosperity."[174] The clergy of Saumur opened their cahier as follows: "Sire, the States-Generals have always produced in the French monarchy the most remarkable results of generous patriotism. . . ."[175] The widespread thanks to Louis XVI for the convocation of the States-General and the almost universal expressions of patriotism were proof that this sentiment was revived and propagated by the king and his councillors when they summoned the national representative body. The electoral period witnessed a rebirth of patriotism.

The cahiers were conscious of this, but in addition about one-fifth of them suggested definite means for propagating patriotism.[176] The press, which is the great modern instrument for all kinds of propaganda, had not yet been developed,[177] and was not thought of for nationalist purposes. The means of patriotic propaganda contemplated by general cahiers were education, national holidays and monuments, and special public honors.

EDUCATION.—The central aim of the contemplated new education was training for citizenship. This fundamental ideal prompted a demand for an increase in law study. According to the nobles of Nivernais, there would be a great change in public life with the assembling of the States-General and the new régime would require more educated men than the old régime.[178] By control of textbooks, moreover, the state could stimulate ideas of citizen-

[172] The nobles of Carcassonne claimed that patriotism was decreasing from day to day (AP, Vol. II, p. 527, art. 7).

[173] *Lettres sur les Anglais* (*Œuvres,* Vol. XXXV; Paris, Baudoin, 1827), p. 213.

[174] AP, Vol. I, p. 701, col. 2.

[175] AP, Vol. V, p. 718.

[176] *Cf.* Table XL, Appendix, p. 280.

[177] *Cf. supra,* pp. 110 *et seq.*

[178] AP, Vol. IV, p. 255, art. 12.

ship.[179] The great means of inculcating patriotism, however, would be school use of the constitution which the States-General would establish. In the worlds of the nobles of Meaux,

> The deputy will ask that after the promulgation of the constitutional laws, the veritable safeguard of liberty and property, the clauses of these laws shall be formed into a kind of catechism, or book of elementary instruction, which will be taught in the parishes, and whose constant use will attach, in a few years, the French people to the law by the indissoluble bond of a national education.[180]

Similar statements were made by numerous cahiers.[181] It was fortunate for the youth of 1789 that the request of the united orders of Montfort l'Amaury was not carried out, for they asked that the resolutions of the States-General be sent to the clergy, who would see that the children of their districts read them and learned them by heart;[182] they did not foresee the prodigious legislative output of the revolutionary assemblies. According to the nobles of St. Mihiel, not only the three *r's* and a religious catechism should be taught in the village schools, but also, "a patriotic catechism, which will explain in a simple and elementary manner the obligations of a citizen, and the rights which derive from the obligations . . . , obedience to the magistrates, devotion to the *patrie,* and to the king. . . ."[183]

Without always specifying methods of training for citizenship, many cahiers expressed the general principle, and asked for the definite inculcation of patriotism. According to the third estate of Lyon, "love of the *patrie,* public spirit, should be from infancy the first feeling [*sentiment*] of the French. . . ."[184] As in so many expressions of national sentiment, the third estate of Nemours gave the most complete statement of patriotism in education. Their cahier asked "that a royal council be established to take measures, constantly and indefinitely, to give a patriotic impulsion to education and to give the proper encouragement necessary for all the schools established."[185]

[179] *Cf. supra,* p. 50.
[180] AP, Vol. III, p. 726, art. 13.
[181] 3 C, 3 N, 4 T, 1 U.
[182] AP, Vol. IV, p. 42, col. 1.
[183] AP, Vol. II, p. 244, col. 1, art. 12.
[184] AP, Vol. III, p. 611, col. 2.
[185] AP, Vol. IV, p. 163, col. 2.

By one means or another, thirty-six cahiers contemplated the propagation of patriotism by means of the schools.[186] The consciousness of the utility of schools for this purpose was strongest in the *generalities* of Paris, Orléans, and Aix.

NATIONAL HOLIDAYS AND MONUMENTS.—The most efficacious method of spreading patriotism is not merely to teach it to children, but to bring it into the daily life of the entire population. Three cahiers of 1789 asked for the institution of a national holiday.[187] In the words of the nobles of Paris *intra-muros,*

> There should be instituted a national fête to perpetuate forever the memory of the day when the constitution will be signed, on which will be founded, beyond all breach, the rights, the happiness and the reciprocal confidence of the monarch and the nation.[188]

The significance of such a suggestion, which appeared only in cahiers from Paris, was increased by the demand, notably among cahiers of the nobles and the third estate, for a reduction of religious holidays.[189] The popular mind was being prepared for a secularization of public holidays. The Fête of the Federation was a fulfillment of the demand for a national celebration.

Mention has been made already of the demand for erection of monuments to Louis XVI.[190] Such statues of the king would not be just so many more baroque figures to decorate the gardens of the palace of Versailles. They would symbolize the unity of the monarch and the nation for a regeneration of France, and would be placed where all citizens could draw inspiration from them. The town of Rouen asked that a monument, dedicated to Louis XVI, be erected on a site to be called the *Place des Etats-Généraux;* they wanted the new monument to surpass all others of the capital city, in order to "show to foreigners and to posterity the importance of the events, and the strength of the sentiments that

[186] This does not include those merely asking for increase of law study. The thirty-six comprise: 8 C, 10 N, 14 T, 2 U, 1 CN, 1 CT.

[187] N. Paris *intra-muros,* T. Paris *intra-muros,* T. Paris *hors-les-murs.*

[188] AP, Vol. V, p. 273, col. 2.

[189] *Cf. supra,* p. 106. N. La Rochelle, for an example of utilitarianism and patriotism. Of the many cahiers mentioning holy days, only three lay cahiers (T—Libourne, Lesneven; U—Marches Communes), favored stricter enforcement, while three cahiers of the clergy were ready for reduction in the number (C—Montargis, Sarreguemines, Sens).

[190] *Cf. supra,* pp. 157-58.

led to the vote for its erection."[191] The *Place de la Concorde* has fulfilled the dreams of the citizens of Rouen, except that it symbolizes the French nation, and not the Bourbon monarchy. While the nobles of Darney asked that the Constitution be engraved on a public monument,[192] the third estate of Paris *hors-les-murs* suggested that a monument commemorating the regeneration of France and the establishment of the constitution be erected in every city of 3,000 inhabitants.[193]

NATIONAL HONORS.—A number of cahiers appreciated the value of patriotic awards. The cahiers that emphasized appointment to public service for merit only, implied some appreciation of this.[194] Some suggested ennoblement for patriotic citizens.[195] The third estate of Villers-Cotterets asked that encouragements of all kinds be given to lawyers, traders, farmers, artists, and that "public distinctions be given to all citizens who have shown themselves worthy by great virtue, talents and service."[196] While the nobles of Reims asked for the establishment of a special patriotic order,[197] the clergy of Poitiers suggested that at each meeting of the States-General, fifty men be designated worthy of the *patrie*.[198] The united orders of Rozières were more inclusive than might have been expected; after asking for rewards for merit in economic affairs, arts and letters, they asked: "that women also receive consideration, when, by virtuous conduct, they are an example to their sex, and, having married, contribute by their conduct to the maintenance of the fortune of the citizens to whom they are united, who give to the State healthy and robust children, well trained in the duties of citizens."[199] According to them, women, too, should receive reward for patriotic service.

Nearly one-fifth of the general cahiers of 1789 asked for the propagation of patriotism by one or more of the foregoing

[191] AP, Vol. V, p. 602, col. 2.
[192] Duhamel, *op. cit.*, Vol. II, p. 369, art. 39.
[193] AP, Vol. V, p. 244, last paragraph.
[194] *Cf. supra*, pp. 86-87.
[195] For example, C. Dourdan, AP, Vol. III, p. 245, art. 13.
[196] AP, Vol. VI, p. 191, art. 3.
[197] AP, Vol. V, p. 527, art. 43.
[198] AP, Vol. V, p. 393, art. 39.
[199] AP, Vol. IV, p. 90, art. 47.

methods.[200] The nobles were more anxious for it than the other two orders, but only two cahiers of the nobles as opposed to five of the third estate made their suggestions particularly concrete.[201] The third estate of Paris *intra-muros* championed all of the various means of patriotic propaganda.

OBSTACLES TO NATIONAL PATRIOTISM

Patriotism toward a national ideal was a complex sentiment in the cahiers of 1789. In the popular consciousness were also other sentiments, two of which were survivals of loyalties that had once been more potent than the national ideal. In 1789, regionalism and class spirit coexisted with national patriotism, and in some cases outweighed national sentiment or formed obstacles to its development.

REGIONALISM.—Regionalism in the cahiers of 1789 was manifested in three ways—by localism, federalism, and provincialism. By localism, we mean a narrow, sectional horizon, and the absence of a national point of view.[202] In cahiers showing localism, general enlightenment did not appear to have penetrated, or else was advisedly rejected. Such cahiers dealt almost exclusively with matters that affected local government and local prosperity, and showed no counterbalancing interest in national welfare. By their concentration upon unfavorable local conditions, these cahiers tended to be pessimistic.

A second type of regionalism was implied in the federalism of many cahiers. Federalism was an emphasis upon decentralization in government, with equality among the provinces of France. Although very nearly all the cahiers asked for the establishment of Provincial-Estates, there was a differing emphasis upon the proper rôle of such bodies. Some took the stand of the nobles of Semur-en-Auxois: inasmuch as

His Majesty has promised to establish Provincial-Estates in the midst

[200] *Cf.* Table XL, Appendix, p. 280.

[201] N—Paris *intra-muros,* Reims; T—Angers, Nemours, Paris *hors-les-murs,* Paris *intra-muros,* Riom.

[202] For example, C. Dieuze, Etienne, *D.I., Cahiers de doléances . . . de Dieuze* (Nancy, 1912), p. 401, or T. St. Flour, AP, Vol. VI, pp. 691 *et seq.*

of the States-General, and to form a durable link between the administration of each province and the general legislation . . .,[203]

democratic Provincial-Estates will be established. Others emphasized the abolition of the intendant and the assumption of his duties by the new elective provincial body.[204] Some would have the States-General adopt general principles or measures for the whole of France, but would leave their local application to the provincial government.[205] According to the third estate of Dourdan,

> Let there be established Provincial-Estates subordinate to the States-General, and charged with the assessment and collection of taxes, their payment to the national treasury, the execution of all public works and the examination of all projects useful for the prosperity of the territory (*pays*) situated within the limits of their jurisdiction.[206]

The strongest expression of federalism, and one which might be reënforced by strong regionalism, was a request that the Provincial-Estates be empowered to pass on legislation of the States-General before it would be valid in the province. According to the nobles of Rouen, of the province of Normandy,

> All laws applicable to the duchy, and which bear directly or indirectly upon its constitution, cannot be promulgated until after examination of them by the Estates and after their free consent.[207]

Such statements implied a provincial referendum on national laws. The desire for a measure of decentralization was fairly widespread in the cahiers of all classes and denoted a survival of some provincial feeling and a desire for a provincial autonomy. In most cases, however, this was subordinated to the national structure.

[203] AP, Vol. II, p. 132, art. 22.

[204] For example, C. Beauvais, N. Angers, T. Poitiers. *Cf.* also *supra,* p. 54.

[205] Among the powers assigned to the Provincial-Estates were: (1) assessment and supervision of taxes; (2) supervision of roads, canals, bridges, and other means of communication; (3) supervision and encouragement of agriculture, industry, and commerce; (4) policing of the province; (5) supervision of municipal government; (6) repairs and improvements; (7) administration of the provincial militia or military units; (8) supervision of forests and water supply; (9) supervision of local education; (10) supervision of royal domains; (11) public welfare. Only a few cahiers suggested that the Provincial-Estates elect the deputies to the States-General (e.g., N. Ponthieu, AP, Vol. V, p. 541). Examples of cahiers that assigned wide powers to the Provincial-Estates are: C. Libourne, N. Bailleul, N. Melun, T. Chartres, T. Beauvais, T. Mans(le), etc.

[206] AP, Vol. III, p. 251, art. 18.

[207] AP, Vol. V, p. 594, art. 10.

Federalism was a phase of national patriotism rather than a real obstacle to it.[208]

It was the third form of regional spirit that presented a true obstacle to national patriotism—provincialism. This not only involved an emphasis upon local autonomy, but also implied a sentiment of loyalty to the province. Provincialism meant that the province and not the national unit was the object of patriotism. It was expressed in a number of ways.

In the first place, a large number of cahiers from the frontier regions conceived of their provinces as entities, with rights and traditions quite as definite as those of the national entity, France. Along the northern frontiers, the three cahiers of Bailleul spoke of Maritime Flanders as separate from the Walloon section, and affirmed the treaties, capitulations, and constitution of the territory.[209] The nobles of Avesnes and of Quesnoy referred to the "genius and character of the inhabitants"[210] of Hainaut, and the third estate of Boulogne made a strong appeal to the traditions of the Boulonnais.[211] The cahiers of the Barrois, Lorraine, Trois-Evêchés, Alsace, and Franche-Comté also referred to provincial traditions.[212] Three cahiers of Provence, of the southeast, spoke of the "Provençal nation,"[213] while two cahiers emphasized the dual citizenship of the people—French and Provençal.[214] Although the loss of texts has deprived us of numerous opinions from the Spanish frontier, the cahiers of Navarre, Béarn, and of the clergy and third estate of Ustaritz looked upon their respective territories as separate entities. The clergy of Ustaritz were particularly vehement: they spoke of the purity of their blood, of the military vigor of the Basques, of the Basque language, customs, and tradi-

[208] Good examples of federalist-national patriotism are the cahiers of the third estates of Poitiers, and Vitry-le-françois.

[209] AP, Vol. II, pp. 170, 172, 174.

[210] N. Avesnes, AP, Vol. II, p. 150-51, art. 4.

[211] AP, Vol. II, p. 432, col. 1.

[212] For example, N. St. Mihiel, AP, Vol. II, p. 236, ch. ii; T. Sedan, AP, Vol. V, p. 727, col. 2; C. Colmar, AP, Vol. III, p. 6, art. 19; N. Besançon, AP, Vol. VI, p. 515, art. 1.

[213] N. Brignoles (mandate, MS, *Arch. Nat.* B III 146, p. 509); N. Sisteron, N. Forcalquier.

[214] N. Forcalquier, T. Marseille.

tions.[215] In Brittany, the refusal of the higher clergy and of the nobles to take part in the national elections had been prompted by their strong feeling not only for class privileges, but especially for Breton traditions and prerogatives.[216] The lower clergy and the third estate of Brittany also expressed some consciousness of Breton traditions.[217] The appeal of cahiers of Normandy to the privileges of that duchy was expressed in no uncertain terms.[218] The nobles and third estate of Corsica spoke of the "Corsican nation."[219]

From the interior provinces of France, only a few cahiers expressed a similar feeling for local "nationality." The nobles of Limoges (Haut-Limousin) spoke of their citizens as good defenders of their *patrie,* and as famed for their sobriety, obedience, and vigor.[220] When the third estate of Château-Thierry (which showed, however, a marked national patriotism) was speaking of education in its district, it said, "Genius exists here. It is possible that a second La Fontaine may be born."[221] The French provinces have continued to this day to be proud of their native sons who have risen to national fame.

Besides references to local traditions and "nationality," cahiers of 1789 betrayed provincialism by insisting upon the rights and privileges guaranteed by the various charters which had been granted at the time of the annexation of the respective provinces to the French kingdom. The nobles of Evreux, in Normandy, prefaced their demands for provincial reform with the statement, "that in addition to the rights common to all Frenchmen, the Normans possess those in particular attached to the constitution of the duchy of Normandy. . ."[222] The nobles of Artois spoke of the "national rights" of their province.[223] The nobles of Besançon

[215] AP, Vol. III, p. 424, arts. 52-53, 55.

[216] *Cf.* the *procès-verbal* of their refusal and protest, AP, Vol. V, pp. 627-29.

[217] *Cf.* on language, *supra,* pp. 47 *et seq.* Cf. also T. Nantes, AP, Vol. IV, p. 99, art. 154, etc.

[218] *Cf.* C. Caudebec-en-Caux, AP, Vol. II, p. 573, col. 1; C. Caen, AP, II, p. 488, col. 2, etc.

[219] AP, Vol. III, pp. 41 *et seq.,* and text, reprinted in *Guide.*

[220] AP, Vol. III, p. 565, col. 1.

[221] AP, Vol. II, p. 674, art. 35.

[222] AP, Vol. III, p. 296, col. 2.

[223] AP, Vol. II, p. 79, preamble.

reclaimed the charter of Franche-Comté.[224] From the opposite corner of France, the nobles of Perpignan (province of Roussillon) gave instructions that,

> After having fixed the general constitution, and previous to any discussion of taxes, the deputies will consider the interest of the province, and will uphold its rights with all the zeal of patriotism . . .[225]

The third estate of Aix, one of the districts which had chosen Mirabeau for deputy, declared that "Our deputies will require that Provence be maintained in its constitution as a state, united, principal and not subaltern."[226] From the nobles of Dijon came a denial that "the States-General of the kingdom would have the right to change or modify in any manner whatsoever the constitution of the provincial régime of the province of Burgundy."[227] The third estate of Nantes made reservation of the rights of Brittany,[228] while the third estate of Mende reserved all "the rights, immunities, prerogatives and privileges" of Languedoc,[229] if the States-General failed to enact national reform. A great many of the cahiers of northeastern France were anxious to maintain certain privileges, bilingual,[230] economic, [231] religious,[232] or administrative.[233]

Various examples of concern for provincial privileges have been cited for different parts of France. Such statements sound more peremptory, however, when isolated from the rest of the cahier. They did occur, however, more frequently in cahiers from the frontier districts of France.

Regionalism, whether indicated by localism, federalism, or provincialism, actually assumed three differing degrees of importance in the cahiers of 1789. There were cahiers that subordinated

[224] AP, Vol. VI, p. 515, col. 1.

[225] AP, Vol. V, p. 372, col. 1.

[226] AP, Vol. I, p. 697, col. 2. Mirabeau himself referred to Marseille as his *patrie*. *Cf. Mémoires,* Vol. V, *Troisième lettre de Mirabeau aux députés et commissaires du tiers de Marseille, 7 avril, 1789.*

[227] *Cf.* p.v., *Bibl. Dijon, Fonds Juigné,* no. 44.

[228] *Cf.* Appendix, p. 322, note 17.

[229] AP, Vol. III, p. 756, art. 7.

[230] *Cf.* language, *supra,* pp. 47 *et seq.*

[231] *Cf.* discussion of interior customs duties, *supra,* pp. 56 *et seq.*

[232] For example, C. Longuyon, MS, *Arch. Moselle,* art. 17, or reprint in *Guide.*

[233] *Cf.* T. Strasbourg, T. Dix Villes, etc., on local government.

regionalism to nationalism; there were others that equated regionalism and nationalism; and there were still others that exalted regionalism above national patriotism.

Three illustrations of the subordination of regional to national interests may here be cited. The joint cahier of the clergy and third estate of Bruyères opened as follows: "Lorraine will find the active principle of her own well-being in the same measures that will regenerate France. . ."[234] With the exception of reservations on sharing the national debt contracted before her annexation, and opposing the abolition of interior customs, this cahier gave a full liberal program of national reform, and thus conformed throughout with the thought of its opening words. A second illustration is afforded by the attitude of the nobles of Mende, of the province of Languedoc, who expressly reserved their provincial rights only if the States-General failed to accomplish a national reorganization.[235] Here, the national welfare was foremost, and the provincial secondary. A further illustration of the relative subordination of regional interests was supplied by the Dauphiné. An article of the cahier drawn up by its Provincial-Estates[236] reserved the rights of the province just as had the nobles of Mende. It is significant, however, that this article did not appear in the printed editions of the cahier, and that the conservative Intermediate Commission of the Provincial-Estates appointed two delegates to go to Paris to uphold the constitution and rights of the Dauphiné.[237] In actual fact, the Dauphiné had been an early leader of the revolutionary movement, and its elections prior to the general convocation had inspired many districts of France, but once the National Assembly was formed, the provincial interests reappeared.[238] Cahiers that took an attitude similar to that of the three examples here cited were a forecast of federalism in the Revolution or of a surviving moderate regionalism.

[234] AP, Vol. IV, p. 11, col. 1.

[235] MS addition to cahier, *Arch. Nat.*, Ba 51, art. 12.

[236] The article appears in the summary preserved in the minutes of the Provincial-Estates; *cf.* AP, Vol. III, p. 81, col. 1.

[237] P.v. of the Commission, *Arch. Isère,* III C 4, March 19, 1789. Supplementary instructions were given to the delegates.

[238] The elections in the Dauphiné were in January, but were subsequently legalized. The organization of the Provincial-Estates which had been effected after the disturbances in the summer of 1788, was held up as a model of democratic representation by many cahiers of 1789.

The second shade of regionalism was that which represented an equality of national and regional concern. In cahiers of this character, demands for provincial referenda or insistence upon provincial privileges were expressed along with confidence in national regeneration. For example, the nobles of Poitiers refused any change in the charter of their province without the consent of the Provincial-Estates,[239] but at the same time they expressed a zeal for national regeneration, and outlined a program for national constitutional government. The cahiers of the nobles of Belley and of the clergy of Soule are also good examples of this type of regionalism.[240]

It was the third type of regionalism which represented an obstacle to national patriotism. There were thirty-seven cahiers in 1789 which put regionalism above national interests,[241] and these cahiers came largely from the frontier districts. Along the Flemish frontier, the cahiers, while jealous of provincial privileges, evinced, in general, considerable French patriotism, although some cahiers of the clergy displayed a stronger regionalism. In the northeastern provinces, regionalism waxed stronger as one approached the frontier. Alsace was more separatist than the Barrois, Lorraine, or Trois-Evêchés. The cahiers of Franche-Comté were about evenly divided between those that placed France first, and those that paralleled national and regional loyalty. Burgundy was very jealous of its privileges and proud of its history, but the majority of its cahiers laid greater emphasis upon national patriotism. Provence was, on the whole, national, but numerous cahiers of its clergy were characterized by narrow interest in local church affairs or in an exclusive class spirit.[242] Nevertheless, some of the strongest expressions of national patriotism to be found anywhere in the cahiers were made by cahiers of the third estate of Provence.[243]

Regionalism was stronger on the Spanish frontier than anywhere else in France. Languedoc was primarily national, but the

[239] AP, Vol. V, p. 397, art. 43.

[240] *Cf.* AP, Vol. II, pp. 497 *et seq.* (Belley is the same district as Bugey and Valromey), and AP, Vol. V, pp. 774 *et seq.*

[241] *Cf.* Table XLVII, Appendix, p. 285.

[242] *Cf. infra,* p. 226.

[243] For example, *cf.* T. Aix, Digne, Draguignan, etc.

districts on the frontier itself showed an ultra-regionalism.[244] None were more separatist than the territories of Béarn and Navarre. In the former case, the Estates of Béarn denied that it was a French province.[245] When they consented to send deputies to the States-General, they did so not because of obedience to the royal convocation or of desire to exercise their right to participate in French affairs, but on the grounds of expediency and the reciprocity of French and Béarnese interests.

Navarre went even further in its regionalism. It was never represented in the States-General or its successor, the National Assembly. The long cahier drawn up by the Provincial-Estates of Navarre was an exposition of the rights and traditions of Navarre, centering in the contention that "Navarre is not a province of the kingdom of France, it is a kingdom apart, submitting to the king of France, but distinct and independent of the kingdom of France."[246] Other districts of the south reserved provincial privileges or status, or gave evidence of Basque loyalties, but balanced this by evidences of a national spirit.

The cahiers of Brittany are only a partial gauge of regional sentiment. The struggle between the orders within the province colored the attitude of the lower clergy and the third estate. The upper classes adhered to class and provincial privileges, while the lower classes were sometimes local in their horizon, and often appealed to rights of the Breton constitution against the upper classes.[247]

The upper classes of Normandy were more insistent upon provincial privileges than the third estate, but even the clergy and nobles placed national interests foremost.

One may add a word about the distribution of regionalism among the classes in France. Among the cahiers of the clergy, those along the Flemish frontier (*generalities* of Amiens and Lille) and from Provence showed more regionalism than the rest of the clergy's. Sectionalism among the nobles was expressed in many

[244] The loss of cahiers is a handicap for the Spanish frontier, *cf.* map, and Appendix, pp. 238-39.

[245] *Cf.* p.v., MS, Provincial-Estates of Béarn, *Arch. Nat.* C 16/24, May 25, 1789.

[246] MS text, *Arch. Nat.* K 692 A.

[247] *Cf.*, for example, use of "*peuple breton*" in contradistinction to higher clergy and nobles. T. Rennes, See and Lessort, *op. cit.*, Vol. IV, p. 250, art. 53.

cahiers of the frontier provinces, but with greater emphasis in Normandy and the northeastern provinces—Franche-Comté, the Barrois, Lorraine, Trois-Evêchés, and Alsace.[248] In cahiers of the third estate, regionalism was scattered geographically, and more often reflected a lack of enlightenment or of a national outlook than regional feeling directly hostile to the nation as such.

CLASS SPIRIT.—Antithetical to national fraternity was *esprit de corps*. Although the cahiers and the procès-verbaux contained many statements of harmony and coöperation among the classes, some few preferred the interests of their own class, and made class spirit an obstacle to national patriotism. The third estate of Nemours recognized the need of change when it said: "Ah! It is not *esprit de corps* that must be cultivated; that has caused all the trouble in France."[249]

In cahiers of the clergy, one often found an appeal to the traditions of the church. According to the clergy of Caen,

> Ministers of a sacred religion which we ought to sustain in all our relations with society, the moment has come when it is necessary to ask the king to protect it effectively . . . against the enemies that attack it.[250]

General statements were reënforced by opposition to renunciation of ecclesiastical privileges,[251] by insistence upon the distinction between clergy and laity,[252] or by absorption in the interests of the church.[253] Class spirit in cahiers of the clergy was less frequently evidenced by a single phrase or demand than by the cumulative effect of the whole cahier.

In cahiers of the nobles, pride in the historic rôle of the nobility was frequently expressed, but without exclusiveness or hostility

[248] We have only one cahier of the nobles for Alsace, N. Colmar.

[249] AP, Vol. IV, p. 167, col. 2.

[250] AP, Vol. II, p. 487, col. 1.

[251] For example, the clergy of Gien made no renunciation whatsoever (*cf.* AP, Vol. III, pp. 398 *et seq.*, and p.v., *Arch. Nat.* Ba 43), while the clergy of Clermont Ferrand first made a blanket promise of pecuniary sacrifices for the welfare of the state, and then reserved the privileges of personal immunity from taxation, etc. (AP, Vol. II, p. 764, col. 2).

[252] For example, C. Nivernais, AP, Vol. IV, pp. 246 *et seq.*

[253] For example, the cahiers of the clergy of the *generality* of Aix were prone to omit political problems and to devote their entire attention to church reform (*cf.* C. Arles (ville), Draguignan, etc.). An example of this elsewhere is C. Mende, AP, Vol. III, pp. 751 *et seq.*

to national coöperation.[254] The nobles sometimes cited their past service for the *patrie* as evidence of their contemporary zeal.[255] At other times, they made their pride an obstacle to reform. The nobles of St. Flour were particularly uncompromising:

> The nobles of Haute-Auvergne, despite their love of the *patrie* (a sentiment which will not cease to animate them), cannot sacrifice their financial privileges. These privileges are a property which the nation cannot touch without the consent of the order. They are the reward of services rendered by the nobles . . .[256]

Class spirit lay behind reservation of feudal rights,[257] financial privileges,[258] and restrictions on eligibility to office.[259]

An exclusive class spirit was less frequent in the cahiers of the third estate than in those of the privileged orders. Their egalitarianism was stronger than their *esprit de corps*.[260] Since the third estate was the most numerous class, their interest was more nearly coincident with that of the entire nation. The most class-conscious demand of the third estate was the stipulation of thirty-four cahiers that its deputies could only be chosen from that class.[261] The third estate of Meaux suggested that each class elect deputies only from its own order,[262] but the other thirty-three were interested primarily in the the third estate. A yet more exclusive spirit was shown by the third estate of Nantes which declared:

> The deputies shall be neither ecclesiastics, nobles, nor newly ennobled; likewise, they shall not be chosen from business men, or tax agents, or from seignorial officers, in case seignorial justice is not suppressed; similarly, the representatives of the intendants and the financial officers shall be excluded.[263]

[254] For example, N. La Rochelle, AP, Vol. III, p. 476, art. 13; N. Crépy-en-Valois, AP, Vol. III, p. 74.

[255] For example, N. Nérac, AP, Vol. I, p. 701 *et seq.*

[256] AP, Vol. VI, p. 690, art. 5.

[257] *Cf. supra,* pp. 114 *et seq.*

[258] For example, N. Cahors, AP, Vol. V, p. 490, col. 1.

[259] *Cf. supra,* pp. 86-87.

[260] *Cf. supra,* pp. 87, 90.

[261] T—Angers, Auch, Auray, Auxerre, Aval, Besançon, Bigorre, Bourges, Caen, Châlon-sur-Saône, Châlons-sur-Marne, Chartres, Coutances, Dax, Dijon, Dôle, Etain, Evreux, Grasse, Gien, Lyon, Mans(le), Mantes, Meaux, Montpellier, Nérac, Paris *hors-les-murs,* Paris *intra-muros,* Saumur, Sens, Rodez, Tartas, Villefranche-en-Rouergue, Vitry-le-françois.

[262] AP, Vol. III, p. 728, art. 5.

[263] AP, Vol. IV, p. 94, art. 17.

The third estate of Dax showed perhaps the narrowest class demands of all cahiers of that order, but combined it with many demands for the nation as a whole.[264] No cahier of the third estate was, however, unwilling to share its gains with the clergy and nobles. Class spirit among cahiers of the third estate ignored rather than denounced the other classes.

Although many cahiers made demands that would benefit primarily their own order, only a small number, twenty-six,[265] made class spirit an obstacle to national patriotism. In this group, the prevalence of class spirit among cahiers of the clergy from the southeast is noticeable.

SUMMARY OF PATRIOTISM

The conception of patriotism manifested in the cahiers of 1789 conforms with the description of eighteenth-century patriotism by Stewart and Desjardins[266] in six respects: its utopian tone, its sacrifice of the individual, its self-criticism, its belief that a return of liberty would revive patriotism, its desire for the development of French resources, and its emphasis upon pacific bonds between France and humanity. The self-criticism, however, was seldom in comparison with other European states, but chiefly with the glorious traditions of the past or with impersonal standards of equality and justice. Similarly, the belief that patriotism would be revived was not tinged, in 1789, with any disparagement of past patriotism. On the other hand, there is little or no evidence in the cahiers of four particular features which Stewart and Desjardins have ascribed to French patriotism of the period: its rationalism, its neglect of French traditions, its substitution of the state for the person of the king as the supreme object of loyalty, and its disparagement of France in comparison with other European states. Rationalism in the cahiers was related to democracy and *étatisme* rather than to patriotism, while an appeal to French traditions was well nigh universal. It was the nation and not the state which was replacing the king as the object of patriotism. To be sure, the distinction between the state and the nation was

[264] AP, Vol. III, pp. 95 *et seq.*
[265] *Cf.* Table XLVIII, Appendix, p. 286.
[266] *Cf. supra,* p. 150 and note 1.

not clearly drawn, but the ideal elements of patriotism indicated something else than the state. Furthermore, we have noted how seldom the cahiers referred to foreign countries, either to borrow from them or to disparage them.

If the conception of patriotism formulated by Stewart and Desjardins does not fit the cahiers, what was the concept of patriotism of these documents? In the first place, we must discount seventy-five cahiers,[267] which were so direct or impersonal that they expressed neither patriotism nor any other sentiment.[268] Such cahiers were geographically scattered, though more frequent in the southern and northeastern districts of France. Of the remaining number, eighty-two should be subtracted.[269] These subordinated national patriotism to regional or class loyalty. Such cahiers were distinctly more frequent in the frontier provinces.

In the remaining three hundred and sixty-five cahiers, two characteristics stood out: the union of the king and nation as the object of patriotism, and the mingling of regional and class loyalty with devotion to national interests. Only a minority retained the feudal conception of personal loyalty to the king, while a large minority ignored the monarch and expressed patriotism to the nation.[270] The survival of medieval loyalties was more noticeable in the retention of some class and sectional spirit than in the attitude toward Louis XVI. The dominant note of almost all these cahiers was national regeneration to be inaugurated by universal coöperation of king and nation, and subordination of province, class, or individual to the common good. This was the prevailing tone of patriotism in the cahiers of 1789.

One must not overlook, however, other elements in the French patriotism of 1789. Patriotism was not directed toward a person, and still less toward a defined place. The *patrie* of most Frenchmen in 1789 was a unity of king and nation augmented by national traditions, enhanced by Gallicanism, conditioned by cosmopolitanism, reënforced by economic patriotism, and tempered

[267] *Cf.* Table XLVI, Appendix, p. 284.

[268] Some distinction should be made between the cahiers that showed local or class interest and those that showed local or class sentiment. A few cahiers showed a national interest without, however, any expression of patriotism.

[269] *Cf.* Table XLVI, Appendix, p. 284.

[270] *Cf. supra,* pp. 152, 160.

by a peaceful and unaggressive spirit. A feature of further significance in the cahiers was their witness to the stimulation of patriotism during the electoral period, and to a growing demand for its positive propagation.

What light do the cahiers of early States-Generals throw upon patriotic sentiment in 1789? In the first place, patriotism in the early cahiers was overwhelmingly bound up with a paternalistic monarch. Praise of Louis XVI was less obsequious than that offered to the king by different orders of early States-Generals.[271] Furthermore, the early cahiers expressed none of the demands or ideas denoting a changing conception of the monarchy or the ascription of greater sanctity to the nation.[272] The king, in the early cahiers, was represented as a benevolent despot, an attitude that survived in only a few cahiers of 1789. If an early cahier expressed a superiority of France over other states of Europe, it was superiority of the kingdom, and not of French life or national existence.[273] The early cahiers manifested a personal patriotism toward the king.

Gallicanism had made marked gains since 1614. In the early cahiers of the clergy, the French church had been divided between loyalty to the French king and loyalty to the Roman Catholic Church headed by the pope,[274] while in 1789, the clergy were loyal to the Gallican church even to the point of desiring greater independence of the pope. The lay orders showed an even more marked Gallicanism.

The early cahiers evinced no cosmopolitanism. Their demands relative to the exercise of French citizenship[275] and the absence of any appeal to natural law or universal principles give greater importance to the evidences of cosmopolitanism in 1789. Neither

[271] For example, *cf.* the introductory paragraphs of T. 1614, Lalourcé and Duval, *op. cit.*, Vol. IV, pp. 270-73; C. 1560, *ibid.*, Vol. I, p. 2; T. 1560, *ibid.*, p. 276; T. 1576, *ibid.*, Vol. II, pp. 185-86.

[272] *Cf. supra*, pp. 152 *et seq.* There were also contrary demands. Treason was an act against the king (e.g., N. 1614, T. 1614, Lalourcé and Duval, *op. cit.*, Vol. IV, pp. 170, 273-74). Early cahiers opposed alienation of the royal domain (e.g., C. 1576, T. 1614, *loc. cit.*, Vol. II, p. 105; Vol. IV, p. 373), etc.

[273] For example, T. 1614, Lalourcé and Duval, *op. cit.*, Vol IV, p. 271.

[274] *Cf. supra*, p. 147, and C. 1614, Lalourcé and Duval, *op. cit.*, Vol. IV, pp. 1 *et seq.* on the *Clergé*.

[275] *Cf. supra*, pp. 33 *et seq.*

the early cahiers nor those of 1789 were militaristic, but some of the latter expressed the need of patriotic defense. The early cahiers were written under the shadow of a waning feudal system, and of civil war. Defense for them was against internal foes, and involved class security rather than external defense.[276] By contrast, therefore, the psychology of national defense in the cahiers of 1789 was more pronounced. Imperialism did not enter into the early cahiers, and despite its relative rarity in 1789, one must note an occasional solicitude at the later date for the French colonies.

The greater importance assigned to national considerations in the economic field was another advance of the cahiers of 1789 beyond the early cahiers. The early ones never stated that they aimed at national prosperity, and for the most part, they merely enumerated reforms affecting agriculture, industry, or commerce, without a national perspective.[277] Although the welfare of specific industries or localities was often sought in 1789, the ultimate aim was economic gain for France. In addition, we have noted some positive expressions of economic patriotism in 1789.[278]

Regionalism and class spirit were both far stronger in the early cahiers. Not only did they more frequently include demands for specific provinces,[279] but regional loyalty was also implied in the absence of a national phraseology. Class spirit in the early cahiers[280] was even more marked than regional. There was no national fraternization expressed in the early cahiers.

The comparison of patriotism in 1789 with that manifested prior to 1614 emphasizes certain striking tendencies in national sentiment on the eve of the Revolution. In the first place, movement of opinion was toward the nation and its welfare as the supreme goal of patriotism. Regional and class loyalties, although still existent, were to be sacrificed for the national good. A far greater consciousness of humanity and of France as part of a world-universe was

[276] See comments by Picot, *op. cit.*, Vol. V, pp. 99 *et seq.*, pp. 217 *et seq.*

[277] For example, T. 1614, Lalourcé and Duval, *op. cit.*, Vol. IV, pp. 385 *et seq.*, pp. 466 *et seq.*

[278] *Cf. supra*, pp. 168 *et seq.*

[279] N. 1560, loc. cit., Vol. I, pp. 69 *et seq.* The appearance of demands for separate provinces in the national cahier for the whole of France is doubly significant. Compare, also, the tone of any early cahier with the cahiers of 1789.

[280] *Cf. supra*, p. 280.

shown in 1789 than at previous periods, although the cahiers, instead of ignoring all national distinctions, brought the world to the threshold of France. Individuals in the eighteenth century had expressed a greater cosmopolitanism, and the common people had attained by 1789 a wider horizon and a greater national tolerance than at earlier dates. Pride in France was not accompanied by jealousy or hatred of other countries, while only a few cahiers manifested the missionary attitude that France should aid other peoples. The propagation of patriotism within France was, however, of vital import in 1789.

Not only does the comparison between the cahiers of 1789 and those of earlier times bring out the general tendencies of patriotism on the eve of the Revolution, but it accentuates the prophetic patriotism of the minority. The patriotism of 1791 was forecast in the superior emphasis upon the nation, upon humanity, upon a national mission abroad and propagation at home, upon economic patriotism, upon secular loyalty, and upon the elimination of province and class. This patriotism was strongest in the *generalities* of Paris, Tours, Amiens, Châlons, and in the third estates of Aix and Rennes.[281] It was this patriotism which the leaders in the National Assembly propagated. It required a threat, from internal as well as foreign foes, to national liberty and to the achievements of the Revolution to forge the chauvinism of the later revolutionary and Napoleonic periods. And it may here be emphasized that monarchism was deeply entrenched with the French masses in 1789 and that the disillusionment of nineteenth-century monarchial revivals was needed to divorce French patriotism from the monarchy.

[281] *Cf.* Table XLV, Appendix, p. 283.

CHAPTER VII

NATIONALISM IN THE GENERAL CAHIERS

Early in our discussion of French nationalism, we noted that it combined four elements: consciousness of nationality, democracy, *étatisme,* and patriotism. In the perspective of four hundred years preceding 1789 and of a century and a half since that year, certain developments of each of these factors as manifested in the general cahiers of 1789 assume prominence.

THE ELEMENTS OF NATIONALISM

The conception of nationality laid prime emphasis upon traditions of French monarchy, French Catholicism, and the French nation. A growing consciousness of the physical unity and the peculiar character both of France and of the French people entered into the conception of nationality, at the same time that cosmopolitanism and religious toleration played a larger part than they had at earlier periods. While the French electorate of 1789 manifested a marked desire for greater unity, especially administrative and economic, the interest of a minority in the numerical increase of Frenchmen was a new note. The desire for uniformity coexisted with individualism.

Democracy was a relative matter on the eve of the Revolution. As compared with earlier centuries, opinion was widespread and insistent for constitutional government, and for popular sovereignty, but the conception of "the people" was still largely aristocratic. According to the majority, sovereignty should be exercised jointly and equally by the three classes of the French nation. Only a minority adhered to a more democratic interpretation, and considered the third estate as sovereign. Democratic principles and agencies within the governmental structure were, however, recommended, and they pointed the way of future democratic advance. In view of French evolution in the entire modern era, democratic tendencies in respect to the classes were even more marked in 1789 than governmental democracy. Although the majority retained the three-class system, many demands signified a widespread desire for political equality, and for greater social and economic equality, while, applied to their logical fullness, numerous demands in the cahiers implied the elimination of existing class distinctions. Individualism, as voiced in the general cahiers, laid emphasis upon the individual in relation to national unity, and not as a member of a particular class. Individualism was a revolt against arbitrary government, but it also implied the equal worth of every citizen of the state. This feature of French democracy became increasingly important in the national consciousness, and has remained to the present time as a safeguard against encroaching *étatisme* by the nation. Individualism and political democracy have become traditions of French nationalism.

The cahiers of 1789 were not *étatist,* but they foreshadowed the future extension of state functions along many lines. As compared with previous centuries, the idea of the exclusive sovereignty of the state and of the elimination of plural sovereignty had gained many adherents. An antipapal sentiment prepared the way for state control of the French church. While tangible suggestions for subordination of the church to the state were relatively inconspicuous, the marked development of a secular spirit was preparing the ground for the Civil Constitution of the Clergy. Some increase in state control of education was also advocated, but the most marked *étatist* advances were along three lines—supreme state control of justice, national defense, and public welfare. In the perspective of modern history, the development of utilitarianism and of humanitarianism shown in 1789 was especially notable, while the seeds of "state socialism" had already been sown. Although liberty—that is to say, anti-*étatisme*—was the keynote of press reform and of majority opinion in the economic field, the demand for governmental publicity was significant, and the cahiers were less concerned with eliminating national regulation of agriculture, industry, and commerce, than with abolishing irregular local applications of mercantilism. Whereas individualism was stronger than *étatisme* on the eve of the Revolution, the right of the state to control everything within its dominion was nowhere denied, and many specific future increases in state power were forecast.

The cahiers afford incontestible evidence of a revival or stimulation of French patriotism on the eve of the Revolution. The dominant note of the patriotism of the majority was loyalty to the king and the nation. The movement of opinion toward an ideal of national patriotism is especially marked when we compare the cahiers of 1789 with earlier ones. Although a large part of the electorate retained some degree of loyalty to class or to province, the majority subordinated such loyalty to national sentiment. Patriotism in the cahiers of 1789 was closely bound up with the French monarchy, and gave no clear indication of the conflicting patriotisms developed three years later by Jacobins and *émigrés*. There were, however, other elements than the king and the nation in the 1789 concept of patriotism. The cahiers evinced Gallicanism, a greater degree of cosmopolitanism than at earlier periods, a lack of chauvinism and imperialism (though some germs of these were present), and also some economic nationalism. A most significant development of patriotism on the eve of the Revolution was the desire for its purposeful propagation. While patriotism involved an optimistic expectation of national regeneration, French traditions were closely associated with it. The most advanced "patriots" foreshadowed the patriotism of the Revolution in their expression of an impersonal, ideal devotion to national welfare.

TYPES OF NATIONALISM IN THE GENERAL CAHIERS

Nationalism is something more than the sum of its elements. It includes a consciousness of the joint existence and mutual interaction of the elements. Throughout the foregoing analysis, attention has been centered upon the outstanding developments of each of four elements. Citations and illustrations from individual cahiers have been chosen for their pertinence to the topic at hand. In reality, however, we have been dealing with five hundred and twenty-two documents, each of which represented the thought of a particular group in a definite locality. What kind or degree of national spirit did each *general* cahier of 1789 evince, and what light does this kind or degree throw upon the whole complex of nationalism on the eve of the Revolution?

The limitations of the cahiers as source materials make a synthesis of their collective spirit very difficult. Each cahier expresses opinions on many subjects, many details of which are irrelevant to our subject. Matters bearing directly on nationalism seldom constitute as much as one-third of the bulk of any cahier. Actually, too, the cahiers comprise a series of articles, arranged without regard to logical sequence, or expressed as brief topics whose interpretation was left to the deputies. Conflicting attitudes sometimes appear in the same cahier,[1] while the philosophical purport of specific demands is not always clear, and may even be contradictory. Furthermore, in view of all the possible subjects for reform, the omission of topics must be taken into consideration in estimating the general trend of each cahier.[2] In seeking a common basis of comparison, one is apt to lose sight of eccentricities of individual cahiers. One must endeavor to estimate the aggregate significance of each cahier in relation to all the others.

Certain general differences between the cahiers of the three classes further complicate the problem of a common standard. The clergy naturally gave more space to religious matters and church reform than did the lay orders. The relative amount of attention devoted to political reform was, therefore, less in cahiers of the clergy than in those of the nobles and of the third estate. In respect to the nobles, their cahiers almost universally asked for vote by order in the States-General, an essentially undemocratic request, and yet this might be offset by demands for really democratic reforms along most other lines. Indeed, not all the nobles were conservative, any more than all the third estate was democratic. The third estate was more apt than the two upper classes to state its demands specifically and directly, and it tended to de-

[1] For example, a cahier of the clergy might combine strict conservatism in church matters with altruism toward the third estate. A cahier of the nobles might combine concern for class privileges with suggestions for democratic machinery of government, or insistence upon constitutional monarchy with paternalistic patriotism. A cahier of the third estate might infuse a demand for democratic sovereignty with a narrow class spirit.

[2] Compare, for example, two extreme cases: N. St. Pierre-le-Moutier, a text of about two hundred words in two articles (possibly not authentic), and T. Nemours (also exceptional), which occupies over one hundred pages of print.

tail a series of reforms rather than to enunciate general principles. It also, as a rule, gave more space to local reforms. Such basic differences between the cahiers of the three orders must be recognized in order to establish a fair basis of comparison.

A general difference between the cahiers from outlying provinces and those from districts centering in Paris should also be noted. The former were almost invariably shorter, and gave less attention to matters relevant to nationalism. A cahier of the *generality* of Nancy may appear exceptionally progressive as compared with others of that *generality,* but in comparison with those of the *generality* of Paris it appears less progressive. The cahiers of 1789 represented opinion of particular groups from all over France, and, despite their limitations and the difficulties in the way, a comparison of their import brings out many interesting features of French nationalism on the eve of the Revolution.

According to Professor Hayes, "humanitarian nationalism" was the first philosophical form of nationalism, and was formulated in the eighteenth century.[3] It was based upon the enlightenment of that century, upon ideas of natural law, reason, progress, and the welfare of mankind, but varied in some of its details with different countries, and different philosophers. In the case of Rousseau, whom Professor Hayes discusses as an eighteenth-century nationalist in France, humanitarian nationalism included doctrines of popular sovereignty, self-determination of peoples, liberty, equality, individualism, a desire for reform and for the development of national institutions, an exaltation of secularism, and a regard for fraternity within and among nations. The cahiers show us that the popular mind in France had not adopted *in toto* just such an humanitarian nationalism of the "enlightenment" as Rousseau typified. Many of the ideas in the cahiers must have been inspired by Rousseau, but the philosophical complex of the masses in 1789, as evidenced by the cahiers, contained elements out of harmony with Rousseau's variety of "humanitarian nationalism." The cahiers were not individual opinions, and therein lies their peculiar value in the present study. Reproducing as they do

[3] Hayes, C. J. H., *The Historical Evolution of Modern Nationalism* (New York, 1931), ch. ii, *passim.*

the collective mind of so many electoral districts, they afford us a gauge of national sentiment for the entire French nation.

Among several essential differences between nationalism in the cahiers of 1789 and the humanitarian nationalism of Rousseau as described by Professor Hayes, was the frequent appeal of the former to French tradition. This appeal was very nearly universal, and dominant over the occasional reference to natural law or to reason. Secondly, attention in the cahiers was centered upon reform in France and was accompanied relatively seldom by altruistic assertions of a resulting benefit to humanity. Furthermore, an exaltation of secular power at the expense of the church had advanced much less among the French people than among "enlightened" philosophers. Although many suggestions of the cahiers pointed to future *étatist* development, only a few were strongly *étatist*. Self-determination of peoples was scarcely intimated in the cahiers, while fraternity in them meant a brotherhood of Frenchmen, rather than of all mankind. A cosmopolitan and humanitarian outlook doubtless contributed to keep the cahiers from expressing hostility to other nations, but the focus of attention for the overwhelming majority of cahiers was the general welfare of France alone. Fraternity with other peoples was negative rather than positive. Humanitarianism in the cahiers meant social betterment and humane policy within France, rather than the welfare of humanity at large.

The comprehensiveness of the reform program outlined in the general cahiers makes it possible to define with more precision than does the general survey of Professor Hayes the nationalism manifested on the eve of the Revolution. Undoubtedly its development and expression were colored by events of the electoral period, but in turn the national spirit prevailing in May, 1789, helped to determine the later course of events. Let us see what general types of nationalism the cahiers displayed.

The general cahiers may be classified in five groups as regards nationalism: (1) those which show no nationalism, and those whose nationalism may be described as (2) "conservative," (3) "intermediate," (4) "progressive," and (5) "radical." These are not hard and fast divisions, nor are they purely arbitrary. Like the colors of the spectrum, they shade from one into another, and yet each degree of nationalism, like every color in the spectrum, has an obviously distinct quality.

To the first of our categories—that which shows no nationalism—belong forty-nine cahiers, devoted to local, regional, or class interests.[4] Some of these may include a few expressions or requests of national import, but every one of them is notably lacking in national spirit and way of thinking. A considerable number of the cahiers of this category came from the clergy of the south, but more came from all classes of the *generalities* of Nancy and Metz.

In our second category—that of "conservative nationalism"—we have put such cahiers as emphasized French history and traditions and defended conservative reforms by an appeal to the past. They would retain the plural sovereignty of the old régime in respect to church versus state, province versus central government, class versus nation. They would not sacrifice historic privileges though they might request ameliorative reforms. They stressed the personal element—loyalty to the king—in their patriotism and tended to identify the reform movement with the monarch. As a whole, they lacked the liberalizing tendencies of cahiers of the other types of nationalism, or if they included any novel elements of national consciousness they subordinated them to the old and conservative. Among the cahiers of "conservative nationalism," there were some differences of emphasis according to the social class from which they came. The clergy laid particular stress upon their own privileges and those of the church, and supported the papal headship of Catholicism. The nobles emphasized the historic rule of their class as a reason for retaining and even extending their political leadership. Among the cahiers of the third estate, there was express or tacit approval of the three-fold class division, although a more equitable status was desired. The "conservative" nationalists of the third estate usually lacked breadth of vision, were satisfied with a very limited national program, and, viewing the king as a paternal benefactor, appealed to him. As the phrase suggests, "conservative nationalism" describes those who looked

[4] *Cf.* accompanying charts and summary pp. 208-13.

backward, and whose national consciousness was trammelled by institutions and loyalties of the old régime.

The third of our categories—the second type of nationalism, "intermediate"—is so-called by reason of its hybrid nature. Cahiers of "intermediate nationalism" comprise those which took the middle ground and those which balanced conservatism along some lines with progressivism along others. They were less insistent upon provincial and class privileges, and they would limit the sacrifices which they would make for the good of the nation. They tended to espouse federalism as a safeguard of the rights of localities, and yet while they would retain class distinctions, they would make each class useful to the state. On the whole, they leaned more clearly than the cahiers of "conservative nationalism" toward constitutional monarchy, and they laid some stress upon guarantees against arbitrary action. While they would increase the power of the state in certain respects, they would decrease it in others. Patriotism in these cahiers was directed toward the king as the national regenerator, or toward the union of king and nation. "Intermediate" nationalist cahiers of the clergy dwelt upon the service of the clergy to the Gallican church, but at the same time jealously guarded its special privileges. The nobles referred less often to their class traditions but were still anxious to maintain some of their privileges. The third estate clung to direct co-operation between the monarch and themselves in the cause of reform. They stressed local needs, but manifested a wider horizon than did that part of the third estate which displayed "conservative nationalism." The middle-class democracy of "intermediate nationalism" was within the framework of the existing class system or of a traditional federal state.

In the same category we have also grouped such cahiers as nicely balanced essentially contradictory demands: those that offset a democratic attitude toward classes by a marked religious conservatism; those that accompanied utilitarianism or humanitarianism with insistence upon French traditions; those that united a plea for popular sovereignty with a defense of regionalism, etc. "Intermediate nationalism" looked both backward and forward.

"Progressive nationalism"—our third type of nationalism, and our fourth category—appears in a number of cahiers which reflect a more self-conscious and comprehensive national spirit than do any of the cahiers in the preceding categories. The cahiers here emphasize national unity even at the sacrifice of provincial and class privileges. They express more clearly and in greater detail the need for the establishment of constitutional monarchy, and they make their definitions of popular sovereignty more democratic. They advocate reforms in the direction of liberty and equality. They would have the constitution guarantee not only national rights, but also safeguard individual rights, and at the same time they would have the state extend its functions over the church, education, and social welfare. In economics, "progressive" cahiers were either mercantilist and liberal together, or exclusively liberal, but in either case, their concern was with the stimulation of economic activity. Secularism, utilitarianism, and humanitarianism were aspects of the national consciousness of these cahiers, and their patriotism was directed toward the king and the nation, toward the nation, or toward a symbolic union of the two, while some cahiers of the group voiced the desirability of increasing patriotism. Each of the four major elements in nationalism received a clearer and more comprehensive treatment in the "progressive" cahiers, while at the same time, these cahiers better appreciated the significance of the four elements. If one of the elements was relatively neglected, others were especially stressed. If some regional feeling was still evidenced, it was more than counterbalanced by the fervor of the democratic spirit. If religious conservatism was shown, it was offset by a particularly marked humanitarianism.

"Progressive" cahiers of the clergy were less anxious for ecclesiastical privileges, and more concerned with ecclesiastical service to the nation. The nobles refrained from treating of their historic rôle, and emphasized their potential patriotic utility. The third estate combined a faith in democracy with altruism toward the other classes. "Progressive nationalism" stood for national unification, greater democracy, *étatisme* along a few lines and a more idealized national patriotism.

"Radical nationalism"—our final category—has been employed

to denote the type of nationalism which appeared in some cahiers and which gripped France when foreign war threatened a few years later. "Radical" cahiers constituted a minority of the whole, and they were the most nationalist of all. In them the concepts of nationality, democracy, *étatisme* and patriotism were all more concrete and more advanced, though not always uniformly radical. Even the most radical cahiers were seldom without some conservative items,[5] while none of the cahiers classified as "radical" expressed extreme opinion on every point. In "radical nationalism," as we here use the phrase, the welfare of the nation took precedence over all other loyalties, and unity and uniformity were forcefully advocated. A national constitution and a national declaration of rights were demanded. A more democratic interpretation of sovereignty was advanced; the popular sovereign should be either majority opinion in the States-General, or the majority of the nation irrespective of class. Several "radical" cahiers of the third estate insisted that this estate alone should be sovereign. In respect to classes, "radical" nationalists either presented more thorough programs for the elimination of class privileges, or made some suggestions that struck at the very existence of the class divisions. Individualism was much more marked in "radical" cahiers than among the others. At the same time, the functions of the state were more widely extended and more carefully defined. A secularized church, state direction of education, state publicity, state stimulation of economic life, and state action for public welfare were championed. Both secularism and humanitarianism were more stressed in these cahiers, while an appeal to universal principles and natural law either accompanied references to French traditions or outweighed them. Patriotism was no longer directed toward the monarch, except as a symbol; it was loyalty to the French nation, or to the ideal of a regenerated France. Patriotism was usually reënforced by Gallicanism, by economic nationalism, and by demands for the propagation of patriotism.

"Radical" cahiers of the clergy and nobles would sacrifice traditional rights in the interest of egalitarianism. The third estate would sometimes ignore the upper classes and call itself the na-

[5] *Cf.*, for example, regional demands of the third estate of Rennes.

tion, but more often it would share the altruism of the clergy and nobles and gradually eliminate class distinctions. The clergy would combine Gallicanism and cosmopolitanism with humanitarianism for France. The nobles would occasionally combine an insistence upon their own major rôle in patriotic service with pleas for individualism and for justice for the third estate. The third estate, in turn, would relate any local interest which it mentioned to the national welfare; it would display the same influence of the enlightenment as was displayed by radical nobles; and it would confine its class consciousness to a desire for leadership in national regeneration.

All the ideals and demands of the cahiers of 1789 which evinced an advance in national consciousness over the earlier cahiers, appeared most frequently in the "radical" group of cahiers. Expression of French traits of character, interest in increase of population, desire for French unity, championship of the elective principle, democratic definition of "the people," equalization of provinces and classes, affirmation of individual rights and freedom of the press, advocacy of governmental publicity, patriotic national defense, economic nationalism with a liberal flavor, exclusive sovereignty of the state, secularism, utilitarianism, humanitarianism, cosmopolitanism, and patriotism toward a national ideal—all of these measures and attitudes appeared in the "radical" cahiers and gave them a tone which distinguished them from the cahiers of the other types of nationalism, "conservative," "intermediate," and "progressive." "Radical nationalism" of the cahiers foreshadowed the nationalism of the subsequent Jacobin Revolution.

THE DISTRIBUTION OF TYPES OF NATIONALISM

	None	*Conservative*	*Intermediate*	*Progressive*	*Radical*
Gen. of Paris	Paris V	Etampes C	Beauvais T	Beauvais C, N	Mantes C, N, T
		Provins C	Meaux C, N	Etampes T	Melun C
		Sens C	Nemours C	Meaux T	Montfort U
			Paris h.m. C	Melun N, T	Nemours T
			Paris i.m. C	Nemours N	Paris h.m. T
			Sens N	Paris h.m. N	Paris i.m. N, T
				Provins N, T	Senlis T
				Senlis N	Sens T

	None	*Conservative*	*Intermediate*	*Progressive*	*Radical*
Gen. of Orléans	Gien C	Chartres C Montargis C Orléans C	Blois C Chartres N Dourdan C, T Vendôme C, N	Gien N, T Orléans T Vendôme T	Blois N, T Chartres T Dourdan N Montargis N, T Orléans N
Gen. of Bourges	Bourges C	Bourges N		Bourges T	
Gen. of Moulins		Guéret C, N	Guéret T Moulins N Nivernais C, N	Moulins C, T Nivernais T St Pierre N	St. Pierre T
Gen. of Lyon				Forez C, N, T Lyon V Villefr. C, N, T	Lyon C, N, T
Gen. of Riom		Riom C St. Flour N	Clermont Fer. C, N St. Flour T		Clermont Fer. T Riom N, T
Gen. of Montpellier	Mende C	Annonay N Beziers C Montpellier C Nîmes C Puy C	Beziers N Mende N Montpellier N Nîmes N Puy T Villeneuve C, N	Annonay C, T Mende T Montpellier T Villeneuve T	Nîmes T
Gen. of Toulouse	Castres C	Carcassonne C Castres N Limoux C Toulouse C	Carcassonne T Castelnaud. C, N Limoux N, T Toulouse N	Castres T Castelnaud. T Toulouse. T	Carcassonne N
Gen. of Perpignan		Perpignan N	Perpignan T		
Gen. of Auch	Béarn CN, T Navarre U	Armagnac T Comminges T Quatre Vallées T Rivière C, N Soule C, N	Armagnac C, N Auch C, N, T Bigorre C Comminges N Foix N Rivière T Soule T	Bigorre T Foix T Rustaing U	

	None	*Conservative*	*Intermediate*	*Progressive*	*Radical*
Gen. of Bordeaux	Bazas C Ustaritz C	Bazas N Condom C Dax C Mont-de-M. C Tartas N Ustaritz N	Agen N, T Bazas T Bordeaux C Castelmoron C, N, T Condom N Dax N Libourne C, N T Mont-de-M. T Nérac C, N Périgord N, T Tartas T Ustaritz T	Agen C Bordeaux N Condom T Dax T Nérac T	Bordeaux T
Gen. of Montauban		Cahors C, N	Cahors T Rodez C, N Villefr. T	Rodez T Villefr. N	
Gen. of Limoges		Limoges N Tulle C	Angoulême C, N Dorat N Limoges C, T Tulle T	Angoulême T Dorat C, T Tulle N	
Gen. of La Rochelle		Saintes C	Saintes T St. Jean. N	La Rochelle N Rochefort. T St. Jean. C, T	La Rochelle T Saintes N
Gen. of Poitiers		Marches Com. U Poitiers C, N	Chatellerault C		Chatellerault T Poitiers T
Gen. of Tours		Loudun N	Loudun C, T	Angers C, N Mans(le) C, N Saumur C, N, T Tours C, T	Angers T Mans(le) T Tours N
Gen. of Caen			Caen C, N Coutances C, N	Caen T Coutances T	
Gen. of Alençon		Châteauneuf.C	Bellême N, T	Alençon C, N, T	Bellême C Châteauneuf. N, T

	None	*Conservative*	*Intermediate*	*Progressive*	*Radical*
Gen. of Rouen		Caudebec C Evreux N Rouen N	Caudebec N Chaumont. N, T Evreux C Rouen C	Caudebec T Evreux T	Rouen V
Gen. of Amiens	Boulogne T Calais C	Boulogne C, N	Amiens C, N Montreuil C, T Ponthieu C	Calais T Montreuil N Ponthieu T St. Quentin C, N, T	Amiens T Calais N Péronne C, NT Ponthieu N
Gen. of Lille	Douai C Lille C	Artois C Bailleul C, T Douai N, T	Artois T Bailleul N Lille N, T	Artois N	
Gen. of Soissons	Crépy. C	Soissons C Vermandois C Villers. C	Crépy. N, T Clermont-en-B. C Villers. N, T	Soissons T Vermandois N, T	Château Th. N,T Clermont-en-B. N,T
Gen. of Châlons		Châlons. N Langres T Vitry N	Châlons. C Chaumont. N Sezanne C, N, T Vitry T	Châlons. T Chaumont. T Reims N, T Troyes C, N, T Vitry C	Chaumont C Reims C
Gen. of Dijon	Gex C, N, T Mâcon C	Belley C Châlon-s-S. C Semur. C Trévoux N	Autun C, N, T Bar-s-S. C, N Belley N, T Châlon-s-S. N Charolles C, N Semur N Trévoux T	Auxerre C Bourg-en-B. U Châlon-s-S. T Charolles T Châtillon. C, N, T Dijon C, N Semur T	Auxerre N, T Bar-s-S. T Dijon T Mâcon N, T
Gen. of Besançon		Besançon N	Amont U, T Aval C, N, T Besançon C Dôle N, T	Besançon T Dôle C	
Gen. of Grenoble			Orange C, T	Dauphiné U	

	None	*Conservative*	*Intermediate*	*Progressive*	*Radical*
Gen. of Aix	Arles C Barcelonnette C, T Castellane C Digne C Draguignan C Grasse C Sisteron C	Aix C Arles NT Digne N Forcalquier C Grasse T Marseille C	Forcalquier N Marseille N, T Sisteron N	Aix N, T	Digne T Draguignan T Forcalquier T Toulon T
Gen. of Rennes	St. Brieuc C, N	Carhaix T Dinan T Lesneven T St. Brieuc T St. Malo C	Lannion T Morlaix T Nantes C Quimper T	Auray T Brest T Dol C Nantes T Ploërmel T Rennes C Tréguier C	Rennes T Vannes T
Gen. of Valenciennes		Avesnes C, N Cambrésis N	Avesnes T Cambrésis T Quesnoy N Valenciennes T		
Gen. of Nancy	Bassigny. U Bitche C Bourmont N Bouzonville T Châtel. N Dieuze C, N La Marche T Lixheim T Longuyon C Mirecourt C Thiaucourt N	Boulay C Bourmont C Bouzonville C, N Bruyères N Château-Salins C Châtel T Dieuze T Longuyon N Nancy C, N Nomény C, N Pont-à-M. C, N Sarreguemines T Thiaucourt C, T	Bar-le-Duc N, T Blamont C Boulay T Bourmont T Briey N Château-Salins T Etain C Fénestrange U La Marche C Lixheim CN Lunéville C, N Longuyon T Mirecourt N, T Nancy T Nomény T Pont-à-M. T St. Mihiel N Sarreguemines N Vézelise C	Briey T Darney N Etain T Neufchâteau T Rozières U St. Dié T St. Mihiel C Sarreguemines C Vézelise T Villers. U	Bruyères CT Etain N

	None	*Conservative*	*Intermediate*	*Progressive*	*Radical*
Gen. of Metz	Longwy T Sarrebourg C Sedan T Sarrelouis CN Thionville C, N, T Vic T	Metz C Vic N	Arches U Longwy C, N Metz N, V Sarrebourg N, T Toul C, N, T Verdun C, N, T Vic C	Metz T Mohon U	
Gen. of Strasbourg		Belfort C, T Colmar C, N, T Dix Villes T Haguenau T Strasbourg T			
Corsica	Corsica	Corsica N, T			

Totals:

None:	49	cahiers.	26 C, 7 N, 11 T, 3 U,* 2 CN.
Conservative:	109	"	51 C, 35 N, 21 T, 1 U, 1 NT.
Intermediate:	179	"	49 C, 65 N, 61 T, 3 U, 1 CN.
Progressive:	121	"	25 C, 28 N, 62 T, 6 U.
Radical:	64	"	7 C, 19 N, 35 T, 1 U, 1 CT, 1 NT.

* The cahier of the *ville* of Paris *intra-muros* represented all three orders and has been counted, therefore, with the united orders. This was an exceptional cahier and does not really represent opinion for Paris.

GENERAL CHARACTER.—The accompanying charts, and the map facing p. 214, indicate the distribution of the various types of nationalism among the classes by *generalities*. A glance at the figures summarizing the charts, shows that the largest opinion in 1789 was "intermediate."[6] This is an evidence of the power of tradition in French consciousness on the eve of the Revolution. While 9 percent showed no nationalism, approximately 21 percent were "conservative"; 34 percent "intermediate"; 23 percent, "progressive"; and 12 percent, "radical." These figures also bring out an interesting balance between "conservative" and "progressive" opinion, with a slight advantage on the "progressive" side of the

[6] *Cf. charts*, pp. 208 *et seq.*

scale. The interest of our five-fold classification lies less in the summary figures, however, than in the class and geographic distribution.

One may be surprised, at first, by the greater conservatism of the clergy than of the nobles.[7] In respect to sharing political power with the third estate, the clergy were more liberal than the nobles, but they were prone to devote so much attention to religion and to church affairs that they failed to express many of the newer national attitudes. Conservatism among the clergy was religious and ecclesiastical, whereas among the nobles it was regional and aristocratic. The great majority of the nobles were of the "intermediate" group, neutralizing radicalism along one line with conservatism along another, or desiring only moderate reform. As might be expected, the third estate leaned strongly to the newer nationalism, but it is significant that an almost equally large number were of the "intermediate" group. The appeal of tradition, or fear of arbitrary power, led many assemblies of the third estate to ask for reform of existing institutions, rather than for a completely new régime. The "progressive" spirit was notably dominant among joint cahiers of the three orders, although joint cahiers of the two privileged orders were usually reactionary.[8] The distribution of types of nationalism among the general cahiers of 1789 helps to explain the ensuing coöperation of the clergy with the third estate in forming the National Assembly, and likewise the clergy's subsequent opposition to the Civil Constitution. It also serves to explain the recalcitrancy of the nobles with respect to the sovereignty of the third estate, their coöperation in establishing a constitutional monarchy, and their defection when a radical movement against privileges gathered headway. We should remember that it was the third estate, reënforced by a few members of the clergy, and by "enlightened" deputies from among the nobility, that supplied the leaders of the Revolution.

The accompanying map indicates graphically the nature of

[7] 77 C as opposed to 42 N showed either no nationalism or a "conservative nationalism."

[8] The nobles and third estate of the town of Arles are an exception to this generalization. They prepared a joint cahier as a requirement of the convocation and not as the result of voluntary union.

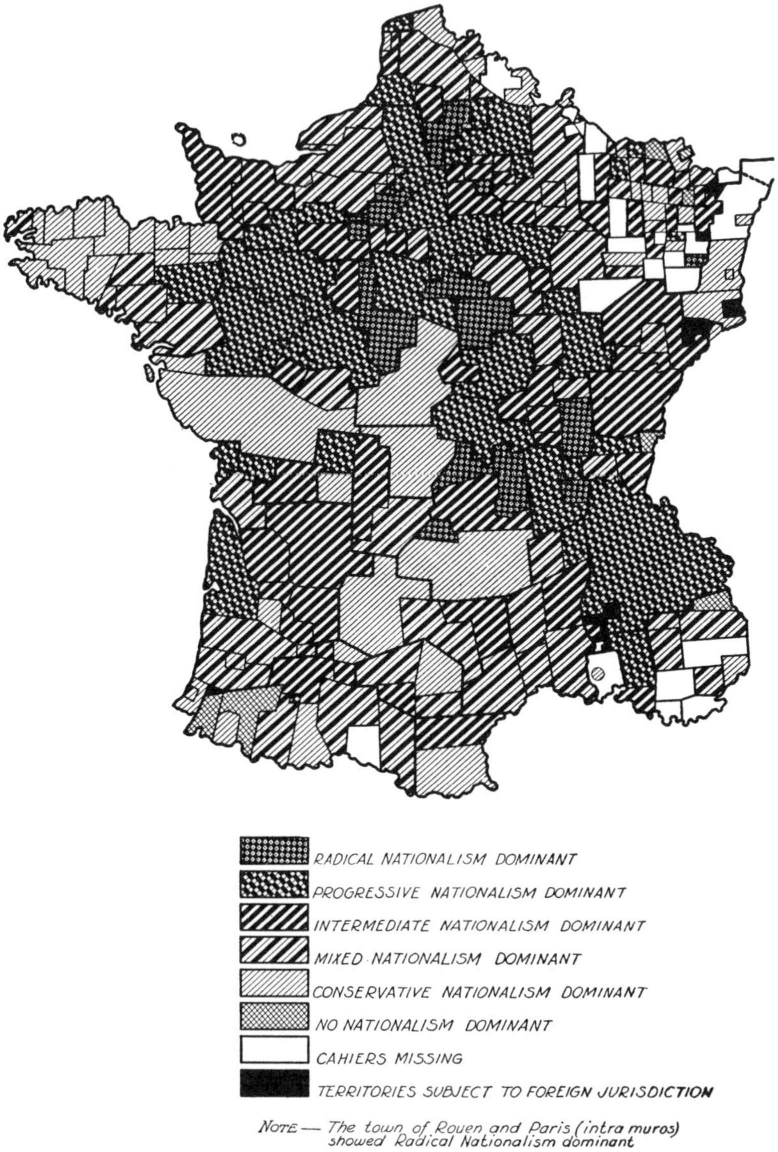

DISTRIBUTION OF DOMINANT NATIONALIST TREND BY BAILLIAGE

Explanation of map is given in Appendix,

nationalist opinion among the several classes of the electoral districts, as well as the general geographical distribution of such opinion. Study of the map reveals, first, numerous differences among the classes within *bailliages,* and second, a lack of unanimity within the *generalities.* Sometimes the clergy and third estate of a *bailliage* displayed the same nationalist trend, sometimes the nobles and third estate.[9] A comparison of Map II with the chart pages 208-13, reveals that in particular districts the two privileged orders were in agreement with each other less often than one of them was in agreement with the third state. The large number of districts where the three classes manifested different types of nationalism is striking, especially in the *generalities* of Montpellier, Toulouse, Auch, Rouen, and Châlons. The diversity of opinion was a prophecy of the tedious discussions of the National Assembly and of its slow achievement of reconstruction in France.

The distribution of national spirit by *generalities* is no less significant than its class dispersion. Nine *generalities* were predominantly "progressive-radical": Paris, Orléans, Moulins, Lyon, La Rochelle, Tours, Alençon, Amiens, and Grenoble, while three others—Châlons, Soissons, and Dijon—were mainly "progressive," though with less agreement among the orders within the several *bailliages,* and consequently with less clearly marked dominance of "progressive nationalism" on the map.[10] In other words, the whole north central area radiating from Paris, stretching through Burgundy and the Dauphiné, and including a disjointed region in the west at La Rochelle, was most nationalist. It was this area that supplied the nationalist program and a large proportion of nationalist leaders for the French Revolution.

Eight *generalities* were largely "intermediate" in their national-

[9] *Cf.* the explanation of the method used in preparing the map, in the Appendix, p. 249. One may repeat here that the various markings indicate the agreement of at least two classes within a district; in the cases of mixed nationalism, none of the three classes agreed. Where one class has been progressive and another radical, the *bailliage* has been represented as progressive.

[10] Compare the chart, pp. 208-13, with the map, p. 214. The dominant "progressive" character of these three *generalities* is disguised by an apparent "intermediate nationalism," arising from the fact that wherever there was difference between the classes we have indicated it as intermediate rather than as progressive.

ism: Montpellier, Toulouse, Bordeaux, Montauban, Limoges, Caen, Rouen, and Besançon. This fact is not indicated on the map as clearly as it should be because of the relatively greater diversity of opinion among the classes within many of the *bailliages*.[11] Nevertheless, the southwest, Normandy and Franche-Comté were "intermediate," ready to join the Revolution or to oppose it, according to the particular problems involved.

Five *generalities* displayed either an even distribution of the different national types, or an even balance between "conservative" and "progressive" districts. These five were the *generalities* of Riom, Auch, Aix, Rennes, and Metz. Each of these represented peculiar conditions. The *generality* of Riom combined a few "radical" cahiers from "enlightened" Riom and Clermont Ferrand with "conservative" cahiers from the mountainous, backward district of St. Flour. In the *generality* of Aix, the loss of cahiers and the contrast of opinion between the classes within *sénéchaussées* present handicaps for an interpretation of opinion. Whereas the cahiers of the clergy evinced "conservative nationalism," if any nationalism at all, some cahiers of the third estate were as "radical" as any in France. Similarly, the *generality* of Auch presented contrasts. Whereas a large number of cahiers were "intermediate," several of those from frontier territories were ultraconservative or regionalist. Besides, in the case of Auch, the classes within a district frequently displayed different types of nationalism. The *generality* of Rennes was likewise exceptional. The loss of cahiers for Brittany does not appear on the map.[12] We find ultraconservatism on the part of the upper clergy and nobility, localism among a large section of the third estate, a divided opinion among the lower clergy, and a very "progressive" spirit among a small section of the third estate. The *generality* of Metz supplied a large number of "intermediate" cahiers, but also many cahiers without any nationalism at all. None of these five *generalities* would be likely to exert a united influence; each subdivision would tend to go its own way.

[11] Compare map, p. 214, and chart, pp. 208-14.

[12] It was impossible to indicate the boundaries of the diocese for the lower clergy as well as the *bailliage* lines for the third estate. Also, where the cahier of only one class is missing, this does not appear on the map.

Whereas the five *generalities* just mentioned afford numerous expressions of "conservative nationalism" or of no nationalism, eight *generalities* were distinctly "conservative:" Bourges, Perpignan, Poitiers, Lille, Valenciennes, Nancy, Strasbourg, and Corsica. The northern, northeastern, and southwestern regions were thus the strongholds of "conservative nationalism," while two or three areas in the central section of the country were only slightly touched by the "progressive" movement.

Elsewhere we have spoken of reservations which should be made in the use of twenty-five cahiers,[13] and here we may speak of the relationship of these dubious cahiers to the foregoing generalizations. For the most part, the twenty-five are so distributed among the different *generalities* and among the different types of nationalism as to leave our general characterizations substantially correct, whether the twenty-five are taken into account or not. Some additional comment seems necessary for two cahiers which are probably more "radical" than the assembly sponsoring them.[14] A protest was made in the assembly of the third estate of Poitiers against some of the very features which led to the classification of their cahier as "radical." The third estate of Nemours acted under "enlightened" leadership, and although there is no evidence that radicalism was forced upon unwilling constituents, still a very radical phraseology in the cahier may have been largely a result of such leadership. About the whole group of dubious cahiers, it might be added that while some were probably more "progressive" than the electoral assemblies to which they were ascribed, others were probably more "conservative," and that the net outcome does not materially modify the generalizations already made concerning the great mass of general cahiers of 1789.

OUTSTANDING NATIONALIST CHARACTERISTICS OF THE GENERALITIES.—Although we have noted the general types of nationalism and their distribution among the classes and electoral districts of France, a closer examination reveals certain dominant trends

[13] *Cf. supra,* p. 12, and list in Appendix, p. 237. This list contained twenty-seven names, but the cahiers of two of the districts have been lost.

[14] T. Nemours, Poitiers. Comments on the other dubious cahiers will be given under their respective *generalities.*

among the cahiers of a single *generality*. These are of special importance for a thorough understanding of the regional evolution of French nationalism.

The *generality* of Paris was the leader in "radical nationalism." Its cahiers were fuller, more "enlightened," and more national than those of most other *generalities*. The nationalists of the *generality* of Paris stressed a formal constitution, a declaration of rights, French traditions, and uniformity. Although emphasizing national severeignty, they were quite moderate in their demands for democratic government. On the other hand, they evinced a fairly democratic attitude in respect of the classes, and laid great stress upon individualism. Utilitarianism and secularism were shown, and humanitarianism was frequent, both in statement and demand. Patriotism was "progressive" or "radical." Gallicanism, cosmopolitanism, and antimilitarism colored the national patriotism, which seldom betrayed federalism or any localism. Traditions of the privileged classes were made to serve the *patrie*. A larger proportion of the cahiers of the *generality* of Paris than of other *generalities* showed an interest in race, in national education, and especially in the propagation of nationalism. All the newer ideas of nationalism may be found here.

In the cahiers of the *generality* of Orléans, the appeal to French traditions was less strong than in the *generality* of Paris, while more cahiers appealed to natural rights. There was marked emphasis upon a formal constitution and especially upon individual rights. While humanitarianism was weak, some of the lay cahiers showed secularism. Democracy, both political and social, was an important note of this area, and so was economic liberalism. While the clergy were more conservative than the corresponding class in the *generality* of Paris, the nobles were very liberal, and the third estate combined with considerable anxiety for its own welfare, a solicitude for democracy. The *generality* of Orléans was concerned with agricultural interests and with reform of local administration, but it also displayed all types of patriotism, from none, or paternalistic, to the most ideal. Whereas there was steadfast support of the monarchy, expressions of patriotism were, on the whole, brief and direct. The nationalism of the *generality* of Orléans, like that of Paris, was predominantly "radical" or "progressive."

The convocation of the *generality* of Bourges was such that, although the *generality* was a fairly large area, it provided only three *general* cahiers, one for each class. The same is true of the *generality* of Perpignan, and of the island of Corsica. In all of these *generalities*, therefore, we have little basis for comparison or generalization, and so we shall pass over them.

The cahiers of the *generality* of Moulins[15] showed a well developed concept of nationality. While the clergy and nobles were generally conservative, the third estate was liberal and egalitarian. The nobles were also strongly humanitarian and secular. The clergy were Gallican in sympathy, and although none of the orders gave many expressions of patriotism, a few cahiers made suggestions for its propagation.

The *generality* of Lyon was entirely "progressive-radical." There was a strongly developed concept of nationality, and a marked interest in uniformity, in a national constitution, and in egalitarian reforms. The cahiers from this *generality* were also strongly humanitarian and *étatist*, while many of them evinced an interest in the broadening of publicity and expressed ardent patriotism.

As we have already said, the cahiers of the *generality* of Riom comprised "enlightened" ones from Riom and Clermont Ferrand, and reactionary ones from St. Flour.[16] In the former, uniformity, economic liberalism, and humanitarianism were especially evident, although there was some regional feeling and a notable lack of democratic spirit. They did, however, ask for patriotic publicity and education, and the cahiers of the nobles displayed a pride in the patriotic rôle of their class. As for the reactionary cahiers of St. Flour, they were characterized by class spirit and localism.

In the *generality* of Montpellier, the clergy and nobles were more conservative than the third estate, but at the same time,

[15] The *bailli* refused to approve the cahier of the nobles of St. Pierre-le-Moutier and he was accused of substituting the short document which is all we possess. It is probable that the nobles were more conservative.

[16] The royal officials interfered in the assembly of the third estate of St. Flour.

the third estate of Nîmes was notably more radical than the third estate in other parts of the *generality*.[17] While the clergy were particularly interested in ecclesiastical affairs, both clergy and nobles displayed considerable class spirit. Gallicanism was, however, strong among all classes. The few cahiers that evinced individualism were very positive in championing it. Sentiment for the province of Languedoc was generally subordinated to national interests. The king was the major object of patriotism, but economic patriotism was more vocal than in neighboring *generalities*. Little appeal was made to French traditions, and almost no humanitarianism or secularism was expressed. The "conservative" cahiers of this *generality* leaned toward the reactionary, while the others were federalist.

The cahiers of Toulouse presented several contrasts. Those of the clergy were undemocratic and strongly favorable to ecclesiastical power, while those of the nobles combined with provincial and class feeling a demand for liberal reforms looking toward the establishment of national sovereignty. The cahiers of the third estate were liberal and more democratic than those of the upper orders, and yet they too showed considerable class spirit. Some cahiers were warmly patriotic and others expressed no such sentiment at all, but regionalism was generally subordinate to national interests. There was little humanitarianism or individualism. Although there was no demand for religious uniformity, there was emphasis on church education. All the cahiers strongly advocated economic liberalism. The cahiers of the *generality* of Toulouse, although chiefly of the "intermediate" group, bordered on the "conservative."

The *generality* of Auch, a frontier area, also presented contrasts. A few of the interior districts were moderate; Béarn and Navarre were regionalist and reactionary; and the loss of cahiers has deprived us of means of gauging opinion in certain neighboring frontier districts. Many cahiers of the *generality* included both a request for confirmation of privileges and a national pro-

[17] There was trouble between the bishop and curates of the assemblies of Puy-en-Velay, and of Beziers. It is possible that the curates would have favored a more liberal cahier. It is uncertain whether the royal officer tampered with the cahier of the third estate of Puy-en-Velay.

gram of reform. In such cahiers, loyalty to Louis XVI formed the patriotic link between provincial traditions and the French nation; and although there was some concern for the substance of individual rights, the conventional phrasing of them was lacking. These cahiers showed little interest in religious uniformity and made no mention of non-Catholics; they evinced little concern for education, and little humanitarianism. The Parlements were approved, and anxiety for accurate notarial records was widespread. With but few demands relative to industry, the point of view for other economic recommendations was liberal.

Most of the cahiers of all classes of the *generality* of Bordeaux were of the "intermediate" type of nationalism.[18] The upper orders appealed to class traditions for patriotic service, while the third estate balanced some class spirit of its own with patriotism toward the king and nation and some interest in individualism. The cahiers of this *generality* was frequently concise, with the result that many questions were not discussed. There was little interest in provincial organization, little Gallicanism, little interest in the army and little in seignorial justice or rural conditions. Economic liberalism received some attention, while the navy elicited some interest.

Among the cahiers of the *generality* of Montauban, there was great emphasis upon the constitution, but little on individual liberty. Patriotism was "conservative" and conditioned by considerable localism. The nobles were patriotic, but very conservative in respect of their own political power. Although some utilitarianism was shown, there was little humanitarianism. Like Bordeaux, Montauban was economically liberal.

The cahiers of the *generality* of Limoges resembled those of the *generalities* of Bordeaux and Montauban, although, on the whole, they were somewhat more "conservative." Limited in topics and terse in style, they combined an interest in the national constitution with localism and made few references to national tradition. Their patriotism was "conservative" but strongly Gal-

[18] It is probable that the nobles of Bordeaux were more conservative than their cahier. The royal officers interfered in the cahiers of the third estate of Mont-de-Marsan and of Périgord, while a coterie of lawyers may have exerted undue influence on the third estate of Agen.

lican. The clergy and third estate were more democratic in the *generality* of Limoges than in the neighboring *generalities,* but the nobles were ultra-aristocratic. Economic liberalism prevailed, although the cahiers of the Limousin were generally pessimistic about their own province. There was almost no humanitarianism.

The *generality* of La Rochelle must be sharply contrasted with its immediate neighbors, for its cahiers resembled those of Paris and the other "progressive-radical" *generalities* in the heart of France. Cosmopolitan, distinctly humanitarian, Gallican, democratic, interested in a formal constitution, federalist, utilitarian—all of these descriptions are applicable to the cahiers of the lay orders of the *generality* of La Rochelle and in only lesser degree to such cahiers of the clergy as have been preserved. All the cahiers of the *generality* displayed consciousness of French nationality and made frequent expressions of patriotism. The classes were patriotic and their patriotism was directed toward king and nation. Liberalism was the dominant note in economic affairs.

Poitiers, like Riom, was a *generality* of divergent opinions. The upper classes were "conservative" and the third estate "radical" or "progressive."[19] The tradition of religious uniformity was strong and some desire for economic uniformity was manifested. All the cahiers were federalist and some were democratic. Cahiers that evinced humanitarianism and cosmopolitanism were markedly developed in these respects. Economic problems called for little attention. Patriotism was conservative.

When we have made the southern circuit of France and arrive at the *generality* of Tours, we return once more to an area where the "progressive nationalism" of the Parisian variety prevailed.[20] Even among the privileged orders, progressivism was the dominant tone. Interest in the constitution and in national uniformity were central. The clergy were anxious for religious uniformity, and Gallicanism was prominent. Although some local demands were

[19] The procedure for the adoption of the cahier of the clergy of Poitiers was irregular. The third estate was more conservative than its cahier.

[20] The original cahiers of the clergy and third estates of Tours have been lost, but the extant summaries are probably accurate. The doubts about the cahiers of the third estate of Loudon do not affect nationalism.

presented, there was no feeling for Touraine as an entity, and little interest in provincial organization. All the classes were much interested in legal reforms and the third estate was particularly opposed to seignorial justice. Humanitarianism and cosmopolitanism characterized most of the cahiers of the *generality* of Tours, while patriotism, when it was expressed, was "progressive."

The *generalities* of Caen and Rouen, both in the province of Normandy, were somewhat alike. The upper classes were "conservative," while the third estate was "progressive." All the cahiers of these *generalities* were interested in a formal constitution and in guarantees of national rights. At the same time, they were solicitous for the rights of Normandy, but these they subordinated to a national patriotism in which the king played the major rôle. The appeal to tradition was especially strong in cahiers of the *generality* of Caen, although some cahiers of the same area also voiced a cosmopolitan philosophy. The desire for the maintenance of the class system was strong throughout Normandy. The cahiers of the *generality* of Rouen evinced some humanitarianism, while those of Caen were more Gallican than those of the neighboring regions. The twofold emphasis upon a national constitution and upon the rights of the province characterized all the Norman cahiers, while those of the third estate sounded a democratic note.

The cahiers of the *generality* of Alençon, between Touraine and the Norman *generalities* of Caen and Rouen, resembled rather the progressive cahiers of Touraine. Alençon was outstandingly democratic, even among the upper classes, and likewise humanitarian and economically liberal. There was also reflected some secularism and utilitarianism. Although reservation for the Norman charter was made, provincial interests were subordinated to national. Patriotism was outspoken, and fraternity among the classes was warmly espoused by some of the cahiers.

The *generality* of Amiens bordered both upon the *generality* of Paris and upon the Flemish frontier and English Channel. Its cahiers were notably patriotic, sometimes toward a paternalistic king and sometimes toward the nation. They made frequent appeal to French traditions, to Gallicanism, or to French territory, and they often ascribed characteristics to the French race. The clergy were exceptionally "progressive" and patriotic.[21] Militarism played some part in these cahiers, and economic liberalism was prominent. Their nationalism showed a federalist tinge. The individual demands of each cahier of the *generality* of Amiens were less striking than the nationalist tone of their ensemble.

The *generality* of Lille also bordered upon the Flemish frontier, but opinion here was less "progressive" than in the *generality* of Amiens. The clergy were distinctly "conservative," both on church rights and upon provincial rights. Contrasted with this, however, was a marked emphasis by the nobles and third estate upon the national constitution. The lay orders were Gallican and showed some militarism and economic nationalism. Much interest in legal reform was displayed. Provincial tradition was strong, but so also was emphasis upon patriotic national reforms. It was usual to approach national reforms from a local point of view. While there was slight humanitarianism, some class spirit and some interest in the broadening of publicity were manifested.

In the *generality* of Soissons,[22] the clergy were socially conservative and even reactionary, but at the same time, Gallican and patriotic. The upper classes were notably altruistic on taxation. All orders showed some class spirit, but usually balanced this by affirmation of national traditions. Many legal reforms were requested, though not from an *étatist* point of view. The *generality* of Soissons was generally federalist. Humanitarianism was prominent and some utilitarianism was expressed. Where individualism was shown, it was very marked. Economic liberalism was dominant, and "progressive" patriotism was frequently and heartily voiced.

In the *generality* of Châlons, unlike that of Soissons, the clergy were unusually liberal.[23] Both the clergy and the third estate of Châlons were democratic. While the nobles of the *generality* clung to seignorial justice, the third estate opposed it. Patriotism toward the king and nation was tempered by devotion to the province of Champagne. Gallicanism played a part in patriotism, and there

[21] The curates of Amiens may have been more "progressive" than the cahier.

[22] There was disorder and interference in the assembly of the third estate of Soissons. Prevailing sentiment may have been more radical than the cahier.

[23] The royal officers had a prominent hand in the cahier of the third estate of Chaumont-en-Bassigny.

were many demands for governmental publicity. The *generality* of Châlons was notably humanitarian and tolerant, and slightly utilitarian. Its cahiers were anxious for national uniformity, but in economic matters they advocated liberalism on the ground that it would be advantageous to Champagne.

The cahiers of the *generality* of Dijon, which comprised the historic province of Burgundy, combined a universal emphasis upon national sovereignty with great interest in provincial government.[24] They were federalist in tendency, rather than regionalist. Interest in province or class was overbalanced by a wide program of national reform. Although emphasis was put upon retention of classes, considerable attention was given to individual rights. Prominent, also, were an humanitarianism, some utilitarianism and secularism, and a desire for national uniformity and education. Patriotism varied from loyalty to the king as the link between Burgundy and the nation, to strong national patriotism. There was an element of Gallicanism and of militarism in some of the patriotic expressions. The cahiers of Gex and of Trévoux, with their strong regionalism and localism and their lack of "enlightenment," were an exception to the general tone of the cahiers of the *generality* of Dijon.

The *generality* of Besançon, which corresponded with the province of Franche-Comté, combined in its cahiers some strongly nationalist demands and attitudes with statements of provincial traditions and aims.[25] The latter, however, were subordinated to the former. The *generality* of Besançon was generally federalist. The clergy and nobles were altruistic, but the third estate evinced considerable class spirit. While these cahiers expressed every type of patriotism, they also evinced strong Gallicanism and some militarism. They were also pronouncedly humanitarian.

The *generality* of Grenoble, consisting chiefly of the province of the Dauphiné, was not fairly represented in the number of *general* cahiers,[26] but such as we possess are liberal in tone. They

[24] The clergy of Dijon may have been more "progressive" than their cahier.

[25] The clergy and nobles of Amont were probably more conservative than the joint cahier of the three orders.

[26] *Cf. supra*, p. 188. For this large area, due to the method of convocation, there should be four general cahiers. One has been lost (N. Orange), while only a summary of the cahier of the Provincial-Estates of the Dauphiné has survived.

set forth a short, but national program, with some federalist leanings. Although the Dauphiné exerted a revolutionary influence prior to the opening of the States-General, its cahier was moderate in tone.

The *generality* of Aix was not a homogeneous unit. The clergy were particularist and self-centered.[27] In the few cahiers of the nobles that exist, some were national, and some regional. They combined altruism for the third estate with championship of the provincial nobility. The third estate was Gallican but anticlerical, and individualistic but not egalitarian. It manifested strong class spirit, and combined a radical national program with a demand for enactment of local reforms by the States-General. Little direct patriotism was expressed, but a few cahiers were "radical" and cosmopolitan, and stressed the propagation of patriotism by national education. National traditions were balanced by Provençal traditions.

The *generality* of Rennes, like that of Aix, represented extremes in its cahiers: on the one hand, those of the upper classes that were selfish, antinational and separatist; and on the other hand, a few of those of the third estate that were among the most "radical" in all France. The "progressive" tone of most of the cahiers of the third estate was unquestionably due to the influence and propaganda of leaders in the provincial struggle against the upper classes. While the upper classes were predominantly regionalist, the lower clergy and third estate were also anxious to safeguard the rights of Brittany. The third estate showed the greatest unity and coöperation among its own members and the strongest class spirit. They desired egalitarian reforms to benefit the common peasant and universally denounced the seignorial régime. A socializing tendency was more marked in Brittany than elsewhere. Except by the few radical cahiers, comparatively little attention was paid to national reorganization. On the other hand, much space was devoted to economic questions, and the merchant marine and colonial trade elicited many articles. The lower classes

[27] The clergy of Draguiguan could not agree on one cahier, so that all the preliminary cahiers were to be given to the deputy. Only two of these were verified by the secretary of the assembly.

were Gallican and humanitarian. While there was little patriotic phraseology, patriotism was generally of an ideal sort.

The *generality* of Valenciennes comprised several small districts along the border of the Austrian Netherlands. Its cahiers combined an interest in the national constitution with detailed recommendations concerning local administration. There was, however, less concern for provincial privileges than among most other *pays d'état*. Loyalty to the king was the common form of patriotism. The nobles betrayed the influence of enlightened constitutional philosophy, while the clergy and third estate made direct, terse demands without reference to any philosophy. There was some humanitarianism and but little concern with religion. Opinion was divided upon economic policy.

Among the relatively large number of cahiers from the *generality* of Nancy, a few were "progressive" in their nationalism, but most were either "conservative" or quite devoid of nationalism.[28] In general, regional and local feeling outweighed national sentiment or rendered it synonymous with retention of the old régime. There was little appeal to French nationality, but some Gallicanism, militarism, and economic patriotism were expressed. Insistence upon a constitutional monarchy was the chief demand which could be called national. The clergy were especially "conservative." On the other hand, it must be borne in mind that a few cahiers of each order and a few of the joint cahiers offered "progressive" programs similar to those of the *generality* of Paris. By and large, however, the Barrois and Lorraine were regionalist and stood for "conservative nationalism."

The *generality* of Metz was exceptional.[29] Its cahiers were less regional than those of Nancy, but also less expressive of national patriotism. Where patriotism was expressed, it meant loyalty to the French nation. Although economically separatist, the *generality* of Metz was less concerned with provincial administration than many another *pays d'état*. There was some individualism,

[28] The cahier of U. Bassigny-Barrois was exceptional, late in composition, and without proper authentication.

[29] *Cf. supra*, p. 216. Note that the various districts of the *generality* of Metz were not all contiguous.

Gallicanism, and militarism, but little humanitarianism and little evident consciousness of French nationality. The *generality* of Metz was, however, more liberal than other sections of the northeast.

The *generality* of Strasbourg was almost more regional than nationalist. Both economically and administratively, the interests of the province were foremost, and yet demands for a national constitutional monarchy were prominent. National reforms were approached from a regional point of view.

In general, we may think of France as composed of three concentric circles, centering in Paris. The inner circle was characterized by "progressive-radical nationalism," the middle circle by "intermediate nationalism," and the outer circle by "conservative nationalism" verging on the absence of nationalism. Such was the distribution of nationalism to which our study points throughout France on the eve of the Revolution.

THE INFLUENCE OF THE GENERAL CAHIERS

Although our chief interest in the cahiers of 1789 is in the national sentiment which they reflected on the eve of the Revolution, we must not forget that they were used by the deputies as guides, and that they exerted, therefore, an influence upon the course of the Revolution, particularly upon the procedure of the States-General and then upon that of the National Assembly.

A comparison of the imperative mandates issued with various cahiers[30] brings out the interesting fact that more of them were directed toward assuring the establishment of constitutional government than toward protecting class or provincial privileges.[31] Of the two hundred and thirty-two imperative mandates for which we possess the corresponding cahiers, 5 per cent were from districts showing no nationalism and 20 per cent were from districts whose nationalism was "conservative," while 37 per cent were "in-

[30] *Cf. supra*, p. 18, for a discussion of the issuance of mandates, of the motives for their issuance, and of their repudiation.

[31] The following figures do not include districts which made the entire cahier imperative. 125 cahiers with imperative mandates required the making of the national constitution before other business (15 C, 65 N, 40 T, 3 U, I CN, 1 NT). Only 32 cahiers made imperative demands for the provinces (8 C, 13 N, 10 T, 1 CN). Vote by order was imperative for 39 cahiers (5 C, 34 N) and vote by head for only 15 (1 C, 12 T, 2 U).

termediate," 23 per cent were "progressive," and 15 per cent were "radical" in the nationalism.[32] These percentages presaged the ensuing struggle for the transformation of the States-General into the National Assembly and the ultimate triumph of "progressive-radical nationalism."

The printing of many of the cahiers in 1789 had a significant bearing upon their influence. The texts of cahiers were much in demand,[33] and their publication helped to swell, with the added weight of their official character, the great volume of political writing published in 1788 and 1789. Two hundred and sixty-three general cahiers were published in 1789, that is to say, less than half of all the general cahiers, but more than half of those now extant.[34] Of this number, fifty-four were cahiers of the clergy; one hundred and five, of the nobles; ninety-two, of the third estate; eight, of the united orders; one, of the clergy and nobles united; one, of the clergy and third estate united; and two, of the nobles and third estate united. It is likely that the cost of printing deterred numerous districts from voting for publication, while the same reason may explain the smaller ratio of printed cahiers from the third estate.

What publication there was, was widely distributed although the frontier *generalities*, especially those of Nancy, Metz, Besançon, Aix, and Rennes, published comparatively few cahiers. Two *generalities*, Lille and Rouen, printed almost all of their cahiers.[35] In six *generalities*, all three orders adopted publication equally:

[32] A comparison of the tables of imperative mandates and of the chart of types of nationalism brings out the following statistics:

No nationalism with imperative mandate: 5 C, 2 N, 3 T, 1 CN—11.
Conservative nationalism with imperative mandate: 18 C, 22 N, 6 T, 1 NT—47.
Intermediate nationalism with imperative mandate: 10 C, 52 N, 22 T, 1 U, 1 CN—86.
Progressive nationalism with imperative mandate: 3 C, 21 N, 24 T, 5 U—53.
Radical nationalism with imperative mandate: 2 C, 15 N, 15 T, 1 U, 1 CT, 1 NT—35.
Total: 232 imperative mandates (19 cahiers, from total of 251, missing).

[33] *Cf. supra*, p. 17.

[34] Compare lists in Appendix, pp. 237-44 and 244-45. Of 615 general cahiers, 263 were printed (not including one colonial document), whereas we now possess 522 general texts. In some cases, the electoral assembly voted to print the cahier but no printed example has survived. The *procès-verbaux* are helpful in the determination of the number of cahiers printed.

[35] Lille printed 11 out of 12 cahiers, Rouen 13 out of 14.

Paris, Limoges, Rouen, Amiens, Lille, and Dijon. Three *generalities* were exceptional in that more cahiers of the third estate than of the nobles were printed: Auch, Valenciennes, and Strasbourg. Although the *generality* of Orléans was "progressive," only one cahier of the third estate was printed as against twelve from the privileged orders.

The different types of nationalism represented among the printed cahiers are significant.[36] Whereas 25 per cent of the cahiers showing no nationalism were printed, and 43 per cent of cahiers, whose nationalism was "conservative," 52 per cent of those of "intermediate nationalism" were printed, 54 per cent of "progressive," and 70 per cent of "radical." This ascending rate toward the "radical" type of nationalism would seem to indicate that the more extreme nationalists were the more active in propagating their nationalism.

When we consider the types of nationalism in relation to the total number of printed cahiers, we discover a somewhat larger number of the more "progressive' and "radical" cahiers in circulation. Out of a total number of printed cahiers, 4 per cent were without nationalism and 19 per cent of "conservative nationalism," while 36 per cent were "intermediate," 25 per cent "progressive" and 17 per cent "radical" in nationalism.[37] It is reasonable to suppose that the printed cahiers circulated locally before they reached other parts of France. From this supposition, it would follow that the more conservative cahiers must have received widespread attention in the *generalities* of Toulouse, Auch, Perpignan, Bordeaux, Montauban, Lille, Valenciennes, Nancy, Metz, and Strasbourg[38]; in other words, in the outlying provinces of France, where regionalism and class spirit were already much in evidence. On the other hand, it would follow also that the radical nationalist spirit would be in the *generalities* of Paris, Orléans (to a lesser degree), Lyon, Tours, and Amiens. Eventually, cahiers of different types must have circulated throughout France. The slightly larger number of "progressive" and "radical" cahiers, and the probability that Parisian cahiers were more widely read

[36] *Cf.* Table XLIX, Appendix, p. 286.
[37] These percentages are calculated from Table XLIX.
[38] *Cf.* the same table.

in the provinces than provincial cahiers in Paris, would appear to give a considerable advantage to the revolutionary forces, while the circulation of texts sent out to the provinces from the more "radical" districts surrounding Paris would be apt to exert a leavening influence in bringing provincial France into line with the capital. Thus, the cahiers, by their publication and circulation, helped to spread the very ideas which came to dominate the National Assembly later in 1789.

A circumstance which may have contributed to the circulation of printed texts, and to the spread of information from Paris among the provinces, was the appointment of committees of correspondence by approximately one hundred electoral assemblies.[39] Such committees were intended to keep in touch with the deputies of the district, to furnish them with information about the *bailliage,* to act as a link between the deputies and the electorate, and to receive information to be disseminated among the constituents.[40] In one sense, the creation of such committees was an attempt to perpetuate the electoral assemblies. The history of these committees has yet to be written, but in view of the motives for their appointment, there is no doubt that they served as centers for the dissemination of knowledge about events at Versailles and Paris.[41] They may also have served as agents for the circulation of the cahiers.

Some distinction should be made between the general influence of the cahiers of 1789 and their actual contents. In view of the later trend of French history, the cahiers appear to us today as very moderate in tone. With our knowledge of subsequent events. we are perhaps disappointed that the cahiers appealed so often to tradition, gave so conservative a definition of popular sovereignty, made so slight an attack on classes, and showed themselves so loathe to eradicate provincial boundaries. We look among the cahiers in vain for the republicanism of '93, the secularism of the Convention, the missionary aggressiveness of the armies of the

[39] *Cf.* list in Appendix, p. 246.

[40] *Cf.*, for example, the reasons for naming such committees: N. Toulon (p.v., *Arch. Nat.* C 24/158), T. Ponthieu (p.v., *Arch. Nat.* C 22/112), N. Perpignan (p.v., *Arch. Nat.* Ba 67), U. Montfort l'Amaury (p.v., *Arch. Nat.* Ba 54).

[41] *Cf.*, especially, T. Marseille (p.v., *Arch. Nat.* C 19/96), and T. Vannes (p.v., *Arch. Nat.* C 25/167).

first Republic, or the violence employed within France to establish the revolutionary reforms. To contemporaries, however, the cahiers of 1789 would appear more revolutionary than to us. What reading matter could a curious citizen obtain during the first months of 1789? There was the *Gazette de France* with its details of the court and its silence on immediate political events. There was the *Mercure de France* with some fuller national news but with chief emphasis on long literary articles. The writings of eighteenth-century philosophers did not have a serviceable concreteness for immediate problems; their theoretical character was in contrast with the swift moving actualities of the moment. Numerous pamphlets appeared, of course, with discussion of current problems, and some of them were more radical than the cahiers, but they all voiced the opinions of individuals. The legal formulae of royal edicts and regulations were so baffling that even the royal officers were often doubtful as to what they meant or how they should be enforced.

Into this situation came the cahiers of 1789. These represented group opinions, and they carried added weight because of their official character. Moreover, their brevity and terseness admitted of quick reading. Such a reading of several cahiers, without attention to the infinite variety of articles, would give a widespread cumulative impression of similarity. The similarity of form, the repetition of demands, and the comprehensiveness of recommendations must have struck many a reader in 1789. And thus the cahiers, themselves moderate in tone, would be a powerful force in making French opinion more "radical." They were, indeed, an important factor in stimulating national consciousness, and spreading the more progressive types of nationalism.

The nationalism of the cahiers of 1789 was the precursor of the nationalism developed during the Revolution, which in turn, foreshadowed the evolution of nationalism during the nineteenth century. Many changes have taken place and yet the puissant French nationalism of post-war Europe displays many characteristics in common with that which transformed the old régime.

Consciousness of nationality is infinitely more acute today than in 1789, and yet its cultural and cosmopolitan aspects were foreshadowed at the earlier period. French national consciousness now combines with an ethnic exclusiveness and a conviction of French superiority, a cosmopolitan patronage of other peoples and a patriotic pride in the contributions of France to the world's civilization. Tradition is as important an element in the French mind at the present time as it was in 1789, but it now includes novel traditions from various revolutions. While France has achieved political democracy and has erected individualist safeguards for her citizens against political and social tyranny, she has retained a large measure of social aristocracy. Birth and station are still criteria, along with wealth and education. Today, while France is eminently *étatist,* she appears, in comparison with her Fascist and Nazi neighbors, a stronghold of liberty and individualism. Honor is still an ideal both of individual and of national action.

Although Church and State have been divorced, the tradition of French Catholicism is well nigh universal in France today. There is, however, the same undercurrent of scepticism and toleration that was felt on the eve of the Revolution. The nation has dethroned its monarch, but it has retained and increased the national patriotism which it evidenced in the cahiers of 1789. Economic nationalism has, to be sure, been forged more firmly by the Industrial Revolution and by the exigencies of twentieth-century warfare, but some of its varied hues were already reflected in the economic spectrum of the cahiers. French imperialism has also increased since 1789, and its basic patriotic psychology was exhibited in a few of the general cahiers. Although Frenchmen have ever been hardy defenders of French soil, the masses of the people today are no more consciously militaristic than in 1789. Deprived of administrative semi-independence, the provinces of France yet retain many distinctly cultural traditions. Contemporary patriotism, still displays an element of regionalism, though much less so now than at the time of the cahiers. Idealism and utilitarianism have been fused in the French mind of the twentieth century, and while humanitarianism is applied today in many French institutions, it also supplies a cosmopolitan motive for the international rôle of contemporary France.

Between 1614 and 1789 occurred fundamental changes in

French national spirit. We would scarcely expect that the period between 1789 and 1934—a period traversed by three major political revolutions, two world wars, an industrial revolution, the rise of a new imperialism, and a prodigious technological and cultural advance—should pass without further nationalist developments and changes. It is remarkable, in the circumstances, that so many of the subsequent developments and changes of French nationalism were foreshadowed by the *general* cahiers of 1789.

APPENDIX

LIST OF GENERAL CAHIERS FOR WHICH SPECIAL RESERVATION ON THEIR VALUE IS MADE

Total: 27 cahiers. 9 C, 3 N, 12 T, 3 U

T. Agen, C. Amiens, U. Amont, U. Bassigny-Barrois, C. Beziers, N. Bordeaux, T. Chaumont-en-Bassigny, U. Dauphiné, C. Dijon, C. Draguignan, T. Loudun, T. Mont-de-Marsan, C. Nantes, T. Nemours, T. Périgord, T. Perpignan, C, T, Poitiers, C, T, Puy-en-Velay, N. St. Pierre-le-Moutier, T. Soissons, T. St. Flour, C, T, Tours.

If we possessed the texts of C. Toulon and N. Hyères, they should also be included in this list.

LISTS OF GENERAL CAHIERS BY GENERALITY

	C	*N*	*T*	*U*	*Total*
Generality of Paris (35)					
Used (33)	10	10	11	2	
Beauvais C, N, T, Etampes C, T, Mantes C, N, T, Meaux C, N, T, Melun C, N, T, Montfort l'Amaury U, Nemours C, N, T, Paris *hors-les-murs* C, N, T, Paris *intra-muros* C, N, T, V,[1] Provins C, N, T, Senlis N, T, Sens C, N, T.					
Missing (2)	1	1			
Etampes N, Senlis C.					
					35
Generality of Orléans (21)					
Used (21)	7	7	7		
Blois C, N, T, Chartres C, N, T, Dourdan C, N, T, Gien C, N, T, Montargis C, N, T, Orléans C, N, T, Vendôme C, N, T.					
					21
Generality of Bourges (3)					
Used (3)	1	1	1		
Bourges C, N, T.					
					3
Generality of Moulins (12)					
Used (11)	3	4	4		

[1] The cahier of the municipality of Paris has been counted among those of all three orders jointly.

	C	N	T	U	Total
Guéret C, N, T, Moulins C, N, T, Nivernais C, N, T, St. Pierre-le-Moutier N, T.					
Missing (1)	1				
St. Pierre-le-Moutier C.					
					12
Generality of Lyon (10)					
Used (10)	3	3	4		
Forez C, N, T, Lyon C, N, T, V, Villefranche-de-Beaujolais C, N, T.					
					10
Generality of Riom (9)					
Used (8)	2	3	3		
Clermont-Ferrand C, N, T, Riom C, N, T, St. Flour N, T.					
Missing (1)	1				
St. Flour C.					
					9
Generality of Montpellier (21)					
Used (19)	7	6	6		
Annonay C, N, T, Beziers C, N, Mende C, N, T, Montpellier C, N, T, Nîmes C, N, T, Puy-en-Velay C, T, Villeneuve-de-Berg C, N, T.					
Missing (2)		1	1		
Beziers T, Puy-en-Velay N.					
					21
Generality of Toulouse (15)					
Used (15)	5	5	5		
Carcassonne C, N, T, Castres C, N, T, Castelnaudary C, N, T, Limoux C, N, T, Toulouse C, N, T.					
					15
Generality of Perpignan (3)					
Used (2)		1	1		
Perpignan N, T.					
Missing (1)	1				
Perpignan C.					
					3
Generality of Auch (29)					
Used (23)	5	6	9	2U 1CN	
Armagnac C, N, T, Auch C, N, T, Béarn CN, T, Bigorre C, T, Comminges N, T, Foix N, T,					

	C	*N*	*T*	*U*	*Total*
Navarre U, Quatre-Vallées T, Rivière-Verdun C, N, T, Rustaing U, Soule C, N, T.					
Missing (6)	4	1		1NT	
Béarn C,[2] Bigorre N, Comminges C, Couserans C, NT, Foix C.					
					29
Generality of Bordeaux (35)					
Used (33)	10	11	12		
Agen, C, N, T, Bazas C, N, T, Bordeaux C, N, T, Castelmoron d'Albret C, N, T, Condom C, N, T, Dax C, N, T, Libourne C, N, T, Mont-de-Marsan C, T, Nérac C, N, T, Périgord N, T, Tartas N, T, Ustaritz C, N, T.					
Missing (2)	1	1			
Mont-de-Marsan N, Périgord C.					
					35
Generality of Montauban (9)					
Used (8)	2	3	3		
Cahors C, N, T, Rodez C, N, T, Villefranche-en-Rouergue N, T.					
Missing (1)	1				
Villefranche-en-Rouergue C.					
					9
Generality of Limoges (12)					
Used (12)	4	4	4		
Angoulême C, N, T, Dorat C, N, T, Limoges C, N, T, Tulle C, N, T.					
					12
Generality of La Rochelle (10)					
Used (9)	2	3	4		
La Rochelle N, T, Saintes C, N, T, St. Jean d'Angely C, N, T, Rochefort T.					
Missing (1)	1				
La Rochelle C.					
					10
Generality of Poitiers (7)					
Used (6)	2	1	2	1U	
Chatellerault C, T, Marches Communes U, Poitiers C, N, T.					

---

[2] Lower Clergy.

	C	*N*	*T*	*U*	*Total*
Missing (1)		1			
Chatellerault N.					
					7
Generality of Tours (15)					
Used (15)	5	5	5		
Angers C, N, T, Loudun C, N, T, Mans (le) C, N, T, Saumur C, N, T, Tours C, N, T.					
					15
Generality of Caen (6)					
Used (6)	2	2	2		
Caen C, N, T, Coutances C, N, T.					
					6
Generality of Alençon (9)					
Used (9)	3	3	3		
Alençon C, N, T, Châteauneuf-en-Thimerais C, N, T, Bellême C, N, T.					
					9
Generality of Rouen (13)					
Used (11)	3	4	4		
Caudebec-en-Caux C, N, T, Chaumont-en-Vexin N, T, Evreux C, N, T, Rouen C, N, V.					
Missing (2)	1		1		
Chaumont-en-Vexin C, Rouen T.					
					13
Generality of Amiens (20)					
Used (20)	7	6	6	1NT	
Amiens C, N, T, Boulogne-sur-Mer C, N, T, Calais C, N, T, Montreuil-sur-Mer C, N, T, Péronne C, NT, Ponthieu C, N, T, St. Quentin C, N, T.					
					20
Generality of Lille (12)					
Used (12)	4	4	4		
Artois C, N, T, Bailleul C, N, T, Douai C, N, T, Lille C, N, T.					
					12
Generality of Soissons (18)					
Used (16)	5	5	6		
Château-Thierry N, T, Crépy-en-Valois C, N, T, Clermont-en-Beauvoisis C, N, T, Soissons C, T, Vermandois C, N, T, Villers-Cotterets C, N, T.					

	C	*N*	*T*	*U*	*Total*
Missing (2)	1	1			
Château-Thierry C, Soissons N.					
					18
Generality of Châlons (21)					
Used (19)	6	6	7		
Châlons-sur-Marne C, N, T, Chaumont-en-Bassigny C, N, T, Langres T, Reims, C, N, T, Sézanne C, N, T, Troyes C, N, T, Vitry-le-françois C, N, T.					
Missing (2)		1		1U	
Langres U, N.					
					21
Generality of Dijon (37)					
Used (36)	11	12	12	1U	
Autun C, N, T, Auxerre C, N, T, Bar-sur-Seine C, N, T, Belley C, N, T, Bourg-en-Bresse U, Châlon-sur-Saône C, N, T, Charolles C, N, T, Châtillon-sur-Seine C, N, T, Dijon C, N, T, Gex C, N, T, Mâcon C, N, T, Semur-en-Auxois C, N, T, Trévoux N, T.					
Missing (1)	1				
Trévoux C.					
					37
Generality of Besançon (11)					
Used (11)	3	3	4	1U	
Amont U, T, Aval C, N, T, Besançon C, N, T, Dôle C, N, T.					
					11
Generality of Grenoble (4)					
Used (3)	1		1	1U	
Dauphiné U, Orange C, T.					
Missing (1)		1			
Orange N.					
					4
Generality of Aix (39)					
Used (24)	10	5	8	1NT	
Aix C, N, T, Arles(ville) C, NT, Barcelonnette C, T, Castellane C, Digne C, N, T, Draguignan C, T, Forcalquier C, N, T, Grasse C, T, Marseilles C, N, T, Sisteron C, N, Toulon T.					

	C	*N*	*T*	*U*	*Total*
Missing (15)	4	6	5		
Arles (*sen.*) C, N, T, Brignoles C, N, T, Castellane N, T, Draguignan N, Hyères C, N, T, Sisteron T, Toulon C, N.					
					39
Generality of Rennes (29)					
Used (20)	6	1	13		
Auray T, Brest T, Carhaix T, Dinan T, Dol C,[2] Lannion T, Lesneven T, Morlaix T, Nantes C[2], T, Ploërmel T, Quimper T, Rennes C,[2] T, St. Brieuc C, N, T, St. Malo C,[2] Tréguier C,[2] Vannes T.					
Missing (9)	3		6		
Fougères T, Hédé T, Hennebont T, Jugon T, Quimper C,[2] Rhuys T, St. Aubin-du-Cormer T, St. Brieuc C,[2] Vannes C.[2]					
					29
Generality of Valenciennes (10)					
Used (7)	1	3	3		
Avesnes C, N, T, Cambrésis N, T, Quesnoy N, Valenciennes V.					
Missing (3)	2		1		
Cambrésis C, Quesenoy C, T.					
					10
Generality of Nancy (93)					
Used (64)	19	18	21	4U 1CN 1CT	
Bar-le-duc N, T, Bassigny-Barrois U, Bitche C, Blamont C, Boulay C, T, Bourmont C, N, T, Bouzonville C, N, T, Briey N, T, Bruyères CT, N, Château-Salins C, T, Châtel-sur-Moselle N, T, Darney N, Dieuze C, N, T, Etain C, N, T, Fenestrange U, La Marche C, T, Lixheim CN, T, Lunéville C, N, Longuyon C, N, T, Mirecourt C, N, T, Nancy C, N, T, Nomény C, N, T, Neufchâteau T, Pont-à-Mousson C, N, T, Rozières U, St. Dié T, St. Mihiel C, N, Sarreguemines C, N, T, Thiaucourt C, N, T, Vézelise C, T, Villers-la-Montagne U.					
Missing (29)	9	11	8	1U	
Bar-le-duc C, Bitche N, T, Blamont N, T,					

[2] Lower Clergy.

	C	N	T	U	Total
Boulay N, Briey C, Charmes C, N, T, Château-Salins N, Châtel-sur-Moselle C, Commercy C, N, T, Darney C, T, Epinal C, N, T, La Marche N, Lunéville T, Neufchâteau C, N, Remiremont U, St. Mihiel T, St. Dié C, N, Vézelise N.					
					93
Generality of Metz (33)					
Used (26)	7	7	9	2U	
Arches and Charleville U, Longwy C, N, T, Metz C, N, T, V, Mohon U, Sarrebourg and Phalsbourg C, N, T, Sedan T, Sarrelouis CN, Thionville C, N, T, Toul C, N, T, Verdun C, N, T, Vic C, N, T.				1CN	
Missing (7)	2	1	1	2U	
Carignan C, NT, Clermont à Varennes U, Mouzon U, Sarrelouis T, Sedan C, N.				1NT	
					33
Generality of Strasbourg (11)					
Used (8)	2	1	5		
Belfort and Huningue C, T, Colmar and Schlestadt C, N, T, Haguenau and Wissembourg T, Dix Villes T, Strasbourg T.					
Missing (3)	1	2			
Belfort and Huningue N, Haguenau and Wissembourg C, N.					
					11
Island of Corsica (3)					
Used (2)		1	1		
Corsica N, T.					
Missing (1)	1				
Corsica C.					
					3
					Total 615
Colonies (9)					
Used (4)			4		
Guadeloupe—Colony; Martinque—Paris committee; Pondichéry; St. Domingue—Paris petition.					

Missing (5) 5
Guadeloupe—Paris committee; Ile de France et de Bourbon; St. Domingue: Colony—N, S, W.
9

Used—158C, 154N, 190T, 14U[3], 3CN, 1CT, 2NT-522

Missing—36C, 28N, 23T, 4U, 2NT-93

Total made in 1789: 615 general cahiers; 9 colonial cahiers.

[3] The cahier of the municipality of Paris has been counted with the united orders.

ALPHABETICAL LIST OF CAHIERS THAT WERE PRINTED IN 1789[1]

Total: 54 C, 105 N, 92 T, 8 U, 1 CN, 1 CT, 2 NT. 263 cahiers
1 colonial document

C, N, T, Agen; N, Alençon; N, Amiens; N, T, Angers; C, N, T, Angoulême; N, T, Annonay; NT, Arles(ville); C, Armagnac; C, N, T, Artois; C, N, T, Auch; T, Auray; C, N, Autun; C, N, T, Auxerre; N, Aval; C, N, T, Avesnes; N, T, Bailleul; T, Bar-le-duc; C, N, T, Bar-sur-Seine; U, Bassigny-Barrois; N, T, Bazas; CN, T, Bêarn; N, Beauvais; T, Belfort and Huningue; N, Bellême; C, N, T, Belley; N, Beziers; T, Bigorre; C, N, Blois; N, Bordeaux; U, Bourg-en-Bresse; N, Bourges; T, Brest; N, T, Briey; CT, N, Bruyères; C, N, Cahors; T, Calais; N, T, Cambrésis; N, Carcassonne; N, Castres; C, N, T, Caudebec-en-Caux; C, N, T, Châlons-sur-Marne; C, N, Chartres; N, T, Château-Thierry; N, T, Châteauneuf-en-Thimerais; N, Chaumont-en-Bassigny; N, T, Chaumont-en-Vexin; N, Clermont-en-Beauvoisis; N, T, Clermont Ferrand; C, N, T, Colmar and Schlestadt; N, T, Comminges; N, Condom; T, Corsica; N, Coutances; N, Crépy-en-Valois; U, Dauphiné; N, T, Dax; C, N, T, Dijon; T, Dix Villes Impériales; C, T, Dôle; C, N, T, Douai; C, N, T, Dourdan; T, Draguignan; T, Etampes; C, N, T, Evreux; N, T, Foix; C, N, T, Forez; N, Gien; C, Libourne; C, N, T, Lille; C, N, T, Limoges; N, Longwy; C, Loudun; N, Lunéville; C, N, T, V, Lyon; N, Mans(le); C, N, T, Mantes; T, Marseilles; C, N, T, Meaux; C, N, Melun; T, Mende; C, N, T, V, Metz; C, N, Montargis;

[1] Not all of these printed texts have come down to us. This list has been checked with the official inventory (Hyslop, B., *Repertoire critique des cahiers de doléances pour les Etats-généraux de 1789*), and contains one or two additions where the assembly voted to print the cahier but no text has survived. The following assemblies voted to print their cahiers, but no copy has survived: C, Auch, N, Avesnes, T, Bazas, C, Blois, N, Bruyères, N, Longwy, T, Rouen, T, St. Brieuc, C, Verdun, T, Villeneuve-de-Berg. We learn from bibliographical sources that the following cahiers were printed: C, T, Caudebec-en-Caux, C, T, Belley, T, Perpignan, T, Ustaritz.

U, Montfort l'Amaury; N, Montpellier; C, N, T, Moulins; N, Nancy; C, Nantes; U, Navarre; C, N, T, Nemours; N, Nérac; N, T, Nîmes; N, T, Nivernais; N, Nomény; N, Orléans; C, N, T, Paris *hors-les-murs;* C, N, T, V, Paris *intra-muros;* N, T, Périgord; C, NT, Péronne; N, T, Perpignan; T, Ploërmel; N, T, Poitiers; C, N, T, Pont-à-Mousson; C, N, T, Ponthieu; C, N, T, Provins; C, T, Puy-en-Velay; N, Quesnoy; N, T, Reims; C, T, Rennes; N, T, Riom; T, Rivière-Verdun; C, N, T, V, Rouen; U, Rozières; C, N, T, St. Brieuc; T, St. Dié; C, St. Malo; C, N, Saintes; N, St. Mihiel; T, St. Pierre-la-Moutier; N, T, St. Quentin; C, N, T, Saumur; T, Sedan; N, Semur-en-Auxois; N, T, Senlis; N, Sens; N, Sézanne; T, Soule; T, Strasbourg; N, Tartas; N, Thionville; C, N, T, Toul; C, N, T, Toulouse; N, Tours; N, T, Trévoux; C, N, T, Troyes; C, N, T, Tulle; N, T, Ustaritz; T, Valenciennes; T, Vannes; N, Vendôme; C, N, T, Verdun; C, N, T, Vermandois; N, T, Villefranche-en-Rouergue; N, T, Villeneuve-de-Berg; U, Villers-la-Montagne; colony of Martinique.

LIST OF CAHIERS WITH IMPERATIVE MANDATES ATTACHED[1]

Total: 251 cahiers, 40 C, 126 N, 73 T, 7 U, 2 NT, 2 CN, 1 CT.

	CNTU		*CNTU*		*CNTU*		*CNTU*
Paris		Lyon		Auch		Montauban	
Beauvais	N	Forez	NT	Armagnac	N	Cahors	CN
Etampes	N	Lyon	NT	Auch	NT	Rodez	N
Meaux	N	Villefr.	N	Béarn	CNT	Villefranche.	N
Melun	C	Riom		Bigorre	N	Limoges	
Montfort	U	Clermont.	NT	Comminges	N	Dorat	N
Nemours	CNT	Riom	N	Foix	N	Limoges	NT
Paris h.m.	N	St. Flour	N	Rivière	NT	Tulle	N
Paris i.m.	N	Montpellier		Rustaing	U	La Rochelle	
Senlis	NT	Annonay	N	Soule	CN	La Rochelle	N
Orléans		Beziers	C	Bordeaux		Saintes	N
Blois	N	Mende	N	Agen	CNT	St. Jean	T
Chartres	N	Montpellier	N	Bazas	CNT	Poitiers	
Dourdan	N	Nîmes	N	Bordeaux	N	Chatelle-rault	NT
Gien	NT	Puy-en-V.	CN	Castel-moron.	CNT	Poitiers	NT
Montargis	CNT	Villeneuve.	NT	Condom	CNT	Tours	
Orléans	CN	Toulouse		Dax	CN	Angers	NT
Vendôme	N	Carcassonne	N	Libourne	NT	Loudun	N
Bourges		Castelnaud.	N	Mont-de-M.	CN	Mans(le)	N
Bourges	NT	Castres	NT	Nérac	CN	Saumur	T
Moulins		Limoux	CNT	Périgord	N	Caen	
Guéret	NT	Toulouse	CN	Ustaritz	C	Caen	NT
Moulins	N	Perpignan				Coutances	NT
Nivernais	CN	Perpignan	NT				

[1] The above list has been arranged alphabetically within *generalities,* as read for this study. In order to conserve space, some of the longer names have been abbreviated. The usual abbreviations have been used. When joint cahiers of two orders were made, the two letters have been joined by a ligature.

	CNTU		*CNTU*		*CNTU*		*CNTU*
Alençon		Reims	N	Brignoles	T	Charmes	N
Alençon	N	Sézanne	N	Forcal-		Château-	
Bellême	CNT	Troyes	N	quier	C	Salins	T
Château-		Vitry.	N	Marseille	C T	Châtel-s-M.	T
neuf.	CNT	Dijon		Toulon	N	Darney	N
Rouen		Autun	N	Rennes		Dieuze	T
Caudebec.	N	Auxerre	T	Auray	T	Epinal	N
Chaumont.	N	Bar-s.-S.	NT	Fougères	T	Etain	N
Evreux	CNT	Belley	NT	Nantes	C T	Fenestrange	U
Rouen	N	Bourg.	N U	Ploërmel	T	La Marche	N
Amiens		Châlon-s.-S.	N	Quimper	C T	Lixheim	C͡N
Amiens	N	Charolles	CNT	Rennes	C	Lunéville	CN
Boulogne	C T	Châtillon	NT	Rhuys	T	Mirecourt	CNT
Calais	N	Dijon	CNT	St. Brieuc	T	Neufchâteau	T
Montreuil	N	Gex	CN	Vannes	T	Pont-à-M.	CN
Péronne	N͡T	Mâcon	NT	Valenciennes		Rozières	U
Ponthieu	NT	Semur.	NT	Avesnes	T	St. Dié	NT
Lille		Trévoux	NT	Cambrésis	CN	Sarreguem.	NT
Artois	N	Besançon		Quesnoy	N	Metz	
Douai	CNT	Amont	N	Valenciennes	T	Metz	TV
Soissons		Aval	NT	Nancy		Mohon	U
Château Th.	T	Besançon	CN	Blamont	C	Sarrebourg	N
Clermont.	N	Dôle	N	Boulay	T	Sedan	T
Crépy.	N	Grenoble		Bourmont	N	Toul	N
Villers.	CN	Dauphiné	U	Bouzon-		Verdun	N
Châlons		Aix		ville	C	Strasbourg	
Chaumont.	NT	Aix	T	Briey	NT	Belfort	NT
Langres	N	Arles (V)	N͡T	Bruyeres	C͡T	Colmar	N

DISTRICTS WHICH CREATED COMMITTEES OF CORRESPONDENCE

Total: 100 cases. 23 C, 32 N, 41 T, 3 U, 1 CN.

N, T, Agen; T. Aix; T. Angers; N. Annonay; T. Auch; T. Avesnes; C. Bailleul; CN. Béarn; C, T, Bellême; C. Besançon; C, T, Bigorre; C. Blamont; N. Bordeaux; C, N, T, Bourmont; C. Bouzonville; C. Cahors; N. Calais; N. Cambrésis; C. Castelmoron d'Albret; T. Castres; C, N, T, Charolles; C, N, T, Chartres; N. Château-Thierry; C, N, T, Châteauneuf-en-Thimerais; N, T, Chatellerault; T. Chaumont-en-Bassigny; C, T, Clermont Ferrand; N. Condom; N. Couserans; T. Dieuze; N. Dijon; N. Dorat; C, N, T, Douai; N, T, Etampes; N. Guéret; T. Lesneven; N, T, Limoux; N. Lyon; T. Marseille; U. Mohon; U. Montfort-l'Amaury; N. Montpellier; C, T, Nantes; T. Nemours; C. Nérac; T. Neufchâteau; N. Nîmes; C. Orléans; N. Périgord; T. Péronne; N, T, Perpignan; T. Ploërmel; N. Poitiers; C. Pont-à-Mousson; T. Ponthieu; N. Puy-en-Velay; T. Quesnoy; C, T, Quimper; T. Reims; C, T, Rennes; T. Rhuys; C, N, Riom; R. Rivière-Verdun; U. Rozières; T. Rustaing; N. Sarrebourg; T. St. Brieuc; T, St. Jean d'Angely; T. Sarreguemines; T. Sedan; C, N, Soule; T. Toul; N. Toulon; T. Trévoux; T. Vannes; N. Villefranche-de-Beaujolais; N. Vitry-le-françois. The colonies of Guadeloupe, Martinique, Pondichéry.

EXPLANATION OF THE MAPS

The outlines for both maps are adapted from the map showing all electoral districts, principal and secondary, in Brette, Armand, *Les Limites et les divisions térritoriales de la France en 1789* (Paris, 1907). The lines of the subdivisions (i.e., secondary *baillages*) of principal *bailliages* have been omitted from the present maps in order to make clear the entire areas represented in all electoral assemblies producing general cahiers. The final drafts of the two maps are the work of T. R. Miller, architect and student at Columbia University.

MAP I. GENERAL ELECTORAL DISTRICTS OF 1789

The aim of Map I is two-fold; first, to show the general electoral districts of 1789, and second, to show their grouping by *generalities.* A geographic disparity between the general election districts of 1789 is at once apparent, as for example the contrast between Poitiers (which, in fact, had seven secondary *bailliages* attached to it) and any of the small districts of the northeast. The population was not necessarily equally disproportionate.

The large Roman numerals indicate the *generalities,* for which a key is given on the map itself. The thirty-two *generalities* are numbered in the order in which the cahiers were read for the analysis of nationalism.

The names of some of the districts were too long to print in the space to which they belong, and a number is substituted in such cases. The assigned numbers correspond with the order in which the general cahiers were read for the present study. As has already been explained, the cahiers were read alphabetically by *generalities,* starting with the *generality* of Paris. Thus, of each *bailliage* were given a number corresponding to its place in the entire series of districts issuing general cahiers, number one would be Beauvais, number two, Etampes, and so forth. Hence, where it has been necessary to give numbers, the number corresponds to the numerical order in which the entire series of cahiers was read. In the *Guide,* a map will be given with the entire series of numbers and a key for the corresponding names. The numbers of the same districts are identical on the present map with those on the map in the *Guide.*

A key to the numbered districts of Map I follows:

A. Arabic Numerals (electoral districts)

6—Montfort l'Amaury
11—Senlis (two sections)[1]
27—Villefranche-de-Beaujolais
29—Riom (two sections)

[1] Because of confusion and ignorance in the royal councils for the convocation and because of the existence of secondary *bailliages,* it sometimes happened that all areas represented in a single general assembly were not contiguous (*e.g.,* Autun, Riom, etc.). Where such has been the case, the number of the *bailliage* is indicated on both areas.

40—Castelnaudary
44—Armagnac (two sections)
53—Rivière-Verdun
54—Rustaing
60—Condom
61—Dax
78—Rochefort-sur-mer
81—Poitiers (two sections)
88—Coutances (two sections)
91—Châteauneuf-en-Thimerais
93—Chaumont - en - Vexin (two sections)
95—Rouen (two sections)
96—Amiens (two sections)
102—St. Quentin
107—Château-Thierry
108—Crépy-en-Valois
109—Clermont-en-Beauvoisis
110—Soissons
112—Villers-Cotterets
113—Châlons-sur-Marne
117—Sézanne (two sections)
119—Vitry-le-françois (two sections)
120—Autun (two sections)
122—Bar-sur-Seine
124—Bourg-en-Bresse
125—Châlon-sur-Saône
127—Châtillon-sur-Seine
163—Lesneven
176—Avesnes (two sections)
182—Blamont
184—Bourmont
186—Briey
187—Bruyères
188—Charmes
189—Château-Salins
190—Châtel-sur-Moselle
191—Commercy
193—Dieuze
194—Epinal
195—Etain
196—Fénestrange
197—La Marche
198—Lixheim
199—Longuyon
200—Lunéville
201—Mirecourt
202—Nancy
203—Neufchâteau
204—Nomény
205—Pont-à-Mousson
206—Remiremont
207—Rozières
209—St. Mihiel
211—Thiaucourt
212—Vézelise
213—Villers-la-Montagne
221—Sarrebourg

The district of Bassigny-Barrois (seventh type of convocation) comprised the two districts of Bourmont and La Marche (184 and 197) and could not, therefore, be indicated separately. The boundaries of the dioceses of the lower clergy in Brittany (*generality* of Rennes) are not given, but the diocesan center has been marked.

B. Small Roman Numerals

The small Roman numerals indicate territories within the frontiers of France but subject to foreign jurisdictions. These were as follows:

I	Avignon
II	Comtat Venaissin
III	Terre de Bidâche
IV	Seigneurie de Mandeure
V	Comté de Montbéliard
VI	Ville de Mulhouse
VII	Comté de Sarre-Verden
VIII	Principalité de Salm
IX	Comté de Sault
X	Seigneurie de Montjoie

MAP II. DISTRIBUTION OF DOMINANT NATIONALIST TRENDS BY BAILLIAGE

The presentation of nationalist trends is a very difficult matter, because, as the chart indicates, opinion was seldom unanimous among the three orders of a *bailliage,* and never so for an entire *generality*. The method finally adopted seemed to give the most accurate picture possible of nationalist trends, without undue violence to exceptions.

The general principle applied in the marking of each *bailliage* is to indicate the type of nationalism which two of the three classes represented. The application of the principle results as follows:

If two classes or all three of a *bailliage* were radical—Radical Nationalism
If two classes or all three of a *bailliage* were progressive—Progressive Nationalism
If one class was radical, and one progressive—Progressive Nationalism
If two classes or all three of a *bailliage* were intermediate—Intermediate Nationalism
If two classes or all three of a *bailliage* were conservative—Conservative Nationalism
If one class was conservative and one without nationalism—Conservative Nationalism
If two classes or all three of a *bailliage* were without nationalism—No Nationalism
If none of the classes represented the same type of nationalism—Mixed Nationalism

A serious difficulty has been encountered in picturing opinion in the *generality* of Rennes (Brittany) where the two upper orders showed no nationalism, and the lower clergy and third estate displayed differing types of nationalism. It was impossible, in this case, to make the same classification as for the rest of France. The balance of opinion between the various cahiers has been pictured.

The map is, necessarily, an incomplete picture of opinion, in that it ignores the third cahier of each *bailliage,* and the white sections representing *bailliages* where the cahiers of at least two orders are missing, leave regrettable gaps among frontier *generalities*. The names of the different districts and the outlines of the *generalities* may be ascertained by comparison with Map No. I.

Despite its shortcomings, Map II gives some picture of the distribution of nationalist trends in the cahiers of 1789. The chief areas of the revolutionary movement and of conservative opposition are demonstrated.

TABLE OF OPINIONS IN THE GENERAL CAHIERS

Explanation:

In order to give a basis of geographic comparison, and at the same time show the distribution of opinion by classes, the following tables have been prepared. The districts are arranged alphabetically within *generalities*. The *generalities* have been listed, always in the same order, first by *pays d'élection* starting with Paris, and moving clockwise, and then by *pays d'états*.

Only the *bailliages* which held the given opinion are named. It has sometimes been necessary to abbreviate the name of a *bailliage*. The full name may be ascertained by comparison with the list by *generality*, in this appendix, pp. 237-43. The usual abbreviations have been used. C—clergy, N—nobles, T—third estate, U—united orders, V—town. Cahiers of towns (except the municipality of Paris) have been counted with the third estate. The letters for joint cahiers are joined by a ligature.

I. CAHIERS ASSIGNING SPECIFIC QUALITIES TO FRENCHMEN, OR REFERRING DIRECTLY TO A NATIONAL CHARACTER, GENIUS, OR SPIRIT

Total: 89 cahiers. 8 C, 53 N, 25 T, 2 U, 1 NT

	CNTU		*CNTU*		*CNTU*		*CNTU*
Paris		Toulouse		Poitiers		Dijon	
Beauvais	NT	Carcassonne	N	Poitiers	N	Autun	N
Mantes	N	Castelnaud.	N	Tours		Auxerre	NT
Melun	T	Castres	N	Tours	N	Châlons.-S.	N
Nemours	T	Toulouse	NT	Alençon		Bourg-en-B.	U
Paris i.m.	NT	Auch		Alençon	T	Mâcon	N
Orléans		Armagnac	C	Caen		Semur.	N
Blois	N	Comminges	N	Caen	CN	Besançon	
Dourdan	C	Foix	N	Coutances	NT	Besançon	NT
Orléans	NT	Rivière-V.	N	Rouen		Aix	
Bourges		Rustaing	U	Rouen	N	Arles(Ville)	N͡T
Bourges	N	Bordeaux		Amiens		Rennes	
Moulins		Condom	N	Amiens	T	Rennes	T
Nivernais	CN	Dax	N	Calais	NT	Malenciennes	
St. Pierre	T	Nérac	N	Montreuil.	CN	Cambrésis	T
Lyon		Périgord	N	Ponthieu	NT	Quesnoy	N
Lyon	N	Ustartiz	N	Lille		Nancy	
Villefr.	CN	Montauban		Artois	N	Bar-le-D.	N
Riom		Villefr.	N	Bailleul	T	St. Mihiel	N
Clermont F.	N	Limoges		Soissons		Vézelise	T
Riom	N	Limoges	N	Clermont.	N	Metz	
Montpellier		La Rochelle		Villers. C.	N	Metz	N
Montpellier	N	La Rochelle	NT	Châlons		Longwy	C
Puy-en-V.	C	Rochefort	T	Châlons.	T	Toul	T
Perpignan		Saintes	N	Chaumont.	N	Verdun	T
Perpignan	NT			Reims	NT		
				Troyes	N		

II. CAHIERS APPEALING TO FRENCH TRADITIONS

This table does not include cahiers whose appeal to class or regional traditions was stronger than their appeal to French national traditions.

Total: 303 cahiers. 97 C, 96 N, 99 T, 8 U, 1 CN, 1 CT, 1 NT

	CNTU
Paris	
Beauvais	CNT
Etampes	C T
Mantes	CNT
Meaux	CNT
Melun	CNT
Montfort.	U
Nemours	C T
Paris h.m.	CNT
Paris i.m.	CNT
Provins	CNT
Senlis	T
Sens	CNT
Orléans	
Blois	C T
Chartres	C T
Dourdan	CNT
Montargis	CNT
Orléans	CNT
Vendôme	C
Bourges	
Bourges	NT
Moulins	
Guéret	C
Moulins	CNT
Nivernais	CNT
St. Pierre	T
Lyon	
Forez	T
Lyon	CNTV
Villefr.	CNT
Riom	
Clermont.	CNT
Riom	CN
St. Flour	NT
Montpellier	
Mende	CNT
Montpell.	CNT
Nîmes	C T
Puy.	C T
Villeneuve.	C
Toulouse	
Carcassonne	CNT
Castres	CN
Limoux	NT
Toulouse	CNT

	CNTU
Perpignan	
Perpignan	T
Auch	
Armagnac	CN
Auch	C
Bigorre	C T
Comminges	N
Foix	N
Rivière.	NT
Rustaing	U
Quatre-V.	T
Soule	T
Bordeaux	
Agen	NT
Bazas	NT
Bordeaux	NT
Condom	CNT
Dax	C T
Libourne	CN
Mont-de-M.	C
Nérac	N
Périgord	N
Tartas	NT
Montauban	
Cahors	C T
Rodez	CN
Villefranche	N
Limoges	
Angoulême	N
Dorat	N
Limoges	CN
La Rochelle	
La Roch.	NT
Saintes	CNT
St. Jean	N
Poitiers	
Chatellerault	C
Marches Com.	U
Poitiers	CNT
Tours	
Angers	NT
Loudun	C T
Mans(le)	C T
Saumur	C
Tours	CN

	CNTU
Caen	
Caen	CNT
Coutances	CN
Alençon	
Alençon	CN
Bellême	CNT
Châteauneuf.	C
Rouen	
Caudebec.	CNT
Chaumont.	NT
Evreux	CN
Rouen	CN V
Amiens	
Amiens	C T
Boulogne	CN
Montreuil	N
Péronne	C
Ponthieu	N
St.Quentin	C
Lille	
Artois	CNT
Bailleul	C
Douai	T
Lille	N
Soissons	
Château Th.	NT
Clermont.	CN
Crépy	CN
Soissons	C
Vermandois	CNT
Villers-Cot.	CNT
Châlons	
Châlons.	CNT
Chaumont.	NT
Langres	T
Reims	CNT
Sézanne	CNT
Troyes	CN
Vitry	CNT
Dijon	
Autun	CNT
Auxerre	C T
Bar-s.-S.	C T
Belley	CN
Bourg-en-B.	U

	CNTU
Châlon-s.-S.	NT
Châtillon	CN
Charolles	C T
Dijon	CNT
Mâcon	NT
Semur	CNT
Besançon	
Amont	U
Aval	C T
Besançon	C T
Dôle	NT
Aix	
Arles (V.)	CNT
Aix	CN
Barcel.	T
Castellane	C
Digne	C
Draguignan	T
Forcalquier	T
Marseille	CN
Rennes	
Brest	T
Lesneven	T
Nantes	T
Quimper	T
Rennes	C
Vannes	T
Valenciennes	
Avesnes	T
Cambrésis	NT
Quesnoy	N
Nancy	
Bar-le-D.	N
Bourmont	T
Boulay	T
Briey	N
Bruyères	CT
Château-S.	C T
Darney	N
Etain	N
Fenestrange	U
La Marche	C
Lixheim	CN
Longuyon	NT
Lunéville	CN
Mirecourt	N
Nancy	CNT

	CNTU		*CNTU*		*CNTU*		*CNTU*
Neufchâ-		Villers.	U	Longwy	C	Strasbourg	
teau	T	Metz.		Thionville	T	Belfort	C
Pont-à-M.	NT	Arches	U	Toul	CN	Corsica	
St.Mihiel	CN	Metz	CN	Verdun	T	Corsica	T

III. SUMMARY TABLE ON RELIGION

Totals: For Uniformity: 124 cahiers. 99 C, 11 N, 11 T, 3 U
For Toleration: 35 cahiers. 1 C, 10 N, 23 T, 1 NT
Both opinions: 44 cahiers. 19 C, 8 N, 16 T, 1 U

A. For Uniformity

	CNTU		*CNTU*		*CNTU*		*CNTU*
Paris		Limoux	C	Tours	C	Dijon	N
Beauvais	C T	Toulouse	C	Caen		Gex	C
Etampes	C	Auch		Caen	C	Mâcon	C
Mantes	C	Armagnac	C	Coutances	C	Semur	C
Meaux	C	Auch	C	Alençon		Besançon	
Melun	C T	Bigorre	C	Alençon	C	Amont	U
Montfort.	U	Rivière.	C	Bellême	C	Aval	C
Nemours	C	Soule	C	Château-		Besançon	CNT
Paris h.m.	C	Bordeaux		neuf.	C	Grenoble	
Paris i.m.	C	Bordeaux	C	Rouen		Orange	C
Sens	C	Castel-		Rouen	C	Aix	
Orléans		moron.	C	Amiens		Arles (V)	C
Chartres	C	Condom	C	Amiens	C	Castell.	C
Montargis	C	Dax	C	Péronne	C	Digne	C
Vendôme	C	Libourne	C	Ponthieu	C	Draguig.	C T
Moulins		Mont-de-		St.Quentin	C T	Forcalq.	C
Nivernais	C	M.	C T	Lille		Grasse	C
Lyon		Nérac	C	Artois	CN	Marseille	C
Forez	C T	Ustartiz	C	Bailleul	C	Rennes	
Lyon	CNTV	Montauban		Douai	CN	Dol.	C
Ville-		Cahors	C	Soissons		Nantes	C T
franche	C	Rodez	N	Soissons	C	Rennes	C
Riom		Limoges		Villers.	C	St.Malo	C
Riom	C	Angoulême	C	Châlons		Valenciennes	
Montpellier		Dorat	C	Chaumont	C	Avesnes	CN
Montpel-		Limoges	C	Langres	T	Quesnoy	N
lier	C	Tulle	C	Sézanne	C	Nancy	
Puy-en-V.	C	Poitiers		Troyes	C	Bitche	C
Villen-		Chatell.	C	Vitry.	C	Bourmont	CN
euve.	C	Marches		Dijon		Etain	C
Toulouse		Com.	U	Autun	C	La Marche	C
Carcas-		Poitiers	C	Auxerre	C	Nancy	C
sonne	C	Tours		Belley	N	Vézelise	C
Castres	CN	Angers	C	Châlon.	C	Metz	
Castel-		Mans(le)	C	Charolles	C	Metz	C
naud.	C	Saumur	C	Châtillon.	C	Strasbourg	
						Belfort	C

B. For Toleration

	C	N	T	U
Paris				
Melun		N		
Provins		N	T	
Orléans				
Blois		N	T	
Montargis		N	T	
Montpellier				
Montpellier			T	
Nîmes			T	
Villeneuve.			T	
Toulouse				
Castres			T	
Castelnaud.			T	
Auch				
Foix			T	
Bordeaux				
Nérac			T	
Périgord			T	
La Rochelle				
La Rochelle		N	T	
Saintes			T	
St. Jean.			T	
Caen				
Coutances		N	T	
Alençon				
Châteauneuf.		N	T	
Rouen				
Caudebec.		N		
Evreux			T	
Amiens				
Amiens			T	
Péronne		N͡	T	
Boulogne	C			
Soissons				
Clermont.		N		
Châlons.				
Troyes		N		
Dijon				
Dijon			T	
Semur			T	
Aix				
Aix			T	
Forcalquier			T	
Valenciennes				
Valenciennes			T	

C. Both Opinions

	C	N	T	U
Paris				
Nemours			T	
Paris h.m.			T	
Paris i.m.			T	
Provins	C			
Orléans				
Blois	C			
Dourdan	C			
Gien	C			
Orléans	C		T	
Bourges				
Bourges			T	
Moulins				
Nivernais			T	
St. Pierre			T	
Riom				
Clermont	C			
Montpellier				
Béziers	C			
Mende	C			
Montpel.			T	
Villeneuve.		N		
Toulouse				
Carcassonne			T	
Bordeaux				
Bazas	C			
Limoges				
Angoulême	C			
Tulle		N		
La Rochelle				
Saintes	C			
Tours				
Angers		N		
Caen				
Caen		N	T	
Rouen				
Evreux	C			
Rouen	C			
Amiens				
Boulogne		N		
Lille				
Lille		N		
Soissons				
Vermandois	C			
Châlons				
Châlons.	C			
Reims	C			
Troyes			T	
Dijon				
Auxerre		N		
Bar-s.-S.			T	
Belley	C			
Bourg-en-E.				U
Châlon-s.-S.		N	T	
Dijon	C			
Semur			T	
Rennes				
Quimper			T	
Rennes			T	
Metz				
Verdun	C			

IV. CAHIERS PROPOSING SOME MEASURE OF NATIONAL EDUCATION

Total: 111 cahiers. 41 C, 31 N, 35 T, 2 U, 1 CT, 1 NT

	C	N	T	U
Paris				
Beauvais	C			
Mantes	C	N	T	
Melun			T	
Nemours			T	
Paris h.m.	C	N	T	
Paris i.m.		N		
Provins	C			
Senlis			T	
Sens	C		T	
Orléans				
Blois		N		
Chartres	C			
Dourdan		N		
Orléans		N	T	
Moulins				
Moulins	C			
Nivernais	C		T	
Lyon				
Forez	C			
Lyon	C	N	T	
Villefranche	C			
Riom				
Clermont.		N		
Riom		N	T	
Montpellier				
Annonay	C		T	
Nîmes		N	T	
Puy-en-V.	C			
Toulouse				
Carcassonne	C	N		
Castelnaud.			T	
Castres		N		
Toulouse	C		T	
Auch				
Rivière-V.			T	
Rustaing				U

	C	N	T	U
Bordeaux				
Bazas	C			
Bordeaux		N	T	
Dax	C			
Nérac			T	
Périgord			T	
Montauban				
Rodez	C			
Limoges				
Angoulême		N		
La Rochelle				
La Rochelle		N	T	
Saintes		N	T	
St. Jean		N		
Poitiers				
Poitiers	C			
Tours				
Angers		N	T	
Mans(le)	C		T	

	C	N	T	U
Caen				
Caen	C			
Rouen				
Caudebec	C	N		
Rouen	C			
Amiens				
Calais		N		
Péronne	C	N	T	
Ponthieu		N		
St.Quentin	C			
Soissons				
Château Th.		N		
Clermont.		N		
Châlons.				
Chaumont.	C			
Langres			T	
Reims	C			

	C	N	T	U
Dijon				
Auxerre		N	T	
Bar-s.-S.	C			
Belley	C	N		
Bourg-en-B.				U
Châtillon	C			
Dijon	C			
Mâcon	C		T	
Trévoux		N		
Besançon				
Aval	C	N		
Dôle	C		T	
Aix				
Aix	C			
Forcalq.	C		T	
Marseille			T	
Sisteron		N		
Rennes				
Rennes			T	

	C	N	T	U
Vannes			T	
Nancy				
Briey			T	
Bruyères	C		T	
Etain		N		
St.Mihiel		N		
Sarreguemines	C			
Vézelise			T	
Metz				
Longwy	C			
Metz	C		T	
Toul	C		T	
Strasbourg				
Colmar	C			
Corsica				
Corsica		N	T	

V. CAHIERS EMPHASIZING UNIFORMITY OF ADMINISTRATIVE AND LEGAL SYSTEMS

Total: 109 cahiers. 17 C, 37 N, 54 T, 1 U

	C	N	T	U
Paris				
Beauvais		N	T	
Etampes			T	
Paris h.m.	C		T	
Paris i.m.	C		T	
Melun		N		
Nemours			T	
Sens	C		T	
Orléans				
Blois	C		T	
Chartres			T	
Dourdan	C			
Montargis			T	
Orléans		N		
Vendôme			T	
Moulins				
Nivernais	C	N		
Lyon				
Lyon	C	N	T	
Villefranche.	C			
Riom				
Clermont		N	T	
Riom		N	T	
Montpellier				
Annonay		N		
Montpellier			T	
Nîmes		N	T	
Puy-en-V.			T	
Toulouse				
Carcass.		N		

	C	N	T	U
Auch				
Auch			T	
Foix			T	
Rustaing				U
Soule	C	N		
Bordeaux				
Bordeaux			T	
Castelmoran			T	
Condom		N		
Dax		N		
Mont-de-M.			T	
Montauban				
Rodez	C			
Villefranche.		N		
Poitiers				
Poitiers			T	
Tours				
Angers		N	T	
Loudun		N		
Mans(le)			T	
Saumur			T	
Tours		N	T	
La Rochelle				
La Rochelle			T	
Alençon				
Châteauneuf.		N		
Caen				
Coutances			T	

	C	N	T	U
Rouen				
Caudebec.		N		
Rouen				V
Amiens				
Amiens			T	
Boulogne		N		
Calais			T	
Montreuil	C			
Lille				
Bailleul		N		
Douai		N	T	
Soissons				
Château Th.		N		
Clermont.		N		
Soissons			T	
Châlons.				
Châlons.			T	
Chaumont.			T	
Reims			T	
Sézanne		N		
Troyes		N		
Vitry			T	
Dijon				
Autun	C			
Auxerre		N		
Bar-s.-S.			T	
Belley		N		
Charolles	C	N		
Châlon-s.-S.			T	
Dijon	C		T	
Trévoux		N		

	C	N	T	U
Besançon				
Aval		N		
Besançon		N	T]	
Aix				
Digne			T	
Draguignan			T	
Forcalquier		N	T	
Sisteron		N		
Valenciennes				
Quesnoy		N		
Rennes				
Brest			T	
Nantes			T	
Quimper			T	
Rennes			T	
St. Brieuc			T	
Vannes			T	
Nancy				
Blamont	C			
Briey			T	
Darney		N		
Etain			T	
Neufchâteau			T	
Vézelise			T	
Metz				
Toul		N		
Verdun	C			
Strasbourg				
Belfort	C			

VI. CAHIERS SHOWING STRONG SENTIMENT FOR ECONOMIC UNIFORMITY

Any cahier making two demands for economic uniformity is included in the following list. Since many more cahiers of the third estate than of the other two orders wanted uniform weights and measures, the composite table shows a large majority for the third estate.

Total: 162 cahiers. 16 C, 30 N, 111 T, 4 U, 1 NT

	CNTU
Paris	
Beauvais	NT
Etampes	T
Mantes	T
Meaux	T
Melun	CN
Montfort	U
Nemours	NT
Paris h.m.	NT
Paris i.m.	NT
Senlis	T
Sens	T
Orléans	
Blois	T
Chartres	T
Dourdan	NT
Gien	T
Montargis	T
Orléans	CNT
Vendôme	T
Bourges	
Bourges	T
Moulins	
Moulins	NT
Nivernais	T
St. Pierre	T
Lyon	
Forez	NT
Lyon	CNTV
Villefranche.	NT
Riom	
Clermont	C T
Riom	C
Montpellier	
Beziers	N
Mende	T
Montpellier	T
Nîmes	T
Puy-en-V.	T

	CNTU
Toulouse	
Castres	NT
Auch	
Auch	T
Bigorre	T
Foix	T
Rivière-V.	C
Bordeaux	
Bordeaux	T
Castelmoron	T
Condom	T
Dax	T
Mont-de-M.	T
Nérac	T
Périgord	T
Tartas	T
Ustaritz	N
Montauban	
Cahors	T
Rodez	T
La Rochelle	
La Rochelle	T
Saintes	T
Rochefort	T
Poitiers	
Marches Com.	U
Poitiers	CNT
Tours	
Angers	NT
Loudun	C
Mans(le)	T
Saumur	T
Tours	T
Caen	
Coutances	T
Alençon	
Bellême	T
Châteauneuf.	NT

	CNTU
Rouen	
Caudebec	T
Rouen	V
Evreux	T
Amiens	
Amiens	CNT
Calais	NT
Montreuil.	T
Ponthieu	T
St.Quentin	NT
Lille	
Bailleul	T
Soissons	
Château Th.	NT
Crépy-en-V.	CNT
Soissons	T
Châlons	
Châlons	T
Chaumont	C T
Langres	T
Reims	C T
Sézanne	T
Troyes	NT
Vitry-le-F.	C T
Dijon	
Autun	NT
Auxerre	C
Belley	T
Bourg-en-B.	U
Châlon-s.-S.	T
Charolles	T
Châtillon.	C
Dijon	T
Semur	NT
Trévoux	NT
Besançon	
Aval	T
Aix	
Aix	T

	CNTU
Arles (V.)	NT
Digne	T
Draguignan	T
Forcalquier	T
Grasse	T
Toulon	T
Rennes	
Auray	T
Brest	T
Carhaix	T
Dinan	T
Lesneven	T
Morlaix	T
Nantes	T
Ploërmel	T
Quimper	T
Rennes	C T
Vannes	T
Lannion	T
Valenciennes	
Avesnes	T
Cambrésis	T
Valenciennes	T
Nancy	
Bourmont	T
Château-S.	T
Dieuze	T
Etain	T
La Marche	T
Nancy	T
Neufchâteau	T
Sarreguemines	N
Metz	
Longwy	NT
Mohon	U
Sarrebourg	N
Verdun	N
Vic	T

VII. CAHIERS OF THE CLERGY AND NOBLES AND OF UNITED ORDERS APPROVING VOTE BY HEAD

Total: 54 cahiers. 32 C, 14 N, 7 U, 1 CT

	CNTU
Paris	
Montfort.	U
Paris i.m.	C
Senlis	N
Orléans	
Dourdan	C
Gien	C
Lyon	
Forez	CN
Lyon	C
Villefranche	C
Montpellier	
Beziers	C
Villeneuve.	C
Perpignan	
Perpignan	N
Auch	
Armagnac	C
Rustaing	U
Bordeaux	
Nérac	C
Limoges	
Dorat	C
Tulle	C
Tours	
Loudun	C
Caen	
Caen	C
Alencon	
Châteauneuf.	N
Amiens	
Amiens	C
Calais	N
Montreuil.	N
Ponthieu	C
Soissons	
Vermandois	N
Châlons.	
Chaumont	C
Langres	N
Sézanne	C
Dijon	
Charolles	C
Châtillon.	C
Besançon	
Amont	U
Aval	C
Besançon	C
Dôle	C
Grenoble	
Dauphiné	U
Aix	
Draguignan	C
Forcalquier	N
Marseille	CN
Rennes	
Dol	C
St. Malo	C
Nancy	
Bruyères	CT
Etain	N
Fénestrange	U
La Marche	C
Mirecourt	N
Remiremont	CN
Rozières	U
Metz	
Mohon	U
Thionville	C
Vic	C
Strasbourg	
Belfort	C

VIII. CAHIERS EMPHASIZING NEED OF EQUAL STATUS AMONG PROVINCES

Total: 121 cahiers. 22 C, 37 N, 58 T, 3 U, 1 NT

	CNTU
Paris	
Beauvais	N
Melun	NT
Montfort.	U
Paris i.m.	T
Nemours	NT
Senlis	N
Orléans	
Chartres	T
Dourdan	C
Gien	T
Montargis	NT
Orléans	NT
Moulins	
Guéret	N
Moulins	NT
St. Pierre.	T
Nivernais	T
Lyon	
Forez	NT
Lyon	CNTV
Villefranche.	C
Riom	
Clermont.	T
Riom	NT
St. Flour	NT
Montpellier	
Nîmes	T
Puy-en-V.	C
Villeneuve.	C
Toulouse	
Carcassonne	CNT
Auch	
Auch	C
Comminges	T
Foix	T
Rivière-V.	T
Soule	T
Bordeaux	
Agen	T
Bordeaux	C
Périgord	N
Montauban	
Rodez	N
Villefranche.	NT
Limoges	
Angoulême	NT
Limoges	NT
Tulle	T
La Rochelle	
Saintes	C T
St. Jean	N
Poitiers	
Marches Com.	U
Poitiers	T
Tours	
Angers	C T
Mans(le)	T
Rouen	
Caudebec.	NT
Rouen	N
Amiens	
Amiens	T
Calais	T
Boulogne	N
Montreuil.	C
Péronne	CNT
St. Quentin	T
Lille	
Bailleul	T
Douai	N
Soissons	
Château Th.	NT
Clermont.	N

	C	*N*	*T*	*U*
Vermandois	C			
Châlons.				
Châlons.		N	T	
Chaumont.		N	T	
Langres			T	
Reims		N	T	
Vitry-le-F.	C	N	T	
Dijon				
Autun	C			
Auxerre		N		
Bar-s.-S.			T	
Belley		N		
Châlon.			T	
Dijon	C		T	
Mâcon		N		
Semur	C			
Besançon				
Aval	C			
Dôle			T	
Aix				
Forcalquier			T	
Toulon			T	
Rennes				
Rennes			T	
Vannes			T	
Valenciennes				
Avesnes	C	N		
Nancy				
Boulay			T	
Bouzonville			T	
Briey			T	
Darney		N		
St. Dié			T	
St. Mihiel		N		
Vézelise	C			
Metz				
Longwy	C			
Mohon				U
Sarrebourg			T	
Toul		N	T	
Vic		N		
Strasbourg				
Belfort	C		T	
Haguenau			T	

IX. DEMAND FOR EQUAL TAX LIABILITY, RENUNCIATION OF PRIVILEGES, OR BOTH

E equal tax liability
R renunciation of privileges
B both demands
X opposed to either or both
Joint cahiers of two orders appear in U column

Totals: Equal tax liability: 58C, 44 N, 164 T, 5 U, 3 CN, 1 CT, 1 NT. 275
Renunciation of privileges: 21 C, 24 N 45
Both demands: 75 C, 80 N, 4 T, 2 U, 1 NT 162
Against either or both: 2 C, 5 N 7

	C	*N*	*T*	*U*
Paris				
Beauvais	E	B	E	
Etampes	B	B	E	
Mantes	B	B	E	
Meaux	B	B	E	
Melun	E	E	E	
Montfort.				B
Nemours	B	E	E	
Paris h.m.	B	B	E	
Paris i.m.	E	E		
Provins	B	B		
Senlis	B	B	E	
Sens	B	R		
Orléans				
Blois	B	B	E	
Chartres	B	B	E	
Dourdan	B	B	E	
Gien	E	R	E	
Montargis	B	E		
Orléans	B	B	E	
Vendôme	B	E	E	
Bourges				
Bourges		E	E	
Moulins				
Guéret	E	X	E	
Moulins	B	R	E	
Nivernais	R	B	E	
St.Pierre		R	E	
Lyon				
Forez	E	B	E	
Lyon	B	B	E	E
Villefranche.	B	B	E	
Riom				
Clermont	R	B	B	
Riom	B	B	B	
St.Flour		X	E	
Montpellier				
Annonay	E	B	E	
Beziers	E	R		
Mende	R	E	E	
Montpellier	R	E	E	
Nîmes	B	B	E	
Puy-en-V.	E	B		
Villeneuve.	B	E	E	
Toulouse				
Carcassonne	E	R	E	
Castelnaud.	B		E	
Castres	R		E	
Limoux	B	R	E	
Toulouse	B	E	E	
Perpignan				
Perpignan		B	E	
Auch				
Armagnac			E	
Auch	E		E	
Béarn				E
Bigorre	E		E	
Foix			E	
Quatre-V.			E	
Rivière-V.	E	B	E	
Rustaing				E
Soule	E	R	E	
Bordeaux				
Agen	B	B	E	
Bazas	B	B	E	
Bordeaux	B	R	E	
Castelmoron.	B	E	E	
Condom	B	E	E	
Dax		B	E	
Libourne			E	
Marsan	B		E	
Nérac	B	B	E	
Périgord		B	E	
Tartas		B		
Ustaritz	B	E		
Montauban				
Cahors	B	B	E	
Rodez	B	B	E	
Villefranche.		X	E	
Limoges				
Angoulême	B		E	
Dorat	E	E		
Limoges	B	R	E	
Tulle	R	B	E	
La Rochelle				
La Rochelle	R	B	E	
Rochefort			E	
Saintes	B	B		
St. Jean	E		E	
Poitiers				
Chatellerault	B	B	E	
Marches-Com.	E			
Poitiers	B	B	E	
Tours				
Angers		B	E	
Loudun	B	B	E	
Mans(le)	E	E	E	
Saumur	B	E	E	
Tours	B	E	E	
Caen				
Caen	E	R	E	
Coutances	B	R	E	

	C	*N*	*T*	*U*
Alençon				
Alençon	E	R	E	
Bellême	B	B	E	
Château-neuf.	E	B		
Rouen				
Caudebec.	R	E	E	
Chaumont.		R	E	
Evreux	B	B	E	
Rouen	B	B		E
Amiens				
Amiens	E	E	E	
Boulogne	R	E	B	
Calais	B	E	E	
Montreuil	E	R	E	
Péronne	B			B
Ponthieu	B	B	E	
St.Quentin	E	E		
Lille				
Artois	B	B	E	
Bailleul		R	E	
Douai		R	E	
Lille	R	B	E	
Soissons				
Château-Th.	E	B	E	
Clermont.	E	B	E	
Crépy	E	B	E	
Soissons	B	E	E	
Vermand.	E	B	E	
Villers Cot.	B	B	E	
Châlons.				
Châlons.	B	B	E	
Chaumont.	E	B	E	
Langres	E	E	E	
Reims	E	E	E	
Sézanne	B	B	E	
Troyes	E	B	E	
Vitry.	B	B	E	
Dijon				
Autun	B	B	E	
Auxerre	B	B	E	
Bar-s.-S.	E	B	E	
Belley	B	B	E	
Bourg-en-B.				B
Châlon-s.-S.	B	E	E	
Charolles	E	E	E	
Châtillon.	B	B	E	
Dijon	B	B	E	
Gex	B	B	E	
Mâcon	B	E	E	
Semur.	B	B	E	
Trévoux	R	B	E	
Besançon				
Aval			E	
Besançon	B		E	
Dôle	R	R	E	
Grenoble				
Dauphiné				E
Orange	B	R		
Aix				
Aix	E	B	E	
Arles(ville)	R			E
Castellane	E	E		
Digne		E	E	
Draguignan	B			
Forcalquier	R	B	E	
Grasse	E	E	E	
Marseilles	E	B	E	
Sisteron	E	B		
Toulon			E	
Rennes				
Auray			E	
Brest			E	
Carhaix			E	
Lesneven			E	
Morlaix			E	
Nantes	E		E	
Ploërmel			E	
Quimper			E	
Rennes	B		E	
St. Brieuc	E	E	E	
St. Malo	E			
Vannes			E	
Valenciennes				
Avesnes	B	B	E	
Cambrésis	R	B	E	
Quesnoy	R	R		
Valencien.			E	
Nancy				
Bar-le-D.	E	B	E	
Bitche	E			
Blamont	E			
Boulay	E		E	
Bourmont	E	X	E	
Bouzonville	E	B	E	
Briey		B	E	
Bruyères		R		E
Château-S.	B		E	
Châtel-s.-M.		X	E	
Darney		E		
Dieuze	E	R	E	
Etain	E	B	E	
Fénes-trange	R	R	E	
La Marche	B			
Lixheim			E	E
Longuyon	E	B	B	
Lunéville	E	B		
Mirecourt	E		E	
Nancy	R	E	E	
Nomény	E	E		
Neufchâteau			E	
Pont-à-M.		E	E	
Remire-mont	E	E	E	
St. Dié			E	
St. Mihiel	E	B	E	
Sarreguem.	R	E	E	
Vézelise	B	E	E	
Villers.				E
Metz				
Longwy	E	E	E	
Metz	E	B	E	
Mohon				E
Sarrebourg		B	E	
Sarrelouis				E
Thionville	B	R	E	
Toul	R	E	E	
Verdun	B	B	E	
Vic	B	E	E	
Strasbourg				
Belfort	B	B	E	
Colmar	R	E	E	
Dix Villes			E	
Haguenau		E	E	
Strasbourg			E	

X. CAHIERS MAKING RESERVATIONS ON THE RENUNCIATION OF PRIVILEGES

Total: 80 cahiers. 29 C, 50 N, 1 T

	C	*N*	*T*	*U*
Paris				
Etampes		N		
Mantes	C			
Paris h.m.		N		
Sens	C			
Orléans				
Gien		N		
Montargis	C			
Bourges				
Bourges		N		
Moulins				
Moulins		N		
Lyon				
Lyon		N		
Riom				
Clermont.	C	N		
Riom		N	T	
St.Flour		N		
Montpellier				
Annonay		N		
Mende	C	N		
Montpell.	C			
Puy-en-V.		N		
Toulouse				
Casteln.	C			
Auch				
Soule		N		
Bordeaux				
Bazas	C	N		
Castelm.	C			
Dax	C	N		
Nérac	C			
Montauban				
Cahors	C			
Limoges				
Angoul.		N		
Limoges		N		
Tulle		N		
Poitiers				
Poitiers		N		

	C	*N*	*T*	*U*
Tours				
Loudun		N		
Alençon				
Alençon		N		
Bellême	C	N		
Rouen				
Evreux	C	N		
Rouen	C	N		
Amiens				
Calais	C			
Montreuil.		N		
Lille				
Artois	C	N		
Bailleul		N		
Soissons				
Crépy.		N		
Soissons	C			
Villers Cot.	C			
Châlons.				
Châlons	C	N		
Sézanne	C	N		
Troyes		N		
Vitry.		N		
Dijon				
Auxerre		N		
Châtillon.	C	N		
Mâcon	C			
Semur	C			
Trévoux		N		
Aix				
Marseille		N		
Sisteron		N		
Valenciennes				
Avesnes		N		
Quesnoy		N		
Nancy				
Bar-le-D.	C			
Briey		N		
Bruyères		N		
Château-S.	C			
Dieuze		N		
Etain		N		
Fénes-trange	C	N		
Longuyon		N		
Nancy	C			
St. Mihiel		N		
Metz				
Metz		N		
Sarrebourg		N		
Thionville		N		
Verdun	C	N		

XI. CAHIERS DEMANDING THE SAME LAW FOR ALL CLASSES

Total: 98 cahiers. 15 C, 11 N, 68 T, 2 U, 1 NT, 1 CT

	C	*N*	*T*	*U*
Paris				
Etampes			T	
Mantes		N	T	
Meaux			T	
Melun			T	
Paris h.m.	C	N	T	
Paris i.m.			T	
Provins	C		T	
Senlis		N	T	
Sens	C			
Orléans				
Chartres			T	
Dourdan		N		
Gien		N	T	
Bourges				
Bourges		N		
Moulins				
Nivernais			T	
St. Pierre.			T	
Lyon				
Forez			T	
Lyon		N		V
Ville-franche.	C			
Montpellier				
Nîmes			T	
Toulouse				
Castelnaud.			T	
Toulouse	C			
Perpignan				
Perpignan			T	
Auch				
Auch			T	
Bigorre			T	
Foix			T	
Bordeaux				
Bordeaux			T	
Tartas			T	
Ustaritz			T	
Montauban				
Rodez			T	
Limoges				
Tulle			T	
La Rochelle				
La Rochelle			T	
Saintes		N		
Rochefort.			T	
Poitiers				
Poitiers			T	
Tours				
Saumur			T	
Caen				
Coutances			T	
Alençon				
Alençon	C		T	
Château-neuf.		N	T	
Rouen				
Caudebec			T	
Evreux			T	
Rouen				V
Amiens				
Amiens			T	
Boulogne			T	
Calais			T	
Péronne		N͡	T	
St.Quentin	C		T	
Lille				
Artois		N	T	
Soissons				
Château-Th.			T	
Dijon				
Autun	C		T	
Auxerre	C		T	
Bourg-en-B.				U
Charolles			T	
Châtillon	C		T	
Dijon	C		T	
Mâcon			T	
Semur			T	
Trévoux		N	T	
Besançon				
Amont				U
Aval			T	
Besançon	C		T	
Dôle	C		T	
Aix				
Toulon			T	
Rennes				
Carhaix			T	
Dinan			T	
Morlaix			T	
Nantes	C		T	
Ploërmel			T	
Quimper			T	
Rennes	C		T	
Vannes			T	
Nancy				
Briey			T	
Bruyères	C͡		T	
Pont-à-M.			T	
St. Mihiel			T	
Sarreguem.			T	
Metz				
Metz			T	
Verdun			T	
Strasbourg				
Belfort			T	

XII. CAHIERS DEMANDING THE DEMOCRATIZATION OF THE CLERGY

Total: 73 cahiers. 59 C, 4 N, 7 T, 3 U

	CNTU		*CNTU*		*CNTU*		*CNTU*
Paris		Castel-		Rouen		Aix	
Beauvais	C	naud.	C	Evreux	C	Arles (V.)	C
Etampes	C	Limoux	CN	Amiens		Digne	C
Mantes	T	Toulouse	CN	Calais	C	Draguig-	
Montfort	U	Auch		Montreuil.	C	nan	C
Nemours	C	Armagnac	C	Lille		Forcal-	
Provins	T	Bigorre	C	Artois	C	quier	C
Sens	C	Bordeaux		Soissons		Grasse	C T
Orléans		Bordeaux	C T	Clermont.	C	Sisteron	C
Vendôme	C	Castelmor.	C	Châlons		Toulon	T
Moulins		Libourne	C	Reims	C	Rennes	
Guéret	C	Mont-de-		Troyes	C	Dol	C
Moulins	C	M.	C	Vitry.	CNT	Nantes	C
Lyon		Nérac	C	Dijon		Nancy	
Lyon	C	Poitiers		Autun	C	Dieuze	C
Montpellier		Poitiers	C	Bar-s.-S.	C	Etain	C
Annonay	C	Tours		Bourg-en-B.	U	La Marche	C
Beziers	C	Mans(le)	C	Châlon.	C	Longuyon	C
Montpel-		Tours	C	Charolles	C	Lunéville	C
lier	C	Caen		Mâcon	C	Villers.	U
Puy-en-V.	C	Coutances	C	Besançon		Metz	
Villen.	CN	Alençon		Aval	C	Verdun	C
Toulouse		Alençon	C			Strasbourg	
Carcas-		Bellême	C			Belfort	C
sonne	C					Haguenau	T

XIII. CAHIERS BY "GENERALITY" THAT DEMANDED NO DISCRIMINATION AGAINST THE THIRD ESTATE

Total: 177 cahiers. 21 C, 13 N, 139 T, 3 U, 1 NT

Paris	15	Auch	7	Alençon	3	Grenoble	1
Orléans	6	Bordeaux	7	Rouen	4	Aix	7
Bourges	1	Montauban	2	Amiens	9	Rennes	13
Moulins	5	Limoges	8	Lille	1	Valenciennes	3
Lyon	5	La Rochelle	3	Soissons	6	Nancy	14
Riom	2	Poitiers	3	Châlons	7	Metz	8
Montpellier	7	Tours	5	Dijon	8	Strasbourg	5
Toulouse	4	Caen	1	Besançon	6	Corsica	1

XIV. CAHIERS THAT WERE MOST STRONGLY DEMOCRATIC

Total: 55 cahiers. 4 C, 5 N, 43 T, 2 U, 1 NT

	CNTU
Paris	
Mantes	NT
Montfort.	U
Nemours	NT
Paris h.m.	T
Paris i.m.	T
Orléans	
Blois	T
Chartres	T
Moulins	
St. Pierre.	T
Lyon	
Forez	T
Lyon	T
Montpellier	
Montpellier	T
Nîmes	T

	CNTU
Auch	
Bigorre	T
Foix	T
Rivière-V.	T
Rustaing	U
Bordeaux	
Bordeaux	T
Castelmoron	T
Limoges	
Angoulême	T
Poitiers	
Chatell.	T
Poitiers	T
Tours	
Angers	T
Mans(le)	T

	CNTU
La Rochelle	
Saintes	T
Alençon	
Alençon	C T
Bellême	C
Château-neuf.	NT
Amiens	
Amiens	T
Péronne	CNT
Ponthieu	N
Châlons	
Chaumont.	T
Reims	CNT
Vitry.	T
Dijon	
Dijon	T
Mâcon	T

	CNTU
Aix	
Digne	T
Draguignan	T
Forcalquier	T
Grasse	T
Toulon	T
Rennes	
Auray	T
Brest	T
Nantes	T
Ploërmel	T
Quimper	T
Rennes	T
Vannes	T
Nancy	
Briey	T

XV. CAHIERS SHOWING MARKED INDIVIDUALISM

Total: 302 cahiers. 49 C, 114 N, 130 T, 5 U, 1 CT, 2 NT
Marked Individualism: 31 cahiers. 3 C, 14 N, 12 T, 1 U, 1 CT

	CNTU
Paris	
Beauvais	N
Etampes	C T
Mantes	CN
Meaux	CNT
Melun	CNT
Montfort.	U
Nemours	NT
Paris h.m.	CNT
Paris i.m.	CNT
Provins	CNT
Senlis	NT
Sens	NT
Orléans	
Blois	NT
Chartres	CNT
Dourdan	NT
Gien	NT
Montargis	NT
Orléans	C T
Vendôme	NT
Bourges	
Bourges	NT

	CNTU
Moulins	
Moulins	C T
Nivernais	NT
St. Pierre.	T
Lyon	
Forez	C T
Lyon	CNTV
Ville-franche.	CN
Riom	
Clermont	C T
Riom	NT
Montpellier	
Annonay	CNT
Beziers	N
Mende	NT
Montpell.	NT
Nîmes	NT
Ville-neuve.	CNT
Toulouse	
Carcass.	NT

	CNTU
Casteln.	T
Limoux	T
Toulouse	NT
Perpignan	
Perpignan	NT
Auch	
Auch	CNT
Bigorre	T
Comminges	N
Foix	T
Quatre-V.	T
Rivière.	NT
Rustaing	U
Soule	T
Bordeaux	
Agen	C T
Bazas	N
Bordeaux	NT
Castel-moron	NT
Dax	NT
Libourne	T
Nérac	C T

	CNTU
Périgord	NT
Tartas	N
Ustaritz	CNT
Montauban	
Cahors	NT
Rodez	CNT
Ville-franche.	NT
Limoges	
Angou-lême	CNT
Dorat	NT
Limoges	T
Tulle	NT
La Rochelle	
La Rochelle	NT
Rochefort.	T
Saintes	CNT
Poitiers	
Chatel-lerault	C T
Poitiers	NT

	CNTU
Tours	
Angers	NT
Loudun	NT
Mans(le)	NT
Saumur	CNT
Tours	CNT
Caen	
Caen	CNT
Coutances	N
Alençon	
Alençon	CNT
Bellême	CN
Châteauneuf.	NT
Rouen	
Caudebec.	CNT
Chaumont.	NT
Evreux	NT
Rouen	N V
Amiens	
Amiens	CNT
Boulogne	N
Calais	NT
Péronne	NT
Ponthieu	NT
St. Quentin	CNT
Lille	
Artois	NT
Bailleul	N
Douai	NT
Lille	CN
Soissons	
Château Th.	NT
Crépy	NT
Clermont.	CNT
Vermandois	CNT
Villers Cot.	NT
Châlons.	
Châlons	CN
Chaumont.	CNT
Reims	CNT
Troyes	CNT
Vitry.	CNT
Dijon	
Autun	CNT
Auxerre	CNT
Bar-s.S.	CNT
Châlon-s.S.	N
Charolles	NT
Châtillon	NT
Dijon	CNT
Mâcon	NT
Semur	NT
Trévoux	N
Besançon	
Aval	N
Besançon	NT
Dôle	NT
Grenoble	
Orange	C T
Aix	
Arles (V.)	NT
Digne	CNT
Draguignan	T
Forcalquier	NT
Marseille	CNT
Sisteron	N
Toulon	T
Rennes	
Auray	T
Brest	T
Lannion	T
Lesneven	T
Nantes	T
Ploërmel	T
Rennes	T
Vannes	T
Valenciennes	
Avesnes	NT
Cambrésis	NT
Quesnoy	N
Valenciennes	T
Nancy	
Briey	NT
Bruyères	CT
Etain	CN
Fénestrange	U
Lixheim	T
Lunéville	N
Longuyon	T
Mirecourt	N
Nancy	NT
Neufchâteau	T
Pont-à-M.	T
Rozières	U
St. Dié	T
St. Mihiel	N
Sarreguem.	N
Vézelise	T
Metz	
Longwy	NT
Metz	N
Mohon	U
Sedan	T
Thionville	N
Toul	T
Verdun	NT
Vic	NT
Strasbourg	
Colmar	C T
Haguenau	T

XVI. CAHIERS EXPRESSLY HOSTILE TO PAPAL INFLUENCE IN THE FRENCH CHURCH

(Hostility to the Concordat, approval of the Pragmatic Sanction, or both.)

Total: 57 cahiers. 8 C, 16 N, 31 T, 2 U

	CNTU
Paris	
Beauvais	CNT
Paris h.m.	T
Orléans	
Blois	T
Chartres	N
Gien	T
Montargis	T
Lyon	
Lyon	N
Montpellier	
Villeneuve.	T
Auch	
Armagnac	NT
Auch	T
Comminges	T
Rivière-V.	T
Bordeaux	
Nérac	T
Limoges	
Angoulême	T
Tulle	N
La Rochelle	
Saintes	T
St. Jean.	N
Rochefort	T
Tours	
Angers	T
Tours	NT
Alençon	
Alençon	T
Rouen	
Evreux	T
Amiens	
Ponthieu	C
St. Quentin	T
Soissons	
Viller-Cot.	C
Lille	
Lille	N
Chalons	
Reims	C
Sézanne	N
Dijon	
Châtillon.	T
Dijon	T
Mâcon	T
Trévoux	T
Besançon	
Dôle	N
Aix	
Aix	N
Digne	C T
Draguignan	T
Forcalquier	NT
Toulon	T
Rennes	
Rennes	T
Vannes	T
Nancy	
Bar-le-D.	N
Bourmont	T
Bouzonville	CN
Château-S.	C
Longuyon	N
Rozières	U
Villers-la-M.	U
Metz	
Metz	NT
Toul	C

XVII. CAHIERS CONCERNED FOR A REGENERATION OF THE MOEURS

Total: 119 cahiers. 74 C, 22 N, 22 T, 1 U

	CNTU		*CNTU*		*CNTU*		*CNTU*
Paris		Bigorre	C	Amiens		Aix	
Beauvais	CN	Comminges	T	Amiens	C	Aix	T
Etampes	C	Soule	N	Boulogne	C	Arles (V.)	C
Mantes	C	Bordeaux		Calais	C	Digne	C
Meaux	C	Bordeaux	C T	Montreuil	C	Forcalq.	C
Melun	CN	Castel-		Ponthieu	C	Sisteron	C
Nemours	T	moron	C	Lille		Rennes	
Paris h.m.	CNT	Condom	C	Artois	C	Lesneven	T
Paris i.m.	C T	Dax	C	Bailleul	C	Nantes	C
Orléans		Mont-de-		Douai	C	Rennes	C
Orléans	CN	Mar.	C	Lille	C	Valenciennes	
Moulins		Nérac	C	Châlons		Quesnoy	N
Moulins	C	Montauban		Langres	T	Nancy	
Lyon		Cahors	C	Troyes	C	Bourmont	CN
Lyon	C T	Rodez	N	Vitry-le-F.	C T	Briey	T
Riom		Villefr.	N	Soissons		Darney	N
Clermont		Limoges		Crépy-en-		Dieuze	C
F.	C	Dorat	C	V.	CN	Etain	C
Riom	C	La Rochelle		Dijon		Nancy	CN
Montpellier		La Rochelle	N	Autun	C	Pont-à-M.	T
Annonay	C	Tours		Auxerre	T	St. Dié	T
Beziers	C	Angers	C	Bar-s.-S.	N	St. Mihiel	CN
Montpel-		Tours	C	Belley	CN	Sarreg.	C
lier	C T	Caen		Bourg-en-B.	U	Vézelise	C T
Nîmes	C	Caen	CN	Châtillon.	C	Metz	
Puy-en-V.	C	Coutances	T	Gex	C	Longwy	C
Toulouse		Alençon		Mâcon	C	Metz	C
Carcassonne	N	Alençon	C	Besançon		Toul	C
Castres	CN	Château-		Besançon	C	Verdun	C
Limoux	C T	neuf.	NT	Dôle	T	Strasbourg	
Toulouse	C T	Rouen		Grenoble		Belfort	C
Auch		Evreux	C	Orange	N	Colmar	C
Armagnac	C	Rouen	CN			Dix Villes	T
Auch	C						

XVIII. CAHIERS SHOWING SECULARISM

Total: 188 cahiers. 16 C, 61 N, 107 T, 3 U, 1 NT
The underlined cahiers are ones showing anti-clericalism, and secularism
Total: 36 cahiers. 14 N, 32 T

	CNTU		*CNTU*		*CNTU*		*CNTU*
Paris		Sens	NT	Bourges		Villefranche.	T
Beauvais	N	Orléans		Bourges	T	Riom	
Etampes	T	Blois	NT	Moulins		Clermont.	NT
Mantes	NT	Chartres	NT	Guéret	NT	St.Flour	T
Melun	N	Dourdan	N	Moulins	T	Montpellier	
Nemours	NT	Gien	NT	Nivernais	T	Annonay	T
Paris h.m.	NT	Montargis	NT	St. Pierre.	NT	Beziers	N
Paris i.m.	NT	Orléans	CNT	Lyon		Mende	N
Provins	CNT	Vendôme	T	Forez	CN	Montpellier	NT

	CNTU
Nîmes	T
Puy-en-V.	T
Villeneuve.	NT
Toulouse	
Carcassonne	T
Castelnaud.	N
Limoux	T
Toulouse	T
Perpignan	
Perpignan	N
Auch	
Armagnac	NT
Auch	T
Comminges	T
Foix	CN
Rivière.	T
Bordeaux	
Agen	T
Bordeaux	T
Castel-moran.	NT
Condom	T
Nérac	T
Périgord	T
Montauban	
Rodez	C
Villefranche	N
Limoges	
Angoulême	T
Limoges	N
Tulle	NT
La Rochelle	
La Rochelle	NT
Rochefort.	T
Saintes	T
St.Jean	N
Poitiers	
Chatellerault	T
Poitiers	T
Tours	
Angers	T
Loudun	CN
Saumur	NT
Tours	NT
Caen	
Caen	T
Coutances	NT
Alençon	
Alençon	NT
Bellême	T
Château-neuf.	NT
Rouen	
Caudebec	T
Evreux	T
Rouen	N
Amiens	
Amiens	T
Boulogne	T
Calais	N
Péronne	CNT
Ponthieu	CNT
Lille	
Artois	T
Bailleul	T
Douai	T
Soissons	
Château Th.	NT
Clermont	T
Crépy.	C
Soissons	T
Vermandois	NT
Villers Cot.	T
Châlons	
Châlons	T
Chaumont	NT
Reims	CNT
Sézanne	N
Troyes	NT
Vitry	C T
Dijon	
Autun	NT
Auxerre	NT
Bar-s.-S.	T
Bourg.en-B.	T
Châtillon	T
Mâcon	N
Besançon	
Aval	NT
Dôle	C T
Aix	
Aix	C T
Digne	C T
Draguignan	T
Forcalquier	NT
Grasse	T
Sisteron	N
Rennes	
Brest	T
Lannion	T
Lesneven	T
Nantes	T
Ploërmel	T
Quimper	T
Rennes	T
Vannes	T
Valenciennes	
Avesnes	T
Cambrésis	T
Quesnoy	N
Nancy	
Bar-le-D.	NT
Bouzon-ville	C T
Briey	T
Château-S.	T
Darney	N
Dieuze	NT
Longuyon	N
Lunéville	N
Nancy	N
Neufchâteau	T
Pont-à-M.	T
Rozières	U
Vézelise	T
Villers-la-M.	U
Metz	
Longwy	T
Metz	N
Mohon	U
Toul	C T
Verdun	T
Strasbourg	
Belfort	T
Colmar	C
Dix Villes	T
Corsica	
Corsica	T

XIX. CAHIERS SHOWING PRONOUNCED ETATISME AS REGARDS THE CHURCH

Total: 56 cahiers. 5 C, 17 N, 32 T, 2 U

	CNTU
Paris	
Beauvais	C
Etampes	T
Mantes	NT
Nemours	NT
Paris h.m.	CNT
Paris i.m.	T
Orléans	
Chartres	T
Gien	T
Montargis	NT
Orléans	CN
Moulins	
Moulins	T
Lyon	
Lyon	N
Montpellier	
Annonay	T
Mende	N
Toulouse	
Castelnaud.	N
Limoux	T
Auch	
Armagnac	C
Comminges	T
Bordeaux	
Nérac	T
La Rochelle	
La Rochelle	N
Saintes	T
Tours	
Angers	T
Saumur	NT
Caen	
Coutances	N
Alençon	
Bellême	T

	C	N	T	U
Amiens				
Amiens			T	
Calais		N		
Lille				
Artois			T	
Châlons				
Reims	C		T	
Vitry-le-F.			T	

	C	N	T	U
Dijon				
Autun		N		
Bourg-en-B.				U
Châtillon.			T	
Aix				
Aix			T	
Digne			T	

	C	N	T	U
Draguignan			T	
Forcalquier			T	
Rennes				
Nantes			T	
Brest			T	
Ploërmel			T	
Rennes			T	
Vannes			T	

	C	N	T	U
Nancy				
Bar-le-D.		N		
Lunéville		N		
Pont-à-M.			T	
St. Mihiel		N		
Villers				U
Metz				
Metz		N		

XX. ETATISME IN EDUCATION

Total: 137 cahiers. 24 C, 40 N, 70 T, 1 U, 1 CT, 1 NT

	C	N	T	U
Paris				
Beauvais			T	
Etampes	C			
Mantes		N	T	
Meaux		N		
Melun	C	N	T	
Montfort				U
Nemours		N	T	
Paris h.m.	C	N	T	
Paris i.m.			T	V
Sens		N		
Orléans				
Dourdan			T	
Orléans		N	T	
Vendôme			T	
Moulins				
Moulins	C	N		
Nivernais		N	T	
Lyon				
Lyon		N	T	V
Riom				
Clermont			T	
Riom			T	
Montpellier				
Annonay			T	
Nîmes	C	N		
Puy-en-V.	C			
Toulouse				
Carcassonne			T	
Castelnaud.			T	
Castres		N		
Limoux			T	
Toulouse		N	T	

	C	N	T	U
Auch				
Auch			T	
Rivière-V.			T	
Soule		N		
Bordeaux				
Agen	C		T	
Bazas			T	
Bordeaux	C		T	
Castelmoron			T	
Condom	C			
Dax		N	T	
Nérac	C	N	T	
Périgord		N	T	
Tartas			T	
Montauban				
Villefranche.		N	T	
Limoges				
Angoulême		N		
Dorat	C			
Tulle			T	
La Rochelle				
La Rochelle		N	T	
Saintes	C	N		
Rochefort.			T	
Poitiers				
Poitiers			T	
Tours				
Angers			T	
Mans(le)			T	
Saumur			T	
Tours		N	T	
Caen				
Caen	C		T	
Coutances			T	

	C	N	T	U
Alençon				
Alençon	C	N	T	
Bellême			T	
Rouen				
Caudebec.	C			
Evreux	C	N		
Rouen	C			
Amiens				
Amiens		N	T	
Boulogne	C			
Calais		N	T	
Péronne		N͡T		
Ponthieu		N		
St. Quentin		N		
Lille				
Douai		N		
Soissons				
Château Th.		N	T	
Clermont.		N		
Vermandois			T	
Châlons.				
Reims		N		
Troyes			T	
Vitry.			T	
Dijon				
Auxerre		N		
Belley	C			
Châlon-s.-S.		N	T	
Mâcon	C			
Besançon				
Besançon		N	T	
Dôle	C		T	
Grenoble				
Orange			T	

	C	N	T	U
Aix				
Aix	C		T	
Digne			T	
Draguignan			T	
Forcalquier			T	
Marseille			T	
Toulon			T	
Rennes				
Morlaix			T	
Rennes			T	
Vannes			T	
Valenciennes				
Quesnoy		N		
Nancy				
Bar-le-D.			T	
Bouzon-ville	C			
Briey			T	
Bruyères			C͡T	
Etain		N		
Nancy		N	T	
Sarregue-mines	C			
Vézelise			T	
Metz				
Metz		N	T	
Sarrebourg.			T	
Strasbourg				
Haguenau			T	
Strasbourg			T	
Corsica				
Corsica		N		

XXI. CAHIERS ASKING FOR PUBLICITY OF GOVERNMENTAL ACTION

Includes publicity for the States-General, Printing, Archives, Laws, Constitution, Budget, Finances, etc.

Total: 200 cahiers. 40 C, 67 N, 86 T, 5 U, 1 CT, 1 NT
Underlined cahiers contained the strongest expressions: 15 cahiers. 2 C, 4 N, 8 T, 1 NT

	CNTU
Paris	
Beauvais	NT
Mantes	C T
Meaux	NT
Montfort	U
Nemours	C T
Paris h.m.	NT
Paris i.m.	NT
Provins	N
Senlis	NT
Orléans	
Blois	C
Chartres	T
Dourdan	CN
Orléans	NT
Montargis	N
Bourges	
Bourges	NT
Moulins	
Moulins	T
Nivernais	T
St. Pierre.	T
Lyon	
Forez	NT
Lyon	CNTV
Riom	
Clermont.	C T
Riom	N
St. Flour	T
Montpellier	
Annonay	N
Beziers	N
Mende	T
Montpellier	C T
Nîmes	T
Puy-en-V.	T
Villeneuve.	N
Toulouse	
Cascassonne	N
Castelnaud.	CN
Castres	T
Limoux	NT
Toulouse	NT

	CNTU
Perpignan	
Perpignan	N
Auch	
Armagnac	C
Auch	NT
Bigorre	T
Comminges	N
Foix	N
Rivière-V.	T
Rustaing	U
Soule	CNT
Bordeaux	
Agen	C
Bordeaux	N
Castelmor.	C
Condom	T
Dax	NT
Libourne	T
Mont-de-M.	T
Périgord	T
Ustaritz	CN
Montauban	
Cahors	C
Rodez	CNT
Limoges	
Angoulême	NT
Dorat	C
Tulle	N
La Rochelle	
La Rochelle	T
Saintes	NT
St. Jean.	N
Poitiers	
Chateller.	T
Poitiers	N
Tours	
Angers	NT
Loudun	N
Mans(le)	N
Saumur	NT
Tours	C T
Caen	
Caen	CNT
Coutances	NT
Alençon	
Alençon	N

	CNTU
Rouen	
Caudebec.	N
Evreux	NT
Rouen	V
Amiens	
Amiens	NT
Péronne	NT
St. Quentin	N
Lille	
Artois	CNT
Bailleul	NT
Douai	CN
Lille	C
Soisons	
Clermont.	C T
Crépy-en-V.	T
Châlons	
Châlons.	C T
Chaumont.	CN
Langres	N
Reims	C
Troyes	CN
Vitry.	C
Dijon	
Autun	T
Auxerre	CNT
Bar-s.-S.	C
Belley	N
Bourg.	U
Châlon-s.-S.	N
Châtillon.	C
Dijon	C T
Mâcon	NT
Semur	NT
Trévoux	N
Besançon	
Amont	U
Aval	NT
Besançon	NT
Grenoble	
Orange	T
Aix	
Aix	NT
Digne	T

	CNTU
Forcalquier	T
Marseille	N
Toulon	T
Rennes	
Auray	T
Carhaix	T
Dol	C
Nantes	T
Ploërmel	T
Rennes	T
St. Brieuc	T
St. Malo	C
Vannes	T
Lannion	T
Valenciennes	
Avesnes	T
Valenc.	T
Nancy	
Bar-le-D.	T
Blamont	C
Bourmont	T
Bruyères	CT
Darney	N
Dieuze	NT
Etain	N
Fénestrange	U
Lunéville	CN
Mirecourt	T
Nancy	C
Neufchâteau	T
St. Mihiel	C
Metz	
Metz	CNT
Sarrebourg	N
Toul	C
Verdun	C T
Strasbourg	
Belfort	T
Colmar	T
Dix Villes	T
Haguenau	T
Strasbourg	T

XXII. CAHIERS ASKING FOR FREEDOM OF THE PRESS

Total: 300 cahiers. 21 C, 120 N, 150 T, 6 U, 1 CN, 2 NT

	CNTU
Paris	
Beauvais	NT
Etampes	T
Mantes	NT
Meaux	NT
Melun	CNT
Montfort.	U
Nemours	NT
Paris h.m.	NT
Paris i.m.	NT
Provins	NT
Senlis	NT
Sens	N
Orléans	
Blois	NT
Chartres	NT
Dourdan	N
Gien	C T
Montargis	NT
Orléans	NT
Vendôme	NT
Bourges	
Bourges	NT
Moulins	
Guéret	NT
Moulins	CN
Nivernais	NT
St. Pierre.	T
Lyon	
Forez	NT
Lyon	CNTV
Villefranche.	NT
Riom	
Clermont	NT
Riom	T
St. Flour	NT
Montpellier	
Annonay	CNT
Beziers	N
Mende	NT
Montpellier	NT
Nîmes	NT
Puy-en-V.	T
Villeneuve.	NT
Toulouse	
Carcassonne	NT
Castelnaud.	NT
Limoux	NT
Toulouse	NT
Perpignan	
Perpignan	NT
Auch	
Armagnac	NT
Auch	NT
Bigorre	T
Comminges	NT
Foix	NT
Rivière-V.	NT
Rustaing	U
Bordeaux	
Agen	CNT
Bordeaux	N
Castelmor.	CN
Condom	NT
Dax	NT
Libourne	NT
Mont-de-M.	T
Nérac	CNT
Périgord	NT
Tartas	NT
Ustaritz	T
Montauban	
Cahors	NT
Rodez	C
Villefranche	NT
Limoges	
Angoulême	CNT
Dorat	NT
Limoges	T
Tulle	NT
La Rochelle	
La Rochelle	NT
Saintes	NT
St. Jean.	N
Rochefort.	T
Poitiers	
Chateller.	T
Poitiers	NT
Tours	
Angers	NT
Mans(le)	C
Saumur	CNT
Tours	NT
Caen	
Caen	NT
Coutances	T
Alençon	
Alençon	CNT
Bellême	NT
Château-neuf.	NT
Rouen	
Caudebec	NT
Evreux	NT
Rouen	N V
Amiens	
Amiens	NT
Boulogne	N
Calais	NT
Montreuil	NT
Péronne	NT
Ponthieu	NT
St. Quentin	NT
Lille	
Artois	NT
Bailleul	NT
Douai	N
Lille	NT
Soissons	
Château Th.	NT
Clermont.	NT
Crépy-en-V.	T
Soissons	T
Vermandois	NT
Villers-C.	NT
Châlons	
Chaumont.	NT
Reims	NT
Sézanne	N
Troyes	NT
Vitry-le-F.	NT
Dijon	
Autun	CNT
Auxerre	N
Bar-s.-S.	NT
Belley	T
Bourg-en-B.	U
Châlon-s.-S.	NT
Charolles	NT
Châtillon	CNT
Dijon	CNT
Mâcon	NT
Semur.	NT
Trévoux	T
Besançon	
Amont	U
Aval	NT
Besançon	NT
Dôle	NT
Aix	
Aix	CNT
Arles(V.)	NT
Digne	CNT
Forcalquier	NT
Grasse	T
Marseille	NT
Sisteron	N
Toulon	T
Rennes	
Brest	T
Dinan	T
Lannion	T
Lesneven	T
Morlaix	T
Nantes	T
Ploërmel	T
Quimper	T
Rennes	T
St. Brieuc	T
Vannes	T
Valenciennes	
Cambrésis	NT
Quesnoy	N
Valenciennes	T
Nancy	
Boulay	T
Bouzon-ville	C
Briey	NT
Château-S.	T
Darney	N
Dieuze	C T
Etain	NT
Lixheim	CN
Longuyon	T
Lunéville	N
Mirecourt	NT
Nancy	CNT
Nomény	NT
Neufchâteau	T
Pont-à-M.	T
St. Dié	T
Sarreguem.	N
Vézelise	T
Villers-la-M.	U
Metz	
Longwy	NT
Metz	NTV
Mohon	U
Sarrebourg	N
Thionville	T
Toul	NT
Verdun	NT
Vic	T
Strasbourg	
Colmar	T
Dix Villes	T
Haguenau	T
Strasbourg	T
Corsica	
Corsica	T

XXIII. CAHIERS ASKING FOR RESTRICTION OF THE PRESS

Total: 110 cahiers. 96 C, 7 N, 7 T

	C	*N*	*T*	*U*
Paris				
Etampes	C			
Mantes	C			
Nemours	C			
Paris h.m.	C			
Paris i.m.	C			
Provins	C	N		
Sens	C			
Orléans				
Blois	C			
Chartres	C			
Dourdan	C			
Montargis	C			
Orléans	C		T	
Vendôme	C			
Moulins				
Moulins	C		T	
Nivernais	C			
Lyon				
Forez	C			
Lyon	C			
Villefranche		N		
Riom				
Clermont	C			
Riom	C			
Montpellier				
Beziers	C			
Mende	C			
Montpellier	C			
Nîmes	C	N		
Puy-en-V.	C			
Villeneuve.	C			

	C	*N*	*T*	*U*
Toulouse				
Castelnaud.	C			
Carcassonne	C			
Castres	C			
Limoux	C			
Toulouse	C			
Auch				
Armagnac	C			
Auch	C			
Comminges			T	
Rivière.	C			
Bordeaux				
Bordeaux	C			
Condom	C			
Dax	C			
Libourne	C			
Mont-de-M.	C			
Montauban				
Cahors	C			
Limoges				
Limoges	C			
Dorat	C			
Tulle	C			
La Rochelle				
Saintes	C			
Poitiers				
Chateller.	C			
Tours				
Angers	C			
Tours	C			
Caen				

	C	*N*	*T*	*U*
Caen	C			
Coutances	C	N		
Alençon				
Alençon	C			
Bellême	C			
Châteauneuf.	C			
Rouen				
Caudebec	C			
Evreux	C			
Rouen	C			
Amiens				
Amiens	C			
Boulogne	C			
Calais	C			
Péronne	C			
Ponthieu	C			
Lille				
Artois	C			
Bailleul	C			
Douai	C			
Lille	C			
Soissons				
Clermont.	C			
Crépy.	C	N		
Soissons	C			
Vermand.	C		T	
Villers Cot.	C			
Châlons.				
Chaumont.			T	
Reims	C			
Troyes	C			
Vitry.	C			

	C	*N*	*T*	*U*
Dijon				
Auxerre	C			
Bar-s.-S.	C			
Châlon.	C			
Charolles	C			
Dijon			T	
Gex	C			
Mâcon	C			
Semur			T	
Besançon				
Besançon	C	N		
Dôle	C			
Aix				
Arles (V)	C			
Digne	C	N		
Draguignan	C			
Forcalquier	C			
Marseille	C			
Rennes				
Dol	C			
Nantes	C			
Rennes	C			
St. Malo	C			
Nancy				
Bourmont	C			
Etain	C			
La Marche	C			
Sarreguem.	C			
Metz				
Longwy	C			
Sarrebourg	C			
Verdun	C			
Strasbourg				
Belfort	C			

XXIV. CAHIERS FAVORING THE NATIONALIZATION OF THE ARMY

Total: 29 cahiers. 1 C, 18 N, 8 T, 1 U, 1 NT

	C	*N*	*T*	*U*
Paris				
Melun	C			
Nemours			T	
Senlis		N	T	
Orléans				
Blois		N		

	C	*N*	*T*	*U*
Lyon				
Lyon		N		
Villefranche.			T	
Montpellier				
Villeneuve.		N		

	C	*N*	*T*	*U*
Toulouse				
Carcass.		N		
Bordeaux				
Agen		N		
Ustaritz		N		

	C	*N*	*T*	*U*
Limoges				
Limoges		N		
Tours				
Angers			T	
Mans(le)			T	
Tours		N		

	CNTU		CNTU		CNTU		CNTU
Amiens		Lille		Dijon		Rennes	
Calais	T	Artois	T	Belley	N	Rennes	T
Montreuil.	N	Douai	N	Trévoux	N	Nancy	
Péronne	NT	Châlons		Besançon		Etain	N
Ponthieu	N	Reims	N	Amont	U		
St. Quentin	N			Aval	N		

XXV. CAHIERS FAVORING UNIVERSAL LIABILITY TO MILITARY SERVICE

Total: 29 cahiers. 3 C, 5 N, 20 T, 1 CN

	CNTU		CNTU		CNTU		CNTU
Paris		Bordeaux		Amiens		Lannion	T
Nemours	T	Castelmor.	T	Ponthieu	T	Morlaix	T
Paris h.m.	N	Condom	T	Soissons		Rennes	C
Paris i.m.	N	Limoges		Château Th.	T	Nancy	
Orléans		Angoulême	N	Châlons.		Lixheim	CN
Montargis	C	Dorat	C	Châlons.	T	Nancy	T
Vendôme	T	Limoges	T	Chaumont.	T	Metz	
Lyon		Poitiers		Vitry-le-F.	T	Toul	T
Forez	T	Poitiers	T	Dijon		Verdun	T
Lyon	N	Tours		Auxerre	T		
Riom		Tours	T	Rennes			
Riom	N			Carhaix	T		

XXVI. CAHIERS MAKING DEMANDS FOR NAVAL DEFENSE

Total: 50 cahiers. 5 C, 17 N, 26 T, 1 NT, 1 CN

	CNTU		CNTU		CNTU		CNTU
Orléans		Libourne	NT	Alençon		Aix	
Blois	N	Nérac	T	Alençon	T	Arles (V.)	NT
Gien	T	Périgord	T	Rouen		Marseille	CNT
Montargis	NT	Tartas	N	Caudebec.	T	Toulon	C T
Orléans	T	Ustaritz	CNT	Amiens		Rennes	
Lyon		Montauban		Boulogne.	N	Auray	T
Lyon	N	Ville-franche.	N	Calais	T	Brest	T
Riom		La Rochelle		Montreuil.	N	Nantes	T
Riom	T	La Rochelle	N	Ponthieu	T	Quimper	T
Montpellier		Saintes	N	Lille		Rennes	T
Montpellier	NT	Poitiers		Bailleul	N	Vannes	T
Auch		Poitiers	T	Dijon		Nancy	
Bigorre	T	Tours		Dijon	C	Lixheim	CN
Comminges	T	Tours	N	Semur.	C	Metz	
Rivière-V.	T	Caen				Sarrebourg	N
Bordeaux		Coutances	N				
Bordeaux	T						

XXVII. OPINIONS FOR AND AGAINST THE GILDS

A. Suppression or Maintenance

X for suppression
M for maintenance
Totals: For suppression: 82 cahiers. 10 C, 17 N, 53 T, 2 U
For maintenance: 46 cahiers. 1 C, 3 N, 40 T, 1 U, 2 NT

	C	*N*	*T*	*U*
Paris				
Beauvais			M	
Etampes			M	
Mantes			M	
Meaux			M	
Melun			X	
Montfort				M
Nemours			X	
Paris h.m.			X	
Paris i.m.		X		
Provins			X	
Senlis			M	
Orléans				
Blois		X	X	
Dourdan			M	
Orléans			X	
Montargis			X	
Vendôme			X	
Bourges				
Bourges			X	
Moulins				
Nivernais			X	
St. Pierre.			X	
Lyon				
Lyon		X	X	
Riom				
Clermont.	X		M	
Riom		X	X	
Montpellier				
Beziers	X			
Montpellier			X	
Nîmes			M	
Villeneuve.			X	
Auch				
Bigorre	X		X	
Foix			X	

	C	*N*	*T*	*U*
Bordeaux				
Agen	X		X	
Bordeaux			M	
Nérac			X	
Périgord		M	M	
Tartas			M	
Montauban				
Cahors		X	X	
Rodez		M		
Villefranche.			X	
Limoges				
Angoulême			M	
La Rochelle				
La Rochelle			X	
Rochefort.			X	
Poitiers				
Chateller.			M	
Poitiers			X	
Tours				
Angers			M	
Loudun			M	
Mans(le)			X	
Saumur	X		X	
Tours		X	X	
Caen				
Caen			M	
Coutances		X	X	
Alençon				
Château-neuf.		X	X	
Rouen				
Caudebec.			X	
Rouen				M
Amiens				
Amiens			M	
Calais			M	
Péronne				M

	C	*N*	*T*	*U*
Ponthieu	X		X	
St. Quen-tin	X		X	
Lille				
Bailleul			M	
Douai			M	
Lille			X	
Soissons				
Clermont.		X		
Verman-dois	X	X	X	
Châlons				
Châlons.			X	
Chau-mont.	X	X	M	
Reims			M	
Troyes			X	
Dijon				
Autun		X	X	
Auxerre	X	X	X	
Bourg-en-B.				X
Trévoux		X		
Besançon				
Besançon			M	
Grenoble				
Orange			M	
Aix				
Arles (V)				M
Digne			X	
Forcalquier			X	
Marseille			M	
Toulon			M	
Rennes				
Auray			X	
Brest			M	
Lesneven			M	
Morlaix			M	

	C	*N*	*T*	*U*
Nantes			M	
Ploërmel			X	
Quimper			M	
Vannes			X	
Valenciennes				
Valenciennes			M	
Nancy				
Boulay			M	
Bouzonville			X	
Briey			X	
Darney		X		
Dieuze			X	
Etain			X	
Fénestrange				X
Lunéville		M		
Mirecourt			X	
Neufchâteau			X	
Pont-à-M.			X	
St. Dié			X	
St. Mihiel		X		
Vézelise			M	
Metz				
Sarrebourg			X	
Thionville			M	
Verdun		X	M	
Vic	M			
Strasbourg				
Colmar			X	
Dix Villes			M	
Strasbourg			M	
Corsica				
Corsica			M	

B. Decision on Suppression or Maintenance left to States-General

Total: 9 cahiers. 1 N, 8 T.
N—Belley
T—Alençon, Dax, Evreux, Metz, Metz(ville), Paris *intra-muros,* Rennes, Villefranche-de-Beaujolais

XXVIII. CAHIERS GIVING BOTH MERCANTILIST AND LIBERAL ECONOMIC DEMANDS

Total: 199 cahiers. 24 C, 48 N, 121 T, 3 U, 1 CN, 2 NT

	CNTU
Paris	
Beauvais	T
Mantes	T
Meaux	T
Melun	CNT
Montfort.	U
Nemours	T
Paris h.m.	CNT
Paris i.m.	C T
Provins	T
Senlis	T
Orléans	
Blois	N
Dourdan	NT
Montargis	T
Orléans	N
Vendôme	T
Bourges	
Bourges	T
Moulins	
Moulins	N
St. Pierre.	T
Lyon	
Forez	T
Lyon	CNTV
Riom	
Clermont.	NT
Riom	NT
St.Flour	N
Montpellier	
Mende	T
Montpellier	CNT
Nîmes	NT
Villeneuve.	T
Toulouse	
Carcassonne	T
Castelnaud.	NT
Castres	NT
Limoux	T
Toulouse	T
Auch	
Auch	C T
Comminges	T
Foix	T
Soule	NT

	CNTU
Bordeaux	
Agen	N
Bordeaux	T
Castelmor.	N
Nérac	T
Périgord	NT
Tartas	T
Ustaritz	CN
Montauban	
Cahors	T
Rodez	N
Villefranche.	T
La Rochelle	
La Rochelle	T
Rochefort.	T
Limoges	
Angoulême	N
Tulle	T
Poitiers	
Chateller.	C T
Poitiers	NT
Tours	
Angers	C T
Loudun	T
Mans(le)	T
Saumur	C T
Tours	NT
Caen	
Caen	T
Coutances	T
Alençon	
Alençon	T
Bellême	T
Rouen	
Caudebec.	T
Chaumont.	T
Evreux	T
Rouen	CN V
Amiens	
Amiens	NT
Calais	NT
Péronne	CNT
Ponthieu	T
Montreuil.	T
St. Quentin	CNT

	CNTU
Lille	
Bailleul	C T
Douai	T
Lille	T
Soissons	
Château Th.	NT
Clermont.	T
Soissons	T
Vermandois	CNT
Villers-Cot.	T
Châlons.	
Châlons.	C T
Chaumont.	C T
Langres	T
Troyes	CNT
Reims	NT
Vitry.	C T
Dijon	
Autun	T
Auxerre	CNT
Bar-s.-S.	NT
Belley	N
Châlon-s.-S.	NT
Dijon	T
Mâcon	N
Semur	N
Bescançon	
Besançon	T
Amont	T
Dôle	C T
Aix	
Aix	T
Arles (V)	NT
Digne	T
Draguignan	T
Forcalquier	T
Grasse	T
Marseille	NT
Toulon	T
Rennes	
Auray	T
Brest	T
Dinan	T
Lannion	T

	CNTU
Lesneven	T
Nantes	T
Morlaix	T
Ploërmel	T
Quimper	T
Rennes	T
St. Brieuc	T
Vannes	T
Valenciennes	
Avesnes	CNT
Cambrésis	T
Quesnoy	N
Valenciennes	T
Nancy	
Boulay	T
Bouzonville	NT
Briey	T
Château-S.	T
Darney	N
Dieuze	T
Etain	CN
Fénestrange	U
Lixheim	CN
Lunéville	CN
Nancy	T
Neufchâteau	T
Pont-à-M.	T
St. Mihiel	N
Sarreguem.	T
Vézelise	T
Metz	
Longwy	N
Mohon	U
Sarrebourg	N
Sedan	T
Toul	T
Verdun	NT
Strassbourg	
Belfort	T
Dix Villes	T
Corsica	
Corsica	T

XXIX. CAHIERS SHOWING MERCANTILIST DEMANDS

Total: 40 cahiers. 11 C, 11 N, 16 T, 2 U

	CNTU		*CNTU*		*CNTU*		*CNTU*
Paris		Caen		Grenoble		Metz	
Beauvais	C	Caen	N	Orange	C T	Longwy	T
Etampes	C T	Lille		Aix		Metz	N V
Orléans		Artois	C	Barcell.	T	Sarrebourg	C T
Dourdan	C	Soissons		Grasse	C	Thionville	T
Riom		Crépy.	N	Rennes		Toul	C
St. Flour	T	Villers-Cot.	CN	Carhaix	T	Vic	C T
Auch		Dijon		Nancy		Strassbourg	
Rivière-V.	N	Belley	T	Bar-le-D.	NT	Colmar	N
Bordeaux		Besançon		Bouzon-		Strasbourg	T
Bordeaux	N	Aval	NT	ville	C	Corsica	
Libourne	N	Dôle	N	Rozières	U	Corsica	T
Ustaritz	T			Villers-la-M.	U		

XXX. CAHIERS SHOWING ONLY LIBERAL ECONOMIC DEMANDS

Total: 139 cahiers. 42 C, 55 N, 40 T, 1 CN, 1 U

	CNTU		*CNTU*		*CNTU*		*CNTU*
Paris		Perpignan		Tours		Dijon	
Beauvais	N	Perpignan	NT	Loudun	CN	Autun	CN
Mantes	C	Auch		Mans(le)	CN	Belley	C
Meaux	N	Armagnac	CNT	Saumur	T	Bourg-en-V.	U
Nemours	N	Auch	N	Tours	NT	Châlon-s.-S.	N
Paris i.m.	N	Bigorre	C T	Caen		Charolles	N
Provins	N	Comminges	N	Coutances	CN	Châtillon.	C
Senlis	N	Foix	N	Alençon		Semur	T
Sens	T	Soule	C	Alençon	CN	Trévoux	NT
Orléans		Bordeaux		Bellême	CN	Besançon	
Blois	T	Agen	C T	Château-		Dôle	C
Chartres	NT	Bazas	NT	neuf.	NT	Aix	
Gien	T	Bordeaux	C	Rouen		Aix	N
Montargis	N	Castelmor.	C T	Caudebec.	C	Rennes	
Orléans	C T	Condom	NT	Evreux	C	Rennes	C
Moulins		Dax	T	Amiens		Valenciennes	
Moulins	T	Libourne	T	Boulogne	NT	Cambrésis	N
Nivernais	CNT	Mont-		Montreuil.	CN	Nancy	
Lyon		de-M.	C T	Ponthieu	CN	Blamont	C
Forez	N	Montauban		St. Quentin	N	Dieuze	N
Villefr.	NT	Cahors	NT	Lille		La Marche	C T
Riom		Rodez	C T	Artois	NT	Mirecourt	T
Clermont.	C	Villefr.	N	Bailleul	N	Nomény	CN
Riom	C	Limoges		Lille	CN	St. Dié	T
Montpellier		Angou-		Soissons		St. Mihiel	C
Annonay	T	lême	C T	Clermont.	CN	Sarreguem.	CN
Beziers	C T	Limoges	CNT	Crépy.	T	Vézelise	C
Puy-en-V.	T	Tulle	N	Soissons	C	Metz	
Villeneuve.	CN	La Rochelle		Châlons.		Longwy	T
Toulouse		La Rochelle	N	Châlons.	N	Sarrelouis	CN
Carcassonne	N	Saintes	CNT	Chaumont.	N	Strasbourg	
Limoux	N	St. Jean.	C	Vitry.	N	Colmar	T
Toulouse	N					Hagenau	T

XXXI. CAHIERS EXPRESSING OPINIONS ON FEUDAL JUSTICE

A abolish R reform D diminish M maintain

Totals: Abolition 71 cahiers. 8 C, 61 T, 2 U
Reform 52 cahiers. 6C, 9N, 35 T, 2 U
Diminution 44 cahiers. 11 C, 6 N, 25 T, 1 U, 1 NT
Maintenance 27 cahiers. 2 C, 23 N, 2 T

	C	*N*	*T*	*U*
Paris				
Beauvais			R	
Etampes			A	
Mantes	A		A	
Meaux			A	
Melun			D	
Montfort				A
Nemours			A	
Paris h. m.	R			
Provins			D	
Sens			A	
Orléans				
Blois	A		A	
Chartres		D	A	
Dourdan			A	
Gien			R	
Montarg.		M	A	
Orléans		R	A	
Vendôme	A		A	
Bourges				
Bourges		M		
Moulins				
Moulins			A	
Nivern.	R		A	
St.Pierre.			A	
Lyon				
Forez	D			
Lyon			R	
Riom				
Clermont		M		
St.Flour			A	
Montpellier				
Annonay			A	
Mende		M	A	
Montpel.			A	
Nîmes			A	
Villeneuve			A	

	C	*N*	*T*	*U*
Toulouse				
Casteln.			A	
Castres		M		
Perpignan				
Perpignan			D	
Auch				
Armagn.			D	
Auch		M		
Béarn			R	
Comming.		M		
Foix			A	
Quat.-V.			R	
Riv.-V.	D		A	
Bordeaux				
Bordeaux			R	
Castelmor.			R	
Condom			R	
Dax		M	R	
Libourne			R	
Marsan	A		R	
Nérac		D	A	
Montauban				
Cahors			A	
Rodez	D			
Limoges				
Angoul.		R	R	
Dorat			R	
Limoges		M		
Tulle			M	
La Rochelle				
La Roch.			D	
Rochef't.			R	
Saintes			R	
Poitiers				
Châtell.	M		A	
Poitiers	D		D	
Tours				
Angers	A	R	A	
Mans(le)			A	
Loudun	D		R	

	C	*N*	*T*	*U*
Saumur			A	
Tours		R	A	
Caen				
Caen			D	
Coutances			A	
Alençon				
Alençon		D	A	
Bellême		D	R	
Châ' neuf.		R	R	
Rouen				
Caudebec.			A	
Chaumont.			D	
Evreux			D	
Amiens				
Amiens		R	D	
Boulogne	D	D		
M'treuil	M		D	
Péronne				D
Ponthieu		M	R	
St.Quen.			M	
Lille				
Artois		M	D	
Bailleul	R		R	
Douai	R		M	
Soissons				
Château-Th.		R		
Clermont			D	
Crépy.			D	
Soissons			D	
Verman.	R	M		
Châlons.				
Châlons.		M	R	
Chaum't	D			
Reims			R	
Troyes	D	M	R	
Vitry.	R	M	R	
Dijon				
Auxerre			R	

	C	*N*	*T*	*U*
Bar-s.-S.			A	
Belley		M		
Bourg.				R
Châl.-s-S.			R	
Charol.	A		A	
Châtil.	D	M	D	
Dijon			R	
Gex		M	R	
Mâcon			D	
Trévoux		M		
Besançon				
Amont			A	
Aval		R	R	
Besançon			R	
Dôle		R	A	
Aix				
Aix			A	
Digne			R	
Drag'n.			A	
Forcalq.			A	
Grasse			A	
Marseille			A	
Toulon			A	
Rennes				
Auray			A	
Brest			A	
Carhaix			A	
Dinan			A	
Lannion			D	
Lesneven			D	
Morlaix			A	
Nantes	A		A	
Ploërmel			A	
Quimper			A	
Rennes			A	
St.Brieuc			A	
Tréguier	A			
Vannes			A	

	C	N	T	U
Valencien.				
Avesnes			A	
Cambrés.		M		
Nancy				
Bar-le-D.		M		
Bouzonv.			D	
Château-S.			D	
Etain			A	
Fénestr.				D
Lixheim			D	
Longuyon		M		
Neufchât.			D	
Rozières				R
St. Dié			R	
St.Mihiel		M		
Vézelise			A	
Metz				
Longwy			A	
Metz		D	D	D
Mohon				A
Sarrebourg			A	
Toul			A	
Verdun			A	
Vic			R	
Strasbourg				
Belfort	D			
Colmar	D		R	
Haguenau			R	

XXXII. CAHIERS DEMANDING REFORM OR ABOLITION OF FEUDAL DUES

Total: 186 cahiers. 33 C, 11 N, 147 T, 4 U, 1 CT

	C	N	T	U
Paris				
Beauvais			T	
Etampes	C		T	
Mantes	C		T	
Meaux			T	
Melun		N	T	
Montfort.				U
Nemours			T	
Paris h.m.	C		T	
Paris i.m.			T	
Senlis			T	
Sens			T	
Orléans				
Chartres		N	T	
Dourdan		N	T	
Gien			T	
Montargis	C		T	
Orléans			T	
Vendôme	C			
Bourges				
Bourges			T	
Moulins				
Guéret			T	
Nivernais			T	
St. Pierre			T	
Lyon				
Forez		N	T	
Lyon			T	V
Villefranche.			T	
Riom				
Clermont.			T	
Riom			T	
St. Flour			T	
Montpellier				
Mende			T	
Montpellier			T	
Nîmes			T	
Villeneuve.			T	
Puy-en-V.			T	
Toulouse				
Castelnaud.			T	
Limoux			T	
Toulouse			T	
Auch				
Béarn			T	
Bigorre	C		T	
Comminges			T	
Foix			T	
Quatre-V.			T	
Rivière-V.			T	
Rustaing				U
Bordeaux				
Agen			T	
Bazas			T	
Bordeaux			T	
Castelmor.	C		T	
Condom			T	
Dax			T	
Libourne			T	
Mont-de-M.	C			
Nérac	C		T	
Périgord			T	
Tartas			T	
Montauban				
Cahors	C		T	
Ville-franche.		N		
Limoges				
Angoulême			T	
Dorat	C		T	
Limoges	C		T	
Tulle			T	
La Rochelle				
La Rochelle			T	
Saintes		N	T	
Poitiers				
Poitiers			T	
Tours				
Angers			T	
Loudun	C		T	
Mans(le)	C		T	
Saumur	C		T	
Tours	C		T	
Caen				
Caen			T	
Coutances			T	
Alençon				
Alençon			T	
Bellême	C		T	
Châteaun.		N	T	
Rouen				
Caudebec.			T	
Chaumont.			T	
Evreux			T	
Amiens				
Amiens			T	
Boulogne.	C			
Calais			T	
Péronne	C			
Ponthieu			T	
St. Quent.	C	N	T	
Lille				
Artois			T	
Bailleul		N	T	
Douai			T	
Soissons				
Château Th.			T	
Clermont.			T	
Crépy.	C	N	T	
Soissons			T	
Verman-dois	C		T	
Châlons.				
Châlons.			T	
Chaumont.			T	
Langres			T	
Sézanne			T	
Troyes			T	
Vitry.	C		T	
Dijon				
Auxerre			T	
Bar-s.-S.			T	
Châlon-s.-S.			T	
Châtillon.			T	
Dijon			T	
Gex			T	
Trévoux			T	
Besançon				
Amont			T	
Aval			T	
Besançon			T	
Dôle			T	

	CNTU
Aix	
Aix	T
Digne	T
Draguignan	T
Forcalquier	T
Grasse	T
Toulon	T
Rennes	
Auray	T
Brest	T
Carhaix	T
Dinan	T
Dol	C
Lannion	T
Lesneven	T
Morlaix	T
Nantes	C T
Ploërmel	T
Quimper	T
Rennes	T
St. Brieuc	T
St. Malo	C
Tréguier	C
Vannes	T
Valenciennes	
Avesnec	C T
Cambrésis	T
Valencien.	T
Nancy	
Bar-le-D.	T
Bourmont	T
Bouzonville	C
Briey	T
Bruyères	CT
Château-S.	C T
Châtel.	T
Dieuze	C T
Etain	T
La Marche	T
Lunéville	C
Longuyon	T
Mirecourt	T
Nancy	T
Neufchâteau	T
Nomény	NT
Pont-à-M.	T
Rozières	U
St. Mihiel	C
Sarreguem.	T
Vézelise	T
Villers.	U
Metz	
Longwy	T
Metz	TV
Thionville	T
Toul	T
Verdun	T
Vic	T
Strasbourg	
Belfort	T
Colmar	T

XXXIII. CAHIERS SHOWING MARKED UTILITARIANISM

Total: 252 cahiers. 70 C, 67 N, 109 T, 2 U, 1 CN, 1 CT, 2 NT
Strong utilitarianism (underlined) 67 cahiers. 13 C, 20 N, 32 T, 2 U

	CNTU
Paris	
Beauvais	CNT
Etampes	C T
Mantes	CNT
Meaux	CN
Melun	C T
Montfort.	U
Nemours	C T
Paris h.m.	C T
Paris i.m.	CNT
Provins	NT
Sens	CNT
Orléans	
Blois	CNT
Chartres	NT
Dourdan	NT
Gien	T
Montargis	CNT
Orléans	CNT
Vendôme	C
Moulins	
Moulins	CNT
Nivernais	NT
St. Pierre.	N
Lyon	
Forez	CNT
Lyon	CNTV
Villefranche.	CN
Riom	
Clermont.	CNT
Riom	NT
St. Flour	N
Montpellier	
Beziers	CN
Mende	C T
Montpellier	C T
Nîmes	NT
Villeneuve.	T
Toulouse	
Carcassonne	NT
Castres	C
Limoux	T
Toulouse	T
Perpignan	
Perpignan	NT
Auch	
Auch	T
Béarn	CN
Bigorre	C
Comminges	N
Foix	N
Rivière.	T
Bordeaux	
Agen	CN
Bordeaux	C T
Castelmor.	T
Condom	C T
Dax	C
Nérac	C T
Périgord	NT
Tartas	T
Montauban	
Cahors	C
Rodez	C T
Villefr.	NT
Limoges	
Angoul.	CN
Dorat	C
Limoges	CN
Tulle	T
La Rochelle	
La Rochelle	NT
Rochefort	T
Saintes	N
St. Jean.	N
Poitiers	
Chatell.	C T
Poitiers	NT
Tours	
Angers	CNT
Loudun	NT
Mans(le)	C T
Tours	CN
Caen	
Caen	T
Alençon	
Alençon	C
Bellême	C T
Châteaun.	CNT
Rouen	
Caudebec.	C
Chaumont.	T
Evreux	CNT
Rouen	CN V
Amiens	
Amiens	CNT
Boulogne	CN
Calais	T
Montreuil.	NT
Péronne	CNT
Ponthieu	CNT
St. Quentin	C
Lille	
Artois	CN
Bailleul	T
Douai	NT
Soissons	
Château. Th.	NT
Clermont.	CNT
Crépy.	N

	CNTU
Soissons	C
Vermandois	CNT
Châlons.	
Châlons.	T
Chaumont.	T
Reims	CNT
Troyes	C T
Dijon	
Autun	C T
Auxerre	N
Bar-s.-S.	NT
Châlon-s.-S.	C T
Châtillon	CN
Dijon	T
Mâcon	N
Semur.	N
Trévoux	NT
Besançon	
Aval	N

	CNTU
Besançon	T
Dôle	NT
Aix	
Aix	C T
Arles	NT
Digne	T
Draguignan	T
Forcalquier	C T
Marseille	NT
Sisteron	C
Rennes	
Auray	T
Brest	T
Dinan	T
Dol	C
Lannion	T
Lesneven	T
Morlaix	T
Nantes	C T

	CNTU
Ploërmel	T
Quimper	T
Rennes	C T
St. Brieuc	T
St. Malo	C
Vannes	T
Valenciennes	
Cambrésis	T
Quesnoy	N
Valencien.	T
Nancy	
Bar-le-D.	T
Bitche	C
Bourmont	T
Bouzonville	T
Briey	C
Bruyères	CT
Château-S.	T
Dieuze	T

	CNTU
Etain	N
Nancy	CN
Neufchâteau	T
Pont-à-M.	T
Rozières	U
St. Dié	T
St. Mihiel	N
Sarreguem.	C
Vézelise	T
Metz	
Longwy	C T
Metz	NTV
Sarrebourg	T
Toul	C
Verdun	T
Strasbourg	
Strasbourg	T
Corsica	
Corsica	NT

XXXIV. CAHIERS DEMANDING THE ABOLITION OF SERFDOM

Total: 45 cahiers. 7 C, 5 N, 31 T, 1 U, 1 NT

	CNTU
Paris	
Mantes	N
Melun	C
Paris h.m.	CNT
Paris i.m.	T
Orléans	
Blois	T
Bourges	
Bourges	T
Moulins	
Moulins	T
Nivernais	T
Lyon	
Lyon	NT

	CNTU
Riom	
Clermont.	T
Montpellier	
Puy-en-V.	T
Toulouse	
Toulouse	T
Limoges	
Tulle	T
Poitiers	
Poitiers	T
Tours	
Loudun	T
Caen	
Caen	C
Alençon	
Châteauneuf.	T

	CNTU
Amiens	
Amiens	T
Péronne	CNT
St. Quentin	C
Lille	
Douai	T
Soissons	
Château Th.	T
Châlons	
Chaumont.	T
Langres	T
Dijon	
Autun	C
Auxerre	C T
Trévoux	T

	CNTU
Besançon	
Dôle	T
Aix	
Digne	NT
Draguignan	T
Valenciennes	
Avesnes	T
Nancy	
Bourmont	T
Rozières	U
Metz	
Metz	T
Verdun	T
Vic	T
Strasbourg	
Belfort	T

XXXV. CAHIERS DEMANDING THE ABOLITION OF SLAVERY

Total: 49 cahiers. 17 C, 11 N, 20 T, 1 NT

	CNTU
Paris	
Beauvais	N
Mantes	CN
Melun	C
Paris h.m.	NT

	CNTU
Paris i.m.	C T
Provins	T
Senlis	T
Orléans	
Blois	C T

	CNTU
Vendôme	T
Bourges	
Bourges	T
Lyon	
Forez	C

	CNTU
Bordeaux	
Bordeaux	C
Mont-de-M.	C
Ustaritz	T

	CNTU
Poitiers	
Chatell.	T
Tours	
Angers	T
Saumur	C
Tours	C
Caen	
Coutances	T
Alençon	
Alençon	C T
Bellême	C
Chateau-neuf.	T
Rouen	
Chaumont.	N
Amiens	
Amiens	NT
Boulogne.	N
Calais	N
Péronne	CNT
Soissons	
Château Th.	NT
Clermont.	N
Vermandois	NT
Châlons	
Reims	C T
Sézanne	C
Dijon	
Charolles	T
Besançon	
Aval	T
Rennes	
Rennes	C T
Valenciennes	
Avesnes	C
Quesnoy	N
Metz	
Metz	C

XXXVI. CAHIERS SHOWING MARKED HUMANITARIANISM

Total: Humanitarianism—341 cahiers. 106 C, 78 N, 146 T, 8 U, 1 CN, 2 NT
Strong Humanitarianism—76 cahiers. 14 C, 18 N, 42 T, 1 U, 1 NT

	CNTU
Paris	
Beauvais	CNT
Etampes	C T
Mantes	CNT
Meaux	C T
Melun	C T
Montfort	U
Paris h.m.	CNT
Paris i.m.	CNT
Nemours	C T
Provins	CNT
Senlis	NT
Sens	NT
Orléans	
Blois	CNT
Chartres	CNT
Dourdan	N
Gien	NT
Montargis	CNT
Orléans	C T
Vendôme	C T
Bourges	
Bourges	NT
Moulins	
Guéret	C T
Moulins	C T
Nivernais	CNT
St. Pierre.	T
Lyon	
Forez	C T
Lyon	CNTV
Villefr.	CN
Riom	
Clermont.	C T
Riom	NT
St. Flour	T
Montpellier	
Beziers	C
Mende	CNT
Montpel-lier	C T
Nîmes	NT
Puy-en-V.	C T
Villeneuve.	CNT
Toulouse	
Carcas-sonne	CN
Castelnaud.	T
Castres	C T
Limoux	C T
Toulouse	C T
Perpignan	
Perpignan	NT
Auch	
Béarn	CN
Bigorre	C T
Foix	T
Rivière-V.	C T
Rustaing	U
Soule	CNT
Bordeaux	
Agen	CN
Bazas	C
Bordeaux	CNT
Castelmor.	C T
Condom	C T
Dax	C
Libourne	C
Marsan	C
Nérac	C T
Périgord	N
Tartas	T
Ustaritz	T
Montauban	
Cahors	CNT
Rodez	CNT
Villefr.	N
Limoges	
Angoulême	NT
Dorat	NT
Limoges	CN
Tulle	T
La Rochelle	
La Roch.	NT
Rochefort.	T
Saintes	CNT
Poitiers	
Chatell.	C T
Marches Com.	U
Poitiers	C T
Tours	
Angers	C T
Loudun	C T
Mans(le)	C T
Saumur	C
Tours	CNT
Caen	
Caen	CNT
Coutances	NT
Alençon	
Alençon	CNT
Bellême	C T
Château-neuf.	CNT
Rouen	
Caudebec.	CNT
Chaumont.	NT
Evreux	CNT
Rouen	C V
Amiens	
Amiens	CNT
Boulogne	CNT
Calais	CNT
Montreuil	T
Péronne	CNT
Ponthieu	C T
St. Quentin	CNT
Lille	
Artois	CNT
Bailleul	NT
Douai	NT
Lille	C
Soissons	
Château Th.	NT
Clermont.	CNT
Crépy.	T
Soissons	C T
Verman-dois	CNT
Villers-Cot.	C T
Châlons	
Châlons.	C T
Chaumont.	C T
Langres	T
Reims	CNT
Sézanne	CNT
Troyes	CNT
Vitry.	C T
Dijon	
Autun	CNT
Auxerre	CNT

	CNTU
Bar-s.-S.	CNT
Belley	CN
Bourg-en-B.	U
Châlon-s.-S.	CNT
Charolles	C T
Châtillon.	CNT
Dijon	C T
Mâcon	NT
Semur	CNT
Trévoux	NT
Besançon	
Amont	TU
Aval	CNT
Besançon	C T
Dôle	NT
Grenoble	
Orange	C
Aix	
Aix	C T
Arles	NT
Digne	CNT
Draguignan	T
Forcalquier	CNT
Marseille	T
Sisteron	C
Toulon	T
Rennes	
Auray	T
Brest	T
Carhaix	T
Lannion	T
Lesneven	T
Morlaix	T
Nantes	T
Ploërmel	T
Rennes	C T
St. Brieuc	T
St. Malo	C
Vannes	T
Valenciennes	
Avesnes	C T
Cambrésis	NT
Quesnoy	N
Valenciennes	T
Nancy	
Bar-le-D.	NT
Bitche	C
Bourmont	T
Château-S.	T
Darney	N
Dieuze	C T
Etain	N
La Marche	T
Nancy	C T
Neufchâteau	T
Pont-à-M.	T
Rozières	U
St. Dié	T
St. Mihiel	CN
Sarreguem.	C
Villers-la-M.	U
Metz	
Metz	C TV
Mohon	U
Sarrebourg	NT
Sedan	T
Thionville	T
Toul	N
Verdun	CNT
Vic	C T
Strasbourg	
Belfort	C T
Strasbourg	T
Corsica	
Corsica	NT

XXXVII. CAHIERS SHOWING A TENDENCY TOWARD STATE "SOCIALISM"

Total: 26 cahiers. 2 C, 6 N, 18 T

	CNTU
Paris	
Mantes	T
Nemours	T
Lyon	
Lyon	NT
Toulouse	
Toulouse	C
Bordeaux	
Agen	N
Dax	N
Amiens	
Calais	T
Lille	
Artois	T
Soissons	
Château-Th.	T
Crépy.	T
Dijon	
Dijon	T
Semur.	N
Besançon	
Dôle	C
Rennes	
Lesneven	T
Rennes	T
St. Brieuc	T
Vannes	T
Valenciennes	
Quesnoy	N
Nancy	
Darney	N
Longuyon	T
Neufchâteau	T
Metz	
Longwy	T
Metz	TV
Strasbourg	
Strasbourg	T

XXXVIII. CAHIERS SHOWING PRONOUNCED GALLICANISM

Total: 190 cahiers. 60 C, 42 N, 85 T, 4 U, 1 NT

	CNTU
Paris	
Beauvais	C T
Etampes	T
Mantes	C T
Meaux	C
Nemours	C T
Paris h.m.	NT
Paris i.m.	NT
Provins	T
Senlis	T
Sens	C
Orléans	
Blois	C T
Chartres	CNT
Gien	T
Montargis	C T
Orléans	T
Moulins	
Guéret	T
Nivernais	C T
St. Pierre	T
Lyon	
Forez	T
Lyon	CN V
Villefranche.	N
Riom	
Riom	CN
St. Flour	N
Montpellier	
Annonay	T
Mende	C T
Nîmes	T
Puy-en-V.	C T
Villeneuve.	C T
Toulouse	
Carcass.	T
Castres	C
Limoux	T
Toulouse	N
Auch	
Armagnac	NT
Bigorre	C
Comminges	NT

	CNTU
Foix	T
Riviére-V.	T
Bordeaux	
Agen	C T
Condom	C
Dax	C
Libourne	C T
Mont-de-M.	C T
Nérac	T
Ustaritz	C T
Montauban	
Cahors	C T
Rodez	C T
Limoges	
Angoulême	T
Dorat	CN
Limoges	CNT
Tulle	N
La Rochelle	
Rochefort.	T
Saintes	C T
St. Jean	N
Poitiers	
Poitiers.	C T
Tours	
Angers	T
Loudun	CNT
Mans(le)	C T
Saumur	C T
Tours	NT

	CNTU
Caen	
Caen	C T
Coutances	N
Alençon	
Alençon	N
Château-neuf.	NT
Rouen	
Evreux	C
Rouen	C V
Amiens	
Amiens	T
Boulogne	C
Calais	N
Péronne	CNT
Ponthieu	C
St. Quentin	CNT
Lille	
Artois	NT
Bailleul	C
Lille	N
Soissons	
Château Th.	T
Clermont.	C
Soissons	C T
Vermandois	CN
Villers-Cot.	C
Châlons.	
Châlons.	N

	CNTU
Chaumont.	C
Reims	C T
Sézanne	N
Troyes	NT
Vitry.	C
Dijon	
Autun	C
Auxerre	T
Bar-s.-S.	T
Belley	C T
Bourg-en-B.	U
Châlon-s.-S.	T
Charolles	T
Châtillon.	C T
Dijon	T
Mâcon	C T
Trévoux	T
Besançon	
Amont	T
Aval	NT
Besançon	C T
Dôle	CNT
Aix	
Aix	CN
Digne	T
Draguignan	T
Forcalquier	NT
Marseille	N
Sisteron	N
Toulon	T

	CNTU
Rennes	
Nantes	C T
Ploërmel	T
Rennes	T
Vannes	T
Nancy	
Bar-le-D.	N
Bourmont.	T
Bouzonville	C
Briey	T
Château-S.	C
Darney	N
Etain	T
Fénestrange	U
La Marche	C
Longuyon	N
Lunéville	CN
Mirecourt	T
Nancy	N
Pont-à-M.	T
Rozières	U
Villers-la-M.	U
Metz	
Longwy	N
Metz	NT
Toul	C
Verdun	NT
Vic	CNT

XXXIX. CAHIERS ASKING FOR ARMY DISCIPLINE IN CONFORMITY WITH FRENCH NATIONAL CHARACTER

Total: 94 cahiers. 1 C, 58 N, 32 T, 2 U, 1 NT

	CNTU
Paris	
Beauvais	NT
Montfort.	U
Nemours	T
Paris i.m.	N
Orléans	
Blois	NT
Orléans	T
Bourges	
Bourges	N
Moulins	
Nivernais	NT
St. Pierre	T

	CNTU
Lyon	
Lyon	N
Villefranche.	N
Riom	
Clermont.	N
Montpellier	
Montpellier	N
Villeneuve.	T
Toulouse	
Carcassonne	NT
Castelnaud.	N
Castres	N
Limoux	NT

	CNTU
Toulouse	NT
Perpignan	
Perpignan	NT
Auch	
Comminges	N
Foix	NT
Rivière-V.	N
Bordeaux	
Bordeaux	N
Condom	N
Dax	N
Nérac	N
Périgord	N

	CNTU
Ustaritz	N
Montauban	
Villefranche.	N
Limoges	
Limoges	N
La Rochelle	
La Rochelle	N
Rochefort.	T
Saintes	N
Poitiers	
Poitiers	N
Tours	
Tours	N

	CNTU
Caen	
Caen	NT
Coutances	NT
Alençon	
Alençon	N
Rouen	
Rouen	N
Amiens	
Amiens	C T
Calais	N
Montreuil.	N
Ponthieu	NT
St. Quentin	T
Lille	
Artois	NT
Bailleul	T
Douai	N
Soissons	
Vermandois	N
Châlons	
Chaumont.	N
Reims	N
Troyes	NT
Vitry.	NT
Dijon	
Autun	NT
Auxerre	NT
Bourg-en-B.	U
Châlon-s.-S.	N
Charolles	NT
Dijon	T
Mâcon	N
Semur	N
Besançon	
Besançon	NT
Dôle	N
Aix	
Arles (V)	N͡T
Toulon	T
Rennes	
Rennes	T
Valenciennes	
Cambrésis	T
Quesnoy	N
Nancy	
Bar-le-D.	N
Bruyères	N
St. Mihiel	N
Vézelise	T
Metz	
Metz	N
Toul	N
Verdun	T

XL. CAHIERS ADVOCATING METHODS FOR THE PROPAGATION OF PATRIOTISM

Total: 100 cahiers. 16 C, 43 N, 35 T, 4 U, 1 CT, 1 NT

	CNTU
Paris	
Beauvais	N
Mantes	NT
Meaux	N
Melun	N
Montfort.	U
Nemours	T
Paris h.m.	T
Paris i.m.	NT
Senlis	NT
Orléans	
Blois	N
Orléans	N
Vendôme	C
Moulins	
Moulins	CN
Nivernais	CN
St. Pierre	T
Lyon	
Forez	N
Lyon	CNT
Riom	
Clermont.	NT
Riom	NT
Montpellier	
Villeneuve	N
Toulouse	
Carcassonne	NT
Perpignan	
Perpignan	N
Auch	
Soule	NT
Bordeaux	
Bordeaux	N
Nérac	N
Limoges	
Angoulême	N
La Rochelle	
La Rochelle	NT
Saintes	N
St. Jean.	N
Poitiers	
Poitiers	C T
Tours	
Angers	T
Mans(le)	N
Saumur	C
Tours	N
Alençon	
Alençon	N
Bellême	N
Rouen	
Rouen	V
Amiens	
Amiens	T
Calais	T
Péronne	N͡T
St. Quentin	N
Lille	
Artois	N
Bailleul	N
Lille	T
Soissons	
Château Th.	N
Villers-Cot.	CNT
Châlons.	
Châlons.	C T
Chaumont.	T
Reims	CN
Dijon	
Autun	C
Bar-s-S.	C
Belley	N
Bourg-en-B.	U
Besançon	
Amont	U
Aval	NT
Besançon	T
Aix	
Aix	CN
Digne	T
Draguignan	T
Forcalquier	C T
Marseille	T
Toulon	T
Rennes	
Rennes	T
Vannes	T
Nancy	
Bar-le-D.	NT
Briey	T
Bruyères	C͡T
Darney	N
Etain	N
Nancy	N
Rozières	U
St. Mihiel	CN
Vézelise	T
Metz	
Longwy	C
Metz	V
Toul	CNT

XLI. CAHIERS SHOWING AN ELEMENT OF MILITARISM IN THEIR PATRIOTISM

Total: 75 cahiers. 3 C, 39 N, 28 T, 2 U, 1 CN, 2 NT

	CNTU
Paris	
Melun	CN
Paris i.m.	N
Provins	N
Orléans	
Blois	N
Gien	T
Montargis	N
Orléans	T
Bourges	
Bourges	N
Lyon	
Lyon	N
Villefranche	T
Riom	
Riom	T
Montpellier	
Montpellier	N
Toulouse	
Carcassonne	NT
Limoux	N
Perpignan	
Perpignan	N
Auch	
Auch	N
Comminges	N
Bordeaux	
Bordeaux	N
Castelmoron	T
Ustaritz	N
Montauban	
Villefranche	N
Limoges	
Limoges	N
Tulle	N
La Rochelle	
La Rochelle	N
Saintes	N
Tours	
Angers	T
Tours	N
Rouen	
Rouen	C
Amiens	
Amiens	T
Boulogne	N
Montreuil	N
Péronne	$\widehat{NT}$
Ponthieu	NT
St. Quentin	T
Lille	
Bailleul	T
Douai	N
Lille	T
Soissons	
Château Th.	NT
Vermandois	N
Châlons.	
Chaumont.	N
Reims	N
Troyes	T
Vitry.	T
Dijon	
Auxerre	NT
Dijon	T
Mâcon	N
Semur	N
Besançon	
Aval	N
Besançon	N
Dôle	N
Aix	
Arles (V.)	$\widehat{NT}$
Barcelonnette	T
Digne	T
Marseille	T
Toulon	T
Rennes	
Auray	T
Brest	T
Carhaix	T
Valenciennes	
Cambrésis	N
Nancy	
Lixheim	$\widehat{CN}$
Pont-à-M.	T
Rozières	U
St. Mihiel	N
Vézelise	T
Villers-la-M.	U
Metz	
Sarrebourg	N
Toul	C T
Verdun	NT

XLII. CAHIERS WHOSE ECONOMIC PATRIOTISM WAS AN IMPORTANT FACTOR OF THEIR NATIONAL PATRIOTISM

Total: 55 cahiers. 2 C, 11 N, 41 T, 1 NT

	CNTU
Paris	
Beauvais	NT
Etampes	T
Nemours	T
Paris i.m.	T
Orléans	
Orléans	N
Lyon	
Lyon	N
Montpellier	
Villeneuve.	T
Auch	
Soule	T
Bordeaux	
Bordeaux	T
Montauban	
Cahors	NT
Limoges	
Angoulême	N
Dorat	N
La Rochelle	
La Rochelle	T
Poitiers	
Poitiers	T
Tours	
Angers	T
Mans(le)	T
Caen	
Caen	T
Rouen	
Caudebec.	T
Rouen	V
Amiens	
Amiens	T
Calais	T
Ponthieu	T
St. Quentin	T
Lille	
Artois	T
Bailleul	NT
Douai	T
Lille	T
Châlons.	
Châlons.	C
Troyes	T
Aix	
Aix	T
Arles	$\widehat{NT}$
Forcalquier	T
Grasse	T
Marseille	N
Rennes	
Brest	T
Dinan	T
Morlaix	T
Nantes	T
Ploërmel	T
Quimper	T
Rennes	T
Vannes	T
Valenciennes	
Cambrésis	T
Quesnoy	N
Nancy	
Briey	T
Etain	N
Longuyon	T
Vézelise	T
Metz	
Sarrebourg	N
Sedan	T
Strasbourg	
Belfort	C
Colmar	T

XLIII. CAHIERS WHOSE PATRIOTISM SHOWED A STRONG ELEMENT OF COSMOPOLITANISM

Total: 90 cahiers. 18 C, 29 N, 38 T, 3 U, 1 CT, 1 NT

	CNTU		*CNTU*		*CNTU*		*CNTU*
Paris		Nîmes	T	Poitiers	T	Dijon	
Beauvais	C	Toulouse		Tours		Autun	C
Mantes	CNT	Carcassonne	N	Angers	N	Bar-s.-S.	T
Melun	C T	Perpignan		Loudun	CN	Belley	N
Nemours	T	Perpignan	N	Mans(le)	C T	Semur	C
Montfort.	U	Auch		Tours	N	Trévoux	NT
Paris h.m.	T	Armagnac	T	Caen		Aix	
Provins	C T	Auch	T	Caen	CNT	Arles (V)	NT
Sens	T	Bigorre	C T	Alençon		Digne	T
Orléans		Rustaing	U	Alençon	N	Draguignan	T
Blois	N	Bordeaux		Amiens		Forcalquier	T
Gien	T	Agen	T	Amiens	C T	Rennes	
Moulins		Bordeaux	N	Calais	N	Lannion	T
Nivernais	CN	Condom	N	Montreuil	N	Rennes	T
St. Pierre.	T	Tartas	N	Ponthieu	NT	Nancy	
Lyon		Limoges		Lille		Briey	N
Lyon	NT	Angoulême	N	Bailleul	T	Bruyères	CT
Riom		Dorat	T	Soissons		Nancy	T
Clermont.	N	La Rochelle		Château Th.	T	St. Mihiel	C
Riom	NT	La Rochelle	NT	Verman-		Metz	
St. Flour	T	Rochefort.	T	dois	C	Longwy	T
Montpellier		Saintes	CNT	Châlons.		Metz	C
Beziers	N	Poitiers ¶		Chaumont.	N	Arches	U
Montpell.	NT	Chatell.	CNT	Reims	C		

XLIV. CAHIERS EVINCING TRADITIONAL PATRIOTISM TOWARD THE KING

Total: 78 cahiers. 36 C, 23 N, 16 T, 3 U

	CNTU		*CNTU*		*CNTU*		*CNTU*
Paris		Montpellier		Limoges		Montreuil.	T
Provins	C	Mende	C	Angoulême	N	Lille	
Orléans		Villeneuve.	C	Limoges	C	Bailleul	C
Dourdan	C T	Toulouse		Poitiers		Douai	C
Gien	N	Castres	N	Marches		Lille	C
Montargis	C	Limoux	C	Com.	U	Soissons	
Orléans	C	Auch		Poitiers	N	Château	
Vendôme	C	Auch	N	Caen		Th.	N
Moulins		Comminges	T	Coutances	CN	Crépy.	NT
Moulins	N	Foix	N	Alençon		Soissons	C T
Lyon		Navarre	U	Alençon	C	Châlons	
Forez	C	Quatre-V.	T	Bellême	CN	Vitry.	NT
Lyon	C	Montauban		Château-		Dinjo	
Villefranche	T	Cahors	C	neuf.	C	Châlon-s.-	
Riom		Rodez	N	Amiens		S.	C
Clermont.	C	Bordeaux		Boulogne.	CNT	Gex	CNT
Riom	T	Périgord	N	Amiens	C	Semur	C
St. Flour	N	Ustaritz	C	Calais	C	Trévoux	T

	CNTU
Besançon	
Aval	C
Grenoble	
Orange	C
Aix	
Barcelon.	C
Sisteron	N
Rennes	
St. Malo	C
Valenciennes	
Avesnes	NT
Cambrésis	N
Nancy	
Châtel.	N
Fénestrange	U
La Marche	C T
Longuyon	N
Mirecourt	C
Thiaucourt	C
Metz	
Longwy	NT
Metz	C
Strasbourg	
Dix Villes	T

XLV. CAHIERS SHOWING PATRIOTISM PRIMARILY TOWARD THE NATION

Total: 113 cahiers. 12 C, 43 N, 52 T, 4 U, 2 NT

	CNTU
Paris	
Beauvais	N
Mantes	T
Melun	T
Montfort.	U
Nemours	NT
Paris h.m.	NT
Paris i.m.	NT
Provins	NT
Senlis	NT
Orléans	
Blois	N
Chartres	N
Dourdan	N
Moulins	
Moulins	T
Nivernais	NT
St. Pierre.	T
Lyon	
Forez	T
Lyon	NT
Riom	
Riom	N
Montpellier	
Montpellier	NT
Villeneuve.	NT
Nîmes	T
Auch	
Comminges	N
Bordeaux	
Agen	T
Bazas	N
Bordeaux	N
Dax	N
Montauban	
Villefranche	N
La Rochelle	
La Rochelle	T
Saintes	NT
Poitiers	
Chatell.	C T
Tours	
Angers	T
Loudun	C
Mans(le)	C T
Saumur	T
Tours	N
Caen	
Caen	C T
Alençon	
Alençon	N
Château-neuf.	NT
Rouen	
Caudebec.	C T
Rouen	C V
Amiens	
Amiens	NT
Calais	NT
Montreuil	N
Péronne	CN͡T
Ponthieu	NT
St. Quentin	T
Lille	
Artois	N
Bailleul	T
Lille	N
Soissons	
Château Th.	T
Clermont.	C
Crépy	C T
Châlons.	
Châlons.	C
Reims	CNT
Troyes	NT
Dijon	
Auxerre	N
Bar-s.-S.	T
Châlon-s.-S.	T
Dijon	T
Mâcon	NT
Semur.	NT
Besançon	
Aval	N
Besançon	T
Aix	
Arles (V)	N͡T
Digne	T
Draguignan	T
Forcalquier	NT
Marseille	N
Toulon	T
Rennes	
Brest	T
Nantes	T
Ploërmel	T
Rennes	T
Nancy	
Bouzonville	N
Briey	NT
Etain	N
Fénestrange	U
Darney	N
Rozières	U
Villers.	U
Metz	
Metz	TV
Toul	CN
Verdun	N

XLVI. COMPOSITE TABLE OF LOYALTIES

P National patriotism strongest (to King, King and Nation, Nation, etc.)

M Mixed loyalties: national patriotism combined with regionalism or class spirit, or both. (This does not include class spirit on the part of the third estate, because such spirit was usually a phase of their national patriotism.)

O Other loyalties, regional, or class, or both, outweigh national patriotism.

X No sentiment shown

	C	*N*	*T*	*U*
Paris				
Beauvais	M	P	P	
Etampes	P		P	
Mantes	P	P	P	
Meaux	P	P	P	
Melun	P	M	P	
Montfort				P
Nemours	X	M	P	
Paris h.m.	P	P	P	
Paris i.m.	P	P	P	O
Provins	M	P	P	
Senlis		P	M	
Sens	P	M	P	
Orléans				
Blois	P	M	P	
Chartres	M	P	P	
Dourdan	P	P	P	
Gien	X	P	X	
Montargis	P	P	P	
Orléans	M	M	P	
Vendôme	M	P	X	
Bourges				
Bourges	O	M	X	
Moulins				
Guéret	P	P	M	
Moulins	P	P	P	
Nivernais	M	P	M	
St. Pierre.		X	P	
Lyon				
Forez	P	X	P	
Lyon	P	P	P	P
Villefranche.	P	X	P	
Riom				
Clermont.	P	M	P	
Riom	O	P	P	
St. Flour		O	O	
Montpellier				
Annonay	X	M	X	
Beziers	O	M		
Mende	M	M	M	
Montpellier	M	M	M	
Nîmes	X	M	P	
Puy-en-V.	M		M	
Villeneuve.	X	M	M	
Toulouse				
Carcassonne	M	P	P	
Castelnaud.	X	X	X	
Castres	X	M	X	
Limoux	M	M	M	
Toulouse	O	M	M	
Perpignan				
Perpignan		M	M	
Auch				
Armagnac	M	X	O	
Auch	M	M	M	
Béarn			O	O
Bigorre	X		M	
Comminges		P	P	
Foix		P	P	
Quatre-V.			M	
Rivière-V.	X	X	M	
Rustaing				M
Soule	M	M	M	
Navarre				O
Bordeaux				
Agen	P	M	M	
Bazas	O	M	M	
Bordeaux	P	P	P	
Castelmoron	X	P	M	
Condom	M	M	P	
Dax	M	P	O	
Libourne	P	X	P	
Mont-de-M.	M		M	
Nérac	X	M	X	
Périgord		M	X	
Tartas		M	O	
Ustaritz	O	X	M	
Montauban				
Cahors	O	O	M	
Rodez	M	M	X	
Villefranche.		M	M	
Limoges				
Angoulême	P	M	X	
Dorat	X	M	M	
Limoges	M	M	X	
Tulle	X	M	O	
La Rochelle				
La Rochelle		M	M	
Saintes	P	P	M	
St. Jean.	X	M	P	
Rochefort.			P	
Poitiers				
Chatell.	P		M	
Marches Com.				M
Poitiers	M	M	M	
Tours				
Angers	X	M	P	
Loudun	P	M	X	
Mans(le)	P	X	P	
Saumur	P	P	P	
Tours	X	M	X	
Caen				
Caen	M	M	M	
Coutances	M	M	P	
Alençon				
Alençon	M	M	X	
Bellême	P	M	M	
Châteauneuf.	M	P	P	
Rouen				
Caudebec.	M	O	M	
Chaumont.		M	M	
Evreux	X	M	O	
Rouen	M	M		P
Amiens				
Amiens	M	P	M	
Boulogne.	O	O	O	
Calais	O	P	P	
Montreuil.	M	M	M	
Péronne	P			P
Ponthieu	P	M	P	
St. Quentin	M	X	M	
Lille				
Artois	O	M	M	
Bailleul	M	M	O	
Douai	O	M	M	
Lille	O	M	P	
Soissons				
Château Th.		M	P	
Clermont.	P	P	P	
Crépy.	M	P	P	
Soissons	P		M	
Vermandois	M	P	P	
Villers-Cot.	X	M	X	
Châlons				
Châlons.	P	M	M	
Chaumont.	P	P	P	
Langres			M	
Reims	P	M	M	
Sézanne	P	M	X	
Troyes	P	M	M	

	C	N	T	U
Vitry.	P	M	M	
Dijon				
Autun	X	X	X	
Auxerre	M	M	M	
Bar-s.-S.	M	M	M	
Belley	M	M	M	
Bourg.				M
Châlon.	M	M	M	
Charolles	X	X	P	
Châtillon.	P	M	M	
Dijon	M	M	P	
Gex	O	O	O	
Mâcon	O	M	M	
Semur.	M	M	P	
Trévoux		M	M	
Besançon				
Amont			O	M
Aval	P	O	M	
Besançon	M	O	M	
Dôle	P	P	M	
Grenoble				
Dauphiné				M
Orange	P		O	
Aix				
Aix	M	P	X	
Arles (V)	O			O
Barcell.	O		M	
Castell.	O			
Digne	O	M	P	
Draguig.	O		M	
Forcalq.	P	M	P	
Grasse	O		M	
Marseille	O	M	M	
Sisteron	O	O		
Toulon			P	
Rennes				
Auray			X	
Brest			P	
Carhaix			O	
Dinan			O	
Dol	X			
Lannion			M	
Lesneven			O	
Morlaix			X	
Nantes	M		M	
Ploërmel			M	
Quimper			M	
Rennes	M		M	
St. Brieuc	O	O	O	
St. Malo	M			
Tréguier	X			
Vannes			M	
Valenciennes				
Avesnes	M	M	P	
Cambrésis		M	M	
Quesnoy		M		
Valencien.			M	
Nancy				
Bar-le-D.		M	M	
Bassigny.				O
Bitche	O			
Blamont	X			
Boulay	O		P	
Bourmont	X	O	X	
Bouzonv.	X	M	X	
Briey		M	P	
Bruyères		M		P
Château-S.	X		X	
Châtel.		M	X	
Darney		M		
Dieuze	O	O	O	
Etain	X	M	X	
Fénestrange				M
La Marche	M		O	
Lixheim			X	P
Longuyon	O	M	M	
Lunéville	X	M		
Mirecourt	O	M	M	
Nancy	M	M	M	
Neufchâteau			X	
Nomény	M	P	P	
Pont-à-M.	M	M	M	
Rozières				M
Sarreguemines	X	X	X	
St. Dié			O	
St. Mihiel	P	M		
Thiaucourt	O	O	O	
Vézelise	P		P	
Villers-la-m.				P
Metz				
Arches				M
Longwy	P	M	O	
Metz	M	M	M	M
Mohon				P
Sarrebourg	O	X	X	
Sarrelouis				X
Sedan			X	
Thionville	O	O	O	
Toul	P	M	M	
Verdun	M	O	P	
Vic	X	O	O	
Strasbourg				
Belfort	O		O	
Colmar	O	O	O	
Dix Villes.			O	
Haguenau			O	
Strasbourg			O	
Corsica				
Corsica		M	M	

Totals:

National Patriotism foremost	145 cahiers.	45 C, 35 N, 59 T, 3 U, 1 CT, 1 CN, 1 NT
Mixed loyalties	220 cahiers.	50 C, 89 N, 73 T, 8 U
Other loyalties	82 cahiers.	33 C, 16 N, 28 T, 3 U, 1 CN, 1 NT
No sentiment	75 cahiers.	30 C, 14 N, 30 T, 1 CN

XLVII. CAHIERS SHOWING REGIONALISM STRONGER THAN NATIONAL SENTIMENT

Total: 37 cahiers. 13 C, 8 N, 12 T, 3 U, 1 CN

	CNTU
Paris	
Paris i.m.	V
Orléans	
Gien	C
Bourges	
Bourges	C
Riom	
St. Flour	T
Auch	
Béarn	C͡NT
Navarre	U
Bordeaux	
Ustaritz	C
Amiens	
Boulogne	T
Montreuil.	NT
Lille	
Douai	C
Lille	C
Dijon	
Gex	CNT
Mâcon	C
Aix	
Arles (V.)	C
Barcelon.	C T
Rennes	
St. Brieuc	CN
Nancy	
Bassigny.	U
Bitche	C
Bourmont	N
Bouzonville	T
Châtel.	N
Dieuze	CN
La Marche	T
Mirecourt	C
Thiaucourt	N
Metz	
Longwy	T
Thionville	NT
Sedan	T
Vic	T

XLVIII. CAHIERS SHOWING CLASS SPIRIT STRONGER THAN NATIONAL SENTIMENT

Total: 26 cahiers. 20 C, 5 N, 1 CN

	C	N	T	U
Bourges				
Bourges	C			
Riom				
Riom	C			
St. Flour		N		
Montpellier				
Mende	C			
Toulouse				
Castres	C			
Bordeaux				
Bazas	C			
Amiens				
Calais	C			
Lille				
Douai	C			
Lille	C			
Dijon				
Mâcon	C			
Aix				
Arles (V.)	C			
Castellane	C			
Digne	C			
Draguignan	C			
Grasse	C			
Sisteron	C			
Soissons				
Crépy	C			
Rennes				
St. Brieuc	C	N		
Nancy				
Châtel.		N		
Dieuze		N		
Longuyon	C			
Metz				
Sarrebourg	C			
Sarrelouis	C͡N			
Thionville	C	N		

XLIX. TYPES OF NATIONALISM REPRESENTED BY THE CAHIERS PRINTED IN 1789

Abbreviations: C conservative I intermediate P progressive R radical X no nationalism

Totals:

Conservative	17 C, 22 N, 9 T, 1 NT	49
Intermediate	20 C, 44 N, 28 T	92
Progressive	9 C, 21 N, 30 T, 4 U	64
Radical	4 C, 16 N, 21 T, 1 U, 1 CT, 1 NT	44
None	3 C, 2 N, 2 T, 3 U, 1 CN	11
		260[1]

	C	N	T	U
Paris				
Beauvais		P		
Etampes			P	
Mantes	R	R	R	
Meaux	I	I	P	
Melun	R	P		
Montfort.				R
Nemours	I	P	R	
Paris h.m.	I	P	R	
Paris i.m.	I	R	R	X
Provins	C	P	P	
Senlis		P	R	
Sens		I		
Orléans				
Blois	I	R		
Chartres	C	I		
Dourdan	I	R	I	
Gien		P		
Montargis	C	R		
Orléans		R		
Vendôme		I		
Bourges				
Bourges		C		
Moulins				
Moulins	P	I	P	
Nivernais		I	P	
St. Pierre.			R	
Lyon				
Forez	P	P	P	
Lyon	R	R	R	P
Riom				
Clermont.		I	R	
Riom		R	R	
Montpellier				
Annonay		C	P	
Beziers		I		
Mende			P	
Montpellier		I		
Nîmes		I	R	
Puy-en-V.	C		I	
Villeneuve.		I	P	
Toulouse				
Carcassonne		R		
Castres		C		
Toulouse	C	I	P	
Perpignan				
Perpignan		C	I	
Auch				
Armagnac	I			
Auch	I	I	I	
Béarn			X	X
Bigorre			P	
Comminges		I	C	
Foix		I	P	
Navarre				X
Rivière-V.			I	
Soule			I	
Bordeaux				
Agen	P	I	I	
Bazas		C	I	
Bordeaux		P		
Condom		I		
Dax		I	P	
Libourne	I			
Nérac		I		
Périgord		I	I	
Tartas		C		
Ustaritz		C	I	
Montauban				
Cahors	C	C		
Villefr.		P	I	
Limoges				
Angoulême	I	I	P	
Limoges	I	C	I	
Tulle	C	P	I	
La Rochelle				
Saintes	C	R		
Poitiers				
Poitiers		C	R	

[1] The discrepancy between this total and the total of cahiers printed is due to the fact that three cahiers have been lost: C, Artois, Verdun; T. Rouen.

	C	*N*	*T*	*U*
Tours				
Angers		P	R	
Loudun	I			
Mans(le)		P		
Saumur	P	P	P	
Tours		R		
Caen				
Coutances		I		
Alençon				
Alençon		P		
Bellême		I		
Châteauneuf.		R	R	
Rouen				
Caudebec.	C	I	P	
Chaumont.		I	I	
Evreux	I	C	P	
Rouen	I	C		R
Amiens				
Amiens		I		
Calais			P	
Péronne	R			R
Ponthieu	I	R	P	
St. Quentin		P	P	
Lille				
Artois	C	P	I	
Bailleul		I	C	
Douai	X	C	C	
Lille	X	I	I	
Soissons				
Château Th.		R	R	
Clermont.		R		
Crépy.		I		
Vermandois	C	P	P	
Châlons.				
Châlons.	I	C	P	
Chaumont.		I		
Reims		P	P	
Sézanne		I		
Troyes	P	P	P	
Dijon				
Autun	I	I		
Auxerre	P	R	R	
Bar-s.-S.	I	I	R	
Belley	C	I	I	
Bourg.				P
Dijon	P	P	R	
Semur.		I		
Trévoux		C	I	
Besançon				
Aval		I		
Dôle	P		I	
Grenoble				
Dauphiné				P
Aix				
Arles (V.)				C
Draguignan			R	
Marseille			I	
Rennes				
Auray			P	
Brest			P	
Nantes	I			
Ploërmel			P	
Rennes	P		R	
St. Brieuc	X	X	C	
St. Malo	C			
Vannes			R	
Valenciennes				
Avesnes	C	C	I	
Cambrésis		C	I	
Quesnoy		I		
Valenc.			I	
Nancy				
Bar-le-D.			I	
Bassigny.				X
Briey		I	P	
Bruyères		C		R
Lunéville		I		
Nancy		C		
Nomény		C		
Pont-à-M.	C	C	I	
Rozières				P
St. Dié			P	
St. Mihiel		I		
Villers.				P
Metz				
Longwy		I		
Metz	C	I	P	I
Sedan			X	
Thionville		X		
Toul	I	I	I	
Verdun		I	I	
Strasbourg				
Belfort			C	
Colmar	C	C	C	
Dix Villes			C	
Strasbourg			C	
Corsica				
Corsica			C	

BIBLIOGRAPHY
AND
LIST OF TEXTS

BIBLIOGRAPHY

The *cahiers de doléances* of 1789 have given rise to a vast amount of historical writing. A complete bibliography of original and reprinted texts has been published recently,[1] and a *Guide* is in preparation which will include a full bibliography of books relating to the general cahiers. Any study of the *cahiers de doléances* must start with the little volume by Champion, *La France d'après les cahiers*,[2] and with the introduction and reprinted sources in Brette, *Recueil de documents relatifs à la convocation des Etats-généraux de 1789*.[3] A full analysis of the documentary aspects of the cahiers will, however, be reserved for the *Guide*.

The aim of the following bibliography is threefold: (1) to list texts of general cahiers, together with indispensable analyses and aids to their study; (2) to provide a select bibliography on the general conditions in France in 1789 and during the Revolution; and (3) to present a select bibliography on nationalism.

In view of the aims of the bibliography, a purely alphabetical list has been avoided and the references have been classified by topics.

I. THE CAHIERS

Original Sources

Archives Nationales.—Three big sections of the National Archives in Paris contain documents on the convocation and texts of the electoral period, including the *cahiers de doléances:* Ba 1-Ba 90; C 14-C 34; B III 1-B III 174. Brette gave a helpful inventory of these series (*op. cit.*, Vol. I, pp. cxxix *et seq.*) but the Tuetey inventory[4] is more specific for the C series. In addition to these three series, certain other cartons have been useful, especially the series of printed texts in AD I 9-AD I 11.

For fuller information on the sources, the reader is referred to the official inventory,[4] and to the *Guide*. All of the cartons here mentioned were used before the reprinted cahiers were analyzed for the present study.

Bibliothèque Nationale.—The National Library in Paris possesses a collection of printed *procès-verbaux* and printed cahiers in the series

[1] *Cf.* bibliography, p. 297, under Hyslop.

[2] *Ibid.*, p. 300.

[3] *Ibid.*, pp. 296-97.

[4] *Ibid.*, p. 297.

Le 23 . . . and Le 24. . . . This collection overlaps to some degree the texts at the National Archives, but also contains some texts that the latter does not. An inventory of the texts is given in the official *Catalogue de l'histoire de la France*, Vol. VI, and *Supplement*, Vol. XIII.

Departmental and Communal Archives and Libraries.—In the effort to find all available texts of the general cahiers of 1789, the author supplemented the sources available in Paris by research in the departmental and communal archives and libraries. Archivists and librarians supplied information by correspondence, and, through the courtesy of the *Archives Nationales* and the *Bibliothèque Nationale*, many documents were sent to Paris for perusal. In addition, the following departmental archives and libraries were visited:

Besançon	*Arch. Doubs, Bib. Mun.*
Bourg-en-Bresse	*Arch. Ain.*
Dijon	*Bib. Mun.* (The Departmental Archives (Côte d'Or) were closed, but necessary information was obtained by correspondence.)
Grenoble	*Arch. Isère, Bib. Mun.*
Laon	*Arch. Aisne.*
Lons-le-Saunier	*Arch. Jura*, Private Collection of M. Cernesson.
Nancy	*Arch. Meurthe-et-Moselle, Bib. Mun.*
Rouen	*Arch. Seine-Inférieure, Bib. Mun.*
Strasbourg	*Arch. Mun., Bib. Mun. et Universitaire de Strasbourg.*
Tours	*Arch. Indre-et-Loire, Bib. Mun.*

British Museum—The Croker Collection on the French Revolution, series F, R, and F.R., was consulted. With one exception (cahier of the clergy of Toulouse) no printed text not already seen in the French collections was discovered.

Reprinted Texts of Cahiers de Doléances of 1789

Archives Parlementaires de 1787 à 1860, edited by Mavidal, J., and Laurent, E., 1st series, 1787-99 (Paris, Paul Dupont, 1867-75, 7 vols.). Vol. VII is an index volume.

This publication, which contains the majority of the texts of the general cahiers, is very defective. A searching criticism of the method and the results achieved by the two editors was made by M. Brette, *op. cit.*, Vol. I, pp. xci *et seq.* Only when the convocation and the nature of the cahiers are understood, can these volumes be properly used.

As an aid to the reader, a separate table of the reprinted texts used for the present study has been made. With the help of this list,[5] one may easily find the authentic text for each cahier, and avoid the spurious or

[5] *Cf. infra*, pp. 312 *et seq.*

incomplete texts which the *Archives Parlementaires* give along with the genuine texts.

Documents inédits sur l'histoire économique de la Révolution française: the Official Series of volumes. The various volumes which are listed here, have been published under the auspices of the Ministry of Public Instruction. For a survey of the volumes which have appeared up to 1928, *cf.* H. E. Bourne, "The Economic History of the French Revolution as a field of study," in *American Historical Review,* Jan., 1928, pp. 315 *et seq.*

The titles of the pertinent volumes are here listed alphabetically by authors. Starred volumes (*) reprint general cahiers. Even where volumes do not reprint general cahiers, the introductions are invaluable commentaries upon the district, and often give useful analyses of the cahiers as documents.

Balencie, G., Les Cahiers de doléances de la sénéchaussée de Bigorre. Dépt. des Hautes-Pyrénées. (Tarbes, Lesbordes, 1925.)

Bligny-Bondurdand, E., Cahiers de doléances de la sénéchaussée de Nîmes pour les Etats-généraux de 1789. Dépt. du Gard. (Nîmes, Chastanier, 1908-9, 2 vols.)*

Bloch, Camille, Cahiers de doléances du bailliage d'Orléans pour les Etats généraux de 1789. Dépt. du Loiret. (Orléans, Imprimerie Orléanaise, 1906-7, 2 vols.)*

Boissonnade, Prosper, Cahiers de doléances de la sénéchaussée d'Angoulême et du siège royal de Cognac. Dépt. de la Charente. (Paris, Imprimerie Nationale, 1907.)*

Boissonnade, Prosper, and L. Cathelineau, Cahiers de doléances de la sénéchaussée de Civray pour les Etats-généraux de 1789. Dépt. de la Vienne. (Niort, St. Denis, 1925.)

Bridrey, Emile, Cahiers de doléances du bailliage de Cotentin. Dépt. de la Manche. (Paris, Imprimerie Nationale, 1907-12.)*

Cathelineau, Léonce, Cahiers de doléances de la sénéchaussée de Niort et des communautés et corporations de St. Maixent pour les Etats généraux de 1789. Dépt. des Deux-Sèvres. (Niort, G. Clouzot, 1912.)

Etienne, Charles, Cahiers de doléances des bailliages des généralités de Metz et de Nancy. Dépt. de Meurthe-et-Moselle. (Nancy, Berger-Levrault, 1907-30.) Vol. I, Bailliage de Vic. Vol. II, Bailliage de Dieuze.* Vol. III, Bailliage de Vézelise.*

Fourastie, Victor, Cahiers de doléances de la sénéchaussée de Cahors. Dépt. du Lot. (Cahors, Imprimerie typographique, 1908.)

Fournier, Joseph, Cahiers de doléances de la sénéchaussée de Marseille pour les Etats généraux de 1789. Dépt. des Bouches-du-Rhône. Marseille, Imprimerie nouvelle, 1908.)*

Gandilhon, Alfred, Cahiers de doléances du bailliage de Bourges et des bailliages secondaires. . . Dépt. du Cher. (Bourges, Tardy-Pigelet et Fils, 1910.) This volume does not give the general cahiers, but the author's comments on the text of the general cahier of the clergy are invaluable.

Godard, M., and Léon Abensour, Cahiers de doléances du bailliage d'Amont. Dépt. de la Haute-Saône. (Besançon, J. Dodivers, 1918-27, 2 vols.)

Guillaume, Abbé, Récueil des réponses faites par les communautés de l'élection de Gap. . . . Dépt. des Hautes-Alpes. (Paris, Imprimerie Nationale, 1908.)

Jouanne, René, Cahier de doléances des corps et corporations de la ville d'Alençon pour les Etats généraux de 1789. Dépt. de l'Orne. (Alençon, Imprimerie Alençonnaise, 1929.)

Laurent, Gustave, Cahiers dé doléances pour les Etats généraux de 1789. Dépt. de la Marne. Vol. I, Bailliage de Châlons-sur-Marne (Epernay, Villers, 1906).* Vols. II, III, Bailliages de Sézanne et Châtillon-sur-Marne (Epernay, Villers, 1911).* Vol. IV, Bailliage de Reims (Reims, Matot-Braine, 1930).

Le Moy, A., Cahiers de doléances des corporations de la ville d'Angers et des paroisses de la sénéchaussée particulière d'Angers pour les Etats généraux de 1789. Dépt. de Maine-et-Loire. (Angers, Burdin et Cie., 1915-16, 2 vols.)

Le Parquier, E., Cahiers de doléances du bailliage d'Arques. Dépt. de la Seine-Inférieure. (Lille, Robbe, 1922.)

——— Cahiers de doléances du bailliage du Havre. Dépt. de la Seine-Inférieure. (Epinal, Imprimerie Lorraine, 1929.)

——— Cahiers de doléances du bailliage de Neufchâtel-en-Bray. Dépt. de la Seine-Inférieure. (Rouen, Cagniard, 1908.)

Lesueur, F., and A. Cauchie, Cahiers de doléances du bailliage de Blois et du bailliage secondaire de Romorantin. . . Dépt. de Loir-et-Cher. (Blois, Emmanuel Rivière, 1907-8, 2 vols.)*

Martin, E., Cahiers de doléances du bailliage de Mirecourt. Dépt. des Vosges. (Epinal, Imprimerie Lorraine, 1928.)*

Mourlot, Félix, Le Cahier d'observations et doléances du tiers-état de la ville de Caen en 1789 (Dreux, Lefebvre, 1912). The introduction to this volume is very useful.

Pasquier, F., and Fr. Galabert, Cahiers paroissiaux des sénéchaussées de Toulouse et de Comminges en 1789 (Toulouse, Privat, 1925-28). This volume was published under the supervision of the committee of Haute-Garonne, and not of the national committee. It is a less satisfactory publication than other volumes of the official series.

Porée, Charles, Cahiers de curés et des communautés ecclésiastiques du

bailliage d'Auxerre. . . Dépt. de l'Yonne. (Auxerre, Imprimerie "L'Universelle," 1927.)
——— Cahiers de doléances du bailliage de Sens. Dépt. de l'Yonne. (Auxerre, Imprimeries "L'Universelle," 1908.)*
Savina, J., and D. Bernard, Cahiers de doléances des sénéchaussées de Quimper et de Concarneau. . . Dépt. du Finistère. (Rennes, Oberthur, 1927.)*
Sée, Henri, and André Lessort, Cahiers de doléances de la sénéchaussée de Rennes. Dépt. d'Ille-et-Vilaine.* (Rennes, Oberthur, 1909-12, 4 vols.) The introduction to these volumes is invaluable for the study of the cahiers as sources, and also for remarks on the district of Rennes.
Vernier, J. J., Cahiers de doléances du bailliage de Troyes et du bailliage de Bar-sur-Seine. Dépt. de l'Aube. (Troyes, P. Nouel, 1909-11, 3 vols.)*

Semi-Official Editions of Cahiers.

Chassin, Charles L., Les Elections et les cahiers de Paris (Paris, Sigaux et Noblet, 1888-89, 4 vols.). This appears in the series called *Collection de documents rélatifs à l'histoire de Paris,* published under the auspices of the Municipal Council.
Dorvaux, N., and Abbé Lesprand, Cahiers des bailliages de Boulay et de Bouzonville, in the series *Documents sur l'histoire de Lorraine* (Metz, 1908, Vol. IX).
——— Cahiers de doléances des communautés de Metz, in the same series (Metz, 1918, Vol. X).
Lesprand, Abbé, in the *Annuaire de la Société d'histoire et d'archéologie lorraine* (Metz, Scriba). Vol. XV, 1903, "L'Election du député et cahier du tiers-état de la ville de Metz en 1789," pp. 158 *et seq.* Vol. XVI, 1904, "Cahiers lorrains de 1789," pp. 175, *et seq.* This gives some texts not reprinted elsewhere.

Unofficial Publications of Texts.

Only the publications necessary to supplement the *Archives Parlementaires* and official publications are here listed.

Charmasse, A. de, Cahiers des paroisses et communautés du bailliage d'Autun pour les Etats généraux de 1789 (Autun, Dejussieu, 1895).
Duhamel, L., Documents rares ou inédits de l'histoire des Vosges (Paris, Dumoulin, 1869, Vol. II).
Faye, H., Cahier du clergé de Touraine pour les Etats généraux de 1789 (Tour, Deslis, 1899).
Hippeau, C., Le Gouvernement de Normandie aux dix-septième et dix-huitième siècles (Caen, Aubry, 1863-69, 9 vols.).

Jérome, L., Les Elections et les cahiers du clergé lorrain aux Etats généraux de 1789 (Paris, Berger-Levrault, 1899). Contains the texts of several cahiers of the clergy in Lorraine which are not reprinted elsewhere, and whose texts have disappeared since the sale of the library of the Seminary of Nancy where M. Jérome found the originals.

Labot, A., Cahiers de doléances du Nivernais (Paris, Librairie internationale, 1866).

Mesnard, Amedée, St. Jean d'Angely sous la Révolution et jusqu'à l'époque contemporaine (Paris, Jouve, 1910). The text of the cahier of the nobles of St. Jean d'Angely is reprinted from a text which has since been lost.

Périn, M. Charles, Cahiers du clergé et du tiers du bailliage de Soissons (Soissons, Fosse Carcosse, 1869).

Poulet, Henri, "Les Cahiers de doléances de Thiaucourt," in *Annales de l'Est,* Vol. XVIII, pp. 253 *et seq.,* (1904).

Proust, Antonin, Archives de l'Ouest. Series A. (Paris, Librairie internationale, 1867-69, 5 vols.)

Récamier, Etienne, Les Députés des communes de Bugey en 1789 et en 1876 (Paris, Charx, 1876). Contains the reprint of the cahier of the third estate of Belley, the original of which has disappeared.

Reuss, Roderigue, L'Alsace pendant la Révolution (Paris, Fischbacher, 1880), Vol. I, pp. 31-66. Reprint of the cahier of the third estate of Strasbourg.

Révolution française, revue d'histoire moderne et contemporaine, La (Paris, from 1880 on). Vol. XXXII, 1897. Texts of the cahiers of N. Bar-le-duc, and T. Verdun.

This quarterly, started in 1880, and after 1887 published under the direction of A. Aulard, has been continued by a society formed by him. The publication has contained many helpful articles to which reference is made in the present volume.

Torcy, Charles de, Recherches sur la Champagne (Troyes, Laloy, 1832).

Vic, Dom Cl. de, and J. Vaissete, Histoire de Languedoc (Toulouse, Privat, 1872-92), Vol. XIV.

Manuals, Guides, Inventories, Dictionaries, Atlases, etc.

Annales historiques de la Révolution française (Reims, from 1908 on). Published by a society, formerly directed by Albert Mathiez.

Boursin, E., et A. Challamel, Dictionnaire de la Révolution française (Paris, Jouvet, 1893).

Brette, Armand, Recueil de documents rélatifs à la convocation des Etats-généraux de 1789 (Paris, Imprimerie nationale, 1894-1915, 4 vols.). These four volumes are indispensable. They contain an inventory of documents, a reprint of the most important ones for the convocation of 1789, and extensive introduction and scholarly footnotes. Volume I deals with the convocation of the States-General. Volume II gives material on the deputies to the States-General. Volumes III and IV give analyses of the elections by district, with critical information on the assemblies, officials, procedure and texts, for sixteen *generalities*. Brette intended to continue the publication and to add volumes for the other seventeen *generalities* but he died prematurely. The gaps have been partly filled by separate volumes in the official series, *Documents inédits,* but much remains to be done.

Brette, Armand, Atlas des bailliages ou juridictions assimilées . . . (Paris, Imprimerie nationale, 1904). This is a separate folio volume to accompany the four volumes cited above.

——— Les Limites et les divisions territoriales de la France en 1789 (Paris, Cornély et Cie., 1907). An indispensable description of the geographic and administrative character of France in 1789, with a few useful maps.

Caron, Pierre, Manuel pratique pour l'étude de la Révolution française (Paris, Picard et Fils, 1912).

Catalogue de l'histoire de France, Bibliothèque impériale (Paris, Didot, 1855-), especially Vols. VI and XIII.

Catalogue général des manuscripts des bibliothèques publiques de France (Paris, Plon, Nourrit et Cie., 1886-1911), 44 vols.

Hatin, Eugène, Bibliographie historique de la présse périodique française (Paris, Firmin Didot, 1866).

Hyslop, Beatrice, *D. I.,* Repertoire critique des cahiers de doléances de 1789 (Paris, Leroux, 1933). This is an inventory of the texts of cahiers.

Lasteyrie, P., and A. Vidier, Bibliographie des travaux historiques et archéologiques (Paris, Imprimerie nationale, 1888-).

Garrett, Mitchell B., A Critical Bibliography of the Pamphlet Literature published in France between July 3 and December 27, 1788 (Birmingham, Howard College, 1925).

Marion, Marcel, Dictionnaire des institutions de la France au dix-septième et dix-huitième siècle (Paris, Picard, 1923).

Révolution française, revue d'histoire moderne et contemporaine, La. Cf. supra, p. 296.

Sanson, Victor, Repertoire bibliographique pour la périodé dite' 'révolutionnaire'(1789-1801) en Seine-Inférieure (Rouen, Schneider, 1911-12, 3 vols.).

Shepherd, William R., Historical Atlas (New York, Holt, 1929, 7th ed.).

Société de l'histoire de la Révolution française. Les Manuscrits rélatifs à l'histoire de la Révolution et de l'Empire dans les bibliothèques publiques des départements (Paris, Rieder, 1913).

Tuetey, Alexandre, Les Papiers des assemblées de la Révolution aux Archives Nationales (Paris, Cornéley et Cie., 1908). This is an inventory of the series C, of the Archives Nationales.

The Early States-Generals

Sources.

The following notations constitute by no means a complete list of all documents now existing, but they form a workable bibliography.

Archives Nationales: K 674, minutes of sessions; T. cahier (1614); T. Paris intra-muros (1588); 1614—T. Vendôme, T. Paris intra-muros; 1596—T. Rouen. Isolated examples of cahiers: Ba 49—T. Mâcon (1560, 1575, 1588); Ba 50—T. Marseille; Ba 1—T. Méry-sur-Seine (1576); B III 3—Amiens (papers).

Bibliothèque Nationale: Le12.10, T. Troyes (1561); Le17.10, University of Paris (1614). Other numbers duplicate K 674 of the *Archives Nationales.* See the general catalogue of the history of France, Vol. VI, for items.

Reprinted Sources

Lalourcé and Duval, Récueil des cahiers généraux des trois ordres aux Etats-généraux (Paris, Barrois, 1789, 4 vols.). Contains reprints of all the national cahiers of the States-Generals from 1560 to 1614.

——— Forme générale et particulière de la convocation et de la tenue des Assemblées nationales ou Etats-généraux de France (Paris, Barrois, 1789, 3 vols.). Reprint of documents on the convocation, accompanied by explanations. Also reprint of several cahiers: T. Blaigny (1576), Vol. II, pp. 103 *et seq.;* T. Blois (1614), Vol. II, pp. 184 *et seq.*; T. Blois (1588), Vol. II, pp. 188 *et seq.*

Mayer, Charles J., Des Etats généraux, et autres assemblées nationales (La Haye et Paris, Buisson, 1788-89, 18 vols.). Contains text of the national cahier for 1484 not given by Lalourcé and Duval, *op. cit.*

Descriptive Works

Danjou, F., and L. Cimber, Archives curieuses de l'histoire de France (Louis XI-Louis XVIII). (Paris, Cimber, 1837), Vol. I (2e. série).

Picot, Georges, Histoire des Etats généraux (Paris, Hachette, 1888, 2d edition, 5 vols.). This work was written to comply with the request of the commission for historical works for a study showing the demands of the French people for the States-Generals, and the effect of the States-Generals on French law and custom. It is a thorough and scholarly study. In view of this excellent work, it seems unnecessary to list other books on the early States-General, which are all fragmentary, one-sided, or otherwise inadequate.

The Convocation and Elections of 1789

For the sources, see Bibliography, p. 291. For more complete references, *cf.* Denys-Buirette, *op. cit.*, under Bibliography, p. 300; Brette, *op. cit.;* Hyslop, B., *Repertoire critique* . . . and the *Guide.* The following is a partial list of the works most useful for the present study.

Boissonnade, Prosper M., St. Domingue à la veille de la Révolution (Paris, Geuthner, 1906).

Bussière, Georges, Etudes historiques sur la Révolution en Périgord (Bordeaux, Lefebvre, 1885).

Champollion-Figéac, A., Chronique dauphinoises, 1754-1794 (Vienne, Savigné, 1884, 3 vols.).

Cochin, Augustin, and Charles Charpentier, La Campagne électorale de 1789 en Bourgogne (Paris, Champion, 1904).

Coussemaker, C. E. de, Les Elections aux Etats-généraux en 1789 dans la Flandre maritime (Paris, Aubry, 1864).

Couturier, H., La Préparation des Etats-généraux de 1789 en Poitou (Poitiers, Société française d'imprimerie et de librairie, 1909).

Delannoy, L., La Convocation des Etats-généraux de 1789 (Paris, Jouve, 1904). Good summary. Emphasizes the haste in the composition of cahiers, and denies that they are a good gauge of public opinion.

Desjardins, Gustave, Le Beauvoisis, le Valois . . . en 1789 (Beauvais, Père, 1869).

Duchâtellier, A., Histoire de la Révolution dans les départements de l'ancien Bretagne (Paris, Desessart, 1836, 6 vols.).

Franceschini, E., and J., "Les Elections aux Etats-généraux de 1789," in *Bull. de la Soc. des Sciences hist. et nat. de la Corse,* Anneé 1920.

Garrett, Mitchell B., The Beginning of the French Revolution (Birmingham, Ala., 1923).

——— "The Call for Information concerning the States-General in 1788," in *American Historical Review,* April, 1932, pp. 506 *et seq.*

Lesort, André, "La Commission de la convocation des Etats-généraux," in *La Révolution française, revue,* 1930, Vol. LXXXIII, pp. 5 *et seq.*

Maréchal, Philippe, La Révolution en Franche-Comté (Paris, Champion, 1903).

Mège, Francisque, "Les Cahiers des bailliages et sénéchaussées d'Auvergne en 1789," in *Revue d'Auvergne,* Vol. XX (Clermont Ferrand, 1903).

——— "La Dernière Année de la province d'Auvergne," in *Memoires de l'Acad. des Science, Belles-Lettres et Arts de Clermont Ferrand,* 1904.

Mireur, F., Les Procès-verbaux des élections . . . des sénéchaussées de Draguignan, Grasse, et Castellane (Draguignan, Olivier et Rouvier, 1891).

Analyses, Criticisms, and Summaries of the Cahiers

Aulard, Auguste, "Quels sont les cahiers de 1789 qui nous manquent?" in *La Révolution française, revue,* 1895, Vol. XXIX, pp. 150 *et seq.* This article is out of date, but is still useful.

Bloch, Camille. L'Assistance et l'état en France à la veille de la Révolution (Paris, Picard, 1908).

Bonnassieux, P., Examen des cahiers de 1789 au point de vue commerciale et industriel (Paris, Berger-Levrault, 1884).

Bourrilly, L., Les Cahiers de l'instruction publique en 1789 (Paris, Delgrave, 1901).

Brette, A., "La Population de la France en 1789," in *La Révolution française,* 1904, Vol. XLVI, pp. 481 *et seq.*

———, "Les Cahiers de 1789 et les Archives Parlementaires," *ibid.,* 1904-5, Vols. XLVII, XLVIII.

———, "Les Cahiers de 1789 considérés comme mandats impératifs," *ibid.,* 1896, Vol. XXXI, pp. 123 *et seq.*

———, "La Verification des pouvoirs à l'Assemblée constituante," *ibid.,* 1893, 1894, Vols. XXV, XXVI.

Champion, Edme, Esprit de la Révolution française (Paris, Schleicher, 1887).

———, "La Conversion de la noblesse en 1789," in *La Révolution française, revue,* 1895, Vol. XXVIII, pp. 5 *et seq.*

———, "Les pouvoirs des députés en 1789," *ibid.,* 1888, Vol. XV, pp. 481 *et seq.*

———, La France d'après les cahiers de 1789 (Paris, Colin, 1897). Excellent, though not exhaustive, study.

Chassin, Charles L., Le Génie de la Révolution (Paris, Librairie internationale, 1864).

———, Les Cahiers des curés en 1789 (Paris, Charavay, 1882).

Clermont-Tonnerre, Comte Stanislas de, Rapport du comité de constitution, contenant le résumé des cahiers rélatif à cet objet. *Cf. Procés-verbal de l'Assemblée nationale constituante, infra,* p. 302, Séance of July 27, 1789.

Denys-Buirette, A., Les Questions religieuses dans les cahiers de 1789 (Paris, Jouve, 1919). A most useful and scholarly study of the cahiers, with an excellent bibliography.

Desjardins, Albert, Les Cahiers de la législation criminelle (Paris, Pedone-Lauriel, 1883).

Duméril, A., Des Voeux des cahiers de 1789 rélatifs à l'instruction publique (Toulouse, Douladoure, 1880).

Dupont de Nemours, Tableau comparatif des demandes contenus dans les cahiers des trois ordres . . . (*s. l.,* 1789).

Grille, François J., Introduction aux mémoires sur la Révolution française; ou, Tableau comparatif des mandats et pouvoirs . . . (Paris, Pichard, 1825, 2 vols.).

Onou, A., "La Valeur des cahiers de 1789 au point de vue économique et social," in *La Révolution française, revue,* Vol. XLIX (1905), pp. 385 *et seq.*

——— "Les Elections de 1789 et les cahiers du tiers-état," *ibid.,* Vols. LVI, LVII (1909).

Picard, Roger, Les Cahiers de 1789 et les classes ouvrières (Paris, Rivière et Cie., 1910). This same volume also appears under the title, Les Cahiers de 1789 au point de vue industriel et commercial.

Poncins, Léon de, Les Cahiers de '89 (Paris, Didier, 1866).

Principes de 1789 et la liberte de la presse, Les, (Paris, Lemerre, 1867). Anonymous.

Prudhomme, L. M., and Mezières, Laurent de, Résumé général ou Extrait des cahiers des pouvoirs, instructions, demandes et doléances . . . (Paris, Publié par une Société de gens de lettres, 1789, 3 vols.).

Sagnac, P., "De la Méthode dans l'étude des institutions d'ancien régime," in *Revue d'histoire moderne et contemporaine,* Oct. 1904, Vol. VI, pp. 13 *et seq.*

——— "Les Cahiers de 1789 et leur valeur," in *Revue d'histoire moderne et contemporaine,* 1907, Vol. VIII, pp. 329 *et seq.*

Sée, Henri, "La Redaction et la valeur historique des cahiers de paroisse," in *Revue historique,* 1910, Jan.-Avril, pp. 292 *et seq.*

Vialay, Amedée, Les Cahiers de doléances du tiers-état aux Etats généraux de 1789 (Paris, Perrin et Cie., 1911).

Wahl, Adalbert, Studien zur Vorgeschichte der franzosischen Revolution (Tübingen, J. C. B. Moler, 1901).

II. FRANCE IN 1789

Sources

Laws

Bulletin des lois, supplemented after the first publication by *Collection des lois depuis 1789 jusqu'au 22 prairial, an II, formant le commencement du Bulletin des lois* (Paris, an XII-1906, 7 vols.).

Anderson, Frank Maloy, The Constitutions and other select Documents illustrative of the History of France, 1789-1901 (Minneapolis, Wilson Co., 1908).

Duvergier, J. B., Collection Duvergier (Paris, 1825-, 24 vols.).

Isambert, F. A., Récueil général des anciennes lois françaises . . . (Paris, Plon, 1822, 29 vols.).

Newspapers.—The dates are those of the numbers used.

Gazette de France, nos. for 1788 and 1789.

Journal des débats et décrets, Aug. 29-Dec., 1789.

Journal des Etats généraux (appeared under different titles), April 27, 1789-Dec., 1789.

Mercure de France, nos. for 1788 and 1789.

Moniteur universel, Le, May 5-Dec., 1789. The numbers prior to November 24, 1789 were reconstructed later by Thuau-Grandville.

Point du Jour, Le, June 19-Dec., 1789.

Minutes of the States-General and National Assembly

Aulard, F. A., Récit des séances des députés des communes de 5 mai à 12 juin, 1789 (Paris, Charavay, 1895).

Biron, Armand L. de G., Lettres sur les Etats-généraux de 1789 (Paris, Mme. Bachelin-Deflorenne, 1865).

Crévecœur, Robert de, Journal d'Adrien Duquesnoy (Paris, Picard, 1894, 2 vols.).

Houtin, Albert, Les Séances des députés du clergé aux Etats-généraux de 1789 (Paris, Rieder, 1916). Diaries of Abbé Thibault, and Chanoine Coster.

Procès-verbal de l'Assemblée nationale constituante, imprimé par son ordre (Paris, *s. d.,* 75 vols.).

Reports in the newspapers cited above, and the collection of printed minutes, reports, etc., and *Bib. Nat.,* Le 27.10, Le 27.11, have also been utilized for the present study.

Memoires, Diaries, Travels, etc. (Selected list)

Bailly, Jean Sylvain, Mémoires d'un témoin de la Révolution (Paris, Levrault, XII-1804, 3 vols.).

Browning, Oscar, Despatches from Paris (London, Foreign Office, 1909-10), Vol. II (1788-90).

Desmoulins, Camille, La France libre (s. l. 1789).

Grönvelt, H. F., Letters containing an Account of the late Revolution in France (London, J. Johnson, 1792). These are letters by Pierre E. L. Dumont, a friend of Mirabeau.

Jefferson, Thomas, Writings (New York, H. A. Washington (editor), Derby and Jackson, 1859, 9 vols.), Vols. II, III.

Mirabeau, Gabriel-Honoré de Riquetti, comte de, Lettres à ses commettants (Paris, Lavillette, 1791).

Morris, Gouverneur, Journal pendant les années 1789, 1790, 1791 et 1792. French translation by E. Pariset (Paris, Plon, 1901). English editions do not give the diary in consecutive form.

Mounier, Jean J., Exposé de la conduite de Mounier (1790); Appel à l'opinion publique (1790); Recherches sur les causes qui ont empêché les français de devenir libres (1792); De l'Influence attribuée aux philosophes, aux francs-maçons (1801).

Staël, Baroness de, Considerations on the Principal Events of the French Revolution (New York, Eastburn, 1818).

Young, Arthur, Voyages en France en 1787, 1788 et 1789 (Paris, Colin, 1931, 3 vols.). Introduction by Henri Sée. This is a part of the series of *Les Classiques de la Révolution française* directed formerly by Albert Mathiez. The introduction and annotations are invaluable.

General Histories of the French Revolution

This list gives only the books that have proved most useful.

Acton, J. E. D. A., Lord, Lectures on the French Revolution (London, Macmillan, 1910).

Aulard, Auguste, Histoire politique de la Révolution française (Paris, Colin, 1926).

Chérest, Aimé, La Chute de l'ancien régime (Paris, Hachette, 1884-86, 3 vols.).

Gottschalk, L. R., The Era of the French Revolution (Boston and New York, Houghton, Mifflin Co., 1929).

Hazen, Charles D., The French Revolution (New York, Holt, 1932, 2 vols.).

Lavisse, Ernest, Histoire de France depuis les origines jusqu'a la Révolution (Paris, Hachette). Vol. IX, Louis XVI, by H. Carré, P. Sagnac, E. Lavisse. Vol. X, La Révolution (1789-1792), by P. Sagnac. Vol. XI, La Révolution (1792-1799), by G. Pariset.

Mathiez, Albert, The French Revolution, translated by C. A. Phillips (New York, Knopf, 1928).

Michelet, Jules, An historical view of the French Revolution, translated by Cocks (London, Bohn, 1860).

General Works Concerning France on the Eve of the Revolution

Boiteau, Paul, Etat de la France en 1789 (Paris, Guillaumin et Cie., 1889).

Lowell, Edward J., The Eve of the French Revolution (New York, Houghton Mifflin Co., 1926, 34th printing).

Tocqueville, Alexis de, The State of Society in France before the Revolution of 1789, translated by H. Reeve (London, Murray, 1868, 3d edition).

Topical Studies of the Eighteenth Century and the Revolution

Philosophy

It has hardly seemed necessary to call attention to the great works of eighteenth-century philosophy, nor to the numerous pamphlets issued on the eve of the revolution. A useful list of the latter is given by Chassin, Le Génie de la Révolution, Vol. I, Appendix, no. 8, p. 410 *et seq.* The most helpful general surveys are listed here:

Becker, Carl, The Heavenly City of the Eighteenth Century (New Haven, Yale University Press, 1932).

Brinton, Crane, The Jacobins (New York, Macmillan, 1930).

Devaille, J., Histoire de l'idée de progrès jusqu'à la fin du dix-huitième siècle (Paris, Alcan, 1910).

Dunning, William A., A History of Political Theories (New York, Macmillan Co., 1921, 4 vols.), vols. II, III.

Henderson, E. T., Symbol and Satire in the French Revolution (New York, Putnam, 1912).

Roustan, M., The Pioneers of the Revolution, translation by F. Whyte (London, Benn, 1926).

Sée, Henri, L'Evolution de la pensée politique en France au dix-huitième siècle (Paris, Giard, 1925).

——— "Les Idées philosophiques du dix-huitième siècle et la literature prérévolutionnaire" in *Revue de Synthèse historique* (Paris, Cerf, 1903), Vol. VII.

——— Les Idées politiques au dix-huitième siècle (Paris, Hachette, 1920).

Wadia, P. A., The Philosophers and the French Revolution (London, Sonnenheim and Co., 1904).

The Government

Babeau, Albert, La Province sous l'ancien régime (Paris, Firmin-Didot, 1894, 2 vols.).

Brissaud, Jean, A History of French Public Law, translated by J. W. Garner (Boston, Little, Brown and Co., 1915).

Cahen, L., and R. Guyot, L'Oeuvre législative de la Révolution (Paris, Alcan, 1913).

Clausel de Coussergues, Du Sacre des rois de France (Paris, Egron, 1825).

Dubreuil, L., L'Idée régionaliste sous la Révolution (Besançon, Millot Frères, 1919).

Glasson, Ernest, Le Parlement de Paris . . . (Paris, Hachette, 1901, 2 vols.).

Lavergne, Léonce de, Les Assemblées provinciales sous Louis XVI (Paris,

Lévy, 1864). A good survey, although the thesis of Renouvin (*cf. infra*), has tended to supersede it.
Léber, Jean M. C., Des cérémonies du sacre (Paris, Baudouin, 1825).
Meuriot, Paul, La Population et les lois électorales en France de 1789 à nos jours (Paris, Berger-Levrault, 1916).
Péré, G., Le Sacre et couronnement des rois de France dans leurs rapports avec les lois fondamentales (Bagnères-de-Bigorre, Péré, 1921). This is the best work on the coronation.
Pichon, T. J., and Gobet, Le Sacre et couronnement de Louis XVI . . . (Paris, Maillet, 1775).
Renouvin, Pierre, Les Assemblées provinciales de 1787 (Paris, Picard and Gabalda, 1921). Excellent thesis.
Seligman, Edmond, La Justice pendant la Révolution (Paris, Plon, 1913, 2 vols.). Thorough analysis of legal system. Contains also an analysis of the cahiers for law and justice.
Watrin, P., La Tradition monarchique d'après l'ancien droit public français (Paris, Savaete, 1916).

The Constitution, Declaration of Rights, etc.

Andrews, G. G., The Constitution in the Early French Revolution (New York, Crofts, 1927).
Gervais, Louis, Du droit de réunion en France et en Angleterre (Montpellier, Firmin et Montane, 1913).
Jellinek, Georges, La Declaration des droits de l'homme et du citoyen (Paris, Fontemoing, 1902).
Lemaire, André, Les Lois fondamentales de la monarchie française d'après les theoriciens de l'ancien régime (Paris, Fontemoing, 1907).
Marcaggi, V., Origines de la declaration des droits de l'homme de 1789 (Paris, Rousseau, 1904).
Samuel, Paul, Du droit de pétition sous la Révolution (Paris, Giard et Brière, 1909).

The National Assembly

Brette, A., "Rélation des évenements depuis le 6 mai jusqu'au 15 juillet 1789," in *La Révolution française, revue,* 1893, Vol. XXIV, pp. 69 *et seq.*, and pp. 162 *et seq.*
Caron, Pierre, "La Tentative de contre-révolution de juin-juillet 1789," in *Revue d'histoire moderne et contemporaine,* 1906-7, Vol. VIII.
Christophelsmeier, C., The First Revolutionary Step, June 17 (University of Nebraska Studies, Lincoln, 1909).
——— The Fourth of August, 1789 (*ibid.,* 1906).
Darling, Mae, The Opening of the Estates-General of 1789 and the First Phase of the Struggle between the Orders (*ibid.,* 1914).

Howie, E. L., The Counter-Revolution of June-July, 1789 (*ibid.*, 1915).

Lacretelle, C. J. D. de, Histoire de la Constituante (Paris, Treuttel et Wurtz, 1821, 2 vols.).

Lameth, A. T. V. de, Histoire de la Constituante (Paris, Moutardier, 1828-29, 2 vols.).

Needham, Jeanette, The Meeting of the States-General (University of Nebraska Studies, Lincoln, 1917).

Religion and the Church

Cf. also Denys-Buirette, *op cit.*, *supra*, p. 300.

Florange, Charles, Les Assemblées du clergé en France avant 1789 . . . (Paris-Lille, Douriez-Bataille, 1927).

Martin, Gaston, La Franc-maçonnerie et la Révolution (Paris, Vivier, 1926).

Mathiez, A., Les Origines des cultes révolutionnaires (Paris, Bellaix, 1904).

Wallon, J. G., Le Clergé de 1789 (Paris, Charpentier, 1876).

Education

Allain, Abbé E., L'Instruction primaire en France avant la Révolution (Paris, Société bibliographique, 1881).

Babeau, Albert, L'Ecole de village pendant la Révolution (Paris, Didier, 1881).

Compayre, G., Histoire critique des doctrines de l'éducation en France (Paris, Hachette, 1879, 2 vols.).

Duruy, Albert, L'Instruction publique et la Révolution (Paris, Hachette, 1882).

Hippeau, Celestin, La Révolution française et l'éducation nationale (Paris, Charavay, 1883).

Sicard, Auguste, L'Education morale et civique avant et pendant la Révolution, 1700-1808 (Paris, Poussielgue, 1884).

Language

Aulard, August, Note in *La Révolution française, Revue,* 1922, vol. 75, p. 160. On the bilingual character of the Sarre valley.

Brenner and Goodyear, Eighteenth-Century French Plays (New York, Century Co., 1927).

Brunot, Ferdinand, Histoire de la langue française des origines à 1900 (Paris, Colin, 1905-32, 7 vols.), especially Vols. V and VI.

Muret, Th. C., L'Histoire par le théâtre, 1789-1851 (Paris, Amyot, 1864-65, 3 vols.).

Petit de Julleville, L'Histoire de la langue et de la litterature française des origines à 1900 (Paris, Colin, 1898, 8 vols.), Vol. VI on Eighteenth Century.

Reuss, Roderigue, Histoire de Strasbourg (Paris, Fischbacker, 1922, 2 vols.).

Rivarol, Antoine de, De l'Universalité de la langue française (reprinted, New York, Ginn, 1919). This essay received a prize from the Academy of Berlin in 1783.

Welschinger, Henri, Le Théâtre de la Révolution (Paris, Charavay, 1880).

The Press

Soederhjelm, Alma, Le Régime de la presse pendant la Révolution française (Paris, Welter, 1900-1, 2 vols.).

Tourneux, M., "Le Régime de la presse de 1789 à l'an VIII," in *La Révolution française, revue,* 1893, Vol. XXV, pp. 193 *et seq.*

The Army

Babeau, Albert A., La Vie militaire sous l'ancien régime (Paris, Firmin-Didot et Cie., 1890, 2 vols.).

Chamborant de Périssat, A. de, L'Armée de la Révolution (Paris, Plon, 1875).

Duruy, Albert, L'Armée royale en 1789 (Paris, Levy, 1888).

Dussieux, L. E., L'Armée en France (Versailles, Bernard, 1884, 3 vols.), especially Vol. II.

Fieffe, Eugène, Histoire des troupes étrangères au service de la France (Paris, Dumaine, 1854, 2 vols.).

Gébelin, Jacques, Histoire des milices provinciales, 1688-1791 (Paris, Hachette, 1881). Excellent.

Hennet, Léon, Les Milices et les troupes provinciales (Paris, Baudouin, 1884). Does not overlap with Gébelin's work.

Mention, Léon, L'Armée de l'ancien régime (Paris, L. H. May, s. d.).

Wilkinson, Spencer, The French Army before Napoleon (Oxford, Clarendon Press, 1915).

The Navy

Chevallier, E., Histoire de la marine française sous la première Republique (Paris, Hachette, 1886).

Doneaud, Alfred, Histoire de la marine française (Paris, Dubuisson, 1865).

Guérin, L., Histoire maritime de la France (Paris, Ledoux, 1843-48, 3 vols.).

Havard, Oscar, Histoire de la Révolution dans les ports de guerre (Paris, Nouvelle Imprimerie Nationale, 1911-13, 2 vols.).

Moireau, A., La Marine française sous Louis XVI (Paris, Hachette, 1884).

Trousset, Jules, Histoire nationale de la marine et des marins français (Paris, Librairie illustrée, s. d.).

Economic Developments

Boissonnade, P. M., Les Etudes rélatifs à l'histoire économique de la Révolution française (Paris, Cerf, 1906). Especially helpful for bibliography.

Cole, Charles W., French Mercantilist Doctrines before Colbert (New York, Richard W. Smith, 1931). Useful for French economic nationalism.

Gomel, Charles, Histoire financière de la Constituante (Paris, Guillaumin, 1896, 2 vols.).

Kovalesky, Maxime, La France économique et sociale à la veille de la Révolution (Paris, Giard et Brière, 1909-11, 2 vols.).

Levasseur, E., Histoire des classes ouvrières et de l'industrie en France avant 1789 (Paris, Rousseau, 1901, 2 vols.).

Loutichisky, I., La Petite Propriété en France avant la Révolution et la vente des biens nationaux (Paris, Champion, 1897).

Marion, Marcel, Histoire financière de la France depuis 1715 (Paris, Rousseau, 1914-28, 6 vols.). Vol. I, Ch. xiv, is on the cahiers.

Martin St. Léon, E., Histoire des corporations de métiers (Paris, Guillaumin et Cie., 1897). Excellent survey.

Palm, Franklin Charles, The Economic Policy of Richelieu (Urbana, University of Illinois, 1922).

Sée, Henri, Economic and Social Conditions in France during the Eighteenth Century, translation by Edwin H. Zeydel (New York, Knopf, 1927). Bibliography useful.

——— L'Evolution commerciale et industrielle de la France sous l'ancien régime (Paris, Giard, 1925).

Zujovic, Milan J., L'Influence du factum économique dans les travaux constitutionnels de la Révolution (Paris, Sagot, 1924). Analysis of egalitarianism.

Social Conditions

Aulard, Alphonse, La Révolution française et le régime féodal (Paris, Alcan, 1910).

Bloch, C., *cf.* p. 300.

Lichtenberger, A., Le Socialisme et la Révolution française (Paris, Alcan, 1899).

Loutchisky, I. V., L'Etat des classes agricoles en France à la veille de la Révolution (Paris, Champion, 1911).

Mathiez, Albert, La Question sociale en 1789 (Paris, Cornély, 1905).
Mathorez, Jules, Les Etrangers en France sous l'ancien régime (Paris, Champion, 1919-21, 2 vols.).
Sée, Henri, La Vie économique et les classes sociales en France au dix-huitième siècle (Paris, Alcan, 1924).

III. NATIONALISM

Nationalism[6]

Barker, Ernest, National Character (London and New York, Harper, 1927).
Hayes, Carlton J. H., Essays on Nationalism (New York, Macmillan, 1926).
——— France, A Nation of Patriots (New York, Columbia University Press, 1930).
——— The Historical Evolution of Modern Nationalism (New York, Smith Inc., 1931).
Van Deusen, Glyndon, Sieyes: His Life and His Nationalism (New York: Columbia University Press, 1932).
Vaussard, Maurice, Enquête sur le nationalisme (Paris, Editions Spes, s. d.).
Zimmermann, J. G., De l'orgueil national, French translation of German text (Paris, Delalain, 1769, 4th edition).
Notes in *La Révolution française, revue.*
Vol. XLVI, 1905, p. 244: on the use of *nationalisme* in 1813.
Vol. XLIX, 1905, pp. 263-64: on the use of *nationalisme* by the Abbé Barruel, in his Mémoires pour servir à l'histoire du jacobinisme (1798).

Nationality

Barzun, Jacques, The French Race (New York, Columbia University Press, 1932).
Buell, R. L., International Relations (New York, Holt, 1925).
Démangeat, Charles, Histoire de la condition civile des étrangers en France . . . (Paris, Joubert, 1844).
Hauser, Henri, Le Principe des nationalités, ses origines historiques (Paris, Alcan, 1916).
Johannet, René, Le Principe des nationalités (Paris, Nouvelle Imprimerie Nationale, 1918).
Joseph, Bernard, Nationality, its nature and problems (London, Allen and Union, 1929).

[6] Professor Hayes' seminar on Nationalism, at Columbia University, afforded invaluable discussion and criticism.

Rose, J. Holland, Nationality as a Factor in Modern History (London, Macmillan, 1916).

Rouard de Card, E., La Nationalité française (Paris, Pedone, 1922).

Van Gennep, Arnold, Traité comparatif des nationalités (Paris, Payot, 1922).

Zangwill, I., The Principle of Nationalities (New York, Macmillan, 1917).

Democracy

Michel, Henri, La Doctrine politique de la démocratie (Paris, Colin, 1901).

Etatisme

D'Argila, Raymond, L'Etatisme industriel (Paris, Imprimerie du Montparnasse, 1929).

Delemer, Adolphe, Le Bilan de l'étatisme (Paris, Payot, 1922).

Michel, Henri, L'Idée de l'état (Paris, Hachette, 1895).

Weill, Georges, Histoire de l'idée laïque en France au dix-neuvième siècle (Paris, Alcan, 1925). Useful introduction.

Patriotism

Eighteenth Century Writings (other than those of the great philosophers). This is a list of works of major importance only.

Caraccioli, Dictionnaire critique, pittoresque et sentencieux . . . (Lyon, Duplain, 1768, 2 vols.).

Discours sur le patriotisme (s. l., 1789). Anonymous. Pamphlet.

Dissertations pour être lues: la première sur le vieux mot de patrie; la seconde sur la nature du peuple, ascribed to the Abbé Gabriel-François Coyer (La Haye, Gosse, 1755).

Encyclopédie ou dictionnaire raisonné des sciences, des arts et des métiers. Publication of this famous encyclopedia was started by D'Alembert and Diderot in 1751. The volumes used for this thesis, were published at Neufchâtel, 1765.

Raup de Baptestin, Mémoire sur un moyen facile et infallible de faire renaître le patriotisme en France (Paris, Desenne, 1789).

More Recent Analyses

Many works were written in France during the World War that are not useful for an historical study. French writers frequently employ the word *patriotisme* as English and American writers use the word "nationalism."

Arnoux, Jules, La Patrie dans l'histoire (Paris, Gedalge, s. d.).

Aubertin, Charles, L'Esprit publique au dix-huitième siècle (Paris, Didier, 1873).

Aulard, A., Le Patriotisme français de la Renaissance à la Révolution (Paris, Chiron, 1921). Ch. iv deals with the cahiers.

Brenner, Clarence D., L'Histoire nationale dans la tragèdie française du dix-huitième siècle (Berkeley, University of California, 1929).

Brunetière, F., L'Idée de patrie (Paris, Hetzel, 1897).

Goyau, Georges, L'Idée de patrie et l'humanitarianisme (Paris, Perrin, 1902).

Poinsot, M. C., and Georges Normandy, Les Poétes patriotiques (Paris, Michaud, 1909).

Rocheblave, Samuel, La Vraie France et l'évolution du patriotisme français (Paris, Bloud et Gay, 1915).

Stewart, Hugh S., and P. Desjardins, French Patriotism in the Nineteenth Century (Cambridge, University Press, 1923). Especially useful for introduction.

Stocks, J. L., Patriotism and the Super-State (London, Swarthmore Press, 1920).

Viaud, J., Les Epoques critiques du patriotisme français (Paris, Bloud, 1910).

LIST OF TEXTS OF GENERAL CAHIERS, ARRANGED ALPHABETICALLY BY DISTRICTS

Inasmuch as the detailed sources for *procès-verbaux* and cahiers have been indicated in the official inventory (Hyslop, B., *Repertoire critique des cahiers de doléances de 1789*) and full information for the general cahiers will be given in the *Guide,* now in preparation, the following table gives only such information as is vitally necessary to the present study.

The names of the districts have been arranged in alphabetical order, and are followed by the names of the *generalities* to which they severally belonged.[1] The Roman numeral after the name indicates to which of the seven types of convocation the district belongs. Where an * is added, this signifies that M. Brette has treated the district in his invaluable volumes on the convocation. (*Cf.* Bibliography, pp. 296-97). Following these items, are three columns, one for each of the three orders of the convocation, clergy, nobles, and third estate, indicating the reprinted or manuscript text used for the present study. In cases where the three or two orders combined to make one cahier, indication is made in the three columns or other appropriate columns are used.

As has already been stated, the majority of the general cahiers were reprinted by the *Archives Parlementaires,* whose edition is, however, defective. Where appreciable changes or additions to the reprinted text are necessary to make it conform to the original text, a G is placed after the page references, and signifies that the corrections of text given in the proposed *Guide* should be consulted.[2] Roman numerals represent volumes; arabic represent pages. This is not true, of course, of manuscript numbers.

In cases where the mandate is a separate document from the *procès-verbal* or the cahier proper, an M is placed in the appropriate column with the indication of where the text may be found.

When some publication other than the *Archives Parlementaires* has been used (either because that publication does not give the text in question, or because a more reliable text is available), the author is given, with a page reference to the full title in the Bibliography.

	Clergy	*Nobles*	*Third Estate*
Agen (Bordeaux) I*	AP, I, 675-79	AP, I, 679-86	AP, I, 686-91
Aix (Aix) I	AP, I, 692-93	AP, I, 693-95 M—*Arch. Nat.* Ba 9	AP, I, 695-7. G

[1] When a district belongs to the second type of convocation, the center of reunion precedes the name of the generality, in a parenthesis.

[2] Many cahiers require minor insertions or rectifications, but only the more important ones are cited here.

	Clergy	Nobles	Third Estate
Alençon (Alençon) I	AP, I, 708-10	AP, I, 710-16	AP, I, 716-20
Amiens (Amiens) I*	AP, I, 732-39	AP, I, 739-44	AP, I, 744-56
Amont (Besançon) I	U.—AP, I, 773-82		T. Supplement—Goddard and Abensour, *cf. supra,* p. 294
Angers (Tours) I*	AP, II, 30-32	AP, II, 32-38	AP, II, 38-45
Angoulême (Limoges) I*	Boissonnade, *D. I.,* 489 *et seq. Cf. supra,* p. 293	*Ibid.,* 498 *et seq.*	*Ibid.,* 481 *et seq.*
Annonay (Montpellier) I	AP, II, 46-47	AP, II, 47-49. G	AP, II, 50-53. G
Arches and Charleville VII	U—MS, *Arch. Nat.* C 33/280, B III 9, p. 683. Reprinted in *Guide*		
Arles (*sénéchaussée*) (Aix) I	*Missing*	*Missing*	*Missing*
Arles (Ville) (Aix) IV	AP, II, 54-56	NT—AP, II, 57-63. M—*Arch. Nat.* B III 10, p. 851	
Armagnac (Auch) I*	AP, II, 64-69	AP, II, 69-72	AP, II, 75-77
Artois (Lille) I	AP, II, 78-79	AP, II, 79-85	AP, VI, 721-24
Auch (Auch) I*	AP, II, 91-94	AP, II, 94-96	AP, II, 96-99
Auray (Vannes-Rennes) VI	. . .	. . .	AP, VI, 112-16. G. M—*cf.* T. Vannes
Autun (Dijon) I	Charmasse, A., 353 *et seq., cf. supra,* p. 295.	*Ibid.,* 343 *et seq.*	*Ibid.,* 328 *et seq.* M—MS, *Arch. Nat.* Ba 16
Auxerre (Dijon) I	AP, II, 108-112	AP, II, 114-19	AP, II, 120-25
Aval (Besançon) I	AP, II, 137-39. G M—*Private Coll.*	AP, II, 139-43	MS, *Private Coll.* Reprinted in *Guide*
Avesnes (Valenciennes) I	AP, II, 148-49	AP, II, 150-51	AP, II, 151-55
Bailleul (Lille) I	AP, II, 168-71. G	AP, II, 171-73	AP, II, 174-78. G
Barcelonnette (Forcalquier, Aix) II	AP, III, 365-66 M—*cf.* Forcalquier	*None made*	AP, III, 366-74

	Clergy	Nobles	Third Estate
Bar-le-duc (Bar-le-duc, Nancy) II	*Missing*	*Revolution française*, 1897. *Cf. supra*, p. 296	AP, II, 193-96
Bar-sur-Seine (Dijon) I	Vernier J. J., III, 445 *et seq., cf.* p. 295	*Ibid.*, 460 *et seq.*	*Ibid.*, 478 *et seq.*[3]
Bassigny-Barrois VII	U—AP, II, 96-98		
Bazas (Bordeaux) I*	AP, II, 266-67	AP, II, 267-68	AP, VI, 494-96. G
Béarn (Auch) III*	CN—AP, VI, 497-500 Lower C.—*Missing*		T—AP, VI, 500-503
Beauvais (Paris) I*	AP, II, 287-94	AP, II, 294-98. G	AP, II, 298-309
Belfort and Huningue (Strasbourg) I	AP, II, 310-15. G	*Missing*	AP, II, 315-18
Bellême (Alençon) I	AP, V, 319-22	AP, V, 323-25	AP, V, 325-29
Belley (Dijon) I	AP, II, 477-79	AP, II, 479-85	Recamier, *cf. supra*, p. 296
Besançon (Besançon) I	AP, II, 333-37	AP, VI, 515-19	AP, II, 337-43
Beziers (Montpellier) I	AP, II, 346-47. Also *cf.* MS, *Arch.Nat.* Ba 21. Reprinted in *Guide*	AP, II, 347-50	*Missing*
Bigorre (Auch) I*	AP, II, 350-54. G	*Missing*	AP, II, 359-65
Bitche (Sarreguemines-Nancy) II	AP, V, 692-93	*Missing*	*Missing*
Blamont (Nancy-Nancy) II	Jérome, 114 *et seq., cf. supra*, p. 296	*Missing*	*Missing* M—MS, *Arch. Nat.* C 21/110
Blois (Orléans) I*	Cauchie et Lesueur, II, 393 *et seq., cf. supra*, p. 294	*Ibid.*, II, 413 *et seq.*	*Ibid.*, II, 447 *et seq.*
Bordeaux (Bordeaux) I*	AP, II, 392-94	AP, II, 394-97	AP, II, 397-405. G

[3] It is more convenient to cite the text given by the *Archives Parlementaires*, pp. 253 *et seq.*, which is not affected by corrections. The editor of the official series does not reprint the cahier in full, due to similarities with the cahier of the town.

	Clergy	*Nobles*	*Third Estate*
Boulay (Sarreguemines-Nancy) II	AP, V, 693-94	*Missing*	Lesprand, in *Annuaire,* 1904, 200 *et seq. Cf. supra,* p. 295
Boulogne-sur-mer (Amiens) I*	AP, II, 415-24	AP, II, 424-31	AP, II, 431-41
Bourg-en-Bresse (Dijon) I	U—AP, II, 452-64. G M—for C and N—*Arch. Nat.* MS, Ba 23		
Bourges (Bourges) I*	*Cf.* Gandilhon, 755, *cf. supra,* p. 294, and AP, VI, 512-14	AP, II, 319-23	AP, II, 323-25
Bourmont (Bar-le-duc, Nancy) II	MS, *Arch. Haute-Marne.* Reprinted in *Guide*	*Idem*	AP, II, 198-201
Bouzonville (Sarreguemines, Nancy) II	AP, V, 694-98	AP, V, 701-3	AP, II, 703-7
Brest (Rennes) VI	...	...	AP, II, 475-76 and 465-75
Briey (Bar-le-duc, Nancy) II	*Missing*	AP, II, 201-4	AP, II, 204-14
Brignoles (Toulon, Aix) II	*Missing*	*Missing*	*Missing*
Bruyères (Mirecourt, Nancy) II	CT—AP, IV, 9-12	MS, *Arch. Vosges.* Reprinted in *Guide*	*Cf.* CT
Caen (Caen) I	AP, II, 486-88	AP, II, 488-92	AP, II, 492-95
Cahors (Montauban) I*[4]	AP, V, 483-88	AP, V, 488-90. G	AP, V, 490-93. M—*Arch. Nat.* C 23/130
Calais (Amiens) I*	AP, II, 504-6	AP, II, 506-10	AP, II, 510-16. G[5]
Cambrésis (Lille) I	*Missing*	AP, II, 517-19	AP, II, 519-23

[4] Cahors is the same as the district of Quercy.

[5] It is preferable to use the text reprinted by Loriquet, *Cahiers de doléances de 1789 dans le département du Pas-de-Calais* (Arras, 1891), Vol. II, p. 513 *et seq.*

	Clergy	Nobles	Third Estate
Carcassonne (Toulouse)	Dom de Vic, XIV, 2538. *Cf. supra,* p. 296	AP, II, 527-31. G	AP, II, 532-35. G
Carhaix (Carhaix, Rennes) VI	...	...	MS, *Arch Finistère.* Reprinted in *Guide*
Carignan (Sedan, Metz) II	*Missing*	NT—*Missing*	
Castellane (Draguignan, Aix) II	AP, III, 272-73	*Missing*	*Missing*
Castelmoron d'Albret (Bordeaux) I*	AP, II, 542-43 M—*Arch. Nat.* Ba 29	AP, II, 543-45	AP, II, 549-and 544-49. M—*Arch. Nat.* C 17/43[2]
Castelnaudary (Toulouse) I	AP, II, 552-53	AP, II, 557-59	AP, II, 559-61
Castres (Toulouse) I	AP, II, 562-63	AP, II, 565-68	AP, II, 569-71
Caudebec-en-Caux (Rouen) I	AP, II, 573-75	AP, II, 575-77. G	AP, II, 577-81
Châlon-sur-Saône (Dijon) I	AP, II, 600-604 M—*Arch. Nat.* C 17/48	AP, II, 604-8	AP, II, 608-13. G
Châlons-sur-Marne (Châlons) I*	Laurent, G., 821 *et seq. Cf. supra,* p. 294	*Ibid.,* 837 *et seq.* M—*Arch. Nat.* C 17/47	*Ibid.,* 845 *et seq.*
Charmes (Mirecourt, Nancy) II	*Missing*	*Missing*	*Missing*
Charolles (Dijon) I	AP, II, 614-15	AP, II, 615-18	AP, II, 618-22. G
Chartres (Orléans) I*	AP, II, 623-26	AP, II, 626-29	AP, II, 629-35
Châteauneuf-en-Thimerais (Alençon) I	AP, II, 638-40	AP, II, 640-51	AP, II, 651-57
Château-Salins (Sarreguemines, Nancy) II	AP, V, 707-9	*Missing*	Lesprand, *Annuaire,* 1904, 220 *et seq. Cf. supra,* p. 295
Château-Thierry (Soissons) I*	*Missing* M—*Arch. Nat* C 17/52	AP, II, 658-68	AP, II, 668-78

	Clergy	*Nobles*	*Third Estate*
Chatellerault (Tours) I*	AP, II, 686-90	*Missing*	AP, II, 690-99
Châtel-sur-Moselle (Mirecourt, Nancy) II	*Missing*	*Arch. Vosges,* MS, Reprinted in *Guide*	*Idem*
Châtillon-sur-Seine (Dijon) I	AP, II, 700-702	AP, II, 702-10	AP, II, 710-19
Chaumont-en-Bassigny (Châlons) I*	AP, II, 720-23	AP, II, 724-26. G	AP, II, 726-29. G
Chaumont-en-Vexin (Rouen) I	*Missing*	AP, II, 730-32	AP, II, 739-43
Clermont à Varennes Verdun, Metz) II	U—*Missing*		
Clermont-en-Beauvoisis (Soissons) I*	AP, II, 744-48	AP, II, 748-54. G	AP, II, 754-58
Clermont Ferrand (Riom) I*	AP, II, 759-66	AP, II, 766-69	AP, II, 769-74
Colmar and Schlestadt (Strasbourg) I	AP, III, 3-7	AP, III, 7-9	AP, III, 9-12. G
Commercy (Bar-le-duc, Nancy) II	*Missing*	*Missing*	*Missing*
Comminges (Auch) I	*Missing*	AP, III, 21-26	AP, II, 26-28
Condom (Bordeaux) I*	AP, III, 33-36	AP, III, 36-38	AP, III, 38-40
Corsica (Corsica) VI	*Missing*	MS, *Private Coll.* French translation reprinted in *Guide*[6]	AP, III, 41-46
Couserans (Auch) V*	*Missing*	NT—*Missing*	
Coutances (Caen) I	Bridrey, E., III, 467 *et seq. Cf. supra,* p. 293	*Ibid.,* 508 *et seq.*	*Ibid.,* 546 *et seq.*
Crépy-en-Valois (Soissons) I*	AP, III, 73-74	AP, III, 74-76	AP, III, 76-79
Darney (Mirecourt, Nancy) II	*Missing*	Duhamel, II, 356 *et seq. Cf.* p. 295	*Missing*

[6] The Italian text was reprinted by the Abbé Letteron, in the Bulletin of *Soc. des Sc. hist. et nat. de la Corse,* Vol. XIV, Appendix II, p. 447.

	Clergy	Nobles	Third Estate
Dauphiné (Grenoble) III	U—AP, III, 80-81. G[7]		
Dax (Bordeaux) I*	AP, III, 87-93	AP, III, 93-95	AP, III, 95-98 M—AP, III, 107-10
Dieuze (Sarreguemines, Nancy) II	Etienne, 401, *et seq. Cf. supra*, p. 293	*Ibid.*, 405 *et seq.*	*Ibid.*, 411 *et seq.*
Digne (Forcalquier, Aix) II	AP, III, 336-40 M—*cf.* Forcalquier	AP, III, 346-47	AP, III, 348-56
Dijon (Dijon) I	AP, III, 123-27	AP, III, 127-30	AP, III, 131-40. G
Dinan (Rennes) VI	...	...	AP, III, 148-51
Dix Villes Impériales (Strasbourg) IV	...	...	*Bib. Colmar.* French translation reprinted in *Guide*
Dol (Rennes) VI	Sée and Lessort, IV, 299 *et seq. Cf. supra*, p. 295	...	...
Dôle (Besançon) I	AP, III, 152-54	AP, III, 154-60	AP, III, 160-68. G
Dorat (Limoges) I*[8]	AP, III, 675-76	AP, III, 676-78	AP, III, 678-81
Douai (Lille) I	AP, III, 174-75	AP, III, 175-79	AP, III, 179-83. G
Dourdan (Orléans) I*	AP, III, 243-46	AP, III, 246-50	AP, III, 250-54
Draguignan (Draguignan, Aix) II	MS, *Arch. Nat.* Ba 39, Reprinted in *Guide*	*Missing*	AP, III, 255-64
Epinal (Mirecourt, Nancy) II	*Missing*	*Missing*	*Missing*
Etain (Bar-le-duc, Nancy) II	MS, *Arch. Meuse.* Reprinted in *Guide*	AP, II, 214-20	MS, *Arch. Meuse.* Reprinted in *Guide*

[7] The original of the cahier of the three orders made in the Provincial-Estates of the Dauphiné has been lost. We possess only the summary incorporated in the *procès-verbal.*

[8] Dorat is the same district as Marche-Basse.

	Clergy	Nobles	Third Estate
Etampes (Paris) I*	AP, III, 279-82	*Missing*	AP, III, 283-89
Evreux (Rouen) I	AP, III, 290-95	AP, III, 295-99	AP, III, 300-303
Fenestrange (Sarreguemines, Nancy) II	U—AP, V, 710-13		
Foix (Auch) I*[9]	*Missing*[10]	AP, IV, 280-81. G	AP, IV, 281-85
Forcalquier (Forcalquier, Aix) II	AP, III, 324-28 M—p.v. of reunion	AP, III, 328-29	AP, III, 329-36
Forez (Lyon) I*	AP, III, 382-83	AP, III, 383-85	AP, III, 385-87
Fougères (Rennes) VI	...	...	*Missing*
Gex (Dijon) I	AP, III, 388-92 M—*Arch. Nat.* C 19/78	AP, III, 392-94	AP, III, 394-97
Gien (Orléans) I*	AP, III, 398-400	AP, III, 400-406	AP, III, 406-12
Grasse (Draguignan, Aix) II	AP, III, 267-68	*Made none*	AP, III, 274-77
Guadeloupe (Colony) VII	One class—AP, VI, 235		
Guéret (Moulins) I*[11]	AP, III, 682-83	AP, III, 684-85	AP, III, 685-86
Haguenau (Strasbourg) I	*Missing*	*Missing*	AP, III, 416-20
Hédé (Fougères, Rennes) VI	...	...	*Missing*
Hennebont (Rennes) VI	...	...	*Missing*
Hyères (Toulon, Aix) II	*Missing*	*Missing*	*Missing*
Ile de Bourbon et de France (Colony) VII	One class—*missing*		
Jugon (St. Brieuc, Rennes) VI	...	...	*Missing*
Lamarche (Bar-le-duc, Nancy) II	AP, II, 220-24	*Missing*	Duhamel, II, 378 *et seq.* *Cf. supra*, p. 295

[9] Foix is the same as the *sénéchaussée* of Pamiers.
[10] The document given by the *Archives Parlementaires* is not a cahier.
[11] Guéret is the same as the district of Haute-Marche.

	Clergy	*Nobles*	*Third Estate*
Langres (Châlons) I*	U—*Missing*[12]	Supplement—*missing*. M—*Arch. Nat.* B III 70, p. 537	Supplement—MS, *Arch. Nat.* Ba 45. Reprinted in *Guide*
Lannion (Morlaix, Rennes) VI	...	...	AP, IV, 76-78
La Rochelle (La Rochelle) I*	*Missing*	AP, III, 471-78. G	AP, III, 479-86
Lesneven (Rennes) VI	...	...	AP, III, 493-99
Libourne (Bordeaux) I*	AP, III, 503-6	AP, III, 506-7	AP, III, 507-9
Lille (Lille) I	AP, III, 522-26	AP, III, 526-32	AP, III, 532-35
Limoges (Limoges) I*[13]	AP, III, 560-64	AP, III, 564-70. G	AP, III, 570-72
Limoux (Toulouse) I	Dom de Vic, XIV, 2615. *Cf. supra*, p. 296	AP, III, 577-79	AP, III, 579-82
Lixheim (Sarreguemines, Nancy) II	CN—AP, V, 713-17		MS, *Arch. Meurthe-et-Moselle*. Reprint in *Guide*
Longuyon (Bar-le-duc) II	MS, *Arch. Moselle*. Reprinted in *Guide*	*Idem*	*Idem*
Longwy (Metz, Metz) II	AP, III, 771-73. G M—p.v., of 3 Orders	MS, *Arch. Moselle*. Reprint in *Guide*	*Idem*
Loudon (Tours) I*	AP, III, 590-94	AP, III, 594-96	AP, III, 596-98
Lunéville (Nancy, Nancy) II	Jérome, p. 97. *Cf. supra*, p. 296. M—*ibid.*, p. 91	AP, IV, 84-86	*Missing*
Lyon (Lyon) I*	AP, III, 599-602. G	AP, III, 602-8	AP, III, 608-15. M—*Arch. Nat.* C 19/90

[12] The document given by the *Archives Parlementaires* is not authentic.
[13] Limoges is the same as Haut-Limousin.

	Clergy	Nobles	Third Estate
Lyon (Ville) IV*			Town—AP, III, 616-18
Mâcon (Dijon) I	AP, III, 621-23	AP, III, 623-28	AP, III, 628-34. G M—*Arch. Nat.* B III 77, p. 284
Mans, Le (Tours) I*	AP, III, 636-40	AP, III, 640-42	AP, III, 642-51
Mantes (Paris) I*	AP, III, 652-61	AP, III, 661-66	AP, III, 666-74. G[14]
Marches Communes (Poitiers) **I***	U—AP, III, 687-89		
Marseille (Aix) I	Fournier, J., 416 *et seq. Cf. supra,* p. 293. M—MS, *Arch. Nat.* C 19/96	*Ibid.,* 408 *et seq.*	*Ibid.,* 358 *et seq.*
Martinique (Colony) VII	One class. Printed edition of 1789. *Bib. Nat.* Le 23. 183. Reprint in *Guide*		
Meaux (Paris) I*	AP, III, 721-25. G	AP, 725-27	AP, III, 727-32
Melun (Paris) I*	AP, III, 733-39	AP, III, 739-43. G	AP, III, 743-50
Mende (Montpellier) I	AP, III, 751-53	AP, III, 753-55. *Cf. Guide* for supplement	AP, III, 755-58
Metz (Metz, Metz) II	AP, III, 759-62	AP, III, 762-65	AP, III, 765-71.
Metz (Ville) IV			Town-Dorvaux and Lesprand, *Annuaire,* 1903, 192. *Cf. supra,* p. 295
Mirecourt (Mirecourt, Nancy) II	Martin, E., 258 *et seq. Cf. supra,* p. 294	*Ibid.,* 261 *et seq.*	*Ibid.,* 250 *et seq.*
Mohon (Sedan, Metz) II	U—AP, V, 729-30		
Montargis (Orléans) I*	AP, IV, 17-20	AP, IV, 20-26	AP, IV, 26-31

[14] The cahier should read for vote by head, and not vote by order.

	Clergy	*Nobles*	*Third Estate*
Mont-de-Marsan (Bordeaux) I*	AP, IV, 32-33	*Missing*	MS, *Arch. Nat.* Ba 54. Reprint in *Guide*[15]
Montfort l'Amaury (Paris) I*	U—AP, IV, 37-43. G		
Montpellier (Montpellier) I	AP, IV, 44-45	AP, IV, 45-49	AP, IV, 49-58
Montreuil-sur-mer (Amiens) I*	AP, IV, 59-61	AP, IV, 61-68	AP, IV, 68-71
Morlaix (Morlaix, Rennes) VI	...	...	AP, IV, 75- and 72-75. G
Moulins (Moulins) I*[16]	AP, II, 442-44	AP, II, 444-47	AP, II, 447-49
Mouzon (Sedan, Metz) II	U—*Missing*		
Nancy (Nancy, Nancy) II	Jérome, 56 *et seq. Cf. supra,* p. 296	AP, IV, 79-84	AP, VI, 644-47
Nantes (Rennes) VI	Printed text, *Bib. Nat.* Le 24. 249. Reprint in *Guide*	...	MS, *Arch. Nat.* Ba 26 *Cf. Guide*[17]
Navarre (Auch) III*	U—MS, *Arch. Nat.* K 692 A. Printed text of 1789—*Bib. Nat.* LK 2. 1161		
Nemours (Paris) I*	AP, IV, 106-9	AP, IV, 109-12	AP, IV, 112-215. G
Nérac (Bordeaux) I*	AP, IV, 230-32	AP, I, 701-3. G. M—*Arch. Nat.* C 21/113	AP, IV, 232-35
Neufchâteau (Mirecourt, Nancy) II	*Missing*	*Missing*	Duhamel, II, 323 *et seq. Cf.* p. 295

[15] The text given by the *Archives Parlementaires* is not the general cahier. (*Cf. Brette, op. cit.,* Vol. IV, pp. 319-20.)

[16] Moulins is the same district as Bourbonnais.

[17] The text given by the *Archives Parlementaires* is the cahier of the *sénéchaussée* of Nantes, whereas the authentic general cahier is a MS. text of the *sénéchaussées* of Nantes and Guérande united. The two texts resemble each other very closely, however.

	Clergy	*Nobles*	*Third Estate*
Nîmes (Montpellier) I	Bligny-Bondurdand, II, 573 *et seq.* *Cf. supra*, p. 293	*Ibid.*, 579 *et seq.*	*Ibid.*, 588 *et seq.*
Nivernais (Moulins) I*	AP, IV, 246-52. G	AP, IV, 252-56	AP, IV, 256-61
Nomény (Nancy, Nancy) II	Jérome, 139 *et seq.* *Cf. supra*, p. 296	AP, IV.[18] G	MS, *Arch. Meurthe-et-Moselle.* Reprint in *Guide*
Orange (Grenoble) I	AP, IV, 266-67	*Missing*	AP, IV, 267-73
Orléans (Orléans) I*	Bloch, C., II, 399 *et seq.* *Cf.* p. 293	*Ibid.*, 422 *et seq.*	*Ibid.*, p. 399 and 287 *et seq.*
Paris *hors-les-murs* (Paris) I*[19]	AP, V, 230-35. G	AP, V, 235-37	AP, V, 237-45
Paris *intra-muros* (Paris) IV*[19]	AP, V, 263-67 Municipality—AP, V, 290-95	AP, V, 271-75	AP, V, 281-90
Périgord (Bordeaux) I*	*Missing*	AP, V, 338-41	AP, V, 342-44. G
Péronne (Amiens) I*	AP, V, 347-55	NT—AP, V, 355-61. G	
Perpignan (Perpignan) I	*Missing*	AP, V, 368-73	AP, V, 373-77. G
Ploërmel (Rennes) VI	. . .	. . .	AP, V, 378-85. G
Poitiers (Poitiers) I*	AP, V, 389-94	AP, V, 394-97	AP, V. 406-15. G
Pondichéry (Colony) VII	One class—AP, VI, 235-36. Also, six *Memoires*, MS, *Arch. Nat.* C 42/368		
Pont-à-Mousson (Bar-le-duc, Nancy) II	AP, II, 228	AP, II, 228-30	AP, II, 230-34
Ponthieu (Amiens) I*	AP, V, 428-30	AP, V, 430-36	AP, V, 436-44. G

[18] Consult Jerome, *op. cit.*, p. 144, note 1, on the confusion of texts in the *Archives Parlementaires.* The latter combined sections of the cahier of the nobles of Nomény with the cahier of the united orders of Rozières. The cahier of the nobles of Nomény actually extends: AP, Vol. IV, p. 87, art. 1—p. 88, art. 10 and p. 92, arts. 11 to the end.

[19] It is more convenient to use the *Archives Parlementaires* for Paris than the volumes by Chassin (*cf. Bibliography*, p. 295).

	Clergy	Nobles	Third Estate
Provins (Paris) I*	AP, V, 445-47. G	AP, V, 447-52	AP, V, 452-55. G
Puy-en-Velay (Montpellier) I	AP, V, 456-68	*Missing.* M—*Arch. Nat.* C 23/129	AP, V, 469-72. G
Quatre-Vallées (Auch) V*	...	...	AP, III, 413-15
Quesnoy (Valenciennes) I	*Missing*	AP, V, 503-7	*Missing*
Quimper (Rennes) VI	*Missing*	...	Savina and Bernard, II, 360 *et seq.*[20] *Cf. supra* p. 295
Reims (Châlons) I*	AP, V, 520-26	AP, V, 526-30	AP, V, 530-35. M—*Arch. Nat.* C 23/133
Remiremont (Mirecourt, Nancy) II	U—*Missing*		
Rennes (Rennes) VI	Sée and Lessort, IV, 287 *et seq. Cf. supra,* p. 295	...	*Ibid.*, p. 239
Rhuys (Vannes, Rennes) VI	...	...	*Missing*
Riom (Riom) I*	AP, V, 561-63	AP, V, 563-68	AP, V,[21] G
Rivière-Verdun (Auch) I*	AP, V, 581-83	AP, V, 583-86	AP, V, 586-89
Rochefort-sur-mer (La Rochelle) V*	...	...	AP, III, 486-90 and supplement, reprinted in *Guide*
Rodez (Montauban) I*	AP, V, 551-54	AP, V, 555-57	AP, V, 557-59
Rouen (Rouen) I	AP, V, 590-94	AP, V, 594-97	*Missing*
Rouen (Ville) IV			AP, V, 597-602
Rozières (Nancy, Nancy) II	U—AP, IV[22]		

[20] The cahier given by the *Archives Parlementaires* is the cahier of the *sénéchaussée* of Quimper, and not of the united districts of Quimper and Concarneau.

[21] *Cf.* Brette, *op. cit.,* Vol. III, p. 638, on cahier of T. Riom. *Cf.* also, *Guide.*

[22] *Cf.* Jérome, *op. cit.,* pp. 127-28, 144, on the text of U. Rozières. It is reprinted in the AP as follows: Vol. IV, p. 91 arts. 1-10, p. 88, arts. 11 to end.

	Clergy	*Nobles*	*Third Estate*
Rustaing (Auch) V	U—AP, II, 366-72		
St. Aubin-du-Cormier, (Fougères, Rennes) VI	...	...	*Missing*
St. Brieuc (St. Brieuc, Rennes) VI	Upper Clergy—AP, V, 627 Lower Clergy —*Missing*	AP, V, 627-29	AP, V, 629-32. G
St. Dié (Mirecourt Nancy) II	*Missing*	*Missing*	Printed text of 1789, *Arch. Haut-Rhin.* Reprint in *Guide*
St. Domingue (Colony) VII	Petition for admittance to National Assembly—MS, *Arch. Nat.* C 86/15. Reprint in *Guide*		
St. Flour (Riom) I*	*Missing*	AP, VI, 690-91[23]	AP, VI, 691-95
St. Jean d'Angely (La Rochelle) I*	AP, V, 633-34	Mesnard, A., 40 *et seq. Cf. supra,* p. 296	AP, XXXII, 521-22
St. Malo (Rennes) VII	Sée and Lessort, IV, 306 *et seq. Cf. supra,* p. 295	...	...
St. Mihiel (Bar-le-duc, Nancy) II	MS, *Arch. Meuse*	AP, II, 235-44	*Missing*
St. Pierre-le-Moutier (Moulins) I*	*Missing*	AP, V, 635	AP, V, 635-42
St. Pol-de-Léon (Rennes) VI	*Made none*	...	...
St. Quentin (Amiens) I*	AP, V, 647-52. G	AP, V, 652-53. M—*Arch. Nat.* Ba 70	AP, V, 653-58
Saintes (La Rochelle) I*	AP, V, 659-65	AP, V, 665-69	AP, V, 669-74[24]
Sarrebourg (Metz, Metz) II	AP, III, 784-85	MS, *Arch. Meurthe-et-Moselle*	*Idem*
Sarreguemines (Sarreguemines, Nancy) II	AP, V, 689-90	AP, V, 690-92	MS, *Arch. Moselle.* Reprint in *Guide*

[23] The only extant text of the cahier is mutilated, as is the reprint.

[24] The cahier of Ile d'Oléron and of the town of Saintes is a part of the general cahier.

	Clergy	Nobles	Third Estate
Sarrelouis (Metz, Metz) II	CN—MS, *Arch. Nat.* B III 87, p. 577. Reprint in *Guide*		*Missing*
Saumur (Tours) I*	AP, V, 718-20	AP, V, 720-23	AP, V, 723-26
Sedan (Sedan, Metz) II	*Missing*	*Missing*	AP, V, 727-28
Semur-en-Auxois (Dijon) I	AP, II, 126-28	AP, II, 128-31. G	AP, II, 131-33
Senlis (Paris) I*	*Missing*	AP, V, 734-36	AP, V, 736-43 and *Mémoire*, 743-47
Sens (Paris) I*	Porée, 787 *et seq. Cf. supra*, p. 295	*Ibid.*, 801 *et seq.*	*Ibid.*, 813 *et seq.*
Sézanne (Châlons) I*	Laurent, 464 *et seq. Cf. supra* p. 294	*Ibid.*, 472 *et seq.* M—*Arch. Nat.* B III 144, p. 272	*Ibid.*, 486 *et seq.*
Sisteron (Forcalquier, Aix) II	AP, III, 361-63	AP, III, 363-65	*Missing*
Soissons (Soissons) I*	AP, V, 768-73	*Missing*	AP, VI, 696-700
Soule (Auch) I*	AP, V, 774-76	AP, V, 776-79	AP, V, 779-83
Strasbourg (Strasbourg) IV	. . .	. . .	Reuss, I, 31-66. *Cf. supra*, p. 296
Tartas (Bordeaux) I*	*Made none*	AP, I, 699-701	AP, I, 704-7
Thiaucourt (Bar-le-duc, Nancy) II	*Annales de l'Est*, 1904, 357 *et seq. Cf. supra*, p. 296	*Ibid.*, 365 *et seq.*	*Ibid.*, 370 *et seq.*
Thionville (Metz, Metz) II	AP, III, 773-74	AP, III, 774-76	AP, III, 776-80 and Lesprand *Annuaire*, 1904, 90 *et seq.*[25]
Toul (Toul, Metz) II	AP, VI, 1-4	AP, VI, 4-8	AP, VI, 8-16. G
Toulon (Toulon, Aix) II	*Missing*	*Missing*	MS, *Arch. Nat.* Ba 81, Reprint in *Guide*[26]

[25] The general assembly adopted the cahier of the town, hence the two documents.
[26] The *Archives Parlementaires* give only the cahier of the town.

	Clergy	*Nobles*	*Third Estate*
Toulouse (Toulouse) I	AP, VI, 28-31	AP, VI, 31-35	AP, VI, 35-38
Tours (Tours) I*[27]	Faye, H., *Cf. supra* p. 295	AP, VI, 39-44; p.v. 44 *et seq.*	AP, VI, 52-54
Tréguier (Rennes) VI	Sée and Lessort, IV, 312 *et seq. Cf. supra,* p. 295	...	...
Trévoux (Dijon) I	*Missing*	AP, VI, 65-68	AP, VI, 68-71
Troyes (Châlons) I*	Vernier, J. J., III, 445 *et seq. Cf. supra,* p. 295	*Ibid.,* 460 *et seq.*	*Ibid.,* 478 *et seq.*
Tulle (Limoges) I*[28]	AP, III, 536-37	AP, III, 537-39. G	AP, III, 540-42
Ustaritz (Bordeaux) I*[29]	AP, III, 423-25	AP, III, 425-27	Reprint in 1874, *Bib. Bayonne.* Reprint in *Guide*
Valenciennes (Valenciennes) IV	...	...	AP, VI, 99-105
Vannes (Vannes, Rennes) VI	*Missing*	...	AP, VI, 100-12
Vendôme (Orléans) I*	AP, VI, 118-20. M—*Arch. Nat.* B III 152, p. 190	AP, VI, 120-22	AP, VI, 122-26
Verdun (Verdun, Metz) II	AP, VI, 126-30	AP, VI, 130-33	*Révolution française,* 1897. *Cf. supra,* p. 296
Vermandois (Soissons) I*	AP, VI, 134-37	AP, VI, 137-44	AP, VI, 144-48
Vézelise (Nancy, Nancy) II	Etienne, 448 *et seq. Cf. supra,* p. 293	*Missing*	Etienne, 457 *et seq. Cf. supra* p. 293
Vic (Toul, Metz) II	AP, VI, 16-18	AP, VI, 18-19	AP, VI, 20-22
Villefranche-de-Beaujolais (Lyon) I*	AP, II, 279-81	AP, II, 281-82	AP, II, 282-86

[27] Both the cahier of the clergy and that of the third estate of Tours come down to us only as a summary of the articles.

[28] Tulle is the same as Bas-Limousin.

[29] Ustartiz is the same as the district of Labour.

	Clergy	Nobles	Third Estate
Villefranche-en-Rouergue (Montauban) I*	*Missing*	AP, VI, 166-69	AP, VI, 169-71
Villeneuve-de-Berg (Montpellier) I	AP, VI, 702-6	AP, VI, 177-82	AP, VI, 707-14. G
Villers-Cotterets (Soissons) I*	AP, VI, 187-88	AP, VI, 189-91. G	AP, VI, 191-93
Villers-la-Montagne (Bar-de-duc, Nancy) II	U—AP, II, 244-46		
Vitry-le-françois (Châlons) I*	AP, VI, 206-11	AP, VI, 715-20	AP, VI, 211-21. G

234 electoral districts and 5 colonies

CAHIERS USED: 158 C, 154 N, 190 T, 14 U,[29] 3 CN, 1 CT, 2 NT—522 cahiers

CAHIERS LOST: 36 C, 28 N, 23 T, 2 NT, 4 U—93 cahiers

TOTAL MADE IN 1789: 194 C, 182 N, 213 T, 18 U, 3 CN, 1 CT, 4 NT—615 general cahiers

COLONIES: USED:4. LOST:5. MADE:9 cahiers

---

[29] The cahier of the municipality of Paris has been counted among those of all three orders jointly.

CORRECTIONS AND ADDITIONS, 1967

The corrections and additions that are being made do not involve revision of the text and its conclusions, but rather, indicate: (1) typographical corrections, (2) cahiers that should now be consulted, were the entire number of available cahiers now analyzed for nationalism, (3) statistical information about the numbers of cahiers, imperative mandates, and where to find the texts.

The same abbreviations will be used as appeared in the original volume. The statistical information will now be the same as in the *Guide,* since a revised edition of it is appearing simultaneously with the revision of this work. Information about the cahiers is more extensive in the *Guide* than in this volume, which was published first and for which a minimum of essential documentary information was supplied. It should be noted that the present volume provides some tables in the appendix not repeated in the *Guide,* since some of the information was incorporated into the Tables on pp. 116-42 of the *Guide,* with corrections and additions.

PAGE

7-8 Note 21. See also Beatrice F. Hyslop, *Le supplément au répertoire critique des cahiers de doléances . . . (Collection de documents inédits sur l'histoire économique de la Révolution française),* Paris, 1952. Collections of parish cahiers have been found, such as for the grand *bailliage* of Rouen, cited in the *Supplément,* and more recently, for Saumur, Belley, etc.

8 Paragraph 2. Correct numbers to 616 and 532.

Note 23. The *Supplément* provides an index for cahiers of the lower clergy and for gilds, pp. 193, 194-95.

Note 24. The general cahier of Rouen had been found between publication of the original edition of this volume and of the *Guide,* which accounts for the difference of one in the number of available cahiers of the third estate. Note additions for statistics, pp. 237-46 and pp. 312-28, especially the summary, p. 328.

9 Paragraph 1. Correct the statistics, although the original figures must be used for the analysis of nationalism. Cahiers missing: 84. 35 C, 26 N, 18 T, 4 U, 1 NT. Cahiers available: 532. 160 C, 156 N, 195 T, 14 U, 3 CN, 1 CT, 3 NT. Note the addition of

PAGE

C, Tartas to the total number of general cahiers and to the number for the clergy.

Paragraph 2. Correct four to six.

Note 29. See the correction of pp. 243-44, *infra,* and the *Guide.* Of the nine made, six are available. Correct text, par. 2, l. 3 to six.

12 Line 3. Since the ten cahiers discovered after the first edition are not being added to the statistics of opinions, the number 522 is being retained. There are now available 532 general cahiers.

14 Note 49. The *Guide* is being published in a revised second edition simultaneously with this new edition. The original edition of the *Guide* was published by Columbia University Press in 1936.

Note 50. Thirty-five texts, not thirty-four, were given in the *Guide,* since the general cahier for the grand *bailliage* of Rouen had been found.

Note 52. Add: see also the *Supplément.*

16 Note 58. No correction needed, but the number of cahiers missing would now be 84. Consult the table (with revision) in the *Guide,* pp. 116-42, for citation of the p.v., or fuller details in the *Répertoire* and *Supplément.*

17 Note 60. Correct to 265 out of 616, allowing for the printed texts of N, Puy-en-Velay and T, Hennebont. See table, with corrections, for pp. 244-45.

18 Note 69. See correction of table of Imperative Mandates, pp. 245-46, and new alphabetical list of these mandates. See also tables corrected for *Guide,* pp. 116-42.

21 Line 3. Correct to read 616.

22 Much has been written on and said about Nationalism since 1934, but since the analysis of the cahiers was based upon the concept described in Chapter II, it is being reprinted as it appeared in the first edition.

35 Note 59. See *Guide,* pp. 180-84, for important addition to text.

165 Note 92. Three out of . . . nine. Add to list of documents for St. Domingue, cahier drawn up by the North, cahier of the West, and "Le Projet de formation des états coloniaux et provinciaux." See *Guide,* correction for p. 137, and *Supplément,* pp. 164-65.

PAGE

208-13 No additions are being made here for the ten general cahiers now available. It is not practical to appraise nationalism in the same way as in 1934. There is no assurance that judgment would remain the same.

214 A few areas in the map facing p. 214 would no longer be white if the cahiers newly available were being added.

217 Note 13. The cahiers that have been found were not listed among those for which reservation on their validity was recorded.

228 Last paragraph, Notes 30, 31; Page 229, Note 32. This paragraph and the notes need revision. See corrected table of Imperative Mandates, p. 333, list of such mandates added to original, pp. 245-46, and alphabetical list of Imperative Mandates (new), pp. 333-34. The new totals are: 53 C, 135 N, 81 T, 6 U, 2 CN, 1 CT, 1 NT—279. The new total results from omission of two given as imperative originally: U, Bourg-en-Bresse; NT, Péronne; and the addition of thirty that should have been indicated as imperative. It should be noted that more assemblies of the nobles than of the clergy and third estate gave Imperative Mandates. Most of these, though not all, were protective of noble privileges. The cahiers from the nobles of Paris, both classified as Radical Nationalism, reenforced their radicalism rather than defending privileges. The results of the revision of Imperative Mandates are as follows: six of the general cahiers now known were then missing, and two Imperative Mandates have been subtracted. Therefore, no nationalism with Imperative Mandate: 9 C, 2 N, 4 T, 1 CN—16; Conservative: 22 C, 23 N, 6 T, 1 NT—52; Intermediate: 14 C, 55 N, 21 T, 1 U, 1 CN—92; Progressive: 3 C, 21 N, 25 T, 4 U—53; Radical: 2 C, 16 N, 18 T, 1 U, 1 CT—38. These changes would have increased the percentage of Progressive and Radical general cahiers with Imperative Mandates.

229 Paragraph 2, Line 5. Read 265 general cahiers were printed, and correct numbers in the next sentence to 106 for the nobles and 93 for the third estate, since N, St. Dié and T, Hennebont were printed.

Note 34. See correction of list for pp. 244-45. The next sentence would now read 616 general cahiers, 265 printed, 532 available.

Note 35. The figure for Rouen remains the same. Had the general cahier for the grand *bailliage* been printed, it would probably not have been missing in 1934.

PAGE

230 Notes 36, 37, 38. Since the two printed cahiers added now were not known in 1934, they are not added to the statistics in this edition.

231 Note 39. The nobles of Sedan, whose cahier is still missing, and two assemblies of the ten new cahiers known chose committees of correspondence—N, Puy-en-Velay; T, Quesnoy. See correction for table, p. 246.

CORRECTIONS FOR TABLES IN APPENDIX

Corrections and additions are provided for documentary lists, but no insertions are being made to the tables of various opinions in the general cahiers.

237-44 *Lists of General Cahiers by Generality.*

238 *Generality* of Montpellier. Extant (20): add N, Puy-en-Velay; N7. Missing (1): omit N, Puy-en-Velay; N 0.

239 *Generality* of Bordeaux. (36) Extant (34): add C, Tartas; C11. Missing (2); C1.

Generality of Montauban. Extant (9): add C, Villefranche-en-Rouergue. Missing (0): omit C, Villefranche-en-Rouergue.

240 *Generality* of Rouen. Extant (12): add T, Rouen; T5. Missing (1): omit T, Rouen; T0.

241-42 *Generality* of Aix. Extant (26): add T, Brignoles, T, Hyères; T10. Missing (13): omit T, Brignoles, T, Hyères; T3.

242 *Generality* of Rennes. Extant (21): add T, Hennebont; T14. Missing (8): omit T, Hennebont; T5.

Generality of Valenciennes. Extant (8): add T, Quesnoy; T4. Missing (2): omit T, Quesnoy; T0.

242-43 *Generality* of Nancy. Extant (65): add N, St. Dié; N19. Missing (28): omit N, St. Dié; N10.

243 *Generality* of Metz. Extant (27): add NT, Carignan; NT 1. Missing (6): omit NT, Carignan; NT0.

243-44 Colonies (9). Extant (6): add St. Domingue, N, W. Missing (3): add St. Domingue, S. Total: 9.

PAGE

244 Correction of summary statistics of general cahiers, though not used for the analysis.

Made: 195 C, 182 N, 213 T, 18 U, 3 CN, 1 CT, 4 NT—616
Missing: 35 C, 26 N, 18 T, 4 U, 1 NT— 84
Extant: 160 C, 156 N, 195 T, 14 U, 3 CN, 1 CT, 3 NT—532
Found since 1934: 2 C, 2 N, 5 T, 1 NT—10
Colonial Cahiers: Made 9, Lost 3, Extant 6

244-45 *Alphabetical List of Cahiers Printed in 1789.*
Total: 54 C, 106 N, 93 T, 8 U, 1 CN, 1 CT, 2 NT—265 cahiers; Insert T, Hennebont, N, St. Dié.

245-46 Corrections for *List of Cahiers with Imperative Mandates Attached.* A number of additions and a few omissions are necessary. It has been deemed helpful for consultation to provide additions by generality; then a list of additions in alphabetical order; and also the entire list arranged alphabetically.

245 Paris: Add T, Etampes. Orléans: Add C, T, Chartres. Riom: Add C, Clermont; C, Riom. Montpellier: Add C, Nîmes; T, Puy-en-Velay. Auch: Add C, Bigorre; N, Couserans. Bordeaux: Add C, Périgord. Limoges: Add N, Angoulême. La Rochelle: Add N, St. Jean d'Angely.

246 Amiens: Omit NT, add T, Péronne. Lille: Add C, Bailleul; C, N, Lille. Soissons: Add C, Clermont-en-Beauvaisis. Dijon: Add C, Autun; N, Auxerre; omit U, Bourg-en-Bresse; add T, Gex. Aix: Add C, Barcelonnette; C, N, T, Digne; C, Sisteron. Valenciennes: Add T, Quesnoy. Nancy: Add N, Neufchâteau; N, Remiremont. Metz: Add T, Sarrelouis. Strasbourg: Add N, Haguenau.

List of Imperative Mandates Added, in Alphabetical Order.

N, Angoulême; C, Autun; N, Auxerre; C, Bailleul; C, Barcelonnette; C, Bigorre; C, T, Chartres; C, Clermont-en-Beauvaisis; C, Clermont Ferrand; N, Couserans; C, N, T, Digne; T, Etampes; T, Gex; N, Haguenau; C, N, Lille; N, Neufchâteau; C, Nîmes; C, Perigord; T, Péronne; T, Puy-en-Velay; T. Quesnoy; N, Remiremont; C, Riom; N, St. Jean d'Angely; T, Sarrelouis; C, Sisteron. Total: 13 C, 9 N, 8 T—30 Imperative Mandates added. Names to be omitted from the list given on pp. 245-46: U, Bourg-en-Bresse; NT, Péronne. Total, 2.

Alphabetical List of Imperative Mandates.

C, N, T, Agen; T, Aix; N, Alençon; N, Amiens; N, Amont; N, T, Angers; N, Angoulême; N, Annonay; NT, Arles(ville); N,

Armagnac; N, Artois; N, T, Auch; T, Auray; C, N, Autun; N, T, Auxerre; N, T, Aval; T, Avesnes; C, Bailleul; C, Barcelonnette; N, T, Bar-sur-Seine; C, N, T, Bazas; CN, T, Béarn; N, Beauvais; N, T, Belfort; C, N, T, Bellême; N, T, Belley; C, N, Besançon; C, Beziers; C, N, Bigorre; C, Blamont; N, Blois; N, Bordeaux; T, Boulay; C, T, Boulogne; N, Bourg-en-Bresse; N, T, Bourges; N, Bourmont; C, Bouzonville; N, T, Briey; T, Brignoles; CT, Bruyères; N, T, Caen; C, N, Cahors; N, Calais; C, N, Cambrèsis; N, Carcassonne; C, N, T, Castelmoron; N, Castelnaudary; N, T, Castres; N, Caudebec; N, Châlon-sur-Saône; N, Charmes; C, N, T, Charolles; C, N, T, Chartres; T, Château-Salins; T, Château-Thierry; C, N, T, Châteauneuf-en-Thimerais; N, T, Chatellerault; T, Châtel-sur-Moselle; N, T, Châtillon-sur-Seine; N, T, Chaumont-en-Bassigny; N, Chaumont-en-Vexin; C, N, Clermont-en-Beauvaisis; C, N, T, Clermont Ferrand; N, Colmar; N, Comminges; C, N, T, Condom; N, Couserans; N, T, Coutances; N, Crépy; N, Darney; U, Dauphiné; C, N, Dax; T, Dieuze; C, N, T, Digne; C, N, T, Dijon, N, Dôle; N, Dorat; C, N, T, Douai; N, Dourdan; N, Epinal; N, Etain; N, T, Etampes; C, N, T, Evreux; U, Fenétrange; N, Foix; C, Forcalquier; N, T, Forez; T, Fougères; C, N, T, Gex; N, T, Gien; N, T, Guéret; N, Haguenau; N, La Marche; N, Langres; N, La Rochelle; N, T, Libourne; C, N, Lille; N, T, Limoges; C, N, T, Limoux; CN, Lixheim; N, Loudun; C, N, Lunéville; N, T, Lyon; N, T, Mâcon; N, Le Mans; C, T, Marseille; N, Meaux; C, Melun; N, Mende; T, V, Metz; C, N, T, Mirecourt; U, Mohon; C, N, T, Montargis; C, N, Mont-de-Marsan; U, Montfort l'Amaury; N, Montpellier; N, Montreuil; N, Moulins; Cl, T, Nantes;[1] C, N, T, Nemours; C, N, Nérac; N, T, Neufchâteau; C, N, Niverais; C, N, Nîmes; C, N, Orléans; N, Paris-hors-les-murs; N, Paris-intra-muros; C, N, Périgord; T, Péronne; N, T, Perpignan; T, Ploërmel; N, T, Poitiers; C, N, Pont-à-Mousson; N, T, Ponthieu; C, N, T, Puy-en-Velay; N, T, Quesnoy; Cl, T, Quimper;[1] N, Reims; N, Remiremont; Cl, Rennes;[1] T, Rhuys; C, N, Riom; N, T, Rivière-Verdun; N, Rodez; N, Rouen; U, Rozières; U, Rustaing; T, St. Brieuc; N, T, St. Dié; N, St. Flour; N, T, St. Jean d'Angely; N, Saintes; N, Sarrebourg; N, T, Sarreguemines; T, Sarrelouis; T, Saumur; T, Sedan; N, T, Semur-en-Auxois; N, T, Senlis; N, Sézannes; C, Sisteron; C, N, Soule; N, Toul; N, Toulon; C, N, Toulouse; N, T, Trévoux; N, Troyes; N, Tulle, C, Ustaritz; T, Valenciennes; T, Vannes; N, Vendôme; N, Verdun, N, Villefranche-de-Beaujolais; N, Villefranche-en-Rouergue; N, T, Villeneuve-de-Berg; C, N, Villers-Cotterêts; N, Vitry-le-françois.

[1] Cl—lower clergy.

PAGE

Total: Correct to read 279 cahiers, 53 C, 135 N, 81 T, 6 U, 1 NT, 2 CN, 1 CT.

246 *Districts which created Committees of Correspondence.*

Add N, Sedan; T, Riom; and correct total: 102 cases. 23 C, 33 N, 42 T, 3 U, 1 CN. Correct R to N, Rivière-Verdun.

250-87 No change is being made, except Note 1, p. 286. T, Rouen has now been found, but was not printed.

292 Lons-le-Saunier. Omit Private Collection of M. Cernesson. These documents have been returned to the Arch. Jura.

293 Official volumes:

Marc Bouloiseau, *Cahiers de doléances du Tiers Etat du bailliage de Rouen,* Rouen, 1960, 2 vols.

295 Semi-official editions of cahiers. Add:

P. d'Arbois de Jubainville, *Cahiers de doléances des bailliages de Longuyon, Longwy, et de Villers-la-Montagne,* Nancy, 1952.

J. Godfrin, *Cahiers de doléances du bailliage de Nancy,* Paris, 1934.

Z. E. Harsany, *Cahiers de doléances du bailliage de Pont-à-Mousson* (Cahiers de doléances des généralités de Metz et de Nancy, t.V), Paris, 1946.

P. Lesprand and L. Bour, *Cahiers de doléances des prévotés bailliagères de Sarrebourg et Phalsbourg et du bailliage de Lixheim pour les Etats généraux de 1789* (Annuaire de la société d'histoire et d'archéologie de la Lorraine, 1935, 1936, 1937), Metz, 1938.

312-28 List of Texts of Cahiers.

314 U, Bassigny-Barrois. Add April text, ms. Arch. Nat. B III, pp. 484-92.

315 U, Bourg-en-Bresse. Read II, 453-64.

T, Brignoles. Omit *Missing*. Add *Bull. soc. études sci. et arch. du Var,* t.44, 1942-43, pp.22-35.

316 NT, Carignan. Omit *Missing*. Add H. Rouy, *Souvenirs sedanais,* t.II, 1888, series 4, pp. 270-75 (under the name of Yvois-Carignan).

N, Castelmoron d'Albret. Read II, 543-44.

N, Castelnaudary. Add AP, II, 555-57 to pages given.

N, Château-Thierry. Add M—AP, II, 567-68; cahier, pp. 658-67.

PAGE

318 U, Dauphiné. Read III, 80-83.

T, Dax. The pages in the AP indicated as a mandate should be looked upon rather as a part of the cahier.

T, Dijon. Read III, 130-40.

319 T, Hennebont. Omit *Missing*. Add edition by Thomas Lacroix, in *Mém. soc. d'histoire et arch. de Bretagne,* t.XXV, 1955, pp. 75-104.

T, Hyères. Omit *Missing*. Add *Bull. soc. études sci. et arch. du Var,* t.44, 1942-43, pp. 36-41.

320 Longuyon and Longwy. See also edition by d'Arbois Jubainville, *Cahiers de doléances des bailliages de Longuyon, Longwy, et de Villers-la-Montagne,* Nancy, 1952.

Lixheim. See also P. Lesprand and L. Bour, *Cahiers de doléances des prévotés bailliagères de Sarrebourg . . . et du bailliage de Lixheim . . .,* Metz, 1938.

321 N, Mirecourt. Add AP, IV, 2-6.

322 T, Nancy. See also J. Godfrin, *Cahiers . . . de Nancy,* p. 487 *et seq.*

323 T, Pont-à-Mousson. See also Z. E. Harsany, *Cahiers . . . de Pont-à-Mousson,* Paris, 1946.

324 N, Puy-en-Velay. Omit *Missing*. Add ms. Arch. dép. Haute-Loire, I B 1759.

T, Quesnoy. Omit *Missing*. Add *Bull. soc. études provinciales de Cambrai,* t.VIII, 1906, pp. 232-44.

T, Rouen. Omit *Missing*. Add *Guide,* pp. 389-91, and Marc Bouloiseau, *Cahiers de doléances du bailliage de Rouen,* t.II, Rouen, 1960.

325 N, St. Dié. Omit *Missing*. Add *Guide,* pp. 398-417.

St. Domingue. Add the following documents: Cahier made in Colony (N, W), Blanche Maurel, *Cahiers de doléances de la colonie de Saint-Domingue* (official collection), Paris, pp. 263-82. Cahier of the West: *Ibid.,* pp. 299-302. "*Le Projet de formation des états coloniaux et provinciaux,* pp. 282-98.

Sarrebourg. Add Edition, P. Lesprand and L. Bour, *Cahiers de doléances des prévotés bailliagères de Sarrebourg . . . ,* Metz, 1938.

326 C, Tartas. Omit *Made none*. Add *Bull. soc. Borda,* t.V, 1881, p. 285.

PAGE

T, Thionville. Read III, 776-79.

327 T, Vannes. Read VI, 107-12.

T, Verdun. Read VI, 127-30.

328 C, Villefranche-en-Rouergue. Omit *Missing*. Add *Mém. soc. des lettres, sci., et arts de l'Aveyron,* t.XVII, 1906-11, pp. 253-81.

U, Villers-la-Montagne. See also edition by d'Arbois Jubainville, *Cahiers de doléances de Longuyon . . . et Villers-la-Montagne,* Nancy, 1952.

Statistics of General Cahiers

Although the figures as given in 1934 were correct for the cahiers read for nationalism, the numbers now available, etc. are repeated here.

Extant:	160 C,	156 N,	195 T,	14 U,	3 CN,	1 CT,	3 NT—	532
Missing:	35 C,	26 N,	18 T,	4 U,			NT—	84
Made:	195 C,	182 N,	213 T,	18 U,	3 CN,	1 CT,	4 NT—	616[1]

Colonies: Extant: 6, Missing: 3, Made: 9.

1 The cahier of C, Tartas has been added to the number made in 1789.

INDICES

GENERAL INDEX

Page references include footnote material if the topic has been mentioned in the text on the page. If a reference occurs only in a footnote, the page and footnote number are given.

INDEX OF GENERAL CAHIERS QUOTED IN TEXT

This is an index of quotations and citations from general cahiers. No attempt has been made to index lists of opinions, or lists of cahiers given in footnotes.